HOW DOES A POEM MEAN?
SECOND EDITION

John Ciardi
Miller Williams

HOUGHTON MIFFLIN COMPANY • BOSTON
Atlanta • Dallas • Geneva, Illinois • Hopewell, New Jersey • Palo Alto • London

Library of Congress Catalog Card Number: 74–11592

Paperbound edition cover photograph by George S. Sheng

Library of Congress Cataloging-in-Publication Data
Ciardi, John, 1916–1986
  How does a poem mean?   *025456*
  Includes index.
  1. American poetry. 2. English poetry. 3. American poetry—History and criticism. 4. English poetry—History and criticism. I. Williams, Miller, joint author. II. Title.
PS586.C53 1975   821'.008   74–11592
ISBN 0–395–20440–2
ISBN 0–395–18605–6 pbk.

Printed in the United States of America

M 14 13 12 11 10 9 8 7 6 5

"South End" from *Collected Poems* by Conrad Aiken. Copyright © 1953, 1970 by Conrad Aiken. Reprinted by permission of Oxford University Press, Inc.

"Ballad of the Hoppy-Toad" from *Prophets for a New Day* by Margaret Walker Alexander, © 1970 by Margaret Walker Alexander. Reprinted by permission of Broadside Press.

"In Memory of W. B. Yeats" by W. H. Auden. Copyright 1940 and renewed 1968 by W. H. Auden. Reprinted from *Collected Shorter Poems 1927-1957*, by W. H. Auden, by permission of Random House, Inc. and Faber and Faber Limited.

"The More Loving One" by W. H. Auden. Copyright © 1960 by W. H. Auden. Reprinted from *Collected Shorter Poems 1927-1957*, by W. H. Auden, by permission of Random House, Inc.

"A Cabin in Minnesota" from *A Probable Volume of Dreams* by Marvin Bell. Copyright © 1969 by Marvin Bell. Reprinted by permission of Atheneum Publishers.

"The Fish" by Elizabeth Bishop. Reprinted with the permission of Farrar, Straus & Giroux, Inc. from *The Complete Poems* by Elizabeth Bishop, copyright © 1940, 1969 by Elizabeth Bishop.

"Medusa" by Louise Bogan. Reprinted with the permission of Farrar, Straus & Giroux, Inc. from *Blue Estuaries* by Louise Bogan, copyright © 1923, 1929, 1930, 1931, 1933, 1934, 1935, 1936, 1937, 1938, 1941, 1949, 1951, 1952, 1954, 1957, 1958, 1962, 1963, 1964, 1965, 1966, 1967, 1968 by Louise Bogan.

"Heaven" and "The Great Lover" by Rupert Brooke. Reprinted by permission of Dodd, Mead & Company, Inc. from *The Collected Poems of Rupert Brooke*. Copyright 1915 by Dodd, Mead & Company, Inc. Copyright renewed 1943 by Edward Marsh. Permission for Canadian rights granted by McClelland and Steward Limited, Publishers.

"We Real Cool" by Gwendolyn Brooks. Reprinted from *The World of Gwendolyn Brooks* by Gwendolyn Brooks, copyright © 1959 by Gwendolyn Brooks, by permission of Harper & Row, Publishers, Inc.

"For Jane" by Charles Bukowski from *The Days Run Away Like Wild Horses over the Hills*, by Charles Bukowski. © 1973 by Charles Bukowski. Reprinted by permission of Black Sparrow Press.

"Style" and "Short Order" by Charles Bukowski from *Mockingbird Wish Me Luck* by Charles Bukowski. © 1972 by Charles Bukowski. Reprinted by permission of Black Sparrow Press.

"The Tragedy of the Leaves" by Charles Bukowski. Reprinted by permission of Lujon Press.

"Two," by Robert Canzoneri, is reprinted from his collection *Watch Us Pass*, and is Copyright © 1968 by the Ohio State University Press.

"Northwest Airlines" by Fred Chappell from *The World Between the Eyes* by Fred Chappell. Copyright 1971 by Fred Chappell. Reprinted by permission of the Louisiana State University Press.

"The Second Coming" by John W. Corrington from *Lines to the South* by John W. Corrington, © 1966 by John William Corrington. Reprinted by permission of the author.

"gee i like to think of dead" © 1925 by E. E. Cummings. Reprinted from his volume *Complete Poems 1913–1962* by permission of Harcourt Brace Jovanovich, Inc.

"And what is love?" and "Lady of anonymous flesh and face" by J. V. Cummingham from *The Exclusions of a Rhyme*. Copyright 1960 by the Swallow Press and reprinted with their permission.

"Socratic" by H. D. (Hilda Doolittle) from *Transition* #4 (July 1927). Copyright 1927 by Norman Holmes Pearson. Reprinted by permission of New Directions Publishing Corporation and Norman Holmes Pearson.

Canto I from *The Inferno*, by Dante Alighieri, translated by John Ciardi. Copyright 1954, by John Ciardi. Reprinted by arrangement with The New American Library, Inc., New York, New York.

Canto I of *The Inferno* by Dante Alighieri. Reprinted from *The Divine Comedy of Dante Alighieri*, translated by Jefferson Butler Fletcher, New York: Columbia University Press, 1951, by permission of the publisher.

Canto I of *The Inferno* by Dante Alighieri, translated by Allan Gilbert. Copyright © 1969 Duke University Press. Reprinted by permission of the publisher.

Canto I of *The Inferno* by Dante Alighieri, translated by Dorothy L. Sayers. Reprinted by permission of David Higham Associates, Ltd.

Canto I of *The Inferno* from *The Divine Comedy* by Dante Alighieri, translated by Charles S. Singleton, Bollingen Series LXXX; vol. 1, *Inferno*, Italian text and translation (copyright © 1970 by Princeton University Press). Reprinted by permission of the publisher.

"Motley" and "The Listeners" from *The Complete Poems* by Walter de la Mare. Reprinted by permission of The Literary Trustees of Walter de la Mare, and The Society of Authors as their representative.

"Reincarnation" and "Gamecock" by James Dickey. Copyright © 1964, 1965 by James Dickey. Reprinted from *Buckdancer's Choice*, by James Dickey, by permission of Wesleyan University Press. "Reincarnation" first appeared in *The New Yorker*.

"I Heard a Fly Buzz When I Died" and "Narrow Fellow in the Grass" by Emily Dickinson. Reprinted by permission of the publishers and the Trustees of Amherst College from Thomas H. Johnson, Editor, *The Poems of Emily Dickinson*, Cambridge, Mass.: The Belknap Press of Harvard University Press, copyright 1951, 1955, by The President and Fellows of Harvard College.

"Meditation for a Pickle Suite" by R. H. W. Dillard from *News of the Nile* by R. H. W. Dillard. Reprinted by permission of the University of North Carolina Press.

"Love Song: I and Thou" by Alan Dugan from *Poems* by Alan Dugan. Copyright 1961 by Alan Dugan. Reprinted by permission of the author.

"The Fury of Aerial Bombardment" from *Collected Poems 1930–1960*, Richard Eberhart. © Richard Eberhart. Reprinted by permission of Oxford University Press, Inc. and Chatto and Windus Ltd.

"The Hippopotamus" and "The Love Song of J. Alfred Prufrock" from *Collected Poems 1909–1962* by T. S. Eliot, copyright 1936, by Harcourt Brace Jovanovich, Inc., copyright 1963, 1964 by T. S. Eliot. Reprinted by permission of the publisher and Faber and Faber Limited.

"The Negro" by James A. Emanual, Sr. from *The Treehouse* by James A. Emanual, Sr. Reprinted by permission of the author and Broadside Press.

"Dirge" by Kenneth Fearing from *New and Selected Poems* by Kenneth Fearing. Reprinted by permission of the Indiana University Press.

"Dog" by Lawrence Ferlinghetti from *A Coney Island of the Mind*. Copyright © 1958 by Lawrence Ferlinghetti. Reprinted by permission of New Directions Publishing Corporation.

"Terrible a Horse at Night" by Lawrence Ferlinghetti from *A Coney Island of the Mind*. Copyright 1955 by Lawrence Ferlinghetti. Reprinted by permission of New Directions Publishing Corporation.

"Time Out" from *The Garbage Wars* by Donald Finkel. Copyright ©

1969, 1970 by Donald Finkel. Reprinted by permission of Atheneum Publishers.

"Stopping by Woods on a Snowy Evening," "Mending Wall," "Departmental," "The Death of the Hired Man," "The Draft Horse," "The Impulse," "Fire and Ice," "The Span of Life," and "Mowing" by Robert Frost. From *The Poetry of Robert Frost*, edited by Edward Connery Lathem. Copyright 1916, 1923, 1930, 1934, 1939, © 1969 by Holt, Rinehart and Winston, Inc. Copyright 1936, 1944, 1951, © 1958, 1962 by Robert Frost. Copyright © 1964, 1967 by Lesley Frost Ballantine. Reprinted by permission of Holt, Rinehart and Winston, Inc.

"War Poet" from *Collected Poems 1936–1961* by Roy Fuller. Reprinted by permission of the author.

"Romantic" from *For a Bitter Season* by George Garrett, by permission of the author and the University of Missouri Press. Copyright 1967 by George Garrett.

"Detroit Conference on Unity and Art" by Nikki Giovanni. Reprinted by permission of William Morrow & Company, Inc. from *Black Feeling, Black Talk, Black Judgement* by Nikki Giovanni. Copyright © 1968, 1970 by Nikki Giovanni.

"I hope I don't have you next semester, but" from *Cabin Fever* by Edwin Godsey. Reprinted by permission of the University of North Carolina Press.

"The Traveler's Curse after Misdirection" from *Collected Poems: 1959* by Robert Graves by permission of Robert Graves. Copyright 1958, 1961 by Robert Graves. Reprinted by permission of Collins-Knowlton-Wing, Inc.

"On Vanity of Earthly Greatness" from *Gaily the Troubadour* by Arthur Guiterman. © 1936 by E. P. Dutton, renewed by Vida Leindo Guiterman 1964. Reprinted by permission of Vida Leindo Guiterman.

"Arriving" from *Traveling on Credit* by Daniel Halpern. Copyright © 1970, 1971, 1972 by Daniel Halpern. Reprinted by permission of the Viking Press, Inc.

"Birdwatchers of America" from *The Hard Hours* by Anthony Hecht. Copyright © 1958 by Anthony E. Hecht. Reprinted by permission of Atheneum Publishers.

"Herself" a poem by John Holmes from a book entitled *Mid-Century American Poets* edited by John Ciardi, copyright 1950 by John Ciardi and reprinted with permission of Twayne Publishers, Inc.

"With Rue My Heart Is Laden" by A. E. Housman. From "A Shropshire Lad"—Authorised Edition—from *The Collected Poems of A. E. Housman*. Copyright 1939, 1940, © 1965 by Holt, Rinehart and Winston, Inc. Copyright © 1967, 1968 by Robert E. Symons. Reprinted by permission of Holt, Rinehart and Winston, Inc.

"Traditional Red" reprinted from *Colonel Johnson's Ride* by Robert Huff, by permission of the Wayne State University Press and the author. Copyright 1959 Wayne State University Press.

"Dream Deferred" by Langston Hughes. Copyright 1951 by Langston Hughes. Reprinted from *The Panther and the Lash*, by Langston Hughes, by permission of Alfred A. Knopf, Inc.

"Early Evening Quarrel" by Langston Hughes. Copyright 1942 by Alfred A. Knopf, Inc. and renewed 1970 by Arna Bontemps and George Houston Bass. Reprinted from *Selected Poems*, by Langston Hughes, by permission of the publisher.

"Good Morning," "Same in Blues," and "Comment On Curb" from *Montage of a Dream Deferred* by Langston Hughes. Reprinted by permission of Harold Ober Associates, Incorporated. Copyright © 1951 by Langston Hughes.

"Island" by Langston Hughes from *Selected Poems*. Reprinted by permission of Harold Ober Associates, Incorporated. Copyright © 1951 by Langston Hughes.

"Letter" from *The Langston Hughes Reader* by Langston Hughes. Reprinted by permission of Harold Ober Associates, Incorporated. Copyright © 1958 by Langston Hughes.

"December 24 and George McBride Is Dead" from *Death of the Kapowsin Tavern* by Richard Hugo. Reprinted by permission of the author.

"Polo Grounds" by Rolfe Humphries from *Collected Poems of Rolfe Humphries*. Reprinted by permission of the Indiana University Press.

"The Death of the Ball Turret Gunner" by Randall Jarrell. Reprinted with permission of Farrar, Straus & Giroux, Inc. from *The Complete Poems* by Randall Jarrell, copyright © 1945, 1969 by Mrs. Randall Jarrell.

"An Elegy Is Preparing Itself" from *Departures* by Donald Justice. Copyright © 1972, 1973 by Donald Justice. Appeared originally in *The New Yorker*. Reprinted by permission of Atheneum Publishers.

"Poem to Be Read at 3 A.M." Copyright © 1967 by Donald Justice. Reprinted from *Night Light*, by Donald Justice, by permission of Wesleyan University Press.

"Cross Ties" from the book *Growing into Love* by X. J. Kennedy. Reprinted by permission of Doubleday & Company, Inc.

"Little Elegy" and "Nude Descending a Staircase" copyright © 1960 by X. J. Kennedy; "On a Child Who Lived One Minute" copyright © 1958 by X. J. Kennedy; "In a Prominent Bar in Secaucus One Day" all from the book *Nude Descending a Staircase* by X. J. Kennedy. Reprinted by permission of Doubleday & Company, Inc.

"Woodchucks" reprinted from *Up Country* by Maxine Kumin. Copyright © 1971 by Maxine Kumin. Reprinted by permission of Harper & Row, Publishers, Inc.

"Mr. Bleany" from *Whitsun Weddings* by Philip Larkin. Reprinted by permission of Faber and Faber Ltd.

"Snake" from *The Complete Poems of D. H. Lawrence* edited by Vivian de Sola Pinto and F. Warren Brooks. Copyright © 1964, 1971 by Angelo Ravagli and C. M. Weekly, Executors of the Estate of Frieda Lawrence Ravagli. All rights reserved. Reprinted by permission of The Viking Press, Inc.

"Ars Poetica," "The End of the World," "You, Andrew Marvell," "Not Marble nor the Gilded Monuments," and "What Riddle Asked the Sphinx" by Archibald MacLeish from *Collected Poems of Archibald MacLeish 1917–1952.* Copyright © 1962 by Archibald MacLeish. Reprinted by permission of Houghton Mifflin Company.

"The Voice of the Studio Announcer" from *The Fall of the City* by Archibald MacLeish. Copyright © renewed 1965 by Archibald MacLeish. Reprinted by permission of Houghton Mifflin Company.

"El Greco" by E. L. Mayo. Copyright © 1939 by The New York Times Company. Reprinted by permission.

"The Couple Overhead" by William Meredith. Copyright © 1964 by William Meredith. Reprinted from *The Wreck of the Thresher and Other Poems,* by William Meredith, by permission of Alfred A. Knopf, Inc.

"Walter Jenks' Bath" by William Meredith. Copyright © 1968 by William Meredith. Reprinted from *Earth Walk: New and Selected Poems,* by William Meredith, by permission of Alfred A. Knopf, Inc.

"A Timepiece" from *A Country of a Thousand Years Peace* by James Merrill. Copyright © 1953, 1970 James Merrill. Appeared originally in *Shenandoah.* Reprinted by permission of Atheneum Publishers.

"The Place of Backs" from *Writings to an Unfinished Accompaniment* by W. S. Merwin. Appeared originally in *The Nation.* Reprinted by permission of Atheneum Publishers.

"Burning Love Letters" from *Selected Poems* by Howard Moss. Copyright © 1954, 1971 by Howard Moss. Reprinted by permission of Atheneum Publishers.

"Lot Later" by Howard Nemerov from *The Next Room of the Dream* © by Howard Nemerov, 1962. Reprinted by permission of The Margot Johnson Agency.

"Truth" by Howard Nemerov from *New and Selected Poems* © by The University of Chicago, 1960. Reprinted by permission of The Margot Johnson Agency.

"Love and Death" by John Nims from *Of Flesh and Bone* by John Frederick Nims, © 1967 by Rutgers The State University, New Brunswick, New Jersey. Reprinted by permission of the Rutgers University Press.

"Love Poem" by John Frederick Nims. Reprinted by permission of William Morrow & Company, Inc. from *The Iron Pastoral* by John Frederick Nims. Copyright © 1957 by John Frederick Nims.

"Permanence in Change" from *Sappho to Valery, Poems in Translation* by John Frederick Nims, © 1971, Rutgers University the State University of New Jersey. Reprinted by permission of the Rutgers University Press.

"Hawk's Way" by Ted Olson. Reprinted by permission of the author.

"Anthem for Doomed Youth," "Anthem for Doomed Youth" (First Draft), "Dulce et Decorum Est," and "Strange Meeting" by Wilfred Owen, *Collected Poems*. Copyright Chatto & Windus, Ltd., 1946, © 1963. Reprinted by permission of New Directions Publishing Corporation and The Executors of the Estate of Harold Owen and Chatto & Windus, Ltd.

"I Move the Meeting Be Adjourned" by Nicanor Parra. Reprinted from *Chile: An Anthology of New Writing*, Miller Williams, editor, The Kent State University Press.

"Do the Dead Know What Time It Is?" from Kenneth Patchen, *Collected Poems*. Copyright 1939 by New Directions Publishing Corporation. Reprinted by permission of New Directions Publishing Corporation.

"The Coming of Dusk Upon a Village in Haiti" by Henry Rago. Reprinted with permission of Macmillan Publishing Co., Inc. from *A Sky of Late Summer* by Henry Rago. Copyright 1954 by Henry Rago. Originally appeared in *The New Yorker*.

"The Rite" from *Cities Burning*, by Dudley Randall, © 1968 by Dudley Randall. Reprinted by permission of Broadside Press.

"Bells for John Whiteside's Daughter," and "Captain Carpenter" by John Crowe Ransom. Copyright 1924 by Alfred A. Knopf, Inc. and renewed 1952 by John Crowe Ransom. Reprinted from *Selected Poems*, Third Edition, Revised and Enlarged, by John Crowe Ransom, by permission of the publisher.

"The Roach" by John Raven from *Blues for Momma and Other Low Down Stuff* by John Raven, © 1971 by John Raven. Reprinted by permission of Broadside Press.

"Naming of Parts" by Henry Reed. Reprinted from *A Map of Verona* by Henry Reed by permission of Jonathan Cape Ltd.

"Deer," "Herring," "Lion," and "You" from "A Bestiary." From Kenneth Rexroth, *Collected Shorter Poems*. Copyright © 1956 by New Directions Publishing Corporation. Reprinted by permission of New Directions Publishing Corporation.

"I passed by the beach," "The mists rise," and "I wish I were close" by Tamabe No Akahito. From Kenneth Rexroth, *One Hundred Poems from the Japanese*. All Rights Reserved. Reprinted by permission of New Directions Publishing Corporation.

"Written on the Wall at Chang's Hermitage" by Tu Fu, "A Friend Advises Me to Stop Drinking" by Mei Yao Ch'en, and "To a Traveler" by Su Tung P'o. From Kenneth Rexroth *One Hundred Poems from the Chinese.* Copyright © 1971 by Kenneth Rexroth. Reprinted by permission of New Directions Publishing Corporation.

"For a Dead Lady" by Edwin Arlington Robinson. Reprinted by permission of Charles Scribner's Sons from *The Town Down the River* by Edwin Arlington Robinson. Copyright 1910 Charles Scribner's Sons.

"Mr. Flood's Party" by Edwin Arlington Robinson. Reprinted with permission of Macmillan Publishing Co., Inc. from *Collected Poems* by Edwin Arlington Robinson. Copyright 1921 by Edwin Arlington Robinson, renewed 1949 by Ruth Nivison.

"My Papa's Waltz" copyright 1942 by Hearst Magazines, Inc.; "Dolor" copyright 1943 by Modern Poetry Association, Inc.; "Night Crow" copyright 1944 by Saturday Review Association, Inc.; "I Knew a Woman" copyright 1954 by Theodore Roethke from *The Collected Poems of Theodore Roethke* by Theodore Roethke. Reprinted by permission of Doubleday & Company, Inc.

"The Farmer's Wife" from Anne Sexton's *To Bedlam and Part Way Back.* Copyright © 1960 by Anne Sexton. Reprinted by permission of Houghton Mifflin Company.

"The Heart" from *The Eye* by Harvey Shapiro, copyright 1953. Reprinted by permission of The Swallow Press.

"Buick" by Karl Shapiro. Copyright 1942 by Karl Shapiro. Reprinted from *Selected Poems,* by Karl Shapiro, by permission of Random House, Inc.

"Scyros" by Karl Shapiro. Copyright 1941 and renewed 1969 by Karl Shapiro. Reprinted from *Selected Poems,* by Karl Shapiro, by permission of Random House, Inc.

"Sir Beelzebub" by Dame Edith Sitwell. Reprinted from *The Collected Poems of Edith Sitwell* by permission of the publisher, The Vanguard Press, Inc. Copyright © 1968 by The Vanguard Press, Inc. Copyright © 1949, 1953, 1959, 1962, 1963 by Dame Edith Sitwell.

"Lying Awake" from *After Experience* by W. D. Snodgrass. Copyright © 1959 by W. D. Snodgrass. Originally appeared in *The New Yorker* and reprinted by permission of Harper & Row, Publishers, Inc.

"An Emblem of Two Foxes" copyright © 1969 by Barry Spacks from *The Company of Children.* Reprinted by permission of Doubleday & Company, Inc.

"Anecdote of the Jar" by Wallace Stevens. Copyright 1923 and renewed 1951 by Wallace Stevens. Reprinted from *The Collected Poems of Wallace Stevens,* by permission of Alfred A. Knopf, Inc.

"Exchange" from *The Diving Bell* (1966) by Dabney Stuart. Reprinted by permission of the author.

"The Lost Pictures" by Hollis Summers. From: *Start from Home* by Hollis Summers © 1972 by Rutgers University, the State University of New Jersey. Reprinted by permission of the Rutgers University Press.

"After Work" by Gary Snyder from *The Back Country*. Copyright © 1968 by Gary Snyder. Reprinted by permission of New Directions Publishing Corporation.

"Some Good Things to Be Said for the Iron Age" by Gary Snyder from *Regarding Wave*. Copyright 1970 by Gary Snyder. Reprinted by permission of New Directions Publishing Corporation.

"A Refusal to Mourn the Death, by Fire, of a Child in London" and "Do Not Go Gentle into That Good Night" by Dylan Thomas. From *The Poems of Dylan Thomas*. Copyright 1946 by New Directions Publishing Corporation, copyright 1952 by Dylan Thomas. Reprinted by permission of New Directions Publishing Corporation. Reprinted by permission of J. M. Dent & Sons Ltd. and the Trustees for the Copyrights of the late Dylan Thomas.

"The One Furrow" from *Song at the Year's Turning* by R. S. Thomas. Reprinted by permission of Granada Publishing Limited.

"I love you and the rosebush" by Armando Uribe. Reprinted from *Chile: An Anthology of New Writing*, Miller Williams, editor, The Kent State University Press.

From "Crass Times Redeemed by Dignity of Souls" by Peter Viereck. Copyright 1948 by *Poetry* under title "A Sort of Redemption." First published in Peter Viereck's book *Terror and Decorum*, N.Y., Scribner's, 1948; Pulitzer Prize for verse, 1949; out of print. Included in reprint of *Terror and Decorum*, 1973, by Greenwood Press, Westport, Conn. and in Peter Viereck's *New and Selected Poems*, Bobbs-Merrill Co., N.Y., 1967 as well as other collections. Copyright by author. Reprinted by permission of the author.

"Poet" by Peter Viereck. Copyright 1947 by Harper's Magazine under the title "Planted Poet." First published in Peter Viereck's book *Terror and Decorum*, N.Y., Scribner's, 1948; Pulitzer prize for verse, 1949; out of print. Included in reprint of *Terror and Decorum*, 1973, by Greenwood Press, Westport, Conn. and in Peter Viereck's *New and Selected Poems*, Bobbs-Merrill Co., N.Y., 1967, as well as other collections. Copyright by author. Reprinted by permission of the author.

"The Visiting Hour" from *New and Selected Poems* by David Wagoner. Reprinted by permission of the Indiana University Press.

"Thank You for the Valentine" from *The Magellanic Clouds* by Diane Wakoski. Copyright 1970 by Diane Wakoski. Reprinted by permission of Black Sparrow Press.

"Aubade: N.Y.C." from *Ungainly Things*, by Robert Wallace. © 1968 by Robert Wallace. Reprinted by permission of the author.

"Original Sin: A Short Story" by Robert Penn Warren. Copyright 1942 by Robert Penn Warren. Reprinted from *Selected Poems: New and Old 1923–1966,* by Robert Penn Warren, by permission of Random House, Inc.

"The Narrative Hooper and L.D.O. Sestina with a Long Last Line" by James Whitehead. Copyright © 1973 by *The Denver Quarterly* and reprinted with their permission.

"A Grasshopper" © 1959 by Richard Wilbur. Reprinted from his volume *Advice to a Prophet and Other Poems* by permission of Harcourt Brace Jovanovich, Inc. First published in *The New Yorker.*

"Mind" by Richard Wilbur from *Things of This World,* © 1956 by Richard Wilbur. Reprinted by permission of Harcourt Brace Jovanovich, Inc.

"Still, Citizen Sparrow," and "A Simile for Her Smile" from *Ceremony and Other Poems* by Richard Wilbur, copyright 1948, 1949, 1950 by Richard Wilbur. Reprinted by permission of Harcourt Brace Jovanovich, Inc.

"A Sort of Song" from William Carlos Williams, *Collected Later Poems.* Copyright 1944 by William Carlos Williams. Reprinted by permission of New Directions Publishing Corporation.

"Between Walls," "The Red Wheelbarrow," and "This Is Just to Say" from William Carlos Williams, *Collected Earlier Poems.* Copyright 1938 by New Directions Publishing Corporation. Reprinted by permission of New Directions Publishing Corporation.

"Before Disaster" from Yvor Winters, *The Giant Weapon (Collected Poems).* Copyright 1943 by New Directions Publishing Corporation. Reprinted by permission of New Directions Publishing Corporation.

"Photographs" by Charles Wright. Copyright © 1970 by Charles Wright. Reprinted from *The Grave of the Right Hand,* by Charles Wright, by permission of Wesleyan University Press.

"Lying in a Hammock at William Duffy's Farm in Pine Island, Minnesota" by James Wright. Copyright © 1961 by James Wright, by permission of Wesleyan University Press.

"Number 13," "Number 22," "Number 51" from *The Great Bear Lake Meditations* by J. Michael Yates. From *Contemporary Poetry of British Columbia,* Delta, B. C.: Sono Nis Press, 1970. Reprinted by permission of the author.

"After Long Silence" by William Butler Yeats. Reprinted with permission of Macmillan Publishing Co., Inc. from *Collected Poems* by William Butler Yeats. Copyright 1933 by Macmillan Publishing Co., Inc., renewed 1961 by Bertha Georgie Yeats. Canadian permission granted by Mr. M. B. Yeats, Miss Anne Yeats and Macmillan Co. of Canada.

"An Irish Airman Forsees His Death" by William Butler Yeats.

Reprinted with permission of Macmillan Publishing Co., Inc. from *Collected Poems* by William Butler Yeats. Copyright 1919 by Macmillan Publishing Co., Inc., renewed 1947 by Bertha Georgie Yeats. Canadian permission granted by Mr. M. B. Yeats, Miss Anne Yeats and Macmillan Co. of Canada.

"Sailing to Byzantium" by William Butler Yeats. Reprinted with permission of Macmillan Publishing Co., Inc. from *Collected Poems* by William Butler Yeats. Copyright 1928 by Macmillan Publishing Co., Inc., renewed 1956 by Bertha Georgie Yeats. Canadian permission granted by Mr. M. B. Yeats, Miss Anne Yeats and Macmillan Co. of Canada.

"The Second Coming" by William Butler Yeats. Reprinted with permission of Macmillan Publishing Co., Inc. from *Collected Poems* by William Butler Yeats. Copyright 1924 by Macmillan Publishing Co., Inc., renewed 1952 by Bertha Georgie Yeats. Canadian permission granted by Mr. M. B. Yeats, Miss Anne Yeats and Macmillan Co. of Canada.

"Ponce de Léon/A Morning Walk" by Al Young from *The Song Turning Back into Itself* by Al Young. Copyright (©) 1965, 1966, 1967, 1968, 1970, 1971 by Al Young. Reprinted by permission of Holt, Rinehart and Winston, Inc.

CONTENTS

APPENDIX

Material for Further Study   385

INTRODUCTION

Most classroom discussion of poetry turns out to be appreciation, free association, paraphrase, or some combination of these.

Appreciation is honorable but not useful. No poet can be offended when teacher, having presented a poem to the class, summarizes it by saying, "Isn't that beautiful? How deep the thought! How lofty the words! How melodic their ring!" The poet must nevertheless feel that he is in the wrong place. Nor, while he is there, can he fail to notice how some of the class squirms uncomfortably in the presence of teacher's enthusiasm, while most of the rest simply sink into apathy.

Suppose a violin virtuoso had performed for the class and teacher commented on his playing in something like the terms of "How beautiful, how deep, how lofty!" The violinist would be left to bow and to smile inanely. He would certainly wish he were somewhere else, ideally among musicians with whom he could discuss bowing, fingering, tempo, tone, and the thousand managements of the instrument that make a beautiful performance possible. Musicians, too, "appreciate" music. But their appreciation is likely to be an unspoken premise beyond which they have much more specific things to say about the music.

"Appreciation" tends to smother the working facts of any art form. One evening Robert Frost spoke to an audience about what he called his "technical tricks." He mentioned, among much more, his use of hendecasyllables, synechdoche, kinds of rhyme, some effective ways of using repetition, and what he called "bright ideas" in metaphor. It was a brilliant exposition of the sort of specific management that occupies the poet as a technician of his form. He had hardly finished when an elderly woman in the audience—clearly a high-minded "appreciator of the beautiful," was on her feet. "Mr. Frost," she said in some agitation, "surely when you are writing one of your bee-oo-ti-ful poems [and her voice lingered over "bee-oot-i-ful"], surely you are not thinking of [and here her voice spat the words indignantly] *technical tricks!*"

She might as well have asked Pablo Casals if he cares about the chords he plays. Frost thought for a second or two, then leaned forward into the microphone and said in a playfully gravelly tone, "I *revel* in 'em!"

Out of some sense of the homage due to abstract beauty the high (and loose and vague) appreciators resist that poet's revel. To look technically at a poem, they argue, is like picking the wings off a butterfly. But what poem ever ceased to be good because someone had analyzed it badly? The purpose of analysis is not to destroy beauty but to identify its sources. There is no such thing as a beautiful object without characteristics. If one cares about the nature of the beautiful object, he is well occupied in studying what makes it beautiful, and that study necessarily demands a look at the artist's management of his art. No one need assume that technique defines a poem. Something in every good work of art defies definition. Yet close, specific discussion of the artist's technique is useful—so useful and necessary that no critic of any consequence has managed his perception of the beautiful without having looked closely at the technical elements of the form. This book is about the beauty of poetry and about the technical sources of that beauty. It is, let me add, about the beauty of poetry and not about its prettiness. The pretty, by a first law of art, is never the beautiful. The two cannot coexist. If the pretty were enough for art, one would only need go to the drugstore and buy a hundred greeting cards in order to establish oneself as an art collector. The point is that all greeting cards are pretty and *therefore* that no greeting card is beautiful. This book is about the difference between the pretty and the beautiful.

Free association is a permissive and pointless way of discussing a poem. I have known many teachers to say to the class, "Read this poem and list your reactions to it."

But is poetry to be taken as a Rorschach blot into which anyone is free to read his own psyche ad lib? Suppose teacher assigned a poem about October and a student, free-associating with it, wrote:

> This poem reminds me of Emmy Lou Doodlemayer, who was my "best girl" in 8th grade. She loved poetry and was born in October. The poem begins "In lieu of summer." I used to call her Lou and I spent a summer with her family at Pigeon Cove. Later she and her family moved to Wappinger Falls.

Is the invented example an exaggeration? If anything, it is a touch more literate than most responses to the invitation to free associate. To accept such stuff as a reasonable discussion of a poem is to be in contempt of everything educators once called "a discipline."

It is true that every good poem stirs random private associations. The words, images, rhythms, forms, and dramatic situations of good poems are haloed by ghosts, and the ability to release them is perhaps the basic source of poetic power. Still nothing will direct a reader to the experience of a poem until he sees that *the ghosts of a poem talk to one another.* The "ghost" (aura, connotation, suggestion, overtone) of every formal element arises in response to the other ghosts of the poem. This book is about such ghosts, and about the poet's techniques for entrapping them and for directing their conversation to one another rather than to random free association.

Paraphrase is not necessarily an evil, and at times it is an indispensable beginning of the discussion of a poem. John Donne's grammar, for example, is so unusually dense (and precise in its density) that paraphrase may well be the teacher's best way of introducing the student to Donne's special idiom. His poem "A Feaver" begins:

> Oh do not die, for I shall hate
> All women so when thou art gone,
> That thee I shall not celebrate,
> When I remember, thou wast one.

Donne is saying something like: "I love you so much that, if you die, womankind will become so worthless a thing (with you subtracted from the total of its merit) that I shall end up thinking poorly of you when I remember that you, too, were a woman." The traffic patterns of Donne's convolute wit may reasonably need a few of the road signs a paraphrase can offer.

But paraphrase can only open the discussion. End the discussion there and nothing has been said about the poem, for a poem does not exist in its subject matter but in its way of transcending the subject matter.

Sometimes, for subject purposes, a poem pretends to be sad, as does Keats' "When I have fears that I may cease to be." What may be called "the performing voice" of the poet is registering Keats' awareness that he is doomed to die young, his talent unfulfilled. When (as the performing voice says it) he thinks about that, everything sinks to nothingness.

But that paraphrase is not so much "what the poem means" as "what the poem pretends to mean for the purposes of its performance." And though the enacted subject is a sad one, the act of performing it is joyous because it leads the poet to true equivalents of his feeling. In art a true equivalence (no matter of what) is always a joyous capture.

Think of an actor who has played a valiant Hamlet, the prince of sadness. The play ends with the corpse of Hamlet being carried offstage by soldiers. Inside that performing corpse is an actor. Is the actor sad because he has been portraying tragedy? Not a bit of it. If the performance was good he will be full of inner exaltation. This book is about that duplicity-beyond-all-paraphrase that is the mark of all good poetry, and about how the poet manages not his subject, but his performance of it.

Appreciation, free association, and simple paraphrase are dull and pointless ways of talking about poetry. Students respond to dullness with boredom or hostility. "I hate that stuff!" they say.

But how can they hate a word? a rhythm? a form? The nineteenth-century laborers who laid track across the continent were called gandy dancers. (There is a surviving jig tune called "The Gandy Dancers' Ball.") The tools of their trade were made by the Gandy Mfg. Co. of Chicago, now defunct. The workers, stretched out along the right of way and swinging their tools in a steady rhythm, must have resembled some tribe at a ritual dance. So they became "gandy dancers." The language itself, from a root deep in all men, had written something like a small poem, or at least like a fine, sharp poetic image. The language had done naturally what poets labor to equal.

There is no way of hating such an excitement of the language sense. It is dullness and vapidity that are hateful. What is sharply specific or richly ambiguous (a different sort of specification) speaks for itself.

Given a reasonably willing student and a competent teacher some sort of aesthetic excitement is bound to follow from the specific discussion of diction, metaphor, rhythm, counterrhythm, and form. These are the basic elements of poetry. So long as the discussion deals with them specifically it deals with exciting human ways of reacting to stimuli.

Once the student has acquired some specific ways of identifying different kinds of diction, metaphor, rhythm, and counterrhythm, he is prepared to discuss form. Form, in essence, is the way one part of a poem (one movement) *thrusts against another across a silence.* The silences of poetry are not hard to identify. Any standard sonnet moves in one direction for twelve lines, then pauses (the pause like a rest in music), then thrusts the final couplet against the first twelve lines, usually in a reversal.

Whenever such a pause and counterthrust happens in a poem *something changes in the handling of the technical elements.* If the student can be taught to identify such changes, he will have identified the poem in action. He will not need to fumble at the question *"What* does this poem mean?" He will, rather, have experienced it as a performance. He will have seen *how* it means.

The first chapters of this book are about diction, metaphor, rhythm, and related matters. The last chapter is about how the poet uses these elements up to the silence the poem entraps and how he changes them for the counterthrust from the other side of his silence.

This revised edition has not substantially changed the text of the first edition. Professor Williams and I have dropped some poems in order to replace them by others that we hope will be more inviting to students. In making these changes we have set out deliberately to pair or to group the poems in a way that was implicit in the first edition but that is systematic in this one. Our rationale for pairing or grouping all the poems in this book starts with the recognition that students, given a single poem, do not know what to think or say about it. They lack a body of poetry with which to compare the poem. If, however, they are given two matched poems and firmly directed to direct their attention to specific likenesses and specific differences, then one poem becomes a measure of the other, *and they have something specific to talk about,* as for example, the differences (and the likenesses) between a nineteenth-century love poem and a twentieth-century love poem.

The teaching principle is, first, that the minimum assignment is always at least two poems, never one alone; and, second, that the discussion must be kept to specific likenesses and differences. This book is about ways of identifying such likenesses and differences. The editors hope the book is also about ways of keeping the discussion interesting.

John Ciardi

CHAPTER ONE
HOW DOES A
POEM MEAN?

"Bitzer," said Thomas Gradgrind, "your definition of a horse."
"Quadruped. Gramnivorous. Forty teeth, namely twenty-four grinders,
four eye-teeth, and twelve incisive. Sheds coat in the spring; in marshy
countries sheds hoofs too. Hoofs hard, but requiring to be shod with iron.
Age known by marks in mouth." Thus (and much more) Bitzer.
"Now girl number twenty," said Mr. Gradgrind, "you know what a
horse is."

Charles Dickens, *Hard Times*

The School of Hard Facts over which Mr. Gradgrind presided was a
school of fixed answers. Mr. Gradgrind would have agreed with a
recent anthologist who wrote that the inspection of a poem should be
as certain as a chemical analysis. Mr. Gradgrind would have assured
himself that he was a first-class critic, of poetry as of horses. "Now girl
number twenty," he would have said looking up from his analysis,
"you know what a poem is."

Today, more than a century later than Mr. Gradgrind's School of
Hard Facts, the idea is still current that the methods of measurement
evolved by the physical sciences can be applied to all human processes.
And there still lingers the belief that a dictionary definition is a satisfac-
tory description of an idea or of an experience.

There are many grounds on which dictionary definitions can be dis-
puted, but only one need concern us here. Bitzer's definition of a horse
was a dictionary definition. Note that it is put almost exclusively in
terms of classification. In those terms, it may do as a table of physical
characteristics of *Equus caballus*. But what can it possibly say of the
experience one has had of the living animal? No horseman ever rode a
"gramnivorous quadruped." No gambler ever bet on one. No sculptor
ever dreamed one out of a block of stone. For horseman, gambler, and

1

sculptor are involved in a living relation to a living animal, *and the kind of relation is expressed in the language each has evolved for his experience.* ("A good winded bay," says the horseman, "but he has a mouth like iron and won't answer to the bit. He's had bad schooling." Or the gambler: "A good four-year-old. Better than his performance to date. And a good mudder. He's due to win, especially on a wet track. And at nice odds." Or the sculptor: "The set of the stone suggested a rearing posture: the line of force curving down the haunches repeated in the straining line of the neck with the mouth held hard-down by the bit.") Whatever the "gramnivorous quadruped" may be to the biologist, these three ways of speaking are three experiences of the living horse. As Tip O'Neill once wrote in a fine sarcastic line: "There's not a wedding in the world that's worth a running horse." Now try the line revised: "There is not a marriage ceremony in existence worthy of comparison with a gramnivorous quadruped of the species *Equus caballus* in rapid motion."

The point is that *the language of experience is not the language of classification.* A boy burning with ambition to become a jockey does not study a text on zoology. He watches horses, he listens to what is said by those who have spent their lives around horses, he rides them, trains them, feeds them, curries them, pets them. He lives with intense feelings toward them. He may never learn how many incisors a horse has, nor how many yards of intestines. What does it matter? He is concerned with a *feel*, a response to, a sense of the character and reaction of the living animal. And zoology cannot give him that. Not all the anatomizing of all the world's horses could teach a man horse sense.

So for poetry. The concern is not to arrive at a definition and to close the book, but to arrive at an experience. There will never be a complete system for "understanding" or for "judging" poetry. Understanding and critical judgment are admirable goals, but neither can take place until the poem has been experienced, and even then there is always some part of every good work of art that can never be fully explained or categorized. It still remains true that the reader who has experienced most fully will finally be the best judge.

Poetry has only a remote place in the gross of our culture. As has, for example, the opera. Therefore, Americans generally need to be taught in school how to experience both poetry and the opera. In Milan, on the other hand, no one need go to school in order to learn how to experience an opera: the Milanese do not study opera, they *inhale* it. And in Chile, people on the streets of Santiago take poetry in the same way, as an essential part of the world they move in. A Milanese and a Chilean would have to go to school to learn, for example, how to watch a football game in an experienceable way. Certainly few people in the United States need to go to that school: in Green Bay it is football that is inhaled as a living thing, and opera and poetry that have to be learned.

If the reader cared enough for poetry, he would have no need to study it. He would live into it. As the Milanese citizen becomes an encyclopedia of opera information, as the Chilean knows his country's poets, as even retarded boys in the United States are capable of reciting endlessly detailed football stories, so those who are passionate for any given thing become alive to it by natural process.

Any teaching of the poem by any other method owes the poem an apology. What greater violence can be done to the poet's experience than to drag it into an early morning classroom and to go after it as an item on its way to a Final Examination? The apology must at least be made. It is the experience, not the Final Examination, that counts. Though one must note with care—as in the case of the football fan —that passionate learning is full of very technical stuff. Why else would football statistics give rise to such heated argument as one can hear throughout the season?

And in poetry there is the step beyond: once one has learned to experience the poem as a poem, there inevitably arrives a sense that one is also experiencing himself as a human being. It must certainly have been this second experience (to put it in another way, the point at which Art for Art's sake becomes Art for Life's sake) that Matthew Arnold had in mind when he wrote: "The grand power of poetry is its interpretative power . . . the power of so dealing with things as to awaken in us a wonderfully full, new, and intimate sense of them, and of our relations with them." But the grand power of a good sermon is also its interpretative power, and a sermon, it must be remembered, is not a poem.

Paradise Lost is, in one sense, a metrical sermon written to justify God's ways to man. So is Michael Wigglesworth's *The Day of Doom,* which is both metrical and heavily—too heavily—rhymed. Wigglesworth was a Puritan clergyman of the Massachusetts Bay Colony and for over two centuries Puritan children memorized large sections of his poem as part of their church training. Wigglesworth's theology is every bit as sound and as comprehensive as Milton's. Yet today *The Day of Doom* is all but unknown except as a scholar's curio. The difference is not in content but in the fact that Milton wrote a poem whereas Wigglesworth wrote only doggerel. Poetry, it follows, is more than simply "something to say." Nor is it simply an elaborate way of saying something or nothing.

W. H. Auden was once asked what advice he would give a young man who wished to become a poet. Auden replied that he would ask the young man why he wanted to write poetry. If the answer was "because I have something important to say," Auden would conclude that there was no hope for that young man as a poet. If on the other hand the answer was something like "because I like to hang around words and overhear them talking to one another," then that young man was at least interested in a fundamental part of the poetic process and there was hope for him.

When one "message hunts" a poem (that is, goes through the poem with no interest except in its paraphraseable content) he is approaching the writing as did the young man with "something important to say." He is giving it the Wigglesworth treatment. The common question from which such an approach begins is "What does the poem mean?" His mind closed on that point of view, the reader tends to "interpret" the poem rather than to experience it, seeking only what he can make over from it into a prose statement (or examination answer) and forgetting in the process that it was originally a poem. Thus, students are too often headed by their teachers in the direction of reciting, almost like Bitzer: "Keats. 'When I have fears that I may cease to be.' Sonnet. Irregular. Consisting of three quatrains and a couplet, the third quatrain consisting of very close rhymes, thus: 'hour, more, power, shore.' Written on the theme of the vanity of earthly wishes, but given a strong romantic coloration of individualistic aspiration for the good pleasures of the world."

Poor Keats!

For "What does the poem mean?" is too often a self-destroying approach to poetry. A more useful way of asking the question is "How does a poem mean?" Why does it build itself into a form out of images, ideas, rhythms? How do these elements become the meaning? How are they inseparable from the meaning? As Yeats wrote:

> O body swayed to music, o brightening glance,
> How can we know the dancer from the dance?

What the poem is, is inseparable from its own performance of itself. The dance is in the dancer and the dancer is in the dance. Or put in another way: where is the "dance" when no one is dancing it? and what man is a "dancer" except when he is dancing?

Above all else, poetry is a performance. Keats' overt subject in his sonnet was his own approaching death. But note this about poetry: Keats took the same *self-delighting pains* in writing about his death as he took in poems on overtly happy subjects, such as "On First Looking into Chapman's Homer" or the "Ode to a Nightingale." Here is the complete sonnet:

> When I have fears that I may cease to be
>   Before my pen has gleaned my teeming brain,
> Before high-pilèd books, in charact'ry,
>   Hold like rich garners the full-ripened grain;
> When I behold, upon the night's starred face,
>   Huge cloudy symbols of a high romance,
> And think that I may never live to trace
>   Their shadows, with the magic hand of chance;
> And when I feel, fair creature of an hour,
>   That I shall never look upon thee more,
> Never have relish in the faery power
>   Of unreflecting love!—then on the shore
> Of the wide world I stand alone, and think
> Till Love and fame to nothingness do sink.

If this sonnet means "the vanity of human wishes given a strong romantic coloration . . . ," why did Keats take the trouble to bring his rhythms to a stop at the end of the fourth and eighth lines and in the middle of the twelfth? Sonnets normally divide into *octet* (the first eight lines) and *sestet* (the final six lines). Note that Keats' divisions occur in a symmetrical pattern. Why did Keats spend so much care on symmetry? What has symmetry to do with "the vanity of earthly wishes"? Why, too, did Keats bother to compare his mind to a field of grain, and the books he felt himself able to write, to storage bins? An elaborate figure. Why did Keats bother to construct it? Why did he search out such striking phrases as "the magic hand of chance"? If Keats were really convinced that all human wishes are vain, why did he wish to phrase his idea with such earthly care? If *nothingness* is all, why bother to make *the something* a poem is?

Robert Frost provided a valuable clue when he spoke of "the pleasure of taking pains." The paradox here is simply verbal. Frost meant precisely what the German critic Baumgarten meant when he spoke of the central impulse toward poetry (and toward all art) as the *Spieltrieb,* the play impulse.

An excellent native example of the play impulse in poetry is the child clapping its hands in response to a Mother Goose rhyme. What does a child care for "meaning"? What on earth is the "meaning" of the following poem?

> High Diddle diddle
> The cat and the fiddle
> The cow jumped over the moon;
> The little dog laughed
> To see such craft
> And the dish ran away with the spoon.

"Preposterous," says Mr. Gradgrind. But the child is wiser: he is busy having a good time with the poem. The poem pleases and involves him. He responds to it in an immediate muscular way. He recognizes its performance at once and wants *to act with it.*

This is the first level of play. As rhythm is the first element of music. The child claps hands, has fun, and the play involves practically no thoughtful activity. Beyond this level of response, there begins the kind of play whose pleasure lies for the poet in overcoming meaningful and thoughtful (and "feelingful") difficulties, and for the reader in identifying with the poet in that activity.

Nor is the word "difficulty" one to be afraid of. Chess is a play activity, yet it is play only because the players deliberately make the game difficult in order to overcome the difficulties. The equation is simple: no difficulty, no fun. No chess player finds any real pleasure in playing an obviously inferior opponent. *Every game ever invented by mankind is a way of making things hard for the fun of it. The great fun, of course, is in making the hard look easy.* Too much difficulty is painful. The freshman football coach does not send his squad to play last year's Rose Bowl winner. Neither does he send it to play grammar school teams. He tries to find opponents who will give his players a real chance to extend themselves, win or lose, and he hopes bit by bit to develop them for harder play.

Learning to experience poetry is not a radically different process from that of learning any other kind of play. The way to develop a poetic sense is by using it. And one of the real joys of the play impulse is in the sudden discovery that one is getting better at it than he had thought he would be.

It is this self-delighting play impulse that the literalist and message hunter overlooks, just as Mr. Gradgrind overlooked the living fun it is to ride a horse, even an undefined horse.

To summarize these same points in more formal terms: *no matter how serious the overt message of a poem, the unparaphraseable and undiminishable life of the poem lies in the way it performs itself through the difficulties it imposes upon itself.* The way *in which* it means is *what* it means.

What for example does a dance "mean"? Or what does music "mean"? Or what does a juggler "mean" when we watch him with such admiration of his skill? All of these forms—and poetry with them—have meaning only as they succeed in being good performances.

One sees a wizard of a poet tossing his words in the air and catching them and tossing them again—what a grand stunt! Then suddenly one may be astonished to find that the poet is not simply juggling cups, saucers, roses, rhymes, and other random objects, but the very stuff of life. And discovering that, one discovers that seeing the poet's ideas flash so in the air, seeing them performed under such control, is not only a reward in itself, but a living experience that deepens every man's sense of life. One finds himself more alert to life, surer of his own emotions, wiser than he would have been without that experience —and he thought he was just watching a show!

But only a poem can illustrate how a poem works. One of the purposes of this volume is to provide beginning students with a reasonable bulk of poems from the great tradition of English and American poetry. But great as are the virtues of wide reading, they amount to nothing unless the reading goes deep as well as wide. It is good to read much. It is even more important to read a little in greater depth, for every poem one reads closely will teach him something about how to read another poem.

What should such a close reading take into consideration?

Here is a poem, one of the master lyrics of American poetry, perhaps the best known poem by an American poet:

Stopping by Woods
on a Snowy Evening

Robert Frost

Whose woods these are I think I know.
His house is in the village, though;
He will not see me stopping here
To watch his woods fill up with snow.

My little horse must think it queer
To stop without a farmhouse near
Between the woods and frozen lake
The darkest evening of the year.

He gives his harness bells a shake
To ask if there is some mistake.
The only other sound's the sweep
Of easy wind and downy flake.

The woods are lovely, dark, and deep,
But I have promises to keep,
And miles to go before I sleep,
And miles to go before I sleep.

Note that the poem begins as a simple description of events, but that it ends in a way that suggests meanings far beyond the specific description. This movement *from the specific to the general* is one of the basic formulas of poetry. Such poems as Yvor Winter's "Before Disaster" (p. 365 and Holmes's "The Chambered Nautilus" (p. 90) follow exactly this progression from the specific to the general, but the generalization in these poems is, in a sense, divided from the specific description or narration, and even seems additional to the specific action rather than intrinsically part of it. It is this sense of division that is signified when one speaks of "a tacked-on moral." Frost, however, is painstakingly careful to avoid the tacked-on moral. Everything in the poem pretends, on one level, to be part of the incident narrated. Yet one cannot miss the feeling that by the end of the poem, Frost has referred to something much more far-reaching than stopping by woods or than driving home to go to bed. There can be little doubt, in fact, that part of Frost's own pleasure in this poem was in making the larger intent *grow out* of the poem rather than in tacking it on. It is in the poem's own performance of itself that the larger meaning is made to emerge from the specific incident. A careful look at that performance will teach a great deal about the nature of poetry.

The poem begins with a situation. A man—knowing Robert Frost, we know it is a Vermont or New Hampshire man—is on his way somewhere at nightfall. It is snowing and as he passes a patch of woods he stops to watch the easy down-drift of the snow into the dark woods. We are told two other things: first that the man is familiar with these parts (he knows who owns these woods and where he lives) and second that no one sees him stop. More could be read into this opening. (For example: why doesn't he say what errand he is on? Why does he say he knows whose woods these are? What is the significance of watching another man's woods in this way?) Such questions can be multiplied almost endlessly without losing real point, but for present purposes let us assume that we have identified scene one of the poem's performance without raising these questions.

Note that the scene is set in the simplest possible terms. We have no trouble sensing that the man stopped because the scene moved him, but he neither tells us that it is beautiful nor that it moved him. A student writer, always ready to overdo, might have said that he was moved to stop and "to fill his soul with the slow steady stately sinking of that crystaline loveliness into the glimmerless profundities of the hushed primeval wood." Frost prefers to avoid such a spate of words, and to speak the incident in the simplest terms.

His choice illustrates two basic principles of writing of which every sensitive reader should be aware. Frost stated the first principle himself in "Mowing" (p. 170) when he wrote "Anything *more* than the truth would have seemed too *weak*" (italics added). Understatement is one of the principal sources of power in English poetry.

The second principle here illustrated is to let the action speak for itself. A good novelist who wishes us to know a character does not tell us that character is good or bad and leave it at that. Rather, he introduces the character, shows him in action, and lets his actions speak for him. This process is spoken of as *characterization in action.* One of the skills of a good poet is to enact his experiences rather than to talk about having had them. *"Show* it, don't *tell* it," he says, "make it happen, don't talk about its happening."

One part of this poem's performance, in fact, is *to act out* (and thereby to make us act out—*feel out, identify with)* just why the speaker did stop. The man is the principal actor of this little "drama of why" and in scene one he is the only character. In scene two (starting with the beginning of stanza two), however, a *foil* is introduced. In drama, a foil is a character who "plays against" a more important character; by presenting a different point of view or an opposed set of motives, the foil moves the more important character to react in ways that might not have found expression without such opposition. The more important character is thus more fully revealed, to the reader and to himself. The foil here is the horse.

The horse forces the first question in the drama of why. Why did the man stop? Until he comes to realize that his "little horse must think it queer" to stop this way, he has not asked himself why he stopped; he simply did. But he senses that the horse is confused by the stop. He imagines how the horse must feel about it—what *is* there to stop for out here in the cold, away from bin and stall and all that any self-respecting horse would value on such a night?

In imagining the horse's question, the man is of course led to examine his own reasons. In stanza two this question arises only as a feeling within the man. In stanza three, however, the horse acts definitely. He gives his harness bells a shake. "What's wrong?" he seems to say, "what are we doing here?"

By now, obviously, the horse, without losing its identity as a horse has also become a symbol. A symbol is something that stands for something else. That something else may, perhaps, be taken as the order of life that does not understand why a man stops in the wintry middle of nowhere to watch snow come down. (Could the dark and the snowfall symbolize a death wish? that hunger for the last rest that man may feel, but not a beast?) So there is the man, there is that other order of life, and there is the third presence—the movement of the inanimate wind and snow (the all-engulfing?) across both their lives—with the difference that the man knows the second darkness of the dark while the horse does not.

The man has no ready answer to this combination of forces. They exist and he feels them—all three of them, himself included. We sense that he would like to remain here longer to ponder these forces, perhaps to yield to their total. But a fourth force prompts him. That fourth force can be given many names. It is almost certainly better, in fact, to give it many names than attempt to limit it to one. Social obligation, responsibility, personal commitment, duty, or just the realization that a man cannot indulge a mood forever—all of these things and more. He has a long way to go and it is time to be getting there (so there's something to be said for the horse, too). We find the man's inner conflict dramatized to this point by the end of scene two (which coincides with the end of stanza three).

Then and only then—his feelings dramatized in the cross-tug of motives he has given form to—does the poet, a little sadly, venture on the comment of his final scene. "The woods are lovely, dark, and deep." The very sound of the syllables lingers over the thought. But there is something to do yet before he can yield to the lovely dark and deep. "Not yet," he seems to say, "not yet." He has a long way to go—miles to go before he can sleep. Yes, miles to go. He repeats the line and the performance ends.

But why the repetition? The first time Frost writes "And miles to go before I sleep" there can be little doubt that he means "I have a long way to go yet before I can get to bed tonight." The second time he says it, however, "miles to go" and "sleep" are suddenly transformed into symbols. What is the "something else" these symbols stand for? Hundreds of people used to ask Mr. Frost that question in one form or another, and Mr. Frost always turned the question away with a joke. He turned it away primarily *because he could not answer it.* He could answer some part of it. But some part is not enough.

For a symbol is like a rock dropped into a pool: it sends out ripples in all directions, and the ripples are in motion. Who can say where the last ripple disappears? One may have a sense that he at least knows approximately the center point of all those ripples, the point at which the stone struck the water. Yet even then he has trouble marking it precisely. How does one make a mark on water? Oh, very well—the center point of "miles to go" is probably approximately in the neighborhood of being close to meaning, perhaps, "the road of life," and "before I sleep" is maybe that close to meaning "before I take my final rest." (That rest in darkness that seemed so temptingly "lovely, dark, and deep" for the moment of the mood.) But the ripples continue to move and the light to change on the water and the longer one watches the more changes he sees. And such shifting and being at the same instant is of the very sparkle and life of poetry. Of poetry and of life itself. For the poem is a dynamic and living thing. One experiences it as one experiences life—as everybody but Mr. Gradgrind experiences life. One is never done with it: every time he looks he sees something new, and it changes even as he watches. And that very sense of continuity in fluidity is one of the kinds of knowledge, one of the ways of knowing, that only the arts can teach, poetry foremost among them.

Frost himself certainly did not ask what the lines "meant." They came to him and he received them; he "felt right" about them. And what he "felt right about" may perhaps be called their "meaning," but it is far more to the point to describe it as "their long possibility of meaning." For the poem is not a statement but a performance of forces, not an essay on life but a reenactment, and just as men must search their lives over and over again for the meaning of their deepest experiences, so the performance of a true poem is endless in being not a meaning but an act of existence.

Now look at the poem in another way. Did Frost know what he was going to do when he began? Considering the poem simply as a piece of juggling one cannot fail to respond to the magnificent turn at the end where, with one flip, seven of the simplest words in the language suddenly dazzle full of never-ending waves of thought and feeling; or—more precisely—of felt thought. Certainly an equivalent stunt by a juggler—could there be such an equivalent—would bring the house down. Was it to cap his performance with that grand stunt that Frost wrote the poem?

Far from it: the fact that must not be overlooked is that *Frost did not know he was going to write those lines until he wrote them.* Then a second fact must be registered: *he wrote them because, for the fun of it, he had got himself into trouble.*

Let us start by saying that Frost began by playing a game with himself. The most usual way of writing a four-line stanza with four feet to the line, is to rhyme the third line with the first, and the fourth line with the second. Even that much rhyme is so difficult that many poets and almost all the anonymous ballad makers do not bother to rhyme the first and third lines at all, settling for two rhymes in four lines. For the fact is that English is a rhyme-poor language. In Italian and in French, for example, so many words end with the same sounds that rhyming is relatively easy. English, being a more agglomerate language, has far more final sounds, hence fewer of them rhyme. When an Italian poet writes a line ending with *vita* (life) he has literally hundreds of possible rhyme words available. When an English poet writes "life" at the end of a line, he can summon "strife, wife, knife, fife, rife" and then he is in trouble. Now "life/strife," and "life/rife" and "life/wife" seem to offer a combination of ideas that are possibly related by more than rhyme. Inevitably, therefore, the poets have had to work, rework, and over-work these combinations until the sparkle has gone out of them. Readers are normally tired of these combinations. When one encounters "life/strife" he is certainly entitled to suspect that the poet did not really want to say "strife"—that if there had been in English such as word as, say, "hife" meaning "infinite peace and harmony," he would gladly have used that word instead of "strife." So one feels that the writing is haphazard: that the rhyme is making the poet say things he doesn't really feel, and which, therefore, the reader does not feel. One likes to see the rhymes fall into place, but he must end up with the belief that it is the poet who is deciding what is said and not the rhyme scheme.

So rhyme is a kind of game, and an especially difficult one in English. As in every game, the fun of rhyme is to set one's difficulties high and then to meet them skillfully. As Frost himself once defined freedom, it consists of "moving easy in harness."

In "Stopping by Woods on a Snowy Evening" Frost took a long chance. He decided to rhyme not two lines, but three in each stanza. Not even Frost could have sustained that much rhyme in a long poem (as Dante, for example, with the advantage of writing in Italian sustained triple rhyme for thousands of lines in *The Divine Comedy*). He would have known instantly, therefore, when he took that first chance, that he was going to write a short poem. He would have had that much foretaste of it. So the first stanza emerged rhymed a a b a. And with the certain sense that this was to be a short poem, Frost decided to take a chance and redouble: in English three rhymes in four lines is enough —there is no need to rhyme the fourth line. For the fun of it, however, Frost set himself to pick up that loose rhyme and weave it into the pattern—thereby accepting the all but impossible burden of quadruple rhyme.

The miracle is that it worked. Despite that enormous freight of rhyme, the poem not only came out as a neat pattern, but managed to do so with no sense of strain. It is this unstrained fulfillment of one's difficulties Frost meant by "moving easy in harness." Despite all his self-imposed restrictions the poem *seems* to go effortlessly. Every word falls into place as naturally as if there were no rhyme restricting the choice.

That ease is part of the success of the performance. One watches the "skill man" juggle two balls, then three, then four—and every addition makes the trick more wonderful, but unless he makes the hard trick *seem* as easy as the easy one, then all is lost.

The real point, however, is not only that Frost took on a hard rhyme trick and made it look easy. It is rather as if a juggler, carried away, had tossed up one more ball than he could really handle—and then amazed himself by actually handling it. So with the real triumph of this poem. Frost could not have known what a stunning effect his repetition of the last line was going to produce. He could not even have known he was going to repeat the line. He simply found himself up against a difficulty he probably had not foreseen: in picking up the rhyme from the third line of stanza one and carrying it over into stanza two, he had created an endless chain-link form. Each stanza left a hook sticking out for the next stanza to catch. So by stanza four, feeling the poem rounding to its end, Frost had to do something about his third-line rhyme.

He might have tucked it back in a third line rhyming with "know/though/snow" of stanza one. That would have worked out to the mathematical symmetry of using each rhyme four times. But though such a device might be defensible in theory, a rhyme repeated after eleven lines is so far from its original rhyme sound that its feeling as rhyme must certainly be lost, and what good is theory if the reader is not moved by the writing?

It must have been in some such quandary that the final repetition suggested itself—a suggestion born of the very difficulty of what the poet had set out to do. So the point beyond mere ease in handling a hard thing: that the very difficulty of the restrictions the poet imposed upon himself offered the opportunity to do better than he had imagined. What—aside from having that happen to oneself—could be more self-delighting than to take part in its happening as an active reader of the poem?

A poem is not simply something printed on the page. A poem is an event, and it happens when a poet and a reader meet inside the form in such a way that the reader makes real for himself those connections between things that the poet saw as real in the construct of his own world and as able to be communicated. The reader makes this confirmation in much the same way that the poet made the suggestion: by using his intellect, imagination, and memory. Reading a poem is an act of participation in the poem. By participating, the reader not only makes the performance whole, but makes it, in one essential sense, uniquely his.

Consider, for instance, a poem with the line "I close my eyes and see a calendar with a date circled in red." This is a complete statement by all the rules of syntax, and not at all obscure, yet there are open places in it for each reader to fill out of his own psyche, as the date in the case of any two readers will surely be a different date, and circled for a different reason. Such perfect incompleteness, suggestion, and ambiguity are among the most valuable devices of the skilled poet; means by which the poem opens to let us in.

You will observe one further point: that the human insight of the poem, and the technicalities of the poetic devices are inseparable. Each feeds the other. This interplay is the poem's meaning, a matter not of *what* it means (nobody can say entirely what a good poem means) but *how* it means—a process one can come much closer to discussing.

Is it too frivolous to have compared this process to the act of juggling? Consider the following parable based on a short story by Anatole France, "The Juggler of Notre Dame."

The juggler wandered France from fair to fair and whenever he saw a chance to earn a few pennies he unrolled his rug, lay on his back, and juggled his paraphernalia with his hands and feet. It was all he knew how to do, he did it well, and he was happy in the doing.

As he grew older, however, misfortunes crowded him. One winter's day, ill and tired, he took refuge in a monastery and by the time he had recovered he decided to remain there. It was a pleasant monastery dedicated to the Virgin and each of the monks and brothers set himself a special task in her honor. One illuminated manuscripts to offer her, another decorated her altar, another raised flowers. Only the juggler had no productive art, only he produced nothing that could be set in place before her and stay tangibly in place. (This rendering takes a few liberties with the original for the sake of making a point.)

Finally, in despair, the juggler took to stealing into the chapel when no one else was about. There he would unroll his rug and juggle before the Virgin's statute. It was all he had to offer, the one thing he could do well.

One day a passing brother discovered the juggler at work before the statue and summoned the other monks in horror to witness the profanation of the chapel. Soon all the windowsills were lined with the heads of outraged monks come to verify the horrible report. They were just about to rush in and put an end to the sacrilege, when before their eyes the Virgin descended smiling from her pedestal and wiped the sweat from the juggler's brow. The offering was acceptable.

A note to residual Gradgrinds: this parable is not a religious excursion. It is an allegory. An allegory is a story in which each character and element is more important as a symbol (as something else) than as its presumably literal self. Then all these symbols put together acquire further meanings by their interaction upon one another. What does the Virgin stand for in poetic terms? What do the monks stand for? The juggler? How does juggling relate to Frost's definition of freedom (in poetry)? Why should juggling produce the miracle? How does the parable mean what it means?

CHAPTER TWO

A BURBLE THROUGH THE TULGEY WOOD

Everyone who has an emotion and a language knows something about poetry. What he knows may not be much on an absolute scale, and it may not be organized within him in a useful way, but once he discovers the pleasures of poetry, he is likely to be surprised to discover how much he always knew without knowing he knew it. He may discover, somewhat as the character in the French play discovered to his amazement that he had been talking prose all his life, that he has been living poetry. Poetry, after all, is about life. Anyone who is alive and conscious must have some information about it.

And like life, poetry is not uniformly serious. True, poetry is the natural language of man's most exalted thoughts. The rhythmic resemblance between prayer and poetry, for example, can hardly be missed. Yet the more exalted the thought, the more careful the poet must be, for poetic high seriousness can fall into a burlesque of itself at a touch. William Wordsworth, for all his great powers as a poet, was yet capable of slipping from the intensely serious into the intensely inane. His "Idiot Boy," an intensely serious ballad about the natural unspoiled goodness of a young idiot, can hardly be said to survive such a line as "Burr, burr—now Johnny's lips they burr," a line in which the poet seeks to render soulfully the blubbering of a happy idiot, and falls into bathos. Percy Bysshe Shelley was similarly capable of a kind of labored excess that could turn sublime intention into ridiculous utterance. His "Epipsychidion" sets out to describe ideal love, but few readers today can suppress a smile at the last line: "I pant, I sink, I tremble, I expire!" So, too, when John Keats addresses an apostrophe to his love and lets slip the exclamation: "Those lips, O slippery blisses!"

Such lapses do not prove that Wordsworth, Shelley, and Keats were bad poets, but that they could strain so hard for high seriousness that their voices cracked. If, however, some poets let themselves fall into unconsciously ridiculous positions, there are always others ready to pick up the slip and to have fun with it. One of the most pompous and flat-footedly moral of the English poets was Robert Southey. The performance of his poems tends always to center around a spike of moral Gradgrindism which the performer proceeds to drive in with such graceless energy that the hammer splits and leaves him holding a shattered stump of the handle. We in the audience see his laborious earnestness, but the act is so clumsy that we cannot resist laughing it off the stage.

Lewis Carroll, the ever-graceful author of *Alice in Wonderland*, had a great gift for such laughter. His "Father William," a direct takeoff on Southey's "The Old Man's Comforts and How He Gained Them," is as devastating a spoof as one may find in English poetry:

The Old Man's Comforts
And How He Gained Them

Robert Southey

"You are old, Father William," the young man cried;
    "The few locks which are left you are gray;
You are hale, Father William,—a hearty old man:
    Now tell me the reason, I pray."

"In the days of my youth," Father William replied,
    "I remembered that youth would fly fast,
And abused not my health and my vigor at first,
    That I never might need them at last."

"You are old, Father William," the young man cried,
    "And pleasures with youth pass away;
And yet you lament not the days that are gone:
    Now tell me the reason, I pray."

"In the days of my youth," Father William replied,
    "I remembered that youth could not last;
I thought of the future, whatever I did,
    That I never might grieve for the past."

"You are old, Father William," the young man cried,
    "And life must be hastening away;
You are cheerful, and love to converse upon death:
    Now tell me the reason, I pray."

"I am cheerful, young man," Father William replied;
    "Let the cause thy attention engage;
In the days of my youth, I remembered my God,
    And He hath not forgotten my age."

Father William

Lewis Carroll

"You are old, Father William," the young man said,
 "And your hair has become very white,
And yet you incessantly stand on your head—
 Do you think, at your age, it is right?"

"In my youth," Father William replied to his son,
 "I feared it might injure the brain;
But now that I'm perfectly sure I have none,
 Why, I do it again and again."

"You are old," said the youth, " as I mentioned before,
 And have grown most uncommonly fat;
Yet you turned a back-somersault in at the door—
 Pray, what is the reason of that?"

"In my youth," said the sage, as he shook his gray locks,
 "I kept all my limbs very supple
By the use of this ointment—one shilling the box—
 Allow me to sell you a couple?"

"You are old," said the youth, "and your jaws are too weak
 For anything tougher than suet;
Yet you finished the goose, with the bones and the beak—
 Pray, how did you manage to do it?"

"In my youth," said his father, "I took to the law,
 And argued each case with my wife;
And the muscular strength which it gave to my jaw
 Has lasted the rest of my life."

"You are old," said the youth, "one would hardly suppose
 That your eye was as steady as ever;
Yet you balanced an eel on the end of your nose—
 What made you so awfully clever?"

"I have answered three questions, and that is enough,"
 Said his father; "don't give yourself airs!
Do you think I can listen all day to such stuff?
 Be off, or I'll kick you downstairs!"

The fun that Carroll had with his spoof is obvious, but it should not
obscure an awareness of his skill in building his poem—his "act," as a
juggler might say. The first question put to Father William, for exam-

ple, accuses Southey of being turned upside down, and Father William's first reply openly accuses Southey of being brainless. There is really not much more one can say against a poet, yet Carroll, having already assassinated Southey, manages to keep his poem lively for three more question-and-answer turns. If each question-and-answer turn is thought of as a scene, what is the principle on which the scenes follow one another? Are they increasingly serious? Increasingly ludicrous? Increasingly trivial? Increasingly revealing of Father William's character? What is the order of progression in Southey's poem? What are the three virtues Southey's old man extolls to the youth, and why did Southey develop them in the order given? Carroll found himself having such fun with his parody that he went on for one more question and answer than the original. What are the four points Carroll makes about Father William's character, and how does each parody comment on the points Southey makes?

Very often, when one is uncertain about a given poem, he may find useful clues to better understanding in other poems by the same poet. Carroll wrote a number of happy parodies, all of them aimed at deflating overserious morality. Another of Carroll's most memorable parodies is "The Crocodile," a spoof of Isaac Watts' "How Doth the Little Busy Bee":

How Doth the Little Busy Bee

Isaac Watts

How doth the little busy bee
   Improve each shining hour,
And gather honey all the day
   From every opening flower!

How skillfully she builds her cell!
   How neat she spreads the wax!
And labors hard to store it well
   With the sweet food she makes.

In works of labor or of skill
   I would be busy too;
For Satan finds some mischief still
   For idle hands to do.

In books, or work, or healthful play,
   Let my first years be passed,
That I may give for every day
   Some good account at last.

The Crocodile

Lewis Carroll

How doth the little crocodile
  Improve his shining tail,
And pour the waters of the Nile
  On every shining scale!

How cheerfully he seems to grin,
  How neatly spreads his claws,
And welcomes little fishes in
  With gently smiling jaws!

Southey's Father William and Carroll's speak in what seem to be the same terms, yet to very different ends. Watts' little busy bee and Carroll's crocodile are also presented in similar terms. Both are described with a kind of pious unctuousness, yet the two are engaged in activities of quite a different moral color. Is it too much to argue that the crocodile is a happy hypocrite piously gobbling up the trusting fishes (including the poor fishes among the readers who are willing to take Watts' prettily shallow morality as a true rule of life)? Is it too much again to claim that the crocodile and Father William have a good deal in common—that both of them, in fact, accuse their originals of hypocrisy?

If Carroll's aim in these two poems is to show the ludicrousness and hypocrisy of the poems he lampoons, how do the lampoons achieve that aim? (How does a poem mean?) Clearly the two old men, the little busy bee, and the crocodile are symbols. Of what? One must never be in a hurry to "define" symbols for, as already noted, symbols are not pat equivalents but areas of meaning. What must not be missed, however, is that the real performance of Carroll's parodies arises from the way the symbol "crocodile" plays against the symbol "little busy bee." How many such interplays of meaning suggest themselves?

Whether or not one can identify Carroll's great skills as a poetic performer, no reader can fail to respond to Carroll's sense of fun. He has such a good time within his own mind that inevitably the reader is made happy in his mind. One of the most unusual and certainly one of the most delightful of Carroll's performances is "Jabberwocky":

Jabberwocky

Lewis Carroll

'Twas brillig, and the slithy toves
  Did gyre and gimble in the wabe;
All mimsy were the borogoves,
  And the mome raths outgrabe.

"Beware the Jabberwock, my son!
   The jaws that bite, the claws that catch!
Beware the Jubjub bird, and shun
   The frumious Bandersnatch!"

He took his vorpal sword in hand;
   Long time the manxome foe he sought—
So rested he by the Tumtum tree,
   And stood awhile in thought.

And, as in uffish thought he stood,
   The Jabberwock, with eyes of flame,
Came whiffling through the tulgey wood,
   And burbled as it came!

One, two! One, two! And through and through
   The vorpal blade went snicker-snack!
He left it dead, and with its head
   He went galumphing back.

"And hast thou slain the Jabberwock?
   Come to my arms, my beamish boy!
O frabjous day! Callooh! Callay!"
   He chortled in his joy.

'Twas brillig, and the slithy toves
   Did gyre and gimble in the wabe;
All mimsy were the borogoves,
   And the mome raths outgrabe.

Everyone knows that "Jabberwocky" is a "nonsense" poem: it may be found so listed in any number of anthologies. The word "jabber" in the title, followed by "wocky" (whatever that may mean) is itself descriptive: if there were such a thing as a "wocky" this is the way it might "jabber."

In case there were any doubt about the fun, Carroll "explains" this poem in *Through the Looking Glass*. There, Alice and Humpty Dumpty discuss it, and Humpty Dumpty, after an unenlightening explanation of "brillig," goes on to explain "slithy": "Well, 'slithy' means 'lithe and slimy.' 'Lithe' is the same as active. You see it's like a portmanteau —there are two meanings packed up in one word." Later he identifies "mimsy" as another portmanteau word, made up of "flimsy and miserable."

And with Humpty Dumpty's encouragement a number of people have hunted through "Jabberwocky" for other portmanteau words and for what has been packed into them. Such word hunting is pleasant enough as a game, and it is clearly founded in the author's own directive. Where, moreover, there is such good reason for believing the poem to be "nonsense," little will be served by denying its character as such. But what is "nonsense"? Is it the same as "non-sense"? Suppose that Carroll had written not a poem but an orchestral scherzo, a simple but brilliant piece of "fun" music: would one be so readily tempted to call such music "nonsense"? Let the Wocky jabber as it will—and beautiful jabber it is—there is still a second sort of performance to which the appearance of "non-sense" gives an especially apt flavor. And that second performance involves a great deal of "sense" if by "sense" one means "meaningful comment upon an identifiable subject."

One must go a long way round to identify the subject and the comment upon it. Even then his identifications cannot be more than good guesses. The long way round, however, has the advantage of rambling through some of the most attractive and most native of English poetry, and it will further serve to raise some basic questions about the nature of the poetic performance.

Assume for the sake of exploration that the performance of "Jabberwocky" does involve "sensible" comment on a subject. What sort of performance is it, and what clues are there to the nature of its subject? The beamish (whatever that is) boy is warned about a monster called The Jabberwock. The boy is warned to shun it, and also the Jubjub bird and the frumious (furious, ruminous, gloomious?) Bandersnatch (who "snatches at banter"?). Instead of shunning it, however, the boy hunts it, slays it, and is welcomed back as a conquering hero. Clearly, the tone of all this is mock heroic.

"Father William" and "The Crocodile" provide any reader with reason enough to look for mockery in Carroll's poems. But what could he be mocking here? A first clue lies in the devices Carroll uses in his poetic performance. The poem is deeply indebted to the techniques of English ballads. Stanzas one and two of "Jabberwocky," for example, utter some sort of dark prophecy. In disregard of that prophecy, the hero goes forth to mortal combat. He succeeds in overcoming his dark fate and returns victorious to a hero's welcome. Variants of this basic action may be found in countless ballads. Sometimes the hero returns victorious to be greeted with joy, sometimes he returns dying to be saluted with a lament, sometimes the action takes a different turn. The pattern itself, however, is unmistakable, and in order to sense meaningfully what Carroll is doing with this pattern, the reader will have to take an excursion through English balladry, both "folk" and "literary."

Folk Ballads and Literary Ballads

The introductions to the various ballads that follow will point out specific characteristics of the form, but a brief guide at the outset will be useful.

The folk ballad is an anonymous product of the native culture, put together by many unknown folk singers. Folk ballads were not set down on paper at their point of origin, but were sung. Others heard the ballads and repeated them. Such singers had no original text to which they felt they must be faithful. They were simply attracted to a moving song story. When they came on something in the ballad that did not suit them, they changed it. When they came on something that seemed unimportant, they simply forgot it. Thus the ballad has gone through a process of evolution by natural selection. No "literary" judges passed upon it. It either made itself unforgettable or it was forgotten. This process of oral transmission through many centuries has amounted to an ethnic experiment in the nature of poetry and of storytelling. It follows that what survives such transmission must be inseparable from the "poetic pulse" of the language. The ballads, therefore, demonstrate principles of poetry and of storytelling in a way that must be basic to both arts. Ballads have been remembered by the culture only because they are memorable.

It is easier to remember the high spots of an action than to remember all the connecting detail: so the folk ballad leaps from peak to peak of the story's action, skipping the incidentals. It is easier to remember an action than it is to keep straight the moral comment upon it: so the folk ballad tends to consist of action for its own sake, and to avoid moralization. It is easier, obviously, to remember an effective image, phrase, or detail than it is to remember an ordinary or ineffective one: so the folk ballad, its weak points weeded out, has become a treasury of a sort of poetry that English-speaking people have found unforgettable. Finally, the folk mind is most likely to be attracted to larger rather than smaller kinds of action: so the folk ballad is full of tales of life and death—of tragic loves, of bloody betrayals, of heroic deeds; and so the action tends to be direct and uncomplicated by subtleties and minor motives.

The literary ballad, as will be discussed on pp. 23–24, is a conscious imitation of the folk form by a single poet.

The following ballads are meant to be read for pleasure. Most of them, moreover—to combine business with pleasure—have some story elements in common with those Carroll uses in "Jabberwocky." In the course of the reading, all such elements should be noted and marked for later discussion.

Johnie Armstrong was a robber baron of the Scottish border. The Scottish king, both jealous and afraid of his power, summoned him to court with all his men under promise of good treatment and then ordered that Johnie and all his men be executed. In almost all of the (much longer) existing folk versions, Johnie not only protests his loyalty to the king and offers him great gifts and armed support, but makes clear his claim that he has raided only the English and never turned his force against a Scottish subject. The King refuses his gifts (once Johnie is dead, all his possessions will be forfeit to the crown) and Johnie and his men go down fighting rather than submit. The last three stanzas, and especially the final one, are great examples of the power of the ballad.

Johnie Armstrong

(Condensed Version)

There dwelt a man in fair Westmorland,
  Johnie Armstrong men did him call.
He had neither lands nor rents coming in,
  Yet he kept eight score men in his hall.

He had horses and harness for them all.
  Their goodly steeds were all milk-white.
O the golden bands all about their necks!
  Their weapons, they were all alike.

The news was brought unto the king
  That there was such a one as he
That lived like a bold out-law,
  And robbed all the north-countree.

The king he writ a letter then,
  A letter which was large and long,
And signed it with his own hand,
  And he promised to do him no wrong.

When this letter came to Johnie,
  His heart was as blythe as birds on the tree:
"Never was I sent for before any king,
  My father, my grandfather, nor none but me.

And if we go the king before,
  I would we went most orderly;
Let everyman wear his scarlet cloak
  Laced up with silver laces three.

Let everyman wear his velvet coat
  Laced with silver lace so white.
O the golden bands all about your necks!
  Black hats, white feathers, all alike."

By the morrow morning at ten of the clock,
  Towards Edenburough gone was he,
And with him all his eight score men.
  Good lord, it was a goodly sight to see!

When Johnie came before the king,
  He fell down on his knee.
"O pardon my sovereign liege," he said,
  "O pardon my eight score men and me!"

"Thou shalt have no pardon, thou traitor strong,
   For thy eight score men nor thee;
For tomorrow morning by ten of the clock
   Both thou and them shall hang on the gallow-tree."

But Johnie looked over his left shoulder,
   Good Lord, what a grievous look looked he!
Saying, "Asking grace of a graceless face—
   Why there is none for you nor me."

But Johnie had a bright sword by his side,
   And it was made of the mettle so free,
That had not the king stept his foot aside,
   He had smitten his head from his fair bodie.

Saying: "Fight on, my merry men all,
   And see that none of you be taine;
For rather than men shall say we were hanged,
   Let them say how we were slain."

Then, God wot, fair Edenburough rose,
   And so beset poor Johnie round,
That four score and ten of his best men
   Lay gasping all upon the ground.

Then like a mad man Johnie laid about,
   And like a mad man then fought he,
Until a false Scot come Johnie behind
   And ran him through the fair bodie.

Saying: "Fight on, my merry men all,
   And see that none of you be taine;
For I will lie down and bleed awhile,
   And then I will rise and fight again."

From Chaucer's time to the eighteenth century, the ballad had a relatively small place in "serious" English poetry, but following the eighteenth century's revival of interest in England's literary antiquities and the wider awareness of the ballad as a form, it was inevitable that poets should find the ballad way of telling a story irresistible. Thousands of ballads, good, bad, and miserably bad were written in the nineteenth century. "Written" here is used literally: each of these ballads was composed by a single man deliberately reworking the ballad form for his own purposes. "The Old Man's Comforts" is a ballad heavily invested with morality. (The folk ballad seldom bothers to draw a moral; its native interest is in telling a story.) Many literary balladeers hoaxed up the ballad form with so much flummery and so many perfumed asides that it tended to die of overdecoration. Others strove for the heroic strain and succeeded only in achieving a mock-heroic pastiche.

Of the ballads that follow, the excerpt from "Marco Bozzaris" may be taken as a fair example of the mock-heroic smother. "A Ballad of Hell" may be taken as a relatively successful, though unmistakably literary imitation, of the pure ballad. "The Yarn of the Nancy Bell" may be taken as a happy example of a poet having fun with the ballad form.

QUESTIONS

Compare the following poems with "Johnie Armstrong." Which elements of the performance of each poem seem to make the difference in tone? The Scottish border lords proudly recorded Johnie Armstrong's death as an example of tyranny resisted, and Halleck certainly sings Bozzaris's praises for the same reason. Is Halleck more interested in the story or in the moral he derives from it?

Assuming that "Marco Bozzaris" were memorable enough to undergo folk transmission, which parts of it might survive and which parts would most probably be dropped in oral transmission? Why?

What differences between ballad and poem can you identify in the language, in the tone, and in the kind of incident? In "Sir Patrick Spens," the description of the crew drowning ("Their hats they swam aboon") is a classic trope known as *synechdoche,* a figure of speech in which a part is used to represent the whole. Note that there are no shrieks of the dying, no final prayers, no moral pronouncements, but simply the statement that long before the Scots lords crossed the water their hats floated above them on the tide. The tremendous last stanza of "Johnie Armstrong" on the other hand is a *hyperbole* (an exaggeration), but a hyperbole made with such understatement (paradoxical as that may seem) that it leaves no sense of overreaching for effect.

Compare Bozzaris's exhortation to his band in stanza three. Had Marine sergeants on Guadalcanal been required to make all their orders quotations from English poetry, and had one of them had to cheer his men on during a battle, would he have been more tempted to quote Bozzaris or Johnie Armstrong? That is to say, which is better "fight talk"?

Marco Bozzaris
(April 20, 1823)

(Excerpt)

Fitz-Greene Halleck

At midnight, in his guarded tent,
  The Turk was dreaming of the hour
When Greece, her knee in suppliance bent,
  Should tremble at his power:

In dreams, through camp and court, he bore
The trophies of a conqueror;
    In dreams his song of triumph heard;
Then wore his monarch's signet ring:
Then pressed that monarch's throne—a king;
As wild his thoughts, and gay of wing,
    As Eden's garden bird.

At midnight, in the forest shades,
    Bozzaris ranged his Suliote band,
True as the steel of their tried blades,
    Heroes in heart and hand.
There had the Persian's thousands stood,
There had the glad earth drunk their blood
    On old Platæa's day;
And now there breathed that haunted air
The sons of sires who conquered there,
With arm to strike, and soul to dare,
    As quick, as far as they.

An hour passed on—the Turk awoke;
    That bright dream was his last;
He woke—to hear his sentries shriek,
    "To arms! they come! the Greek! the Greek!"
He woke—to die midst flame, and smoke,
And shout, and groan, and sabre-stroke,
    And death-shots falling thick and fast
As lightnings from the mountain-cloud;
And heard, with voice as trumpet loud,
    Bozzaris cheer his band:
"Strike—till the last armed foe expires;
Strike—for your altars and your fires;
Strike—for the green graves of your sires;
    God—and your native land!"

They fought—like brave men, long and well;
    They piled that ground with Moslem slain,
They conquered—but Bozzaris fell,
    Bleeding at every vein.
His few surviving comrades saw
His smile when rang their proud hurrah,
    And the red field was won;
Then saw in death his eyelids close
Calmly, as to a night's repose,
    Like flowers at set of sun.

Come to the bridal-chamber, Death!
    Come to the mother's, when she feels,

ranged: drew up into battle formation, arranged.

For the first time, her first-born's breath;
   Come when the blessed seals
That close the pestilence are broke,
And crowded cities wail its stroke;
Come in consumption's ghastly form,
The earthquake shock, the ocean storm;
Come when the heart beats high and warm
   With banquet-song, and dance, and wine;
And thou art terrible—the tear,
The groan, the knell, the pall, the bier,
And all we know, or dream, or fear
   Of agony, are thine.

But to the hero, when his sword
   Has won the battle for the free,
Thy voice sounds like a prophet's word;
And in its hollow tones are heard
   The thanks of millions yet to be.
Come, when his task of fame is wrought—
Come, with her laurel-leaf, blood-bought—
   Come in her crowning hour—and then
Thy sunken eye's unearthly light
To him is welcome as the sight
   Of sky and stars to prisoned men:
Thy grasp is welcome as the hand
Of brother in a foreign land;
Thy summons welcome as the cry
That told the Indian isles were nigh
   To the world-seeking Genoese,
When the land wind, from woods of palm,
And orange groves, and fields of balm,
   Blew o'er the Haytian seas.

Bozzaris! with the storied brave
   Greece nurtured in her glory's time,
Rest thee—there is no prouder grave,
   Even in her own proud clime.
She wore no funeral-weeds for thee,
   Nor bade the dark hearse wave its plume
Like torn branch from death's leafless tree
In sorrow's pomp and pageantry,
   The heartless luxury of the tomb;
But she remembers thee as one
Long loved, and for a season gone;
For thee her poet's lyre is wreathed,
Her marble wrought, her music breathed;
For thee she rings the birthday bells;
Of thee her babes' first lisping tells;

For thine her evening prayer is said
At palace-couch and cottage-bed;
Her soldier, closing with the foe,
Gives for thy sake a deadlier blow;
His plighted maiden, when she fears
For him, the joy of her young years,
Thinks of thy fate, and checks her tears:
   And she, the mother of thy boys,
Though in her eye and faded cheek
Is read the grief she will not speak,
   The memory of her buried joys,
And even she who gave thee birth,
Will, by their pilgrim-circled hearth,
   Talk of thy doom without a sigh:
For thou art Freedom's now, and Fame's:
One of the few, the immortal names,
   That were not born to die.

All criticism of poetry begins fundamentally with "I like it" or "I don't like it." It seems impossible to imagine a reader of "A Ballad of Hell" (p. 29) who does not find himself liking the heroine. She certainly performs superbly the role of the ballad heroine, and finding her unforgettable, the reader can scarcely forget the poem. Yet certainly, had the ballad undergone folk transmission, a number of its details would have disappeared. Both the heroine and Sir Patrick receive alarming letters and take action as a result of them. The time between the receipt of the letter and the beginning of the consequent action may reasonably be called—by analogy to a play—"the letter scene." Compare the two Letter Scenes. Which is the more effective performance? Could anything be added to Sir Patrick's reaction to make it more effective? Could anything be subtracted from the heroine's?

In general, could anything well be added to Sir Patrick or subtracted from "A Ballad of Hell"? What would you add or take out? How long does the heroine take to kill herself? How long might she have taken had she been a true ballad product? How long does it take her to get to hell, once she has died? How "devilish" is the devil? Compare the heroine's defiance of the devil and of hell with Johnie Armstrong's defiance of the Scottish king.

"Sir Patrick Spens" (or Spence) is certainly the best known of the Scottish ballads and may well be taken as a model for the ballad form. We have modernized the language, but a few points of difficulty remain. In stanza three "a broad letter" probably means "an official letter, a royal command." In stanza eight "shoon" means "shoes" and "aboon" means "above." "Their hats they swam aboon" means "Their hats floated above them" (that is, the crew sank leaving their hats floating on the surface).

Sir Patrick Spens

The King sits in Dumferling town,
  Drinking the blood-red wine:
"O where will I get good sailors
  To sail this ship of mine?"

Up and spoke an old knight,
  Sat at the King's right knee:
"Sir Patrick Spens is the best sailor
  That sails upon the sea."

The King has written a broad letter,
  And signed it with his hand,
And sent it to Sir Patrick Spens,
  Was walking on the sand.

The first line that Sir Patrick read
  A loud laugh laughed he:
The next line that Sir Patrick read,
  A tear blinded his ee.

"O who is this has done this deed,
  This ill deed done to me,
To send me out this time of the year
  To sail upon the sea?

Make haste, make haste, my merry men all,
  Our good ship sails at morn."
"O say not so, my master dear,
  For I fear a deadly storm.

Late, late last night I saw the new moon
  with the old moon in her arm,
And I fear, I fear, my master dear,
  That we will come to harm."

O our Scots nobles were right loth
  To wet their cork-heeled shoon;
But long ere all the play was played,
  Their hats they swam aboon.

O long, long will their ladies sit
  With their fans into their hand,
Before they see Sir Patrick Spens
  Come sailing to the land.

O long, long will the ladies stand
  With their gold combs in their hair,
Waiting for their own dear lords,
  For they'll see them no mair.

Half-o'er, half-o'er to Abadour
  'Tis fifty fathoms deep,
And there lies good Sir Patrick Spens
  With the Scots lords at his feet.

A Ballad of Hell

John Davidson

"A letter from my love today!
  Oh, unexpected, dear appeal!"
She struck a happy tear away
  And broke the crimson seal.

"My love, there is no help on earth,
  No help in heaven; the dead-man's bell
Must toll our wedding; our first hearth
  Must be the well-paved floor of hell."

The color died from out her face,
  Her eyes like ghostly candles shone;
She cast dread looks about the place,
  Then clenched her teeth and read right on.

"I may not pass the prison door;
  Here must I rot from day to day,
Unless I wed whom I abhor,
  My cousin, Blanche of Valencay.

"At midnight with my dagger keen,
  I'll take my life; it must be so.
Meet me in hell tonight, my queen,
  For weal and woe."

She laughed, although her face was wan,
  She girded on her golden belt,
She took her jewelled ivory fan,
  And at her glowing missal knelt.

Then rose, "And am I mad?" she said.
　　She broke her fan, her belt untied;
With leather girt herself instead,
　　And stuck a dagger at her side.

She waited, shuddering in her room,
　　Till sleep had fallen on all the house.
She never flinched; she faced her doom:
　　They two must sin to keep their vows.

Then out into the night she went,
　　And, stooping, crept by hedge and tree;
Her rose-bush flung a snare of scent,
　　And caught a happy memory.

She fell, and lay a minute's space;
　　She tore the sward in her distress;
The dewy grass refreshed her face;
　　She rose and ran with lifted dress.

She started like a morn-caught ghost
　　Once when the moon came out and stood
To watch; the naked road she crossed,
　　And dived into the murmuring wood.

The branches snatched her streaming cloak;
　　A live thing shrieked; she made no stay!
She hurried to the trysting-oak—
　　Right well she knew the way.

Without a pause she bared her breast,
　　And drove her dagger home and fell,
And lay like one that takes her rest,
　　And died and wakened up in hell.

She bathed her spirit in the flame,
　　And near the center took her post;
From all sides to her ears there came
　　The dreary anguish of the lost.

The devil started at her side,
　　Comely, and tall, and black as jet.
"I am young Malespina's bride;
　　Has he come hither yet?"

"My poppet, welcome to your bed."
　　"Is Malespina here?"
"Not he! Tomorrow he must wed
　　His cousin Blanche, my dear!"

"You lie, he died with me tonight."
"Not he! it was a plot" . . . "You lie."
"My dear, I never lie outright."
"We died at midnight, he and I."

The devil went. Without a groan
  She, gathered up in one fierce prayer,
Took root in hell's midst all alone,
  And waited for him there.

She dared to make herself at home
  Amidst the wail, the uneasy stir.
The blood-stained flame that filled the dome,
  Scentless and silent, shrouded her.

How long she stayed I cannot tell;
  But when she felt his perfidy,
She marched across the floor of hell;
  And all the damned stood up to see.

The devil stopped her at the brink.
  She shook him off; she cried, "Away!"
"My dear, you have gone mad, I think."
  "I was betrayed: I will not stay."

Across the weltering deep she ran;
  A stranger thing was never seen:
The damned stood silent to a man;
  They saw the great gulf set between.

To her it seemed a meadow fair;
  And flowers sprang up about her feet;
She entered heaven; she climbed the stair;
  And knelt down at the mercy-seat.

Seraphs and saints with one great voice
  Welcomed that soul that knew not fear.
Amazed to find it could rejoice,
  Hell raised a hoarse, half-human cheer.

    To illustrate the great vitality of the ballad and its diffusion through many cultures, the ballad of Edward is here reproduced in a Scottish form and also in a version recorded in North Carolina. The two texts are taken from Albert B. Friedman's *The Viking Book of Folk Ballads of the English Speaking World* (New York, Viking, 1956). "Lord Randal" is added as an example of a similar but independent ballad. It also exists in many Scottish, English, and American forms, and Mr. Friedman thinks it may originally have been transplanted from Italy. The form of text A of "Edward" follows Mr. Friedman's text without modernization. The following note is excerpted from his introduction to the ballad:

Entirely developed through dialogue, the ballad manages to generate enormous dramatic tension. As a result, there is no more powerful climax in any ballad than the surprise revelation of the mother's guilt in the last lines of "Edward." Some scholars suspect the folk tradition had literary assistance here. . . . The "Edward" story has proved too "strong" for the American folk: a brother or a brother-in-law, not the sufferer's father, is the victim in American versions, and the mother has no share in the crime. . . . The American ballad may be nearer the original form of the story since a brother was also the victim in the lost English or Scottish version from which the Scandinavian ballads on this theme descended. In A, Edward intends to go into exile. Another Scottish version has him setting his foot in a "bottomless boat," thus suggesting that in an ancient form of the story Edward submitted himself to exposure in an open boat, a medieval punishment for fratricide. Text B from North Carolina represents the American tradition.

Edward
Text A

"Why dois your brand sae drap wi' bluid,
               Edward, Edward?
Why dois your brand sae drip wi' bluid?
   And why sae sad gang yee, O?"
"O, I hae killed my hauke sae guid,
               Mither, mither,
O, I hae killed my hauke sae guid,
   And I had nae mair bot hee, O."

"Your haukis bluid was nevir sae reid,
               Edward, Edward,
Your haukis bluid was nevir sae reid,
   My deir son I tell thee, O."
"O, I hae killed my reid-roan steid,
               Mither, mither,
O, I hae killed my reid-roan steid,
   That erst was sae fair and frie, O."

"Your steid was auld, and yee hae gat mair,
               Edward, Edward,
Your steid was auld, and yee hae gat mair,
   Sum other dule ye drie, O."
"O, I hae killed my fadir deir,
               Mither, mither,
O, I hae killed my fadir deir,
   Alas, and wae is mee, O!"

"And whatten penance wul yee drie for that,
    Edward, Edward?
And whatten penance wul yee drie for that?
 My deir son, now tell me, O."
"Ile set my feit in yonder boat,
    Mither, mither,
Ile set my feit in yonder boat,
 And Ile fare ovir the sea, O."

"And what wul yee doe wi' your towirs and your ha',
    Edward, Edward?
And what wul yee doe wi' your towirs and your ha',
 That were sae fair to see, O? "
"Ile let thame stand tul they doun fa',
    Mither, mither,
Ile let thame stand tul they doun fa',
 For here nevir mair maun I bee, O."

"And what wul yee leive to your bairns and your wife,
    Edward, Edward?
And what wul yee leive to your bairns and your wife,
 When yee gang ovir the sea, O?"
"The warldis room, late them beg thrae life,
    Mither, mither,
The warldis room, late them beg thrae life,
 For thame nevir mair wul I see, O."

"And what wul yee leive to your ain mither deir,
    Edward, Edward?
And what wul yee leive to your ain mither deir?
 My deir son, now tell me, O."
"The curse of hell frae me sall yee beir,
    Mither, mither,
The curse of hell frae me sall yee beir,
 Sic counseils yee gave to me, O."

Text B

"How comes that blood all over your shirt?
My son, come tell it to me."
"It's the blood of my little guinea pig—
O mother, please let me be.
It's the blood of my little guinea pig—
O mother, please let me be.

"Your guinea pig's blood is not so red.
My son come tell it to me."
"It's the blood of my little hunting dog
That played in the field for me . . ."

---

brand: sword. **sae:** so. **haukis:** hawk's. **dule:** dole, grief. **drie:** endure. **bairns:** children. **the warldis room:** the world's room; the length and breadth of the world. **thrae:** through. **gang:** go. **sic counseils:** such counsels.

"Your dog lies yonder, O my son,
And this it could not be."
"It is the blood of my old roan horse
That pulled the plow for me . . ."

"How comes that blood all over your shirt?
My son, come tell it to me."
"It's the blood of my little brother Bill
Who I killed in the field today."

"And what will you do when your father comes home?
My son, come tell it to me."
"I'll put my feet in the bottom of a boat
I'll put my feet in the bottom of a boat
And sail across the sea.
And sail across the sea."

Lord Randal

"O where hae ye been, Lord Randal, my son?
  O where hae ye been, my handsome young man?"
"I hae been to the wild wood; mother, make my bed soon,
  For I'm weary wi' hunting, and fain wald lie down."

"Where gat ye your dinner, Lord Randal, my son?
  Where gat ye your dinner, my handsome young man?"
"I din'd wi' my true-love; mother, make my bed soon,
  For I'm weary wi' hunting, and fain wald lie down."

"What gat ye to your dinner, Lord Randal, my son?
  What gat ye to your dinner, my handsome young man?"
"I gat eels boil'd in broth; mother, make my bed soon,
  For I'm weary wi' hunting, and fain wald lie down."

"What became of your bloodhounds, Lord Randal, my son?
  What became of your bloodhounds, my handsome young
  man?"
"O they swell'd and they died; mother, make my bed soon,
  For I'm weary wi' hunting, and fain wald lie down."

"O I fear ye are poisoned, Lord Randal, my son!
  O I fear ye are poisoned, my handsome young man!"
"O yes! I am poison'd; mother, make my bed soon,
  For I'm sick at the heart, and fain wald lie down."

A number of folk ballads have the hero's mother questioning him on
his return home about the details of his journey. In some instances, the
hero has committed a crime, and in some has been with a woman.

"Billy Boy" is an American example of such a ballad. "Lord Randal" and "Edward" are versions from Scotland. Which of the ballads do you prefer? How would you explain your preference?

Billy Boy

"O where have you been, Billy Boy, Billy Boy,
  O where have you been, Charming Billy?
"I have been to seek a wife, she's the joy of my life,
  She's a young thing and cannot leave her mother."

"Did she ask you to come in, Billy Boy, Billy Boy,
  Did she ask you to come in, Charming Billy?"
"Yes she asked me to come in, she has dimples in her chin,
  She's a young thing and cannot leave her mother."

"Did she set for you a chair, Billy Boy, Billy Boy,
  Did she set for you a chair, Charming Billy?"
"Yes, she set for me a chair, she has ringlets in her hair,
  She's a young thing and cannot leave her mother."

"Can she bake a cherry pie, Billy Boy, Billy Boy,
  Can she bake a cherry pie, Charming Billy?"
"She can bake a cherry pie quick as a cat can wink its eye,
  She's a young thing and cannot leave her mother."

"Did you ask her to be your wife, Billy Boy, Billy Boy,
  Did you ask her to be your wife, Charming Billy?"
"Yes I asked her to be my wife, and live with me all my life,
  She's a young thing and cannot leave her mother."

"How old is she, Billy Boy, Billy Boy,
  How old is she, Charming Billy?"
"Three times six and three times seven, three times twenty and eleven,
  She's a young thing and cannot leave her mother."

Since the present chapter is, among other things, a ramble through some specimen English ballads, there is no reason to avoid inviting bypaths. The "Lyke-Wake Dirge" is very far indeed from "Jabberwocky," but certainly it must not be omitted from any discussion of the ballad tradition, though it is not strictly speaking a ballad but a folk dirge for a departed soul; as moving a knell for the departed as any in the English language.

The idea of the "lyke-wake" survives in the modern Irish wake, the custom of sitting up with the dead. "Lyke" meant body or corpse. In this dirge, the soul is described as going first to "Whinny-muir," a moor grown with "whins" or thorny furze bushes. If in life the departed had "given shoes" (been generous) his soul would have them now; if not, the thorns would prick him to the bone. "Brig o' Dread" is bridge of dread, between this world and the next. The idea of a bridge to immortality, or a bridge between the real world and the world of fairyland, was not uncommon in medieval literature.

A Lyke-Wake Dirge

This ae nighte, this ae nighte,
—*Every nighte and alle,*
Fire and sleet and candle-lighte,
And Christe receive thy saule.

When thou from hence away art past,
—*Every nighte and alle,*
To Whinny-muir thou com'st at last;
And Christe receive thy saule.

If ever thou gavest hosen and shoon,
—*Every nighte and alle,*
Sit thee down and put them on;
And Christe receive thy saule.

If hosen and shoon thou ne'er gav'st nane
—*Every nighte and alle,*
The whinnes sall prick thee to the bare bane;
And Christe receive thy saule.

From Whinny-muir when thou may'st pass,
—*Every nighte and alle,*
To Brig o' Dread thou com'st at last;
And Christe receive thy saule.

From Brig o' Dread when thou may'st pass,
—*Every nighte and alle,*
To Purgatory fire thou com'st at last;
And Christe receive thy saule.

If ever thou gavest meat or drink,
—*Every nighte and alle,*
The fire sall never make thee shrink;
And Christe receive thy saule.

If meat or drink thou ne'er gav'st nane,
—*Every nighte and alle,*
The fire will burn thee to the bare bane;
And Christe receive thy saule.

This ae nighte, this ae nighte,
  —*Every nighte and alle,*
Fire and sleet and candle-lighte,
  And Christe receive thy saule.

"The Yarn of the Nancy Bell" was written in 1866 and offered to *Punch* but was rejected on the grounds that cannibalism was too offensive a theme. By "a theme" one generally understands "what the writer set out to say." To what extent did the writer set out to write about cannibalism?

Is it possible that his real intent was to write a parody of Coleridge's "Ancient Mariner" (p. 55)?

How "real" is the cannibalism? Note that in the first line of stanza eleven the survivors had neither "wittles [victuals] nor drink." Yet in stanza eighteen it is clear that the cook not only has water, but a very large kettle, salt and pepper, shallot (along with something to chop it with) and sage and parsley—practically an epicure's kitchen. Could one explain this contradiction to Mr. Gradgrind's satisfaction?

The Yarn of the Nancy Bell

William Schwenck Gilbert

'Twas on the shores that round our coast
  From Deal to Ramsgate span,
That I found alone on a piece of stone
  An elderly naval man.

His hair was weedy, his beard was long,
  And weedy and long was he,
And I heard this wight on the shore recite
  In a singular minor key:

"Oh, I am a cook and a captain bold,
  And the mate of the *Nancy* brig,
And a bo'sun tight, and a midshipmite,
  And the crew of the captain's gig."

And he shook his fists, and he tore his hair,
  Till I really felt afraid,
For I couldn't help thinking the man had been drinking,
  And so I simply said:

"Oh elderly man, it's little I know
  Of the duties of men of the sea,
And I'll eat my hand if I understand
  However you can be

Deal and Ramsgate: Seaside resorts on the coast of Kent.

At once a cook, and a captain bold,
    And the mate of the *Nancy* brig,
And a bo'sun tight, and a midshipmite,
    And the crew of the captain's gig."

Then he gave a hitch to his trousers, which
    Is a trick all seamen larn,
And having got rid of a thumping quid,
    He spun this painful yarn:

"'Twas in the good ship *Nancy Bell*
    That we sailed to the Indian Sea,
And there on a reef we came to grief,
    Which has often occurred to me.

And pretty nigh all the crew was drowned
    (There was seventy-seven o'soul),
And only ten of the *Nancy's* men
    Said 'Here!' to the muster-roll.

There was me and the cook and the captain bold,
    And the mate of the *Nancy* brig,
And the bo'sun tight, and a midshipmite,
    And the crew of the captain's gig.

For a month we'd neither wittles nor drink,
    Till a-hungry we did feel,
So we drawed a lot, and, accordin' shot
    The captain for our meal.

The next lot fell to the *Nancy's* mate,
    And a delicate dish he made;
Then our appetite with the midshipmite
    We seven survivors stayed.

And then we murdered the bo'sun tight,
    And he much resembled pig;
Then we wittled free, did the cook and me,
    On the crew of the captain's gig.

Then only the cook and me was left,
    And the delicate question, 'Which
Of us two goes to the kettle?' arose,
    And we argued it out as sich.

For I loved that cook as a brother, I did,
    And the cook he worshiped me;
But we'd both be blowed if we'd either be stowed
    In the other chap's hold, you see.

---

thumping quid: of chewing tobacco. **seventy-seven o' soul:** seventy-seven souls.

'I'll be eat if you dines off me,' says Tom;
　'Yes, that,' says I, 'you'll be—'
'I'm boiled if I die, my friend,' quoth I;
　And 'Exactly so,' quoth he.

Says he, 'Dear James, to murder me
　Were a foolish thing to do,
For don't you see that you can't cook *me*,
　While I can—and will—cook *you*!'

So he boils the water, and takes the salt
　And the pepper in portions true
(Which he never forgot) and some chopped shallot,
　And some sage and parsley too.

'Come here,' says he, with a proper pride
　Which his smiling features tell,
''Twill soothing be if I let you see
How extremely nice you'll smell.'

And he stirred it round and round and round,
　And he sniffed at the foaming froth;
When I ups with his heels, and smothers his squeals
　In the scum of the boiling broth.

And I eat that cook in a week or less,
　And—as I eating be
The last of his chops, why, I almost drops,
　For a wessel in sight I see!

　　　　·　·　·　·　·　·

And I never larf, and I never smile,
　And I never lark nor play,
But sit and croak, and a single joke
　I have—which is to say:

'Oh, I am a cook and a captain bold,
　And the mate of the *Nancy* brig,
And a bos'sun tight, and a midshipmite,
　And the crew of the captain's gig!'"

In a Prominent Bar in Secaucus One Day
To the tune of "The Old Orange Flute"
or the tune of "Sweet Betsy from Pike"

X. J. Kennedy

In a prominent bar in Secaucus one day
Rose a lady in skunk with a topheavy sway,
Raised a knobby red finger—all turned from their beer—
While with eyes bright as snowcrust she sang high and clear:

"Now who of you'd think from an eyeload of me
That I once was a lady as proud as could be?
Oh I'd never sit down by a tumbledown drunk
If it wasn't, my dears, for the high cost of junk.

"All the gents used to swear that the white of my calf
Beat the down of the swan by a length and a half.
In the kerchief of linen I caught to my nose
Ah, there never fell snot, but a little gold rose.

"I had seven gold teeth and a toothpick of gold,
My Virginia cheroot was a leaf of it rolled
And I'd light it each time with a thousand in cash—
Why the bums used to fight if I flicked them an ash.

"Once the toast of the Biltmore, the belle of the Taft,
I would drink bottle beer at the Drake, never draft,
And dine at the Astor on Salisbury steak
With a clean tablecloth for each bite I did take.

"In a car like the Roxy I'd roll to the track,
A steel-guitar trio, a bar in the back,
And the wheels made no noise, they turned over so fast,
Still it took you ten minutes to see me go past.

"When the horses bowed down to me that I might choose,
I bet on them all, for I hated to lose.
Now I'm saddled each night for my butter and eggs
And the broken threads race down the backs of my legs.

"Let you hold in mind, girls, that your beauty must pass
Like a lovely white clover that rusts with its grass.
Keep your bottoms off barstools and marry you young
Or be left—an old barrel with many a bung.

"For when time takes you out for a spin in his car
You'll be hard-pressed to stop him from going too far
And be left by the roadside, for all your good deeds,
Two toadstools for tits and a face full of weeds."

All the house raised a cheer, but the man at the bar
Made a phonecall and up pulled a red patrol car
And she blew us a kiss as they copped her away
From that prominent bar in Secaucus, N.J.

Kennedy has written a takeoff on the traditional ballad, drawing on
several worn props and characters and putting them in a contemporary
setting in order to create an interesting and amusing story, partly by
means of the contrasts. The barroom confession, the wise and kindly

prostitute, the elaborate advice to the young—these are what a vaude-villian would have called "old chestnuts." Another exposure to them for their own sakes would not be likely to excite much interest in a modern reader. What objects and expressions does the author intro-duce into the poem to pull it into the twentieth century and thereby cause us to look at it in a new way?

Compare Kennedy's poem with the following one by Ransom, which also replays the traditional ballad, but in a language that also has an antique ring about it. Does the more appropriate language of Ransom's poem have anything to do with the fact that Kennedy's poem is more amusing? Would it be accurate to call either of the poems a satire? Do either the lady or Captain Carpenter represent anyone or anything beyond themselves; that is, is either of them a symbol?

Captain Carpenter

John Crowe Ransom

Captain Carpenter rose up in his prime
Put on his pistols and went riding out
But had got wellnigh nowhere at that time
Till he fell in with ladies in a rout.

It was a pretty lady and all her train
That played with him so sweetly but before
An hour she'd taken a sword with all her main
And twined him of his nose for evermore.

Captain Carpenter mounted up one day
And rode straightway into a stranger rogue
That looked unchristian but be that as may
The Captain did not wait upon prologue.

But drew upon him out of his great heart
The other swung against him with a club
And cracked his two legs at the shinny part
And let him roll and stick like any tub.

Captain Carpenter rode many a time
From male and female took he sundry harms
He met the wife of Satan crying "I'm
The she-wolf bids you shall bear no more arms."

Their strokes and counters whistled in the wind
I wish he had delivered half his blows
But where she should have made off like a hind
The bitch bit off his arms at the elbows.

And Captain Carpenter parted with his ears
To a black devil that used him in this wise
O Jesus ere his threescore and ten years
Another had plucked out his sweet blue eyes.

Captain Carpenter got up on his roan
And sallied from the gate in hell's despite
I heard him asking in the grimmest tone
If any enemy yet there was to fight?

"To any adversary it is fame
If he risk to be wounded by my tongue
Or burnt in two beneath my red heart's flame
Such are the perils he is cast among.

"But if he can he has a pretty choice
From an anatomy with little to lose
Whether he cut my tongue and take my voice
Or whether it be my round red heart he choose."

It was the neatest knave that ever was seen
Stepping in perfume from his lady's bower
Who at this word put in his merry mien
And fell on Captain Carpenter like a tower.

I would not knock old fellows in the dust
But there lay Captain Carpenter on his back
His weapons were the old heart in his bust
And a blade shook between rotten teeth alack.

The rogue in scarlet and grey soon knew his mind
He wished to get his trophy and depart
With gentle apology and touch refined
He pierced him and produced the Captain's heart.

God's mercy rest on Captain Carpenter now
I thought him Sirs an honest gentleman
Citizen husband soldier and scholar enow
Let jangling kites eat of him if they can.

But God's deep curses follow after those
That shore him of his goodly nose and ears
His legs and strong arms at the two elbows
And eyes that had not watered seventy years.

The curse of hell upon the sleek upstart
That got the Captain finally on his back
And took the red red vitals of his heart
And made the kites to whet their beaks clack clack.

"Ballad of the Hoppy-Toad" is another recent poem after the fashion of the folk ballad. Margaret Walker tells the story of a man with dark powers—a conjure man or a witch man—setting about to cast a spell, and how the spell is broken. A careful reader will be able to figure the meaning of the unfamiliar expressions in the context of the language and action.

Ballad of the Hoppy-Toad

Margaret Walker

Ain't been on Market Street for nothing
With my regular washing load
When the Saturday crowd went stomping
Down the Johnny-jumping road,

Seen Sally Jones come running
With a razor at her throat,
Seen Deacon's daughter lurching
Like a drunken alley goat.

But the biggest for my money,
And the saddest for my throw
Was the night I seen the goopher man
Throw dust around my door.

Come sneaking round my doorway
In a stovepipe hat and coat;
Come sneaking round my doorway
To drop the evil note.

I run down to Sis Avery's
And told her what I seen
"Root-worker's out to git me
What you reckon that there mean?"

Sis Avery she done told me,
"Now honey go on back
I knows just what will hex him
And that old goopher sack."

Now I done burned the candles
Till I seen the face of Jim
And I done been to Church and prayed
But can't git rid of him.

Don't want to burn his picture
Don't want to dig his grave
Just want to have my peace of mind
And make that dog behave.

Was running through the fields one day
Sis Avery's chopping corn
Big horse come stomping after me
I knowed then I was gone.

Sis Avery grabbed that horse's mane
And not one minute late
Cause trembling down behind her
I seen my ugly fate.

She hollered to that horse to "Whoa!
I gotcha hoppy-toad."
And yonder come the goopher man
A-running down the road.

She hollered to that horse to "Whoa"
And what you wanta think?
Great-God-a-mighty, that there horse
Begun to sweat and shrink.

He shrunk up to a teeny horse
He shrunk up to a toad
And yonder come the goopher man
Still running down the road.

She hollered to that horse to "Whoa"
She said, "I'm killing him.
Now you just watch this hoppy-toad
And you'll be rid of Jim."

The goopher man was hollering
"Don't kill that hoppy-toad."
Sis Avery she said "Honey,
You bout to lose your load."

That hoppy-toad was dying
Right there in the road
And goopher man was screaming
"Don't kill that hoppy-toad."

The hoppy-toad shook one more time
And then he up and died
Old goopher man fell dying, too.
"O hoppy-toad," he cried.

The story is told in a language as unsophisticated and relaxed as Ransom's language in "Captain Carpenter" is cultivated and "correct." This does not mean that Walker is less careful in the control of her lines, or that her story is less carefully delivered. The level of a poem's language has nothing to do with whether or not the poem is a good poem, but the appropriateness of the language to the situation in the poem has a great deal to do with it. Why do you think the poets chose to tell their stories in the idioms they used?

Jabberwocky Revisited

With some knowledge of the ballad in his background, one is prepared to see in "Jabberwocky" a number of devices that might not have been visible at first reading. The first stanza of "Jabberwocky," for example, is unmistakably based on a ballad motif that may be called "the opening contest of dark forces" (see the beginning of "Marco Bozzaris"). The second stanza reinforces the dark mood of the opening forces with a ballad motif that may be called "the dark warning" (see stanza seven of "Sir Patrick Spens"). Stanzas three through five describe some vastly heroic action of arms (see Johnie Armstrong's final battle). Stanza six presents the hero returning in triumph (see Halleck's final windy salute to Bozzaris.) The beamish boy was luckier than Bozzaris, but both receive an accolade.

Carroll, however, uses these heroic patterns only to blow them up by exaggeration into the mock heroic. The Jabberwock and the frumious Bandersnatch may be dark forces, but they are more ridiculous than frightful. The conquering hero, a bit of an "uffish" oaf at best, does not ride back in state but goes "galumphing back." He is greeted not as "Bozzaris! with the storied brave!" but as my "beamish boy." Nor can one fail to note that the final voice, like the hero himself, is slightly cracked and queer.

But what is Carroll inflating so carefully into a kind of ultimate ridiculousness? Carroll's is a playful mind, and playful poets always tend to be evasive. As Robert Frost wrote of his neighbor in "Mending Wall":

> I could say "Elves" to him,
> But it's not elves exactly, and I'd rather
> He said it for himself.

Carroll, like Frost, would rather the reader said it for himself. And while a discerning reader will take care not to define rigidly what was meant to be felt rather than defined, Carroll has left clues enough to guide such a reader's guesses. We have already observed that Carroll found a special delight in deflating such pompous moral hypocrisies as many Victorian readers warmed to in Southey and Watts. And no one who has read Carroll's *Alice* can have failed to note the number of pompous bugaboos that present themselves to Alice only to be deflated by her natural logic. The Duchess is one such bugaboo. She confuses Alice at first and gives her a great deal of trouble, but Alice has only to say at the end "Why, you're nothing but a pack of cards," and the whole elaborate pretense of Wonderland blows up. The Jabberwocky, the Jubjub bird, and the Bandersnatch are also bugaboos. Is it too far-fetched to speculate that all of Carroll's bugaboos are related, and that all of them have their origin in Carroll's sense of the grotesque pompousness of a great deal of Victorian morality and social pretense?

So, over and over again, Carroll finds delight in deflating the pompous. Nothing deflates pomposity as does ridicule. And nonsense is one of the natural languages for ridiculing non-sense. Had Carroll set out with the announced aim of writing a ballad that would express a deep personal sense of one part of the Victorian character, it is impossible to imagine how he could have done better than he does in "Jabberwocky." Nonsense is the surface of the poem and its language of attack. But the very use of nonsense makes excellent sense. The nonsense surface performance is one part of a meaningful comment upon an identifiable subject. "Jabberwocky" is a happy and a graceful performance, but it is unmistakably—like almost everything else Carroll wrote—also a direct satire upon the mental habits of his own age. As noted, Carroll refuses to say directly that the subject is X or is not X. He might say X, but it's not X exactly. And he'd rather you said it for yourself. Nevertheless that second performance is certainly there: an effort (very much like that a choreographer might make for a Victorian Ballet Suite) to find poses, groupings, and actions that would present an accurately ridiculous sense of what was ridiculous in Carroll's age. "Jabberwocky" may be read with perfect coherence as a series of postures that interpret Victorian pomposity.

This function of poetry as a series of interpretive pictures is too seldom recognized and then usually too late in one's awareness of the poetic process, but the idea of this function is certainly not hard to grasp. Had there survived from Early and Middle English times only a series of ballad fragments, snatches describing sea captains drowned on impossible voyages, robber barons cheering the battle as they lay dying, betrayed lovers, sons cursing their mothers, and such like, there can be no doubt that the reader of such fragments would emerge with some rather definite impressions of what the age valued, that is, of how it felt about its mortal problems, and of *what sort of picture it had of itself.*

Most readers tend to lose sight of this force in poetry—of this subsurface release of pictures from the psyche—because they tend to think of poems as made of words only. As they tend to think that all thinking is done with words. Words are inseparable from poetry and forever ready to release unforeseeable magic into the poetic performance. But no poem is made of words alone. Just as no thought exists in words alone. Feelings, suggestions, images arise out of the words and run free of them.

Nor, finally, are words our only language. Music is a language capable of communication. So is painting. Watch a good mechanic listening to an engine that has come in for repair; can there be any doubt that the engine's noises are "talking" to the man, telling him what he needs to know? What the mechanic has in his mind is probably an intimate diagram of the engine's parts. He listens, relates the sounds to the picture in his mind, and comes to a conclusion: a pure case of a nonverbal thought process.

Or suppose that there existed somewhere a religious order that imposed a vow not only of eternal silence but against all verbalization even of one's thoughts. Initiates, suppose further, must pray a certain number of hours each day but *they must dance their prayers*. (The temple dancers of certain religious sects, for that matter, come close to doing exactly that.) Can there be any doubt that the kinds of postures and the sequences of actions such dancers fall into could constitute not only a language but a language susceptible of great refinement?

In very much this way, the performance of a good poem is very likely to contain under its verbalization a dance of images, postures, and attitudes, and such motions, both separately and in their sequences, are an indispensable part of the poetic performance—a deep part, and a complicated one to discuss outside itself, but a part to which one cannot help responding whether or not he realizes what he is responding to. Pattern is a profound and active part of every man's life. The dance of such patterns through his mind may even be the fundamental basis of all his thinking. But though that idea may be a difficult one to grasp in such terms as these, there is fortunately no difficulty in grasping examples of this sort of life performance. The temple dancers are one such illustration. The revealing gestures a badly trained public speaker makes on a platform—gestures that are from his basic nervous pattern and that have only the most tenuous connection with the words he may be speaking (or no connection at all if he is fidgeting through the recital of a memorized "piece")—are another such illustration. There are the words in his mouth and there are the patterns of fidget-and-twitch from his basic nervous life.

A poem has a similar sort of existence in that it has both a surface of words and an inner nervous life, but in a good poem there is the essential difference that the words and the nervous dance are two closely related parts of one thing.

"Jabberwocky" is an example of just such a poem. The surface of nonsense words goes happily on in its own self-entertaining way. But under the words there is a release of grotesque postures and pictures that amount to a series of dance caricatures of the moral flaws in the poet's age, as he sees them. What must finally be seen is that the dance occurs not only under but with the words, one reinforcing the other. And though thousands upon thousands of readers have found delight in "Jabberwocky" without being aware of this interplay, it is exactly this interplay that has been the source of their delight.

CHAPTER THREE

BY RIPPLING POOLS

"Symbolism" may be a frightening, or at least a mysterious, word. It may even be that a few, not necessarily representative, critics of poetry have used "symbolism" and similar terms in somewhat the way medieval alchemists used elaborate symbols—as a way of keeping the discussion private while releasing the suggestion that they were possessed of profound and secret knowledge. Actually, once the alchemist's mysterious symbols are explained they generally turn out to be nothing more mysterious than signs for "salt," "iron," or for some simple chemical process.

Argument by analogy is not argument in good intellectual order unless the analogy can be shown to be apt at all points. It would be absurd to imply that literary criticism and alchemy are the same thing. The analogy may still illustrate the general principle that not everything surrounded by a mysterious aura need be taken as mysterious. The fact is we have already discussed symbolism. At this point we have merely added a technical name to the discussion. Basically, a *symbol* is *something that stands for something else.* A traffic light is a fixed symbol: it uses three different colors to stand for three commands. A dollar bill is also a symbol, but though it seems a fixed and clear symbol, it stands for a theory of wealth and of money exchange that economists do not yet pretend wholly to understand. One can see, therefore, that even simple symbols tend to represent "areas of meaning in motion" rather than static equivalents. It follows that symbolism should offer a natural sort of language to the poet, interested as he must be to keep his "meaning" in motion.

The poems that follow in the present ramble include some of the best known narrative poems in the English language. Each one tells a story or part of a story. Read them for the pleasure to be found in a story well told. But as an exercise in more perceptive reading, concentrate on identifying and examining the force of every symbolic element in the narrative. Such a reading will demonstrate clearly that symbolism, far from being a mysterious and unknown device, is an essential part of good fictional technique. Coleridge's albatross, for example, in "The Rime of the Ancient Mariner," is a symbol. Its symbolic nature begins in the fact that it seems from the start to signify something more than its literal self. That symbolic nature is further made clear in the fact that it goes on adding significances (the widening of the ripples) as the story progresses. Far from being mysterious, this device is so common that few if any storytellers have ever managed to hold an audience long without such symbolic assistance.

The beginning reader will also see, on little reflection, that he himself is constantly using symbolism and that human communication would be impossible without it. The flag of the United States is a symbol made up of a complex of symbols. Taken in the most literal way, the fifty stars, the thirteen stripes, and the three colors, all have precisely fixed meanings. Each of the stars, for example, is assigned to represent one particular state, and no other, in the order of the state's admission into the union.

Any flag manual will run on with pages of such exact specifications. Thus, these literal and fixed meanings may be taken as a code. It is worth noting, too, that in the legislation that established this flag as the symbol of the United States, and in the discussion preceding the legislation, all of these code symbols had to be discussed in more or less literal terms. Such discussion and legislation would not necessarily be unemotional, but it would certainly have to be considerably less emotional than, let us say, the present-day orator's attitudes toward the flag.

It seems clear that not only in poetry but in history itself—which is to say in the very motion of men's lives—symbols acquire emotional expansion and intensity in the process of being sustained over a period of time. As the flag became associated with more and more of the nation's struggles and triumphs, it tended to become less and less evidently the predetermined legislative code it was at birth, and increasingly the symbol of a much broader emotional force. That emotional force, moreover, became so powerful that in many ways the flag tended to lose its character as a symbol and to become a living force in itself. Everyone today is familiar with the—unfortunately very bad—sculpture of the Marines raising the flag on Iwo Jima. It is difficult to believe that those Marines afire with the life and death of battle were consciously concerned with symbolism. Hoisting the flag is, of course, a symbolic action. But those Marines were mortally involved in what certainly must have seemed to them a self-sufficient action. The enmarveling power of all symbolism is exactly in the way symbols tend to become forces in themselves. They never do, in fact, lose their secondary character as representatives of whole other areas of meaning, but in the illusion of one's received sense impressions, as in the illusion of art, the emotional force of a powerfully developed symbol seems to become a force in itself. One of the qualifications of a good reader is his ability to receive that emotional force *as if* it were self-evidently itself, without losing sight of the secondary symbolic force. For convenience it will be useful to think of these two forces as the *literal force* of the symbol on the one hand, and its *symbolic force* on the other.

There is another quality of symbolism that any man can recognize from his own life once his awareness has been directed to it. In few, if any, of his life activities does a man feel one way and only one way about anything. His total attitude tends to be made up of a whole complex of conflicting attitudes. A simple example of a man possessed of conflicting attitudes is the situation of a voter who after long analysis of a national election announced: "I'm going to hold my nose and vote the straight Democratic ticket." Endless examples of attitudes made up of conflicting feelings lie about and in every man's life. No one likes to pay taxes, yet he knows it is his duty to pay them, as he also knows that those taxes buy for him the necessary services of government, as he also knows that it still hurts to pay them—he ends up by grumbling about the hopeless complexity of the forms he must fill out, lets out several hot pronouncements about more efficiency in government, and he pays. John loves Elizabeth, but he knows that Jane is also attractive and has money besides: he finally marries Elizabeth but he still regrets, if only a very little bit, that Elizabeth is poor. Frank is William's assistant in the advertising agency and thinks of himself as William's good friend. William falls ill, and Frank—who happens to be badly in debt —realizes that he will receive a substantial promotion should William fail to recover. Frank is a decent fellow and would never dream of wishing William ill. And still he realizes that his promotion can come about only through the elimination of William. And still he likes William. You may be sure that when Frank visits the hospital with a large basket of fruit, he is feeling more than one way at once.

So with symbols: in "Ballad of Hell," the golden belt symbolizes life and faith; the leather girt symbolizes (as a counter-symbol) resistance and death. As the heroine wore both, there is a pulling both ways that adds an undercurrent of tension to a good reading of the poem. Also, when we read the line "she bathed her spirit in the flame," we must take the flame to mean at once punishment for excessive passion and the drive of passion itself—certainly opposing thrusts.

This way of multifeeling is termed *ambivalence* by psychologists and critics. It is possible to argue that ambivalence is not necessarily a universal characteristic of poetry, but without involving needless critical subtleties at this point, ambivalence may certainly be asserted to be so pervasive in poetry that it is safe enough to assume its presence in some measure in every poem we shall here examine. The symbol, because it tends, like those ripples on the pond, to expand in all directions (and "all" must include opposite directions), is certainly the most natural way of expressing ambivalence.

All the immediately following poems tell a story of some sort and all to some extent use symbolism. For present purposes the symbolic elements may be defined as (1) areas of refusal to be specific in order to emphasize some larger possibility of meaning, or (2) devices introduced into the poem in whole or in part to stand for something else.

Eliot's "yellow smoke" in "The Love Song of J. Alfred Prufrock" (p. 78) serves to keep an area of the poem free from specification, open to a wide range of possible meaning, to the same end as the unspecified circled date on the calendar. De la Mare's Traveler (note that Traveler is capitalized) in "The Listeners" (p. 52) has almost no specific characteristics, nor have the Listeners. The astonishing suggestiveness of the poem arises from the fact that de la Mare has given his principal actors so little specific identity that they not only have to suggest *something* else but somehow seem to suggest almost *everything* else.

"The Listeners," one may well argue, is not even remotely about a man riding up to an empty house at night and knocking on the door. All that about his horse and the house and the forest's ferny floor has only an illusory connection with what the poem is *about*. The incident is simply what the poem is doing. More precisely, the incident is what the poem pretends to be doing while it is actually doing something else—a kind of poetic performance that should become instantly clear if one turns to Brooke's "Heaven" (p. 252) and asks: "Is this poem about fish?" The poem has a great deal to say about fish, but any reader who can believe that Brooke's performance in this poem is literally about fish, is a reader forever lost to poetry.

With such touchstones to identify nearly pure cases of one sort of poetic performance and another, it should be possible for a willing reader to sense the way the other poems here presented perform in a mixed way. Robinson's "Mr. Flood's Party (p. 71)," for example, presents an incident and a character in great detail. Old Eben Flood securely, drunkenly singing with "only two moons listening" becomes a specific and unforgettable person. Yet his very name is a pun—Eben Flood, ebb 'n flood, the going and the coming tide. Of what? Of life, and feeling, of the old order and the new, of the world that changes out from under a man leaving him silly and tragic and lovable and lost—all that and more, to the last ripple at the last edge of the pool at whose center this sort of thought first stirred.

QUESTIONS

In an approximate way the following questions might be asked of all these poems. For the sake of clarity, let the questions be phrased in terms of the albatross in "The Rime of the Ancient Mariner." The albatross is simply one example of a thing not wholly specified and suggestive of something else. By changing the referent from "albatross" to whatever element seems pertinent in the specific poem, the same questions will serve for all.

What is the albatross if taken literally? (How might Gradgrind identify it?)

How is the albatross transformed into a symbolic force? (How does it come to acquire meanings that would elude Gradgrind?)

Does the albatross have its symbolic force at the beginning, or does it enter strictly as its literal self?

Does that symbolic force seem to expand (do the ripples spread) as the poem progresses, and if so, how? by what devices? What are some of the areas of implication released by the albatross at the end of the narrative, and which of those areas was not present—at least not immediately visible—in the beginning?

Are such symbolic elements as the albatross simply embellishments or do they have an essential part in the narrative performance?

In what ways does the albatross set up counter-symbols? That is, what do you find in the poem that represents a state opposite to that represented by the albatross? Has the poet thrust these symbols into the poem for a specific purpose, or does the reader feel they are tied to the albatross and the mariner by natural circumstance?

There is an additional point for the willing reader to consider. In the most common sort of discussion of poetry, the structure and performance of a poem are treated as if they were more or less like the structure and performance of an expository essay. The poem, that is, is parsed out as if it consisted of a series of topic assertions that are developed and left behind in the process of moving on to the next assertion, and as if the true key to the poem were to be found in a logical analysis of its statements, almost as if they were so many syllogisms.

It is far better to think of the poem as a kind of thematic structure, like music, moving forward, but harking back upon itself, one theme playing against the other. This essentially thematic quality of poetic structure must be discussed in a detailed way later, but any reader willing to keep his imagination open to this possibility beforehand must certainly be invited to do so.

Poems for Study: Symbols

In each of the following poems, identify the object or situation that seems to represent something else not directly mentioned, and note how the meaning of the poem—the importance of the poem—expands when the presence of the second element is recognized.

The Listeners

Walter de la Mare

"Is there anybody there?" said the Traveler,
  Knocking on the moonlit door;
And his horse in the silence champed the grasses
  Of the forest's ferny floor.

And a bird flew up out of the turret,
  Above the Traveler's head:
And he smote upon the door again a second time;
  "Is there anybody there?" he said.
But no one descended to the Traveler;
  No head from the leaf-fringed sill
Leaned over and looked into his gray eyes,
  Where he stood perplexed and still.
But only a host of phantom listeners
  That dwelt in the lone house then
Stood listening in the quiet of the moonlight
  To that voice from the world of men:
Stood thronging the faint moonbeams on the dark stair
  That goes down to the empty hall,
Hearkening in an air stirred and shaken
  By the lonely Traveler's call.
And he felt in his heart their strangeness,
  Their stillness answering his cry,
While his horse moved, cropping the dark turf,
  'Neath the starred and leafy sky;
For he suddenly smote on the door, even
  Louder, and lifted his head:—
"Tell them I came, and no one answered,
  That I kept my word," he said.
Never the least stir made the listeners,
  Though every word he spake
Fell echoing through the shadowiness of the still house
  From the one man left awake:
Aye, they heard his foot upon the stirrup,
  And the sound of iron on stone,
And how the silence surged softly backward,
  When the plunging hoofs were gone.

Original Sin: A Short Story

Robert Penn Warren

Nodding, its great head rattling like a gourd,
And locks like seaweed strung on the stinking stone,
The nightmare stumbles past, and you have heard
It fumble your door before it whimpers and is gone:
It acts like the old hound that used to snuffle your door and moan.

You thought you had lost it when you left Omaha,
For it seemed connected then with your grandpa, who
Had a wen on his forehead and sat on the veranda

To finger the precious protuberance, as was his habit to do,
Which glinted in sun like rough garnet or the rich old brain bulging
   through.

But you met it in Harvard Yard as the historic steeple
Was confirming the midnight with its hideous racket,
And you wondered how it had come, for it stood so imbecile,
With empty hands, humble, and surely nothing in pocket:
Riding the rods, perhaps—or Grandpa's will paid the ticket.

You were almost kindly then, in your first homesickness,
As it tortured its stiff face to speak, but scarcely mewed.
Since then you have outlived all your homesickness,
But have met it in many another distempered latitude:
Oh, nothing is lost, ever lost! at last you understood.

It never came in the quantum glare of sun
To shame you before your friends, and had nothing to do
With your public experience or private reformation:
But it thought no bed too narrow—it stood with lips askew
And shook its great head sadly like the abstract Jew.

Never met you in the lyric arsenical meadow
When children call and your heart goes stone in the bosom—
At the orchard anguish never, nor ovoid horror,
Which is furred like a peach or avid like the delicious plum.
It takes no part in your classic prudence or fondled axiom.

Not there when you exclaimed: "Hope is betrayed by
Disastrous glory of sea-capes, sun-torment of whitecaps
—There must be a new innocence for us to be stayed by."
But there it stood, after all the timetables, all the maps,
In the crepuscular clutter of *always, always,* or *perhaps.*

You have moved often and rarely left an address.
And hear of the deaths of friends with a sly pleasure,
A sense of cleansing and hope which blooms from distress;
But it has not died, it comes, its hand childish, unsure,
Clutching the bribe of chocolate or a toy you used to treasure.

It tries the lock; you hear, but simply drowse:
There is nothing remarkable in that sound at the door.
Later you hear it wander the dark house
Like a mother who rises at night to seek a childhood picture;
Or it goes to the backyard and stands like an old horse cold in the
   pasture.

Compare Warren's use of the nightmare to de la Mare's use of the
Traveler. Does the fact that Warren has chosen to describe the relation-
ship of "you" to the haunting presence render the poem more or less
effective than de la Mare's poem, or is the effect simply different?
Which poem do you prefer? Why?

At the end of Part IV the Mariner in Coleridge's "The Rime of the Ancient Mariner" breathes forth unawares a blessing upon the creatures of the deep and immediately the guilty weight of the Albatross falls from him and sinks "Like lead into the sea."

Students are often tempted to interpret this action as symbolizing the Mariner's forgiveness and release from pain. But to accept this interpretation is to ignore the words of the spirit at the end of Part V: "The man hath penance done, And penance more will do." The Mariner suffers when the Albatross is about his neck, and he continues to suffer when he is released from its weight. Obviously, however, the nature of his suffering has changed. Until love touches his soul he suffers in one way. As soon as love has touched him the mood changes: a sleep refreshes him and he wakens from it to a visitation and a whole new motion of events.

The key to an understanding of this change lies in basic Christian theology, in which love is the beginning of redemption. Until love touches the Mariner he has suffered as a damned soul suffers, without hope. As soon as love touches him his sufferings become a penance rather than a doom. Penance is a state of grace, for, however painful it may be, it leads to salvation. The Mariner has not been released from pain at the moment the Albatross falls from him, nor is he admitted into Heaven, his sin forgiven: he has rather passed from the state of Hell (pain without purification) to the state of Purgatory (purifying penance).

How many other religious symbols can be related to this center of the poem? How many Christ symbols are suggested in connection with the Albatross? Can the shooting of the Albatross reasonably be related to Original Sin? Does the fact that the crew comes to condone the Mariner's act in shooting the Albatross implicate them in the act? If so, why? Why does Coleridge allow a brief spell of improved weather to follow the death of the Albatross? What does the crew then do to the Mariner when things begin to deteriorate? Why? If the Mariner has committed something like Original Sin, that fact would suggest that he is a sort of Adam—what then must the crew symbolize?

The Rime of the Ancient Mariner

Samuel Taylor Coleridge

PART I

An ancient Mariner meeteth three Gallants bidden to a wedding-feast, and detaineth one.	It is an ancient Mariner, And he stoppeth one of three. "By thy long gray beard and glittering eye, Now wherefore stopp'st thou me?
	The Bridegroom's doors are opened wide, And I am next of kin; The guests are met, the feast is set: May'st hear the merry din."

He holds him with his skinny hand,
"There was a ship," quoth he.
"Hold off! unhand me, gray-beard loon!"
Eftsoons his hand dropt he.

The Wed-
ding-Guest
is spell-
bound by the
eye of the
old sea-
faring man,
and con-
strained to hear
his tale.

He holds him with his glittering eye—
The Wedding-Guest stood still,
And listens like a three years' child:
The Mariner hath his will.

The Wedding-Guest sat on a stone:
He cannot choose but hear;
And thus spake on that ancient man,
The bright-eyed Mariner.

"The ship was cheered, the harbor cleared,
Merrily did we drop
Below the kirk, below the hill,
Below the lighthouse top.

The Mariner
tells how the
ship sailed
southward
with a good
wind and fair
weather, till
it reached
the Line.

The sun came up upon the left,
Out of the sea came he!
And he shone bright, and on the right
Went down into the sea.

Higher and higher every day,
Till over the mast at noon—"
The Wedding-Guest here beat his breast,
For he heard the loud bassoon.

The Wed-
ding-Guest
heareth the
bridal music;
but the Mar-
iner con-
tinueth his
tale.

The bride hath paced into the hall,
Red as a rose is she;
Nodding their heads before her goes
The merry minstrelsy.

The Wedding-Guest he beat his breast,
Yet he cannot choose but hear;
And thus spake on that ancient man,
The bright-eyed Mariner.

The ship
driven by a
storm toward
the south
pole.

"And now the storm-blast came, and he
Was tyrannous and strong:
He struck with his o'ertaking wings,
And chased us south along.

With sloping masts and dipping prow,
As who pursued with yell and blow
Still treads the shadow of his foe,
And forward bends his head,
The ship drove fast, loud roared the blast,
And southward aye we fled.

And now there came both mist and snow,
And it grew wondrous cold:
And ice, mast-high, came floating by,
As green as emerald.

The land of
ice, and of
fearful
sounds where
no living
thing was to
be seen.

And through the drifts the snowy clifts
Did send a dismal sheen:
Nor shapes of men nor beasts we ken—
The ice was all between.

The ice was here, the ice was there,
The ice was all around:
It cracked and growled, and roared and howled,
Like noises in a swound!

Till a great
sea-bird,
called the
Albatross,
came
through the
snow-fog,
and was re-
ceived with
great joy and
hospitality.

At length did cross an Albatross,
Thorough the fog it came;
As if it had been a Christian soul,
We hailed it in God's name.

It ate the food it ne'er had eat,
And round and round it flew.
The ice did split with a thunder-fit;
The helmsman steered us through!

And lo! the
Albatross
proveth a
bird of good
omen, and
followeth the
ship as it re-
turned north-
ward through
fog and
floating ice.

And a good south wind sprung up behind;
The Albatross did follow,
And every day, for food or play,
Came to the mariners' hollo!

In mist or cloud, on mast or shroud,
It perched for vespers nine;
Whiles all the night, through fog-smoke white,
Glimmered the white moon-shine."

The ancient
Mariner in-
hospitably
killeth the
pious bird of
good omen.

"God save thee, ancient Mariner!
From the fiends, that plague thee thus!—
Why look'st thou so?"—"With my cross-bow
I shot the Albatross.

PART II

"The Sun now rose upon the right:
Out of the sea came he,
Still hid in mist, and on the left
Went down into the sea.

And the good south wind still blew behind,
But no sweet bird did follow,
Nor any day for food or play
Came to the mariners' hollo!

His ship-
mates cry out

against the ancient Mariner, for killing the bird of good luck.

And I had done a hellish thing,
And it would work 'em woe:
For all averred, I had killed the bird
That made the breeze to blow.
'Ah wretch!' said they, 'the bird to slay,
That made the breeze to blow!'

But when the fog cleared off, they justify the same, and thus make themselves accomplices in the crime. The fair breeze continues; the ship enters the Pacific Ocean, and sails northward, even till it reaches the Line

Nor dim nor red, like God's own head,
The glorious Sun uprist:
Then all averred, I had killed the bird
That brought the fog and mist.
' 'Twas right,' said they, 'such birds to slay,
That bring the fog and mist.'

The fair breeze blew, the white foam flew,
The furrow followed free;
We were the first that ever burst
Into that silent sea.

The ship hath been suddenly becalmed.

Down dropt the breeze, the sails dropt down,
'Twas sad as sad could be;
And we did speak only to break
The silence of the sea!

All in a hot and copper sky,
The bloody Sun, at noon,
Right up above the mast did stand,
No bigger than the Moon.

Day after day, day after day,
We stuck, nor breath nor motion;
As idle as a painted ship
Upon a painted ocean.

And the Albatross begins to be avenged. A Spirit had followed them; one of the invisible inhabitants of this planet, neither departed souls nor angels; concerning whom the learned Jew, Josephus, and the Platonic Constantinopolitan, Michael Psellus, may be consulted.

Water, water, everywhere,
And all the boards did shrink;
Water, water, everywhere
Nor any drop to drink.

The very deep did rot: O Christ!
That ever this should be!
Yea, slimy things did crawl with legs
Upon the slimy sea.

About, about, in reel and rout
The death-fires danced at night;
The water, like a witch's oils,
Burnt green, and blue, and white.

They are very
numerous,
and there is
no climate
or element
without one
or more.
The ship-
mates, in their
sore distress,
would fain
throw the
whole guilt
on the ancient
Mariner: in
sign whereof
they hang
the dead sea-
bird round
his neck.

And some in dreams assured were
Of the Spirit that plagued us so:
Nine fathom deep he had followed us
From the land of mist and snow.

And every tongue, through utter drought,
Was withered at the root;
We could not speak, no more than if
We had been choked with soot.

Ah! well a-day! what evil looks
Had I from old and young!
Instead of the cross, the Albatross
About my neck was hung.

PART III

The ancient
Mariner
beholdeth a
sign in the
element
afar off.

"There passed a weary time. Each throat
Was parched, and glazed each eye.
A weary time! a weary time!
How glazed each weary eye,
When looking westward, I beheld
A something in the sky.

At first it seemed a little speck,
And then it seemed a mist;
It moved and moved, and took at last
A certain shape, I wist.

A speck, a mist, a shape, I wist!
And still it neared and neared:
As if it dodged a water-sprite,
It plunged and tacked and veered.

At its nearer
approach, it
seemeth
him to be a
ship; and at
a dear ran-
som he
freeth his
speech from
the bonds of
thirst.

With throats unslaked, with black lips baked,
We could nor laugh nor wail;
Through utter drought all dumb we stood!
I bit my arm, I sucked the blood,
And cried, 'A sail! a sail!'

With throats unslaked, with black lips baked,
Agape they heard me call;
Gramercy! they for joy did grin,
And all at once their breath drew in,
As they were drinking all.

A flash of
joy;
And horror
follows.
For can it be
a ship that
comes on-
ward with-
out wind or
tide?

'See! see! (I cried) she tacks no more!
Hither to work us weal;
Without a breeze, without a tide,
She steadies with upright keel!'

The western wave was all a-flame;
The day was well nigh done!
Almost upon the western wave
Rested the broad bright Sun;
When that strange shape drove suddenly
Betwixt us and the Sun.

It seemeth him but the skeleton of a ship.

And straight the Sun was flecked with bars
(Heaven's Mother send us grace!)
As if through a dungeon-grate he peered
With broad and burning face.

Alas! (thought I, and my heart beat loud)
How fast she nears and nears!
Are those her sails that glance in the Sun,
Like restless gossameres?

And its ribs are seen as bars on the face of the setting Sun. The Spectre-Woman and her Death-mate, and no other on board the skeleton-ship. Like vessel, like crew! Death and Life-in-Death have diced for the ship's crew, and she (the latter) winneth the ancient Mariner.

Are those her ribs through which the Sun
Did peer, as through a grate?
And is that Woman all her crew?
Is that a Death? and are there two?
Is Death that woman's mate?

Her lips were red, her looks were free,
Her locks were yellow as gold:
Her skin was as white as leprosy,
The nightmare Life-in-Death was she,
Who thicks man's blood with cold.

The naked hulk alongside came,
And the twain were casting dice;
'The game is done! I've won! I've won!'
Quoth she, and whistles thrice.

No twilight within the courts of the Sun.

The Sun's rim dips; the stars rush out:
At one stride comes the dark;
With far-heard whisper, o'er the sea,
Off shot the spectre-bark.

We listened and looked sideways up!
Fear at my heart, as at a cup,
My life-blood seemed to sip!
The stars were dim, and thick the night,
The steersman's face by his lamp gleamed white;
From the sails the dew did drip—
Till clomb above the eastern bar
The horned Moon, with one bright star

At the rising of the Moon,

Within the nether tip.

One after
another,

One after one, by the star-dogged Moon,
Too quick for groan or sigh,
Each turned his face with a ghastly pang,
And cursed me with his eye.

Four times fifty living men
(And I heard nor sign nor groan)
With heavy thump, a lifeless lump,
They dropped down one by one.

His ship-
mates drop
down dead.

But Life-in-
Death
begins her
work on the
ancient
Mariner.

The souls did from their bodies fly—
They fled to bliss or woe!
And every soul, it passed me by,
Like the whizz of my cross-bow!"

PART IV

The Wed-
ding-Guest
feareth that
a Spirit is
talking to
him;

"I fear thee, ancient Mariner!
I fear thy skinny hand!
And thou art long, and lank, and brown,
As is the ribbed sea-sand.

I fear thee and thy glittering eye,
And thy skinny hand, so brown."—
"Fear not, fear not, thou Wedding-Guest!
This body dropt not down.

But the
ancient
Mariner as-
sureth him
of his bodily
life, and pro-
ceedeth to
relate his
horrible pen-
ance.

Alone, alone, all, all alone,
Alone on a wide, wide sea!
And never a saint took pity on
My soul in agony.

The many men, so beautiful!
And they all dead did lie:
And a thousand thousand slimy things
Lived on; and so did I.

He despiseth
the creatures
of the calm.

And envieth
that they
should live,
and so many
lie dead.

I looked upon the rotting sea,
And drew my eyes away;
I looked upon the rotting deck,
And there the dead men lay.

I looked to heaven, and tried to pray;
But or ever a prayer had gusht,
A wicked whisper came, and made
My heart as dry as dust.

I closed my lids, and kept them close,
And the balls like pulses beat;
For the sky and the sea, and the sea and the sky
Lay like a load on my weary eye,
And the dead were at my feet.

The cold sweat melted from their limbs,
Nor rot nor reek did they:
The look with which they looked on me
Had never passed away.

An orphan's curse would drag to hell
A spirit from on high;
But oh! more horrible than that
Is the curse in a dead man's eye!
Seven days, seven nights, I saw that curse,
And yet I could not die.

The moving Moon went up the sky,
And nowhere did abide:
Softly she was going up,
And a star or two beside—
Her beams bemocked the sultry main,
Like April hoar-frost spread;
But where the ship's huge shadow lay,
The charmed water burnt alway
A still and awful red.

Beyond the shadow of the ship,
I watch the water-snakes:
They moved in tracks of shining white,
And when they reared, the elfish light
Fell off in hoary flakes.

Within the shadow of the ship
I watched their rich attire:
Blue, glossy green, and velvet black,
They coiled and swam; and every track
Was a flash of golden fire.

O happy living things! no tongue
Their beauty might declare:
A spring of love gushed from my heart,
And I blessed them unaware:
Sure my kind saint took pity on me,
And I blessed them unaware.

The selfsame moment I could pray;
And from my neck so free
The Albatross fell off, and sank
Like lead into the sea.

PART V

"Oh sleep! it is a gentle thing,
Beloved from pole to pole!
To Mary Queen the praise be given!
She sent the gentle sleep from Heaven,
That slid into my soul.

By grace of
the holy
Mother, the
ancient,
Mariner is
refreshed
with rain.

The silly buckets on the deck,
That had so long remained,
I dreamt that they were filled with dew;
And when I awoke, it rained.

My lips were wet, my throat was cold,
My garments all were dank;
Sure I had drunken in my dreams,
And still my body drank.

I moved, and could not feel my limbs;
I was so light—almost
I thought that I had died in sleep,
And was a blessed ghost.

He heareth
sounds and
seeth strange
sights and
commotions
in the sky
and the
element.

And soon I heard a roaring wind:
It did not come anear;
But with its sound it shook the sails,
That were so thin and sere.

The upper air burst into life!
And a hundred fire-flags sheen,
To and fro they were hurried about!
And to and fro, and in and out,
The wan stars danced between.

And the coming wind did roar more loud,
And the sails did sigh like sedge;
And the rain poured down from one black cloud;
The Moon was at its edge.

The thick black cloud was cleft, and still
The Moon was at its side:
Like waters shot from some high crag,
The lightning fell with never a jag,
A river steep and wide.

The loud wind never reached the ship,
Yet now the ship moved on!
Beneath the lightning and the Moon
The dead men gave a groan.

The bodies of the ship's crew are inspired, and the ship moves on.

They groaned, they stirred, they all uprose,
Nor spake, nor moved their eyes;
It had been strange, even in a dream,
To have seen those dead men rise.

The helmsman steered, the ship moved on;
Yet never a breeze up blew;
The mariners all 'gan work the ropes,
Where they were wont to do;
They raised their limbs like lifeless tools—
We were a ghastly crew.

The body of my brother's son
Stood by me, knee to knee:
The body and I pulled at one rope
But he said nought to me."

But not by the souls of the men, nor by daemons of earth or middle air, but by a blessed troop of angelic spirits, sent down by the invocation of the guardian saint.

"I fear thee, ancient Mariner!"
"Be calm, thou Wedding-Guest!
'Twas not those souls that fled in pain,
Which to their corses came again,
But a troop of spirits blest:

For when it dawned—they dropped their arms,
And clustered round the mast;
Sweet sounds rose slowly through their mouths,
And from their bodies passed.

Around, around, flew each sweet sound,
Then darted to the Sun;
Slowly the sounds came back again,
Now mixed, now one by one.

Sometimes a-dropping from the sky
I heard the sky-lark sing;
Sometimes all little birds that are,
How they seemed to fill the sea and air
With their sweet jargoning!

And now 'twas like all instruments,
Now like a lonely flute;
And now it is an angel's song,
That makes the heavens be mute.

It ceased; yet still the sails made on
A pleasant noise till noon,
A noise like a hidden brook

In the leafy month of June,
That to the sleeping woods all night
Singeth a quiet tune.

Till noon we quietly sailed on,
Yet never a breeze did breathe:
Slowly and smoothly went the ship,
Moved onward from beneath.

Under the keel nine fathom deep,
From the land of mist and snow,
The Spirit slid: and it was he
That made the ship to go.
The sails at noon left off their tune,
And the ship stood still also.

The Sun, right up above the mast,
Had fixed her to the ocean:
But in a minute she 'gan stir,
With a short uneasy motion—
Backwards and forwards half her length
With a short uneasy motion.

Then like a pawing horse let go,
She made a sudden bound:
It flung the blood into my head,
And I fell down in a swound.

How long in that same fit I lay,
I have not to declare;
But ere my living life returned,
I heard and in my soul discerned
Two voices in the air.

'Is it he?' quoth one, 'Is this the man?
By Him who died on cross,
With his cruel bow he laid full low
The harmless Albatross.

The Spirit who bideth by himself
In the land of mist and snow,
He loved the bird that loved the man
Who shot him with his bow.'

The other was a softer voice,
As soft as honey-dew:
Quoth he, 'The man hath penance done,
And penance more will do.'

The lonesome Spirit from the south pole carries on the ship as far as the Line, in obedience to the angelic troop, but still requireth vengeance.

The Polar Spirit's fellow-daemons, the invisible inhabitants of the element, take part in his wrong; and two of them relate, one to the other, that penance long and heavy for the ancient Mariner hath been accorded to the Polar Spirit, who returneth southward.

PART VI

First Voice

" 'But tell me, tell me! speak again,
Thy soft response renewing—
What makes that ship drive on so fast?
What is the ocean doing?

Second Voice

'Still as a slave before his lord,
The ocean hath no blast;
His great bright eye most silently
Up to the Moon is cast—

If he may know which way to go;
For she guides him smooth or grim.
See, brother, see! how graciously
She looketh down on him.'

First Voice

'But why drives on that ship so fast,
Without or wave or wind?'

Second Voice

'The air is cut away before,
And closes from behind.

Fly, brother, fly! more high, more high!
Or we shall be belated:
For slow and slow that ship will go,
When the Mariner's trance is abated.'

I woke, and we were sailing on
As in a gentle weather:
'Twas night, calm night, the Moon was high,
The dead men stood together.

All stood together on the deck,
For a charnel-dungeon fitter:
All fixed on me their stony eyes,
That in the Moon did glitter.

The pang, the curse, with which they died,
Had never passed away:
I could not draw my eyes from theirs,
Nor turn them up to pray.

And now this spell was snapt: once more
I viewed the ocean green,
And looked far forth, yet little saw
Of what had else been seen—

The Mariner hath been cast into a trance; for the angelic power causeth the vessel to drive northward faster than human life could endure.

The supernatural motion is retarded; the Mariner awakes, and his penance begins anew.

The curse is finally expiated.

Like one, that on a lonesome road
Doth walk in fear and dread,
And having once turned round walks on,
And turns no more his head;
Because he knows a frightful fiend
Doth close behind him tread.

But soon there breathed a wind on me,
Nor sound nor motion made:
Its path was not upon the sea,
In ripple or in shade.

It raised my hair, it fanned my cheek
Like a meadow-gale of spring—
It mingled strangely with my fears,
Yet it felt like a welcoming.

Swiftly, swiftly flew the ship,
Yet she sailed softly too:
Sweetly, sweetly blew the breeze—
On me alone it blew.

And the ancient Mariner beholdeth his native country.

Oh! dream of joy! is this indeed
The light-house top I see?
Is this the hill? is this the kirk?
Is this mine own countree?

We drifted o'er the harbor-bar,
And I with sobs did pray—
O let me be awake, my God!
Or let me sleep alway.

The harbor-bay was clear as glass,
So smoothly it was strewn!
And on the bay the moonlight lay,
And the shadow of the Moon.

The rock shone bright, the kirk no less,
That stands above the rock:
The moonlight steeped in silentness
The steady weathercock.

And the bay was white with silent light
Till rising from the same,
Full many shapes, that shadows were,
In crimson colors came.

The angelic spirits leave the dead bodies,

A little distance from the prow
Those crimson shadows were:
I turned my eyes upon the deck—
Oh, Christ, what I saw there!

Each corse lay flat, lifeless and flat,
And, by the holy rood!
A man all light, a seraph-man,
On every corse there stood.

*And appear
in their own
forms of light.*

This seraph-band, each waved his hand;
It was a heavenly sight!
They stood as signals to the land,
Each one a lovely light;

This seraph-band, each waved his hand,
No voice did they impart—
No voice; but oh! the silence sank
Like music on my heart.

But soon I heard the dash of oars,
I heard the Pilot's cheer;
My head was turned perforce away,
And I saw a boat appear.

The Pilot and the Pilot's boy,
I heard them coming fast:
Dear Lord in Heaven! it was a joy
The dead men could not blast.

I saw a third—I heard his voice:
It is the Hermit good!
He singeth loud his godly hymns
That he makes in the wood.
He'll shrieve my soul; he'll wash away
The Albatross's blood.

PART VII

*The Hermit
of the Wood.*

"This Hermit good lives in that wood
Which slopes down to the sea.
How loudly his sweet voice he rears!
He loves to talk with marineres
That come from a far countree.

He kneels at morn, and noon, and eve—
He hath a cushion plump:
It is the moss that wholly hides
The rotted old oak-stump.

The skiff-boat neared: I heard them talk,
'Why, this is strange, I trow!
Where are those lights so many and fair,
That signal made but now?'

'Strange, by my faith!' the Hermit said—
'And they answered not our cheer!
The planks look warped! and see those sails,
How thin they are and sere!
I never saw aught like to them
Unless perchance it were

Brown skeletons of leaves that lag
My forest-brook along;
When the ivy-tod is heavy with snow,
And the owlet whoops to the wolf below,
That eats the she-wolf's young.'

'Dear Lord! it hath a fiendish look—
(The Pilot made reply)
I am a-feared'—'Push on, push on!'
Said the Hermit cheerily.

The boat came closer to the ship,
But I nor spake nor stirred;
The boat came close beneath the ship,
And straight a sound was heard.

Under the water it rumbled on,
Still louder and more dread:
It reached the ship, it split the bay;
The ship went down like lead.

Stunned by that loud and dreadful sound,
Which sky and ocean smote,
Like one that hath been seven days drowned

My body lay afloat;
But swift as dreams, myself I found
Within the Pilot's boat.

Upon the whirl, where sank the ship,
The boat spun round and round;
And all was still, save that the hill
Was telling of the sound.

I moved my lips—the Pilot shrieked
And fell down in a fit;
The holy Hermit raised his eyes,
And prayed where he did sit.

I took the oars: the Pilot's boy,
Who now doth crazy go,
Laughed loud and long, and all the while

His eyes went to and fro.
'Ha! ha!' quoth he, 'full plain I see,
The devil knows how to row.'

And now, all in my own countree,
I stood on the firm land!
The Hermit stepped forth from the boat,
And scarcely he could stand.

The ancient
Mariner
earnestly en-
treateth the
Hermit to
shrieve him;
and the
penance of
life falls on
him.

'O shrieve me, shrieve me, holy man!'
The Hermit crossed his brow.
'Say quick,' quoth he, 'I bid thee say—
What manner of man art thou?'

Forthwith this frame of mine was wrenched
With a woful agony,
Which forced me to begin my tale;
And then it left me free.

And ever
and anon
throughout
his future life
an agony
constraineth
him to travel
from land to
land,

Since then, at an uncertain hour,
That agony returns:
And till my ghastly tale is told,
This heart within me burns.

I pass, like night, from land to land;
I have strange power of speech;
That moment that his face I see,
I know the man that must hear me:
To him my tale I teach.

What loud uproar bursts from that door!
The wedding-guests are there:
But in the garden-bower the bride
And bride-maids singing are:
And hark the little vesper bell
Which biddeth me to prayer!

O Wedding-Guest! this soul hath been
Alone on a wide, wide sea;
So lonely 'twas that God himself
Scarce seemed there to be.

O sweeter than the marriage-feast,
'Tis sweeter far to me,
To walk together to the kirk
With a goodly company!—

To walk together to the kirk,
And all together pray,
While each to his great Father bends,
Old men, and babes, and loving friends,
And youths and maidens gay!

Farewell, farewell! but this I tell
To thee, thou Wedding-Guest!
He prayeth well, who loveth well
Both man and bird and beast.

He prayeth best, who loveth best
All things both great and small;
For the dear God who loveth us,
He made and loveth all."

The Mariner, whose eye is bright,
Whose beard with age is hoar,
Is gone: and now the Wedding-Guest
Turned from the Bridegroom's door.

He went like one that hath been stunned,
And is of sense forlorn:
A sadder and a wiser man,
He rose the morrow morn.

And to teach, by his own example, love and reverence to all things that God made and loveth.

Mr. Flood's Party

Edwin Arlington Robinson

Old Eben Flood, climbing alone one night
Over the hill between the town below
And the forsaken upland hermitage
That held as much as he should ever know
On earth again of home, paused warily.
The road was his with not a native near;
And Eben, having leisure, said aloud,
For no man else in Tilbury Town to hear:

"Well, Mr. Flood, we have the harvest moon
Again, and we may not have many more;
The bird is on the wing, the poet says,
And you and I have said it here before.
Drink to the bird." He raised up to the light
The jug that he had gone so far to fill,
And answered huskily: "Well, Mr. Flood,
Since you propose it, I believe I will."

Alone, as if enduring to the end
A valiant armor of scarred hopes outworn,
He stood there in the middle of the road
Like Roland's ghost winding a silent horn.
Below him, in the town among the trees,
Where friends of other days had honored him,
A phantom salutation of the dead
Rang thinly till old Eben's eyes were dim.

Then, as a mother lays her sleeping child
Down tenderly, fearing it may awake,
He set the jug down slowly at his feet
With trembling care, knowing that most things break;
And only when assured that on firm earth
It stood, as the uncertain lives of men
Assuredly did not, he paced away,
And with his hand extended paused again:

"Well, Mr. Flood, we have not met like this
In a long time; and many a change has come
To both of us, I fear, since last it was
We had a drop together. Welcome home!"
Convivially returning with himself,
Again he raised the jug up to the light;
And with an acquiescent quaver said:
"Well, Mr. Flood, if you insist, I might.

"Only a very little, Mr. Flood—
For auld lang syne. No more, sir; that will do."
So, for the time, apparently it did,
And Eben evidently thought so too;
For soon amid the silver loneliness
Of night he lifted up his voice and sang,
Secure, with only two moons listening,
Until the whole harmonious landscape rang—

"For auld lang syne." The weary throat gave out,
The last word wavered; and the song being done,
He raised again the jug regretfully
And shook his head, and was again alone.
There was not much that was ahead of him,
And there was nothing in the town below—
Where strangers would have shut the many doors
That many friends had opened long ago.

Ulysses

Alfred, Lord Tennyson

It little profits that an idle king,
By this still hearth, among these barren crags,
Matched with an aged wife, I mete and dole
Unequal laws unto a savage race,
That hoard, and sleep, and feed, and know not me.
I cannot rest from travel: I will drink
Life to the lees: all times I have enjoyed
Greatly, have suffered greatly, both with those
That loved me, and alone; on shore, and when
Through scudding drifts the rainy Hyades

Vext the dim sea. I am become a name;
For always roaming with a hungry heart
Much have I seen and known: cities of men
And manners, climates, councils, governments,
Myself not least, but honored of them all,—
And drunk delight of battle with my peers,
Far on the ringing plains of windy Troy.
I am a part of all that I have met;
Yet all experience is an arch wherethrough
Gleams that untraveled world, whose margin fades
For ever and for ever when I move.
How dull it is to pause, to make an end,
To rust unburnished, not to shine in use!
As though to breathe were life! Life piled on life
Were all too little, and of one to me
Little remains: but every hour is saved
From that eternal silence, something more,
A bringer of new things; and vile it were
For some three suns to store and hoard myself,
And this gray spirit yearning in desire
To follow knowledge like a sinking star,
Beyond the utmost bound of human thought.
   This is my son, mine own Telemachus,
To whom I leave the scepter and the isle—
Well-loved of me, discerning to fulfill
This labor, by slow prudence to make mild
A rugged people, and through soft degrees
Subdue them to the useful and the good.
Most blameless is he, centered in the sphere
Of common duties, decent not to fail
In offices of tenderness, and pay
Meet adoration to my household gods,
When I am gone. He works his work, I mine.
   There lies the port; the vessel puffs her sail;
There gloom the dark, broad seas. My mariners,
Souls that have toiled, and wrought, and thought with me—
That ever with a frolic welcome took
The thunder and the sunshine, and opposed
Free hearts, free foreheads—you and I are old;
Old age hath yet his honor and his toil.
Death closes all; but something ere the end,
Some work of noble note, may yet be done,
Not unbecoming men that strove with Gods.
The lights begin to twinkle from the rocks;
The long day wanes; the slow moon climbs; the deep
Moans round with many voices. Come, my friends,
'Tis not too late to seek a newer world.
Push off, and sitting well in order smite
The sounding furrows; for my purpose holds
To sail beyond the sunset, and the baths

Of all the western stars, until I die.
It may be that the gulfs will wash us down;
It may be we shall touch the Happy Isles,
And see the great Achilles, whom we knew.
Though much is taken, much abides; and though
We are not now that strength which in old days
Moved earth and heaven, that which we are, we are—
One equal temper of heroic hearts,
Made weak by time and fate, but strong in will
To strive, to seek, to find, and not to yield.

Identify the objects in "Mr. Flood's Parts" and "Ulysses" that serve
as symbols. Could the old men themselves serve as symbols? Of what?

The Death of the Hired Man

Robert Frost

Mary sat musing on the lamp-flame at the table,
Waiting for Warren. When she heard his step,
She ran on tiptoe down the darkened passage
To meet him in the doorway with the news
And put him on his guard. "Silas is back."
She pushed him outward with her through the door
And shut it after her. "Be kind," she said.
She took the market things from Warren's arms
And set them on the porch, then drew him down
To sit beside her on the wooden steps.

"When was I ever anything but kind to him?
But I'll not have the fellow back," he said.
"I told him so last haying, didn't I?
If he left then, I said, that ended it.
What good is he? Who else will harbor him
At his age for the little he can do?
What help he is there's no depending on.
Off he goes always when I need him most.
He thinks he ought to earn a little pay,
Enough at least to buy tobacco with,
So he won't have to beg and be beholden.
'All right,' I say, 'I can't afford to pay
Any fixed wages, though I wish I could.'
'Someone else can.' 'Then someone else will have to.'
I shouldn't mind his bettering himself
If that was what it was. You can be certain,
When he begins like that, there's someone at him
Trying to coax him off with pocket money—
In haying time, when any help is scarce.
In winter he comes back to us. I'm done."

"Sh! not so loud: he'll hear you," Mary said.

"I want him to: he'll have to soon or late."

"He's worn out. He's asleep beside the stove.
When I came up from Rowe's I found him here,
Huddled against the barn door fast asleep,
A miserable sight, and frightening, too—
You needn't smile—I didn't recognize him—
I wasn't looking for him—and he's changed.
Wait till you see."

          "Where did you say he'd been?"

"He didn't say. I dragged him to the house,
And gave him tea and tried to make him smoke.
I tried to make him talk about his travels.
Nothing would do: he just kept nodding off."

"What did he say? Did he say anything?"

"But little."

        "Anything? Mary, confess
He said he'd come to ditch the meadow for me."

"Warren!"

       "But did he? I just want to know."

"Of course he did. What would you have him say?
Surely you wouldn't grudge the poor old man
Some humble way to save his self-respect.
He added, if you really care to know,
He meant to clear the upper pasture, too.
That sounds like something you have heard before?
Warren, I wish you could have heard the way
He jumbled everything. I stopped to look
Two or three times—he made me feel so queer—
To see if he was talking in his sleep.
He ran on Harold Wilson—you remember—
The boy you had in haying four years since.
He's finished school, and teaching in his college.
Silas declares you'll have to get him back.
He says they two will make a team for work:
Between them they will lay this farm as smooth!
The way he mixed that in with other things.
He thinks young Wilson a likely lad, though daft
On education—you know how they fought
All through July under the blazing sun,

Silas up on the cart to build the load,
Harold along beside to pitch it on."

"Yes, I took care to keep well out of earshot."

"Well, those days trouble Silas like a dream.
You wouldn't think they would. How some things linger!
Harold's young college-boy's assurance piqued him.
After so many years he still keeps finding
Good arguments he sees he might have used.
I sympathize. I know just how it feels
To think of the right thing to say too late.
Harold's associated in his mind with Latin.
He asked me what I thought of Harold's saying
He studied Latin, like the violin,
Because he liked it—that an argument!
He said he couldn't make the boy believe
He could find water with a hazel prong—
Which showed how much good school had ever done him.
He wanted to go over that. But most of all
He thinks if he could have another chance
To teach him how to build a load of hay—"

"I know, that's Silas' one accomplishment.
He bundles every forkful in its place,
And tags and numbers it for future reference,
So he can find and easily dislodge it
In the unloading. Silas does that well.
He takes it out in bunches like big birds' nests.
You never see him standing on the hay
He's trying to lift, straining to lift himself."

"He thinks if he could teach him that, he'd be
Some good perhaps to someone in the world.
He hates to see a boy the fool of books.
Poor Silas, so concerned for other folk,
And nothing to look backward to with pride,
And nothing to look forward to with hope,
So now and never any different."

Part of a moon was falling down the west,
Dragging the whole sky with it to the hills.
Its light poured softly in her lap. She saw it
And spread her apron to it. She put out her hand
Among the harplike morning-glory strings,
Taut with the dew from garden bed to eaves,
As if she played unheard the tenderness
That wrought on him beside her in the night.
"Warren," she said, "he has come home to die:
You needn't be afraid he'll leave you this time."

"Home," he mocked gently.

"Yes, what else but home?
It all depends on what you mean by home.
Of course he's nothing to us, any more
Than was the hound that came a stranger to us
Out of the woods, worn out upon the trail."

"Home is the place where, when you have to go there,
They have to take you in."

"I should have called it
Something you somehow haven't to deserve."

Warren leaned out and took a step or two,
Picked up a little stick, and brought it back
And broke it in his hand and tossed it by.
"Silas has better claim on us you think
Than on his brother? Thirteen little miles
As the road winds would bring him to his door.
Silas has walked that far no doubt today.
Why doesn't he go there? His brother's rich,
A somebody—director in the bank."

"He never told us that."

"We know it, though."

"I think his brother ought to help, of course.
I'll see to that if there is need. He ought of right
To take him in, and might be willing to—
He may be better than appearances.
But have some pity on Silas. Do you think
If he had any pride in claiming kin
Or anything he looked for from his brother,
He'd keep so still about him all this time?"

"I wonder what's between them."

"I can tell you.
Silas is what he is—we wouldn't mind him—
But just the kind that kinsfolk can't abide.
He never did a thing so very bad.
He don't know why he isn't quite as good
As anybody. Worthless though he is,
He won't be made ashamed to please his brother."

"I can't think Si ever hurt anyone."

"No, but he hurt my heart the way he lay
And rolled his old head on that sharp-edged chair-back.
He wouldn't let me put him on the lounge.
You must go in and see what you can do.

I made the bed up for him there tonight.
You'll be surprised at him—how much he's broken.
His working days are done; I'm sure of it."

"I'd not be in a hurry to say that."

"I haven't been. Go, look, see for yourself.
But, Warren, please remember how it is:
He's come to help you ditch the meadow.
He has a plan. You mustn't laugh at him.
He may not speak of it, and then he may.
I'll sit and see if that small sailing cloud
Will hit or miss the moon."

It hit the moon.
Then there were three there, making a dim row,
The moon, the little silver cloud, and she.

Warren returned—too soon, it seemed to her—
Slipped to her side, caught up her hand and waited.

"Warren?" she questioned.

"Dead," was all he answered.

The Love Song of J. Alfred Prufrock

T. S. Eliot

S'io credesse che mia risposta fosse
A persona che mai tornasse al mondo,
Questa fiamma staria senza piu scosse.
Ma perciocche giammai di questo fondo
Non torna vivo alcun, s'i'odo il vero,
Senza tema d'infamia ti rispondo.*

Let us go then, you and I,
When the evening is spread out against the sky
Like a patient etherized upon a table;
Let us go, through certain half-deserted streets,

---

* The motto of this poem is taken from Dante's *Inferno,* XXVII, lines 58–63. The lines are spoken by Guido da Monteforno, who sinned by giving false and ungodly counsel, a sin of the tongue. In hell he is enclosed in a tongue of flame and can speak only by shaking (inhaling) the life of the flame. Dante asks the invisible sinner who he is. In earthly pride, Guido would not have answered for fear of tainting his honor, but since there is no honor in hell, and since no one returns from there to tell the truth, he will hide nothing.

If I believed my answer would be made
To one who could ever climb to the world again,
This flame would shake no more. But since no shade [soul]
Ever returned—if what I am told is true—
From this blind world into the living light,
Without fear of dishonor, I answer you.

Questions: Why this motto? In what way are Prufrock and Guido related to one another?

The muttering retreats
Of restless nights in one-night cheap hotels
And sawdust restaurants with oyster-shells:
Streets that follow like a tedious argument
Of insidious intent
To lead you to an overwhelming question. . . .
Oh, do not ask, "What is it?"
Let us go and make our visit.

In the room the women come and go
Talking of Michelangelo.

The yellow fog that rubs its back upon the window-panes,
The yellow smoke that rubs its muzzle on the window-panes,
Licked its tongue into the corners of the evening,
Lingered upon the pools that stand in drains,
Let fall upon its back the soot that falls from chimneys,
Slipped by the terrace, made a sudden leap,
And seeing that it was a soft October night,
Curled once about the house, and fell asleep.

And indeed there will be time
For the yellow smoke that slides along the street,
Rubbing its back upon the window-panes;
There will be time, there will be time
To prepare a face to meet the faces that you meet;
There will be time to murder and create,
And time for all the works and days of hands
That lift and drop a question on your plate;
Time for you and time for me,
And time yet for a hundred indecisions,
And for a hundred visions and revisions,
Before the taking of a toast and tea.

In the room the women come and go
Talking of Michelangelo.

And indeed there will be time
To wonder, "Do I dare?" and, "Do I dare?"
Time to turn back and descend the stair,
With a bald spot in the middle of my hair—
(They will say: "How his hair is growing thin!")
My morning coat, my collar mounting firmly to the chin,
My necktie rich and modest, but asserted by a simple pin—
(They will say: "But how his arms and legs are thin!")
Do I dare
Disturb the universe?
In a minute there is time
For decisions and revisions which a minute will reverse.

For I have known them all already, known them all:
Have known the evenings, mornings, afternoons,
I have measured out my life with coffee spoons;
I know the voices dying with a dying fall
Beneath the music from a farther room.
  So how should I presume?

And I have known the eyes already, known them all—
The eyes that fix you in a formulated phrase,
And when I am formulated, sprawling on a pin,
When I am pinned and wriggling on the wall,
Then how should I begin
To spit out all the butt-ends of my days and ways?
  And how should I presume?

And I have known the arms already, known them all—
Arms that are braceleted and white and bare
(But in the lamplight, downed with light brown hair!)
Is it perfume from a dress
That makes me so digress?
Arms that lie along a table, or wrap about a shawl,
  And should I then presume?
  And how should I begin?

          .   .   .   .   .   .

Shall I say, I have gone at dusk through narrow streets
And watched the smoke that rises from the pipes
Of lonely men in shirt-sleeves, leaning out of windows? . . .

I should have been a pair of ragged claws
Scuttling across the floors of silent seas.

          .   .   .   .   .   .

And the afternoon, the evening, sleeps so peacefully!
Smoothed by long fingers,
Asleep . . . tired . . . or it malingers,
Stretched on the floor, here beside you and me.
Should I, after tea and cakes and ices,
Have the strength to force the moment to its crisis?
But though I have wept and fasted, wept and prayed,
Though I have seen my head (grown slightly bald) brought in
    upon a platter,
I am no prophet—and here's no great matter;
I have seen the moment of my greatness flicker,
And I have seen the eternal Footman hold my coat, and snicker,
And in short, I was afraid.

And would it have been worth it, after all,
After the cups, the marmalade, the tea,
Among the porcelain, among some talk of you and me,

Would it have been worth while,
To have bitten off the matter with a smile,
To have squeezed the universe into a ball
To roll it toward some overwhelming question,
To say: "I am Lazarus, come from the dead,
Come back to tell you all, I shall tell you all"—
If one, settling a pillow by her head,
   Should say: "That is not what I meant at all;
   That is not it, at all."

And would it have been worth it, after all,
Would it have been worth while,
After the sunsets and the dooryards and the sprinkled streets,
After the novels, after the teacups, after the skirts that trail along
   the floor—
And this, and so much more?—
It is impossible to say just what I mean!
But as if a magic lantern threw the nerves in patterns on a screen:
Would it have been worth while
If one, settling a pillow or throwing off a shawl,
And turning toward the window, should say:
   "That is not it at all,
   That is not what I meant, at all."

      .   .   .   .

No! I am not Prince Hamlet, nor was meant to be;
Am an attendant lord, one that will do
To swell a progress, start a scene or two,
Advise the prince; no doubt, an easy tool,
Deferential, glad to be of use,
Politic, cautious, and meticulous;
Full of high sentence, but a bit obtuse;
At times, indeed, almost ridiculous—
Almost, at times, the Fool.

I grow old. . . . I grow old. . . .
I shall wear the bottoms of my trousers rolled.

Shall I part my hair behind? Do I dare to eat a peach?
I shall wear white flannel trousers, and walk upon the beach.
I have heard the mermaids singing, each to each.

I do not think that they will sing to me.

I have seen them riding seaward on the waves
Combing the white hair of the waves blown back
When the wind blows the water white and black.
We have lingered in the chambers of the sea
By sea-girls wreathed with seaweed red and brown
Till human voices wake us, and we drown.

The Eve of St. Agnes

John Keats

St. Agnes' Eve—Ah, bitter chill it was!
The owl, for all his feathers, was a-cold;
The hare limped trembling through the frozen grass,
And silent was the flock in woolly fold:
Numb were the Beadsman's fingers while he told
His rosary, and while his frosted breath,
Like pious incense from a censer old,
Seemed taking flight for heaven, without a death,
Past the sweet Virgin's picture, while his prayer he saith.

His prayer he saith, this patient, holy man;
Then takes his lamp, and riseth from his knees,
And back returneth, meager, barefoot, wan,
Along the chapel aisle by slow degrees:
The sculptured dead, on each side, seem to freeze,
Imprisoned in black, purgatorial rails:
Knights, ladies, praying in dumb orat'ries,
He passeth by, and his weak spirit fails
To think how they may ache in icy hoods and mails.

Northward he turneth through a little door,
And scarce three steps, ere Music's golden tongue
Flattered to tears this aged man and poor;
But no—already had his death-bell rung:
The joys of all his life were said and sung;
His was harsh penance on St. Agnes' Eve:
Another way he went, and soon among
Rough ashes sat he for his soul's reprieve,
And all night kept awake, for sinners' sake to grieve.

That ancient Beadsman heard the prelude soft;
And so it chanced, for many a door was wide,
From hurry to and fro. Soon, up aloft,
The silver, snarling trumpets 'gan to chide:
The level chambers, ready with their pride,
Were glowing to receive a thousand guests.
The carved angels, ever eager-eyed,
Stared, where upon their heads the cornice rests,
With hair blown back, and wings put crosswise on their breasts.

At length burst in the argent revelry,
With plume, tiara, and all rich array,
Numerous as shadows haunting faerily
The brain new-stuffed, in youth, with triumphs gay
Of old romance. These let us wish away,
And turn, sole-thoughted, to one Lady there,
Whose heart had brooded, all that wintry day,

On love, and winged St. Agnes' saintly care,
As she had heard old dames full many times declare.

They told her how, upon St. Agnes' Eve,
Young virgins might have visions of delight,
And soft adorings from their loves receive
Upon the honeyed middle of the night,
If ceremonies due they did aright;
As, supperless to bed they must retire,
And couch supine their beauties, lily white;
Nor look behind, nor sideways, but require
Of Heaven with upward eyes for all that they desire.

Full of this whim was thoughtful Madeline:
The music, yearning like a God in pain,
She scarcely heard: her maiden eyes divine,
Fixed on the floor, saw many a sweeping train
Pass by—she heeded not at all: in vain
Came many a tiptoe, amorous cavalier,
And back retired; not cooled by high disdain,
But she saw not: her heart was otherwhere;
She sighed for Agnes' dreams, the sweetest of the year.

She danced along with vague, regardless eyes,
Anxious her lips, her breathing quick and short:
The hallowed hour was near at hand: she sighs
Amid the timbrels, and the thronged resort
Of whisperers in anger or in sport;
'Mid looks of love, defiance, hate, and scorn,
Hoodwinked with faery fancy; all amort,
Save to St. Agnes and her lambs unshorn,
And all the bliss to be before tomorrow morn.

So, purposing each moment to retire,
She lingered still. Meantime, across the moors,
Had come young Porphyro, with heart on fire
For Madeline. Beside the portal doors,
Buttressed from moonlight, stands he, and implores
All saints to give him sight of Madeline,
But for one moment in the tedious hours,
That he might gaze and worship all unseen;
Perchance speak, kneel, touch, kiss—in sooth such things have
    been.

He ventures in: let no buzzed whisper tell,
All eyes be muffled, or a hundred swords
Will storm his heart, Love's feverous citadel:
For him, those chambers held barbarian hordes,
Hyena foemen, and hot-blooded lords,
Whose very dogs would execrations howl
Against his lineage; not one breast affords

Him any mercy in that mansion foul,
Save one old beldame, weak in body and in soul.

Ah, happy chance! the aged creature came,
Shuffling along with ivory-headed wand,
To where he stood, hid from the torch's flame,
Behind a broad hall pillar, far beyond
The sound of merriment and chorus bland.
He startled her: but soon she knew his face,
And grasped his fingers in her palsied hand,
Saying, "Mercy, Porphyro! hie thee from this place;
They are all here tonight, the whole bloody-thirsty race!

"Get hence! get hence! there's dwarfish Hildebrand:
He had a fever late, and in the fit
He cursed thee and thine, both house and land:
Then there's that old Lord Maurice, not a whit
More tame for his gray hairs—Alas me! flit!
Flit like a ghost away."—"Ah, Gossip dear,
We're safe enough; here in this arm-chair sit,
And tell me how—" "Good saints! not here, not here!
Follow me, child, or else these stones will be thy bier."

He followed through a lowly arched way,
Brushing the cobwebs with his lofty plume;
And as she muttered "Well-a—well-a-day!"
He found him in a little moonlight room,
Pale, latticed, chill, and silent as a tomb.
"Now tell me where is Madeline," said he,
"O tell me, Angela, by the holy loom
Which none but secret sisterhood may see,
When they St. Agnes' wool are weaving piously."

"St. Agnes! Ah! it is St. Agnes' Eve—
Yet men will murder upon holy days.
Thou must hold water in a witch's sieve,
And be liege-lord of all the Elves and Fays
To venture so: it fills me with amaze
To see thee, Porphyro!—St. Agnes' Eve!
God's help! my lady fair the conjurer plays
This very night: good angels her deceive!
But let me laugh awhile,—I've mickle time to grieve."

Feebly she laugheth in the languid moon,
While Porphyro upon her face doth look,
Like puzzled urchin on an aged crone
Who keepeth closed a wondrous riddle-book,
As spectacled she sits in chimney nook.
But soon his eyes grew brilliant, when she told

His lady's purpose; and he scarce could brook
　　Tears, at the thought of those enchantments cold,
And Madeline asleep in lap of legends old.

Sudden a thought came like a full-blown rose,
　　Flushing his brow, and in his pained heart
　　Made purple riot: then doth he propose
　　A stratagem, that makes the beldame start:
　　"A cruel man and impious thou art!
　　Sweet lady, let her pray, and sleep and dream
　　Alone with her good angels, far apart
　　From wicked men like thee. Go, go! I deem
Thou canst not surely be the same that thou didst seem."

　　"I will not harm her, by all saints I swear!"
　　Quoth Porphyro: "O may I ne'er find grace
　　When my weak voice shall whisper its last prayer,
　　If one of her soft ringlets I displace,
　　Or look with ruffian passion in her face.
　　Good Angela, believe me, by these tears;
　　Or I will, even in a moment's space,
　　Awake, with horrid shout, my foemen's ears,
And beard them, though they be more fanged than wolves and
　　bears."

　　"Ah! why wilt thou affright a feeble soul?
　　A poor, weak, palsy-stricken, churchyard thing,
　　Whose passing-bell may ere the midnight toll;
　　Whose prayers for thee, each morn and evening,
　　Were never missed." Thus plaining, doth she bring
　　A gentler speech from burning Porphyro;
　　So woeful, and of such deep sorrowing,
　　That Angela gives promise she will do
Whatever he shall wish, betide her weal or woe.

　　Which was, to lead him, in close secrecy,
　　Even to Madeline's chamber, and there hide
　　Him in a closet, of such privacy
　　That he might see her beauty unespied,
　　And win perhaps that night a peerless bride,
　　While legioned fairies paced the coverlet,
　　And pale enchantment held her sleepy-eyed.
　　Never on such a night have lovers met,
Since Merlin paid his Demon all the monstrous debt.

　　"It shall be as thou wishest," said the Dame:
　　"All cates and dainties shall be stored there
　　Quickly on this feast-night: by the tambour frame
　　Her own lute thou wilt see: no time to spare,

For I am slow and feeble, and scarce dare
On such a catering trust my dizzy head.
Wait here, my child, with patience: kneel in prayer
The while. Ah! thou must needs the lady wed,
Or may I never leave my grave among the dead."

So saying she hobbled off with busy fear.
The lover's endless minutes slowly passed;
The dame returned, and whispered in his ear
To follow her; with aged eyes aghast
From fright of dim espial. Safe at last
Through many a dusky gallery, they gain
The maiden's chamber, silken, hushed and chaste;
Where Porphyro took covert, pleased amain.
His poor guide hurried back with agues in her brain.

Her faltering hand upon the balustrade,
Old Angela was feeling for the stair,
When Madeline, St. Agnes' charmed maid,
Rose, like a missioned spirit, unaware:
With silver taper's light, and pious care,
She turned, and down the aged gossip led
To a safe level matting. Now prepare,
Young Porphyro, for gazing on that bed;
She comes, she comes again, like ring-dove frayed and fled.

Out went the taper as she hurried in;
Its little smoke, in pallid moonshine, died:
She closed the door, she panted, all akin
To spirits of the air, and visions wide:
No uttered syllable, or, woe betide!
But to her heart, her heart was voluble,
Paining with eloquence her balmy side;
As though a tongueless nightingale should swell
Her throat in vain, and die, heart-stifled, in her dell.

A casement high and triple-arched there was,
All garlanded with carven imageries,
Of fruits, and flowers, and bunches of knot-grass,
And diamonded with panes of quaint device,
Innumerable of stains and splendid dyes,
As are the tiger-moth's deep-damasked wings;
And in the midst, 'mong thousand heraldries,
And twilight saints, and dim emblazonings,
A shielded scutcheon blushed with blood of queens and kings.

Full on this casement shone the wintry moon,
And threw warm gules on Madeline's fair breast,
As down she knelt for Heaven's grace and boon;

Rose-bloom fell on her hands, together prest,
And on her silver cross soft amethyst,
And on her hair a glory, like a saint:
She seemed a splendid angel, newly drest,
Save wings, for heaven:—Porphyro grew faint:
She knelt, so pure a thing, so free from mortal taint.

Anon his heart revives: her vespers done,
Of all its wreathed pearls her hair she frees;
Unclasps her warmed jewels one by one;
Loosens her fragrant bodice; by degrees
Her rich attire creeps rustling to her knees:
Half-hidden, like a mermaid in sea-weed,
Pensive awhile she dreams awake, and sees,
In fancy, fair St. Agnes in her bed,
But dares not look behind, or all the charm is fled.

Soon, trembling in her soft and chilly nest,
In sort of wakeful swoon, perplexed she lay,
Until the poppied warmth of sleep oppressed
Her soothed limbs, and soul fatigued away;
Flown, like a thought, until the morrow-day;
Blissfully havened both from joy and pain;
Clasped like a missal where swart Paynims pray;
Blinded alike from sunshine and from rain,
As though a rose should shut, and be a bud again.

Stolen to this paradise, and so entranced,
Porphyro gazed upon her empty dress,
And listened to her breathing, if it chanced
To wake into a slumberous tenderness;
Which when he heard, that minute did he bless,
And breathed himself: then from the closet crept,
Noiseless as fear in a wide wilderness,
And over the hushed carpet, silent, stept,
And 'tween the curtains peeped, where, lo!—how fast she slept.

Then by the bed-side, where the faded moon
Made a dim, silver twilight, soft he set
A table, and, half anguished, threw thereon
A cloth of woven crimson, gold, and jet:—
O for some drowsy Morphean amulet!
The boisterous, midnight, festive clarion,
The kettle-drum, and far-heard clarinet,
Affray his ears, though but in dying tone:—
The hall-door shuts again, and all the noise is gone.

And still she slept an azure-lidded sleep,
In blanched linen, smooth, and lavendered,
While he from forth the closet brought a heap

Of candied apple, quince, and plum, and gourd;
With jellies soother than the creamy curd,
And lucent syrops, tinct with cinnamon;
Manna and dates, in argosy transferred
From Fez; and spiced dainties, every one,
From silken Samarcand to cedared Lebanon.

These delicates he heaped with glowing hand
On golden dishes and in baskets bright
Of wreathed silver: sumptuous they stand
In the retired quiet of the night,
Filling the chilly room with perfume light.—
"And now, my love, my seraph fair, awake!
Thou art my heaven, and I thine eremite:
Open thine eyes, for meek St. Agnes' sake,
Or I shall drowse beside thee, so my soul doth ache."

Thus whispering, his warm, unnerved arm
Sank in her pillow. Shaded was her dream
By the dusk curtains:—'twas a midnight charm
Impossible to melt as iced stream:
The lustrous salvers in the moonlight gleam;
Broad golden fringe upon the carpet lies:
It seemed he never, never could redeem
From such a stedfast spell his lady's eyes;
So mused awhile, entoiled in woofed phantasies.

Awakening up, he took her hollow lute,—
Tumultuous,—and, in chords that tenderest be,
He played an ancient ditty, long since mute,
In Provence called, "La belle dame sans mercy":
Close to her ear touching the melody;—
Wherewith disturbed, she uttered a soft moan:
He ceased—she panted quick—and suddenly
Her blue affrayed eyes wide open shone:
Upon his knees he sank, pale as smooth-sculptured stone.

Her eyes were open, but she still beheld,
Now wide awake, the vision of her sleep:
There was a painful change, that nigh expelled
The blisses of her dream so pure and deep
At which fair Madeline began to weep,
And moan forth witless words with many a sigh,
While still her gaze on Porphyro would keep;
Who knelt, with joined hands and piteous eye,
Fearing to move or speak, she looked so dreamingly.

"Ah, Porphyro!" said she, "but even now
Thy voice was at sweet tremble in mine ear,
Made tuneable with every sweetest vow;

And those sad eyes were spiritual and clear:
How changed thou art! how pallid, chill, and drear!
Give me that voice again, my Porphyro,
Those looks immortal, those complainings dear!
Oh, leave me not in this eternal woe,
For if thou diest, my Love, I know not where to go."

Beyond a mortal man impassioned far
At these voluptuous accents, he arose,
Ethereal, flushed, and like a throbbing star
Seen 'mid the sapphire heaven's deep repose;
Into her dream he melted, as the rose
Blendeth its odor with the violet,—
Solution sweet: meantime the frost-wind blows
Like Love's alarum, pattering the sharp sleet
Against the window-panes; St. Agnes' moon hath set.

'Tis dark: quick pattereth the flaw-blown sleet.
"This is no dream, my bride, my Madeline!"
'Tis dark: the iced gusts still rave and beat:
"No dream, alas! alas! and woe is mine!
Porphyro will leave me here to fade and pine.
Cruel! what traitor could thee hither bring?
I curse not, for my heart is lost in thine,
Though thou forsakest a deceived thing;—
A dove forlorn and lost with sick unpruned wing."

"My Madeline! sweet dreamer! lovely bride!
Say, may I be for aye thy vassal blest?
Thy beauty's shield, heart-shaped and vermeil-dyed?
Ah, silver shrine, here will I take my rest
After so many hours of toil and quest,
A famished pilgrim,—saved by miracle.
Though I have found, I will not rob thy nest,
Saving of thy sweet self; if thou think'st well
To trust, fair Madeline, to no rude infidel.

"Hark! 'tis an elfin-storm from faery land,
Of haggard seeming, but a boon indeed:
Arise—arise! the morning is at hand;—
The bloated wassailers will never heed;—
Let us away, my love, with happy speed;
There are no ears to hear, or eyes to see,—
Drowned all in Rhenish and the sleepy mead:
Awake! arise! my love, and fearless be,
For o'er the southern moors I have a home for thee."

She hurried at his words, beset with fears,
For there were sleeping dragons all around,
At glaring watch, perhaps, with ready spears—

Down the wide stairs a darkling way they found;
In all the house was heard no human sound.
A chain-drooped lamp was flickering by each door;
The arras, rich with horseman, hawk, and hound,
Fluttered in the besieging wind's uproar;
And the long carpets rose along the gusty floor.

They glide, like phantoms, into the wide hall;
Like phantoms, to the iron porch they glide,
Where lay the Porter, in uneasy sprawl,
With a huge empty flagon by his side:
The wakeful bloodhound rose, and shook his hide,
But his sagacious eye an inmate owns:
By one, and one, the bolts full easy slide:—
The chains lie silent on the footworn stones;
The key turns, and the door upon its hinges groans.

And they are gone: aye, ages long ago
These lovers fled away into the storm.
That night the Baron dreamt of many a woe,
And all his warrior-guests with shade and form
Of witch, and demon, and large coffin-worm,
Were long be-nightmared. Angela the old
Died palsy-twitched, with meager face deform;
The Beadsman, after thousand aves told,
For aye unsought-for slept among his ashes cold.

The Chambered Nautilus

Oliver Wendell Holmes

This is the ship of pearl, which, poets feign,
   Sails the unshadowed main,—
   The venturous bark that flings
On the sweet summer wind its purpled wings
In gulfs enchanted, where the Siren sings,
   And coral reefs lie bare,
Where the cold sea-maids rise to sun their streaming hair.

Its webs of living gauze no more unfurl!
   Wrecked is the ship of pearl!
   And every chambered cell,
Where its dim dreaming life was wont to dwell,
As the frail tenant shaped his growing shell,
   Before thee lies revealed,—
Its irised ceiling rent, its sunless crypt unsealed!

Year after year beheld the silent toil
   That spread his lustrous coil;

Still, as the spiral grew,
He left the past year's dwelling for the new,
Stole with soft step its shining archway through,
   Built up its idle door,
Stretched in his last-found home, and knew the old no more.

Thanks for the heavenly message brought by thee,
   Child of the wandering sea,
   Cast from her lap forlorn!
From thy dead lips a clearer note is born
Than ever Triton blew from wreathèd horn!
   While on mine ear it rings,
Through the deep caves of thought I hear a voice that sings:—

Build thee more stately mansions, O my soul,
   As the swift seasons roll!
   Leave thy low-vaulted past!
Let each new temple, nobler than the last,
Shut thee from heaven with a dome more vast,
   Till thou at length art free,
Leaving thine outgrown shell by life's unresting sea!

The treatment of the nautilus gets very close to metaphor, as we are told within the structure of the poem exactly what the nautilus should be taken to represent, even though we are never told so explicitly at the time the nautilus is being described. It should be borne in mind that all poetry finally is about people, and that therefore any vision of creatures other than man must be taken as representative of human beings. Whether the creature is seen as symbol or metaphor is to some degree a matter of definition, and therefore somewhat arbitrary. As will be pointed out later in the discussion of metaphor and image, symbols generally are taken to stand for abstractions without sensory qualities, ideas, or states of existence larger in their import than the concrete symbol itself. A thing known through metaphor is usually concrete and accessible to the senses; it is, in fact, its sensory aspect which a metaphor most often exploits as an image. It is because the nautilus in its activity symbolizes the human soul (if not an abstract, then certainly not something perceptible to the senses, and a considerably more expansive entity than the nautilus) that the representation is to be taken as symbolic.

Mending Wall

Robert Frost

Something there is that doesn't love a wall,
That sends the frozen-ground-swell under it
And spills the upper boulders in the sun,
And makes gaps even two can pass abreast.

The work of hunters is another thing:
I have come after them and made repair
Where they have left not one stone on a stone,
But they would have the rabbit out of hiding,
To please the yelping dogs. The gaps I mean,
No one has seen them made or heard them made,
But at spring mending-time we find them there.
I let my neighbor know beyond the hill;
And on a day we meet to walk the line
And set the wall between us once again.
We keep the wall between us as we go.
To each the boulders that have fallen to each.
And some are loaves and some so nearly balls
We have to use a spell to make them balance:
"Stay where you are until out backs are turned!"
We wear our fingers rough with handling them.
Oh, just another kind of outdoor game,
One on a side. It comes to little more:
There where it is we do not need the wall:
He is all pine and I am apple orchard.
My apple trees will never get across
And eat the cones under his pines, I tell him.
He only says, "Good fences make good neighbors."
Spring is the mischief in me, and I wonder
If I could put a notion in his head:
"*Why* do they make good neighbors? Isn't it
Where there are cows? But here there are no cows.
Before I built a wall I'd ask to know
What I was walling in or walling out,
And to whom I was like to give offense.
Something there is that doesn't love a wall,
That wants it down." I could say "Elves" to him,
But it's not elves exactly, and I'd rather
He said it for himself. I see him there,
Bringing a stone grasped firmly by the top
In each hand, like an old-stone savage armed.
He moves in darkness as it seems to me,
Not of woods only and the shade of trees.
He will not go behind his father's saying,
And he likes having thought of it so well
He says again, "Good fences make good neighbors."

What are the symbolic elements in "Mending Wall"? Is it possible that not only objects, such as the wall, but the confrontation between the two men, might have symbolic meaning?

Do you prefer the symbolic meaning of a poem to be spelled out, as in "The Chambered Nautilus," or left for the reader to recognize, as in Frost's poem? Why?

Identify the symbolic elements in each of the following poems, and discuss what abstract and expanded meaning lies back of the symbol.

I Heard a Fly Buzz When I Died

Emily Dickinson

I heard a fly buzz when I died;
    The stillness round my form
Was like the stillness in the air
    Between the heaves of storm.

The eyes beside had wrung them dry,
    And breaths were gathering sure
For that last onset, when the king
    Be witnessed in his power.

I willed my keepsakes, signed away
    What portion of me I
Could make assignable,—and then
    There interposed a fly,

With blue, uncertain, stumbling buzz,
    Between the light and me;
And then the windows failed, and then
    I could not see to see.

Love Song: I and Thou

Alan Dugan

Nothing is plumb, level, or square:
    the studs are bowed, the joists
are shaky by nature, no piece fits
    any other piece without a gap
or pinch, and bent nails
    dance all over the surfacing
like maggots. By Christ
    I am no carpenter. I built
the roof for myself, the walls
    for myself, the floors
for myself, and got
    hung up in it myself. I
danced with a purple thumb
    at this house-warming, drunk
with my prime whiskey: rage.
    Oh I spat rage's nails
into the frame-up of my work:
    it held. It settled plumb,
level, solid, square and true
    for that great moment. Then
it screamed and went on through,

skewing as wrong the other way
God damned it. This is hell,
   but I planned it, I sawed it,
I nailed it, and I
   will live in it until it kills me.
I can nail my left palm
   to the left-hand crosspiece but
I can't do everything myself.
      I need a hand to nail the right,
a help, a love, a you, a wife.

Night Crow

Theodore Roethke

When I saw that clumsy crow
Flap from a wasted tree,
A shape in the mind rose up:
Over the gulfs of dream
Flew a tremendous bird
Further and further away
Into a moonless black,
Deep in the brain, far back.

The Rite

Dudley Randall

"Now you must die," the young one said,
"and all your art be overthrown."
The old one only bowed his head
as if those words had been his own.

And with no pity in his eyes
the young man acted out his part
and put him to the sacrifice
and drank his blood and ate his heart.

Traditional Red

Robert Huff

Returning after dark, I thought,
The house will have grown small: noises
In the barn I knew, wood and field,
All tree tops visible. My eyes,
I thought, lied then or will lie now;

My ears, even my ears, will tell
Me: small. Then half awake I waited,
Half afraid of the sound light makes
With frost on windowpanes. But night
Birds carried fifteen years away
Like an abandoned nest, put them
To rest somewhere I couldn't see
Without undoing anything,
And when I woke the dawn I saw
Was on the farm as positive as God.

A rooster dipped in sunlight raised
His crown, called to the steaming barn,
Gigantic, red, until my blood
Roared for stupidity, and I
Ran down the path humble with hens
To kneel and stare dumb wonder
At his size. My pride! my pride! O
Jesus, bright dove call! I knelt there
In his thunder, white and small, watched
Whose tops I couldn't see for light,
Dense, golden, moving hosts of leaves
Answering that red cry. And when
I turned I saw the farm house roof
Raking an iron rooster through the sky.

I Move the Meeting Be Adjourned

Nicanor Parra

Translated by Miller Williams

Ladies and gentlemen:
I have only one question:
Are we children of the sun or of the earth?
Because if we are only earth
I don't see why
we continue to film the picture:
I move the meeting be adjourned.

Anecdote of the Jar

Wallace Stevens

I placed a jar in Tennessee,
And round it was, upon a hill.
It made the slovenly wilderness
Surround that hill.

The wilderness rose up to it,
And sprawled around, no longer wild.
The jar was round upon the ground
And tall and of a port in air.

It took dominion everywhere.
The jar was gray and bare.
It did not give of bird or bush,
Like nothing else in Tennessee.

Birdwatchers of America

Anthony Hecht

> I suffer now continually from vertigo, and today, 23rd of
> January, 1862, I received a singular warning: I felt the wind of
> the wing of madness pass over me.
>
> Baudelaire, *Journals*

It's all very well to dream of a dove that saves,
    Picasso's or the Pope's,
The one that annually coos in Our Lady's ear
    Half the world's hopes,
And the other one that shall cunningly engineer
The retirement of all businessmen to their graves,
    And when this is brought about
Make us the loving brothers of every lout—

But in our part of the country a false dusk
    Lingers for hours; it steams
From the soaked hay, wades in the cloudy woods,
    Engendering other dreams.
Formless and soft beyond the fence it broods
Or rises as a faint and rotten musk
    Out of a broken stalk.
There are some things of which we seldom talk;

For instance, the woman next door, whom we hear at night,
    Claims that when she was small
She found a man stone dead near the cedar trees
    After the first snowfall.
The air was clear. He seemed in ultimate peace
Except that he had no eyes. Rigid and bright
    Upon the forehead, furred
With a light frost, crouched an outrageous bird.

The Visiting Hour

David Wagoner

Strip off your clothes and give them to a man
In a uniform, hurry to take a shower,
Put on a starchy, stark-white coverall
That can stand up by itself, then keeping in line,
March to the visitor's room.

It has lamps, rugs, curtains, movable furniture,
And a woman among some women, looking at you
And wearing a dress and holding out her arms
(Which may be entered against her)
And shutting and opening her mouth for an hour.

Standing behind his bullet-proof glass, the guard
Has been instructed to stare, but stares at the wall,
The ceiling, or between your bodies
As if recalling games on television.
What you can do is act like him for her:

Your eyes must look at something common between you—
A crack, a flower on a cushion.
Your hands may touch each other item by item
In order, checking down the list of reminders.
You may reach for almost anything but conclusions.

When a bell rings, there is nothing left to answer,
No one is calling or waiting, nothing is ready—
The time has simply gone, and the time has come
To say goodbye like scouts of opposing factions
From opposite closing doors.

From the corridor, you'll enter an empty room
To be stripped and searched for imaginary objects:
Stooping, squatting, and squinting, the guards go through
Your closets and blind alleys
To catch you keeping what you can never get.

The long way back will take you past a gate
Where you can see a man outside in a tower.
His searchlight, his eyes, his rifle
All turn toward you if you stop to wave.
He must know you to let you out. He doesn't know you.

And in Cell Block D, nobody wants to shoot you.
Those tiers with railings
Rise forty feet like the face of a motel
With ice on every floor. Like venetian blinds,
The catwalks show you mounting, kneeling, or lying.

The guards in the gallery simply look and listen
Over their sights if you thumb your nose or scream
Or try to throw something far enough to reach them.
They'll put your name on a list; then visitors
Will have to imagine you for years and years.

Lying Awake

W. D. Snodgrass

This moth caught in the room tonight
Squirmed up, sniper-style, between
The rusty edges of the screen;
Then, long as the room stayed light,

Lay here, content, in some cornerhole.
Now that we've settled into bed
Though, he can't sleep. Overhead,
He hurls himself at the blank wall.

Each night hordes of these flutterers haunt
And climb my study windowpane;
Fired by reflection, their insane
Eyes gleam; they know what they want.

How do the petulant things survive?
Out in the fields they have a place
And proper work, furthering the race;
Why this blind fanatical drive

Indoors? Why rush at every spark,
Cigar, headlamp or railway warning
To knock off your wings and starve by morning?
And what could a moth fear in the dark

Compared with what you meet inside?
Still, he rams the fluorescent face
Of the clock, thinks that's another place
Of light and families, where he'll hide.

We'd ought to trap him in a jar,
Or come, like the white-coats, with a net
And turn him out toward living. Yet
We don't; we take things as they are.

Photographs

Charles Wright

One of my father; he stands
In hunting clothes in front
Of our house; two dogs
Nuzzle the fingers of
His outstretched hand;
Under his right arm
The shotgun that now is mine
Gleams in the sunlight—
I cannot tell if he leaves
Or if he is just returned.

. . . .

One of my mother, and blurred;
Sunday; the afternoon
Is smoky and overcast;
Standing beside the lake,
She balances on a rock
At the waterline, gazing out;
Someone is in a boat
Taking her picture; she
Is waiting for them to land.
The water . . . The shoreline . . . .

. . . .

This one of me at six
At play in the backyard—
Marbles of some sort;
The ring is quite visible
In the August dust;
I have Ups, and am fudging;
Off to one side,
A group of three boys:
One is my brother and one
Is someone I do not know.

. . . .

I shut the album hard.
What good are these now?
They do not answer *What next?*
Or *What was I trying to prove?*
They do not explain us:
Such poses are unrecorded—
They lurk like money, just
Out of reach, shining
And unredeemed:
And we hold such poses forever.

The One Furrow

R. S. Thomas

When I was young, I went to school
With pencil and foot-rule
Sponge and slate,
And sat on a tall stool
At learning's gate.

When I was older, the gate swung wide;
Clever and keen-eyed
In I pressed,
But found in the mind's pride
No peace, no rest.

Then who was it taught me back to go
To cattle and barrow,
Field and plough;
To keep to the one furrow,
As I do now?

A Cabin in Minnesota

Marvin Bell

Nothing like that road runs from me
which leads up-map through the bleak
brackish erasure in Northern Minnesota

almost to Canada where our plans stopped.
"No use pretending, we're not going,"
and you took up the road to Minneapolis

and beyond, and rolled back the miles,
and then spied through the wrong end
of the tube in the direction of that cabin

which took its last tiny breath and expired
in a clutch of blankets, the fire gone out,
no one nearby, no wood on the way.

CHAPTER FOUR
THE
WORDS OF POETRY

Something about Words

Poetry is made of not-words.
Karl Shapiro

Few people in any age use their own language to the limit of its re-
sources. One manages to get himself understood in one way or
another, and for most people that seems to do. When, occasionally, one
is moved to wonder about a particular word, he may go so far as to turn
to the dictionary. He then "looks up what the word means" and he
thereby "builds his vocabulary." He has found out about the word.

A good dictionary is, of course, indispensable to anyone who hopes
to use the language well. But the dictionary itself cannot be wholly
useful until one realizes four basic qualities of all words. They are
qualities not simply of words in poetry but of words used in any con-
text. The good poet makes deliberate and impassioned use of these
qualities, but had human history not produced a single poem, these
qualities would still be observable as living forces of the language. Once
one is aware of these qualities his very use of a dictionary will be
changed, for he will then be appraising in a very different way what the
dictionary tells him.

1. A word is a feeling.   Words do, to be sure, have areas of agreed-upon
"meaning," or "dictionary definitions." "Rat," for example, is the label
agreed upon in English to identify a rodent that resembles a mouse but
is larger and marked by a different sort of tooth structure. This "iden-
tifying" function of the word is its *denotation*.

But what has happened to the word when a gangster refers to an
accomplice as "a rat," or when he makes the word into a verb and says

"he ratted on me," that is, "he gave information against me to the police"? The gangster does not mean that his accomplice is a rodent resembling a mouse but larger and having a different tooth structure. For man, the language animal, not only invents words as labels (denotations), but tends to associate the word with the thing it labels. Most people think of rats as despicable, vicious, and filthy. So the word takes on that "feel." The gangster is not at all concerned with the zoological classification of genus Rattus. He has dropped the denotation in order to use the feeling of the word (*connotation*).

The following are more or less random examples of different labels used to identify the same objects. What is the difference in feeling implied in using one label instead of another?

Label A	Label B	Label C
Fish	Finny folk	Denizens of the deep
Earth	*La machine ronde* ("the round machine")	The little O, the earth
Alderman John J. McGinnis	That man four-square	That thieving skunk
Can of cat food	Ground fish heads	Pussy-Purr Preparation
Digitaria sanguinalis	Crab Grass	Pestiferous weeds
Elizabeth Jukes	Sweetie pie	Big Bess

These examples will demonstrate that we commonly select language for its feeling (connotation) rather than for purposes of identification (denotation). That is to say we are often less concerned with identifying a thing than we are with expressing a feeling toward it. If I point to a candidate and say Yes and you point to a candidate and say No, we have both pointed to the same person but we have expressed different feelings about him. So with Alderman John J. McGinnis in the table above. Neither Label A nor Label B is really intended to identify him. Each label is a different vote. Each seeks to persuade to a different course of action toward Mr. McGinnis.

But man is a suggestible animal and it often happens not only that his attitudes influence his labels, but that his labels influence his attitudes. Were one to pose as a strolling reporter and stop every mother out pushing a baby carriage to ask her, "Are you willing to have your child killed in the defense of our national policy?" he would probably get a negative answer. Were he to ask instead, "Do you believe we should defend our national policy at all cost?" he would probably get a largely affirmative set of answers. We are all likely to feel well disposed toward defending "our national policy," and mothers seem to have strong feelings against having their children killed. Yet the phrase "at all cost" in question two must certainly include the cost of killing some sons of some mothers, and to that extent the two questions are the same. It is the emphasis and the aura of the question that change the response.

One last instance. In England a man "stands" for Parliament. In America he "runs" for Congress. "Standing" certainly seems to suggest a process rather different from "running." Is there any merit in the argument that a major difference between American and English politics can be summed up in the difference of feeling (connotation) released by these two words? The speculation is more important than the answer. What must be understood is the fact that if "meaning" equals "denotation" ("identification"), then everyone uses many words without "meaning," selecting them primarily for the way they feel rather than for their accuracy.

The difference between this process in normal speech and in poetry is simply that the poet makes his selections with more acute attention to the various forces within the word. For the person who is language sensitive, every word has its own personality. "Billingsgate," "riparian," "pismire," "omnium-gatherum," "rasp," "bang," "bodacious," "lazy Susan," "crepuscular"—every word releases its own aura of feeling.

2. A word involves the whole body. An inseparable but special part of the feeling of words lies in the fact that they have to be produced by a human body—with an exception noted for parrots and the like. The act of producing a word involves breath and muscle, and various kinds of muscular activity tend to produce various kinds of feeling. Thus, aside from all other considerations, the bodily involvement in sounding the word is a distinct part of the word's personality. "Elate" feels one way and "thud" feels another. So for sheets, burble, spit, clack, snip, bang, buzz, alleluia, prestidigitation, indubitably, liquescent, ululate, majestic, and anything else one cares to cite from the total language—some words involve more specific and more localized muscular play than others, and some have their denotations more involved in the resulting sound than others, but every word has a muscular feel of its own. When the muscular play tends more or less definitely to enact the denotation of the word as in "prestidigitation" or "oily" (one has only to protract the "oi" sound to produce an oily suggestion), then the word may be called *mimetic.* When the sound of a word imitates the sound of what the word denotes (as in buzz, link, splash, crunch), then the word may be called *onomatopoetic.* Any conversation attentively listened to will offer examples of both kinds of words. The more excited the conversation becomes, the easier it will be to see in the emphases and gestures of the speakers how the muscles and the nervous system are involved in the process of speech and its meaning.

3. A word is a history. Languages die but words tend to be immortal. Catchwords, slang, and technical terms often disappear after a brief run, but many become established parts of the language, and once so established they persist. Hosts of Greek and Latin words are in use in dozens of the world's present-day languages. It is mainly the order in which words are used, the ways in which they are joined together (*syntax*), and their inflections that change. Like the stones of an ancient ruin, the words fall out of their original organization but survive to be used again, though they are often chipped or even broken in the process. There is hardly a tenement hovel in the old section of modern

Rome that was not built in part with stones from ancient ruins. There is hardly a phrase in a modern American's vocabulary that has not been built up from pieces fallen out of other languages.

To the attentive collector of ancient fragments, however, each unit tends to keep its history. It is so and more so with words, for the history tends to remain in them as an immediate and intrinsic force. Thus a person sensitive to language could conceivably object to the sentence "On the eighth day we arrived at our mid-ocean rendezvous and re-fueled." "Arrive" is simply a slightly changed way of spelling and pronouncing the Latin *ad ripa,* meaning "to the shore." It offends the history of a perfectly good word to speak of "arriving" at mid-ocean.

And just as a firm awareness of the history of words leads one to more precise usage, so can it yield rewarding pleasures. Hearing a New England farmer calling in his cows with a "Ho! Boss! Ho! Boss!" one may be both surprised and delighted to realize that what he is hearing is almost pure Greek. Centuries before Christ, the same cry rang over the hills of Greece, the call meaning literally "The Cow! The Cow!" One may take such awareness as simply ornamental information, or he may find in it a moving example of the continuity of human experience. For the poet, as for anyone passionately concerned with words as living forces, the realization is bound to have a touch of excitement in it.

Often, an awareness of a word's history will not only make clear but will dramatize its meaning. "Supercilious" is an Anglicized form of Latin *supercilium* (*super,* "above," and *cilium,* "eyelid"); hence, an eye-brow. Hence a supercilious expression is "an eyebrow expression," one with raised eyebrows. Nor need one know Latin to come by such an awareness. Good dictionaries not only define words but give their his-tories in brief. Anyone truly concerned to make his speech precise will stop to learn such roots when he consults the dictionary. Having done so, he is less likely to be tempted into such unhistorical imprecisions as the construction, "A supercilious wave of the hand."

Chaucer, at one point, refers to "Christ sterved [starved] on the cross." In Chaucer's day *sterven*—from Anglo Saxon *steorfan,* which in turn derived from Old Norse—meant any slow death, as by exposure, torture, hunger, or thirst. "To starve" acquired its present limited meaning long after Chaucer's day. Towns under attack were often be-sieged and "starved out." That is, they were exposed to slow death by being shut off from the means of life. As it happened, however, it was almost invariably the food that gave out first in those days of no refrig-eration and poor storage. Thus "to die of lack of food" came to usurp the whole meaning of the original word. In sensitive usage, however, the old meaning is still there, still available for some situation in which it can enrich the total communication. "The starved thief of the wind and the hanging tree," is an invented example. Were it an authentic line of poetry, its effect would depend on many allusions. Nor does the writing demand full awareness of such allusions: the general sense of the line is suggestive even when its "meaning" has not been located. But certainly there is an added richness hidden away in "starved" and waiting for the reader who can unlock it. Many poets like to hide away such happy additions: they do not insist that every reader respond to them; it is enough that such touches delight the writer and are ready to delight the reader who is able to respond to them.

Denham's lines on Cowley (p. 136) and John Donne's "Holy Sonnet XIV" (p. 224) provide examples of how richly a deep sense of the history hidden in words can sharpen and excite the language, teaching the reader precisions and distinctions of which he had not been aware.

Turn to Donne's sonnet for a close reading, and then notice especially the word "usurp," which we now understand to mean "to take for one's own use what belongs to another." The word holds the roots, though, for "to make use of" and "to rape," which enrich the role of the word in the context of the poem's sexual metaphor. In a dictionary that gives the origins of words, look also at "labor," "prove," "betroth," and "enthrall."

With a few exceptions every word traced back far enough is either a metaphor or an onomatopoeia. Nor can an awareness of that fact fail to suggest a deep truth about the nature of man's mind and of his sense of the universe. Let us leave onomatopoeia out of present consideration, and consider only specimens of the metaphors, that is, the pictures, locked up in words. "Hippopotamus" is from the Greek *hippo* ("horse") and *potamos* ("river"), hence "the river horse." "Billingsgate" ("foul and vituperative language") is derived from the name of a London fishmarket (compare: "swore like a fishwife") and conceals within it a picture of the whole wrangling, competitive, and coarse squabbling of a penny-grabbing street market. A semirelated word, "aspersion," on the other hand ("a calumny, a calumnious remark") is from latin *ad* ("to, toward") and *spargere* ("to sprinkle"). The distinctions revealed by the histories of these words permit precision of usage that is not possible to those who lack a sense of word history. "My opponent has interpreted my remarks as an aspersion upon his character and has given substance to the interpretation by his own spew of billingsgate." Note how nicely the word "spew" trumps the hidden "sprinkle" in "aspersion."

The following words all have some area of denotation in common. In a good dictionary (preferably the many volumed *Oxford English Dictionary* available in the library, though *The American Heritage Dictionary* will do) look up the *history* of each word. Note how the word's history makes possible distinctions that are not apparent in the simple dictionary definition.

vituperation	objurgation
condemnation	execration
denunciation	abuse
censure	invective
criticism	obloquy
vilification	scurrility
calumniation	

Note especially that an awareness of the word's history eventually identifies the word's meaning in terms of a root picture or root metaphor. This picture-making power, already touched upon, is the fourth indispensable function in determining the feel of the word.

4. *A word is a picture.* The word "daisy" points to a common flower and lightly conceals the root picture "day's eye." "Goodbye" is the noise socially agreed upon for basic leave-taking, and just behind it sounds the benediction from which it is derived: "God be wi' ye." A "gossip" was originally the person who stood with you when you were baptized, or your "God-sibling," your brother- or sister-in-God, and therefore the one to whom you confided your most intimate secrets —secrets eventually called "God-sibling talk" or "gossip talk" and finally "gossip." As soon as one takes into account this picture behind the word, there simply are no synonyms anymore. The whole idea of synonyms is an invention of the habit of dictionary definition. Conceivably there might be sets of identical twins among the words of the world, but they are rare by the very nature of language. For all practical purposes words are most richly conceived as individuals, each with its own history, each with its own locked-in picture.

The problem of the translator will illustrate. The English verb "to burke" is derived from the practices of a famous felon of Edinburgh, one William Burke, well hanged in 1829. Burke began as a corpse-snatcher for a medical school, and when newly buried corpses were unprocurable, or when it became too dangerous to steal them from the guarded graveyards, he simplified matters by making his corpses to order. As a result of its derivation the word "to burke" means, in its fully extended sense, "to smother a victim by pinching his nose between the fingers while pressing the butt of the palm against his mouth in such a way as to produce a corpse with no visible signs of violence and therefore readily saleable to a medical school." It must be obvious without further investigation that there is small chance of finding any word in any other language that has exactly the same dramatization as "to burke."

What is less obvious is that no two words—unless they are derived from the same roots, or except by extraordinary chance, can have the four basic qualities here discussed in anything like the same combination. Each word is "peculiarly" itself. (A happy word, "peculiar," in that it derives from Latin *peculium*, "private property." "Private," moreover, is from *privatus*, "apart from the state," that is, not held in common.") A certain amount of redundance in the roots may help to underline the idea: *every word is peculiarly its exclusive self apart from all common holding.* Within the "state" of common usage, words may seem to have some parts of their dictionary definitions in common, but never within their peculiar private properties.

Even as simple a word as "daisy" is untranslatable. In French, for example, the flower is called a *marguerite*, a pleasant enough suggestion of girls named Marguerite. It is, moreover, derived from Greek *margaron*, "pearl." Two happy pictures in themselves—but what has happened to the lovely English picture, "day's eye"?

Anyone who listens carefully to common speech is bound to realize that though most people respond as if instinctively to the feeling and to the muscular quality of words, few pay attention to the histories and the root pictures words can release. Those neglected qualities are there, however, and the poets have always found them a self-delighting source of excitement. The reader without some awareness of these qualities must inevitably remain insensitive to a substantial part of the life of a good poem.

Look up the following words in one of the dictionaries mentioned above. Pay special attention to their derivations (histories) and to their root pictures. Note how many of them you have used over and over without real awareness of all their meanings.

explicit	publish	algebra
buckaroo	establish	amen
two bits	rhododendron	gentle
progress	aspiration	subscribe
agony	ambition	clown
sympathy	jargon	pants
nice	distinguish	comfort

The Word in the Poem

> So spake the enemy of mankind, enclosed
> In serpent, inmate bad, and toward Eve
> Addressed his way, not with indented wave,
> Prone on the ground, as since, but on his rear
> Circular base of rising folds, that towered
> Fold above fold a surging maze; his head
> Crested aloft, and carbuncle his eyes;
> With burnished neck of verdant gold, erect
> Against his circling spires that on the grass
> Floated redundant.
>
> from *Paradise Lost*

John Milton had a peculiar problem in the foregoing passage from *Paradise Lost* in which he describes the serpent's approach to Eve. Milton's theology demanded the belief that the serpent was condemned to crawl on its belly for its crime in tempting Eve. It follows, then, that serpents originally moved in some other way, and that theological point forces Milton to invent a rather fanciful rear-wheel drive, the details of which he well advisedly keeps a bit vague.

Readers with long memories may recall that something very much like the same point was raised in the course of the famous evolution trial in Tennessee as part of the defending attorney's cross-examination of witnesses. An assiduous digger through European archives, moreover, might well expect to turn up a number of ponderous essay treatises on snake locomotion before and after. By the world's evidence, then, as well as his own conviction, Milton is dealing with facts. There was a time not too long since when the study of such facts was very nearly all there was to the study of poetry in our universities, and there is still a marked tendency among many readers to think they have made a sufficient contact with the poem when they have identified and placed such central facts.

Because the natural form for the exposition of facts seems to be the essay, such a fact-centered reading of poetry may be thought of as "the essay approach." The true nature of a poem's performance of itself, however, is so lightly concerned with its essay content, that it may reasonably serve the purposes of good reading to pretend that there are no facts in the poem. A poet must believe *something* passionately enough to have strong feelings about it, but what that something is in actual fact is the item of least consequence as far as participating in the poetic performance is concerned.

The essay has satisfied its essential requirements when it has followed the facts—facts, opinions, argument, all in general that it "has to say." Music, on the other hand, follows itself, the first sound calling the second into being, and it the third, and so on until those inner calls become feelingly involved and feelingly solve themselves. Music has no facts. It is its own fact.

Poetry does, as noted, involve itself with facts, but the poetic essence is so much nearer that of music than it is that of the essay, that to stress facts in poetry is often the quickest way to lose sight of the poem. *The essence of a poem is that one thing in it requires another.* As far as the words of poetry are concerned that inner requirement is so little a matter of external meaning (denotation) and so much an inner dialogue of connotations (feelings, sounds, and historical and pictorial roots) that it will at least serve to redress the balance to pretend that denotation has no function, and to practice the experience of a poem in something like pure musical terms.

The French critic Boileau called the essence of poetry a *je-ne-sais-quoi,* an "I-don't-know-what." Line by line and passage by passage the poem comes to the poet from sources he feels strongly but does not pretend to understand. At least at the beginning of the poem. Very soon, however, whatever comes to him from the *je-ne-sais-quoi* had better start coming in response to what he has already written down or he is not going to have a poem. Maybe the first line comes from nowhere. And maybe the second comes from a second theme nowhere. But whatever part of what follows continues to come to him from his nowhere, it has to come from those first lines as well. The poem, that is, is forever generating its own context. Like a piece of music, it exists as a self-entering, self-generating, self-complicating, self-resolving form.

To answer to that musicality within the structure of the poem is to answer to the poem itself. Milton's rear-wheel snake passage, ridiculous as its essay content is bound to seem, is an example of poetry elevated to sublimity by the rich and powerful development of its diction into musiclike themes.

The first characteristic of Milton's diction here is precision. Note especially the rightness of "indented." Milton wished to ascribe to the post-Paradisal snake a wavelike motion. Now a wave may be conceived in many ways—as a single peak, as a trough and crest, as a long roller. But the clear historical meaning of "indented" is "cut into toothlike points." For Milton—so passionate a Latinist that he could speak of "elephants endorsed with towers"—that root image of "indented" establishes all. For clearly a single wave cannot be indented. At least two are required to make an indentation. In poetry, the force of a given sense is readily extended: as soon as the pluralness of the wave is established, the suggested picture at once becomes not a picture of two waves but of many.

Parenthetically, it must be noted that the process of selection going on in the poet's mind (or the recognition of that process in the mind of a good reader) is not spread out across a paragraph of description. It is most likely to happen as an instantaneous, surprising, and happy discovery. The rightness of the choice is felt in many ways at once. It is the explanation that labors, not the poem. The one point of the explanation is to guide the reader back to the poem with a sharper awareness of what he must learn to experience instantaneously.

Now note the last phrase, "floated redundant." As the snake rears its jeweled head, the remaining coils lie on the grass as if they floated. "Floated," of course, once more suggests the wave image, and in combination with "redundant" it urges a picture of many slow coils lying at ease on the waters, resting but still keeping a slow, endless, easy motion.

But why "redundant"? Why not "superfluous"? "remaining"? "excessive"? Milton's choice was partly determined by the sound of the word, to be sure, but much more urgently because of the picture hidden in the Latin roots of the word (*redundare,* "to overflow"; from *unda,* "a wave"). "Superfluous" also means "to overflow" but with a single, continuous outward motion, as of a river rather than with the better-related suggestion of a wave's surging and receding motion.

Quite clearly Milton has chosen his words not only, nor even primarily, for the rightness of their denotation (essaywise) but for the interconnection of their connotations (musically); not for their exactness to the "facts" but for the way they follow from other words in the passage. "Floated redundant," for example, might factually have been expressed "sprawled out in excess loops and coils"; but then the interplay of one wave suggestion with another would have been lost. The point cannot be made often enough that it is exactly such interplays that determine the poem as a poem, and that such interplays, far from being merely ornamental, are inseparable from the poem's "meaning." They *are* the meaning, and if they are not there is no defense for poetry, nor any meaningful way of preferring it to embroidery, crossword puzzles, or the day's prose from Washington.

Having located "indented wave" and "floated redundant" as specific kinds of watery motion, one may now look back and see that "surging," too, is at root a watery motion. Its base picture is of a spring bubbling up, its waters agitated in all directions around it. Thus in nine-and-a-fraction lines, that suggestion of watery motion has been three times urged upon the reader. What could be more like the way in which the fragments of a musical theme are picked up, dropped, and picked up again? If the jargon is not objectionable, this sort of poetic development may reasonably be called an "overtone theme." Just as certain characters in opera are identifiable by a musical theme that accompanies them through the action, so the serpent is carried through this description to the theme of a constant wavering watery motion.

And having noted one theme, the reader can hardly fail to note another: the snake also moves like an oriental monarch. His elevation is regal: ("towered," "crested aloft," "spires"). His ornaments are all magnificence: ("crested"—that is, crowned; "carbuncled"—that is, diamonded; and "gold"). Thus the theme of watery motion is accompanied by a theme of regal splendor. Again the poem performs itself much as does a piece of music.

And much as in a piece of music, the two themes join. Waves "tower" and kings may be said to "tower" above men. "Crested aloft" suggests a wave at peak, and it also means "crowned on high."

Now if one rereads the passage he can note three groupings of overtone themes: watery motion, regal splendor, and the two together. Arranged in three columns the words and phrases that might be related to each of these themes would appear so:

Watery motion	Regal splendor and Watery motion	Regal splendor
indented wave	towered	carbuncled
circular base	crested aloft	burnished
rising folds		gold
fold upon fold		circling spires
surging maze		
floated redundant		

Whatever the value of such a tabulation, it cannot fail to make clear, first, that a unified principle of selection is at work in this diction, and second, that the words are being selected from inside their connotations and in answer to one another's connotations, rather than from inside their denotation.

For a poem, it must be understood, is a made thing. It does not *record* reality nor even imagination; it *selects* from them. The ideal newspaper account of an incident, for example, aims at recording what happened; a good short story selects and shapes. Whatever the short story's takeoff from fact, it must end by shaping itself to itself. The fact that a given event happened in "real life" does not make it happen in an art form; art is its own way of happening. A good painting is neither a photograph nor a blueprint but an interpretation and an intensification achieved by emphasizing some things, subordinating others, and by following the inner requiredness of the composition. For that matter, even a photographer selects. Nature does not care where and in what sequence as seen from what vantage point the mountains of Maine fall into the sea or thrust up again as islands: they are simply there. But let the most amateur photographer decide to take a photo of that coastline, and the instant he has framed it in his viewfinder he begins to move the camera about in the attempt to find a relation within the frame. Put a dab of paint on an endless surface and it does not matter where it falls. But put a frame around it, and immediately the one dab requires another, and the two a third, until some sort of composition has been achieved.

These scattering examples are all to the point that every art form presents its material within a convention and a limitation, and that the material does not exist meaningfully in that art form until it has become involved in the inner requiredness of its formal limitations. Until the perception of a poem becomes a perception of that inner requiredness, the poem has not come into view. To paraphrase a statement by I. A. Richards, "One talks about the subject of a poem when he does not know what to do with the poemness of the poem." That "poemness" exists nowhere but in the poem's performance of itself from itself into itself.

A simpler and perhaps more pointed example of this inner relationship of words within the poem occurs in Keats' "The Eve of St. Agnes" (p. 82). In stanza XXVI, Keats is faced with a delicate problem, for in a poem concerned with idealized love, Keats finds himself describing the hero in the potentially satyrlike situation of hiding in a closet and watching the heroine undress for bed. The tone is delicate, yet the material in this particular scene has been the immemorial property of coarse humor from fabliaux to burlesque show. Keats' original work sheets, now in the collection of Harvard's Houghton Library, trace out in interesting detail the poet's difficulties in making his choices.

With Porphyro looking on from the closet, Madeline enters, says her prayers, and prepares for bed. The tone of that opening description is all airiness and delicacy:

> . . . her vespers done,
> Of all its wreathed pearls her hair she frees;
> unclasps her warmed jewels one by one;

Keats' choice of adjectives has been much and justly praised. "Wreathed" is light, graceful, ideal, with a suggestion of a halo about it. And "warmed" (warmed by her flesh) is precisely the kind of rich sensuous yet not sensual detail Keats loved to lavish upon his poems. All goes well so far.

But Keats has already survived one difficulty. The first draft of the manuscript reads not as above in the third line, but "Unclasps her bosom jewels." This reading Keats immediately struck out. One must note in the final version that though Madeline undresses in this stanza, there is not one word that mentions flesh. Certainly there is no reason except the narrowest kind of prurience against mentioning "bosom" as a fact of the world. But the word does not fit the mood Keats is seeking to establish. The flesh remains in the revised line, but it is sublimated and suggested in the richness of "warmed" rather than baldly stated.

In the next line Keats encounters exactly the same difficulty, but here his trouble is more persistent. He begins:

> Loosens the bodice from her . . .

But what can she loosen her bodice from, other than the naked fact Keats is seeking to avoid? He crosses out that reading and tries again even more disastrously:

> Loosens her bursting bodice . . .

But he realizes at once that "bursting" will not do. In succeeding attempts he tries:

> Loosens her bodice lace-strings . . .

then:

> Loosens her bodice, and her bosom bare . . .

then:

> Loosens her fragrant bodice and doth bare
> Her . . .

And in this last form, he has conquered most of his problem, but "bare" as demanded by the rhyme with "hair" is still wrong. At this point Keats backed up, inserted a new rhyme word into line two, and seems to have gone straight to the perfection of his final version:

> Anon his heart revives: her vespers done,
> Of all its wreathed pearls her hair she frees;
> Unclasps her warmed jewels one by one;
> Loosens her fragrant bodice; by degrees
> Her rich attire creeps rustling to her knees:
> Half-hidden, like a mermaid in sea-weed,
> Pensive awhile she dreams awake and sees,
> In fancy, fair St. Agnes in her bed,
> But dares not look behind, or all the charm is fled.

Two things seem to emerge clearly from a careful look at Keats' choices and revisions here. First, Keats seems originally to have conceived of Madeline as definitely buxom, *but no hint of that original conception survives the revisions.* Keats seems to have changed, or at least to have suppressed his original conception of the facts, and to have done so with no hint of unfaithfulness to facts, but rather in a joyous pursuit of something else. *Poets seem easily inclined to change the denotations of what they write about in order to control the connotations.*

The second fact to emerge from such a work-sheet examination is the care with which those connotations have been related to one another. "Wreathed . . . warmed . . . fragrant" release an intimately interrelated series of connotations. "Wreathed" establishes the lightness and grace of the theme. "Warmed" richly suggests the vitality of Madeline's bodily presence. And "fragrant" repeats exactly that suggestion. "Warmed" and "fragrant," in a sense, are brother-and-sister words, and they are cousins of "wreathed."

It is upon such "family" relations within words that the poet lavishes his love and attention. Milton, a Latinist, "felt" his words most richly in terms of their root sense. Keats, a lover of the sensuous fact of the world, "felt" his words in terms of the sensations they released. Both were concerned with the way their words worked in context with one another. Both used words as poets dream of doing, with a kind of life words rarely possess except in poetry.

The Phrase as a Form

Words are, in one sense, distinct units. In another, however, they are forever shaping themselves into rhythmic phrases in which the words themselves become parts of a large unit. This tendency of words to form together is a basic process in all language. Poetry makes rich use of this force but the force itself is prepoetic and is best illustrated by such forms as the battle cry and the proverb, forms of intense and direct natural language in which the phrasing is *muscular, irreducible,* and *memorable.*

The *muscularity* of good phrasing is obvious at a glance. "Saint George and the Dragon for Merrie England" is not simply a statement; it is a rhythmic unit to which a man on a horse can swing his sword arm. The phrase involves the whole body in its muscular spasm. And that muscular spasm is far more important than the precise meaning of the statement. The cry is intimately linked with an action. Its function is to make the muscles twitch. A captain leading his men into battle sounds the cry waving his sword over his head and his men give it back in a single animal roar as they rush forward. Does the statement have meaning? A philosophical captain might have gathered his men quietly about him and said in thoughtful tones: "Men of England, here at this brink of battle, let us summon to mind the triumphant image of Saint George the Dragon slayer, and with him ever in our minds as a symbol of our high heritage, let us move resolutely against the foe. Thank you." Is that statement the same thing? Unfortunately the paraphrase has taken the muscular twitch from it. There is about the same difference between the paraphrase and the original statement as there is between the Official Rule Book for Intercollegiate Football and the kick-off of the Rose Bowl game.

The fact is that battle cries have no real need to mean, only to be. (See Archibald MacLeish's "Ars Poetica," p. 281.) Here are a few of the many battle cries men have fought and died to. Self-evidently the power of such phrasing is not in its paraphrasable meaning:

> *Courage mes amis, le diable est mort!*
> *Banzai!* (The literal meaning is something like "May you live a thousand years.")
> *Ding how!* (The literal meaning is something like "perfect.")
> Bonnie Dundee!
> Hundred and third!

Examples could be multiplied indefinitely, but it should be amply clear that whatever meaning might be locked into the cry (as in "Remember the Alamo!") the real function of such a cry is to release pent-up emotion. Any noise will serve so long as those who cry it are emotionally identified with it. The bark and snarl of dogs is essentially a battle cry.

What is reduced to a single outburst in such cries is used in much more subtle ways in poetic phrasing, but the basic principle of all such phrasing remains firm: *good language involves the body; the more powerful and the more simple its emotion, the greater the bodily involvement is likely to be.*

The language of such cries is also *irreducible.* One cannot find an excess word in them. Proverbs are generally subtler examples of basic phrasing than are battle cries, but the same irreducibility of the phrase is the basis of their effect. "A bird in the hand is worth two in the bush." "Be sure to sell your horse before he dies." "Pretty is as pretty does." "A stitch in time saves nine." The proverb or the proverb-shaped poetic line can be extended into long passages of paraphrase. The second example above is a line from a Robert Frost poem. How many words would one need to write in order to explain everything the line means? The essence of its success is exactly that it says so much in so little. Every word counts: remove any one and the meaning is lost. A whole area of meaning has been reduced to what must certainly be the fewest possible words.

And partly because such phrasing is indeed irreducible, it is also *memorable.* The memorableness of proverbs is assisted by their rhythms, by their turns of phrase, and by their ability to convert a thought into a picture. "A stitch in time saves nine," for example, is rhythmically definite and inevitably suggests some picture of a "nine-stitch rip" as opposed to the same fabric kept whole by the timely taking of a single stitch. A proverb is essentially a rhythmic word portrait of a thought. Still, were the rhythm to become too complex, or the portrait to run to too many words, the force would be lost. For all of these reasons, its irreducibility first among them, the proverb seems to hook onto the memory almost by itself.

These qualities of *muscularity, irreducibility,* and *memorableness,* are forces from the very beginnings of language. In every good poem they continue to work as sources of powerful emotional effects.

The Language of Poetry

Neither the deadness of bad poetry nor the liveliness of good poetry can be located exclusively in the way the poet uses words. Yet certainly whatever is most characteristic of a good poet must begin with a special sensitivity to language. As in Auden's measure of the potential poet, the man must want to hang around words in order to overhear them talking to one another. That "hanging around," however, is not a passive occupation. The poet's necessary sensitivity involves a lifetime of bringing his joyous attention to the ways in which words whisper to one another. And the words of good poetry must be those of the poet's native tongue, the words that echo most deeply into his memory and response.

Thus one may hear poets speaking of words in ways that are not immediately clear; of "hard" words and "soft" ones, of "thin" or "echoing" or "square" words. There is a feeling at the root of such talk, but the labels themselves lack precision. The fact that deeply felt things are often the hardest to define must not, however, obscure the point that such strange talk arises from a real feeling and that those who have such feelings most urgently are likely to use the language in the most living way.

Robert Burns is perhaps the outstanding example of a poet who had a genius for the quality of one sort of language and almost none whatever for the quality of another. His poems in Scottish dialect ring true to the very roots of the language. His poems in English are never more than merely correct. Burns could overhear the broad Scots words talking to one another, hear their echoes to the depths of his consciousness, but he had no such feeling for the sound and echo of English. Here, for example, are the first three stanzas of a poem in his native language:

To James Smith
(stanzas 1–3)

Robert Burns

Dear Smith, the sleest, paukie thief,
That e'er attempted stealth or rief,
Ye surely hae some warlock-breef
    Owre human hearts;
For ne'er a bosom yet was prief
    Against your arts.

For me, I swear by sun and moon,
And every star that blinks aboon,
Ye've cost me twenty pair o' shoon

sleest: slyest. **paukie:** cunning, sly. **warlock-breef:** wizard's contract (with the devil). **prief:** proof. (Sense: no human heart could fail to answer to the quality of your friendship.) **aboon:** above. **shoon:** shoes. (Sense: Burns has worn out twenty pairs of shoes walking to Smith's house and finds himself more and more drawn to Smith with each new pair of shoes he wears out on that road.)

Just gaun to see you;
And ev'ry ither pair that's done,
Mair taen I'm wi' you.

That auld, capricious carlin, Nature,
To make amends for scrimpit stature,
She's turned you aff, a human creature
On her first plan,
And in her freaks, on ev'ry feature,
She's wrote, "The Man."

The language of such a dialect poem is, of course, a difficulty, but the notes should take care of that. Even beyond the strangeness of the language, however, the poem requires careful attention. One is not used to reading of friendship in these (antipoetic) terms. Were the turning of the poem closer to the standard copybook sentiments on friendship, one might run his eyes over it once lightly and perceive all there is in it. Fortunately for the reader's pleasure, the poem is close to life rather than to the copybook. It does require some effort (perhaps as much effort of the attention as it takes to play a tight hand of bridge). Yet despite the effort, there can be no mistaking the liveliness of the poem. One has the sense that only a man who has actually walked many miles (and many times) to the house of his friend could have written of his friendship in this way. One has the sense, too, that the description in stanza three—at once tender and humorous—could only have beeen drawn from a man the poet knew well and loved dearly. And with this depth of feeling, the words come alive. Burns did not have to go to school to learn to use words in this way, and no school could have taught him. For the character and depth of the words echo up from the subconscious of the language. They are leaping, laughing, tender, easy, dear words to Burns. No matter that he could not have defined their quality as he felt it. What counts is that he did feel it. Here on the other hand are the first three stanzas of a Burns poem in English, this one also written to a specific and known person:

Verses
Intended to Be Written
Below a Noble Earl's Picture

(Stanzas 1–3)

Robert Burns

Whose is that noble dauntless brow?
And whose that eye of fire?
And whose that generous princely mien
Even routed foes admire?

carlin: old woman. **scrimpit stature:** scanty and slight of build, not tall. (Sense: To make amends for having made you so small, Nature, in one of her freaks of mood, has stamped your every feature with qualities that say "This is a Man.")

Stranger, to justly shew that brow
And mark that eye of fire,
Would take His hand, whose vernal tints
His other works admire.

Bright as a cloudless summer sun,
With stately port he moves;
His guardian seraph eyes with awe
The noble ward he loves.

"Verses" is a "poetic" or fashionable poem, a standard sort of inscriptive piece out of the copybook of eighteenth-century manners, though rather badly overdone. Only God's hand, the second stanza asserts, painting on something like the same scale on which He paints the world's greenery, could portray the noble Earl—surely a gross, insincere, and even irreverent bit of flattery. Heaven knows what Burns hoped to gain by it, but his need was at times great and servility was one of the ways of moving an influential patron to provide the means of life.

But the point to be made is one of diction. It is almost impossible, if not absolutely impossible, for a poet to cheat emotionally in this way without betraying himself in the flatness and triteness of his language. There is not a phrase in the poem that is not cliché ridden. "Noble brow" and "dauntless brow" are both clichés: Burns gives the reader both for good measure. Pausing for a single cliché in "eye of fire," he once more doubles the charge with "generous princely mien." Then, to round off the first stanza, he reaches blithely into the file of poetic stereotypes for the image of the last line. And so on through "vernal tints," "bright sun," "cloudless summer," "stately port" (for "stately bearing"), and "noble ward." There is no sort of pleasure in counting the insincerities a good poet may fall into, but sooner a small offense than to allow clichés to go unrecognized for lack of sufficient examples. There is not one of these phrases that could not be compiled a hundred times over from the works of a hundred bad poets before and since Burns.

One may argue, to be sure, that such a piece of rhymed flattery composed in the hope of bread must necessarily be stilted. The fact is, however, that Burns always tended to fall into lifeless and unconvincing language when he wrote in English. Here, for example, is a lament in English of exactly the sort he wrote so well in Scottish dialect. Like all of Burns' Scottish lyrics, it was specifically meant to be sung:

A Mother's Lament for the Death of Her Son
Tune—"Finlayston House"

Robert Burns

Fate gave the word, the arrow sped,
And pierced my darling's heart;
And with him all the joys are fled

Life can to me impart!
By cruel hands the sapling drops,
    In dust dishonour'd laid:
So fell the pride of all my hopes,
    My age's future shade.

The mother-linnet in the brake
    Bewails her ravish'd young;
So I, for my lost darling's sake,
    Lament the live-day long.
Death, oft I've feared thy fatal blow,
    Now fond, I bare my breast,
O, do thou kindly lay me low
    With him I love at rest.

Despite Burns' successes with such songs in the Scottish dialect, there is no life in this one. Death as the arrow that pierces the heart, the young man as the sapling chopped down before it could become a tree, the mother bird lamenting her lost fledgling, the baring of the mourner's own breast to the stroke of death—all are worn poetic counters. And, inseparably, the diction goes slack as the impulse goes dead, overfamiliar phrase following overfamiliar phrase.

"Poetry," wrote John Wheelwright, "is a way of knowing." Language, one might paraphrase, is a way of feeling. It has been said somewhere that one can write poetry only in the language in which he first learned to say "Mamma," and the fact is that though some prose writers (Joseph Conrad, to mention one outstanding example) have distinguished themselves in an acquired language, no poet has ever done so. This fact, and the example of Burns' failures in his English poems, will suggest how deeply the language of good poetry must be felt, and how many shadings of response must go into the selection of the right and moving word. The language must not only be overheard, it must be overheard echoing all the way back to one's birth, before the poet can achieve a way of speaking that reveals to the reader not only how well an experience may be perceived, but how well the language can be spoken by one who is life involved in it.

1. A sense of the whole language stirring.   If it is understood that language used at its full depth involves complications as profound and as undefinable as those of life itself, it will then be possible to discuss some questions of language in poetry that will at least help to phrase the final question. That final question, it must be remembered, remains a fundamental one. What is the nature of poetic language? What is the nature of life? How does the planet come to be inhabited? These are all fundamental questions and they are fundamental precisely because they are finally unanswerable. What matters is to raise the question in the most meaningful way possible.

The fact that a good poem will never wholly submit to explanation is not its deficiency but its very life. One lives every day what he cannot define. It is feeling that is first. What one cannot help but sense in good poetry is a sense of the whole language stirring toward richer possibilities than one could have foreseen. To consider some of the impressions that can be isolated from that total feeling, and to speculate on their possible causes, is at least to enter the question of how language functions in a poem. One must remember, however, that such impressions do not exist in isolation in the poem. To separate them for analysis is pointless unless one then attempts to put them back in context. One does not take a poem apart for the love of dissection but only in order to put it back together more meaningfully.

2. Language and diction. The Irish critic Donald Davie makes a useful distinction between *language* and *diction.* Certain poets, he points out, give off a sense that any word in the language could find a place in their works. Others, on the other hand, deliberately exclude certain words. Their work, as Davie puts it, gives off a sense "of words thrusting to be let into the poem but being fended off from it."

In the process of such fending off these poets are, in essence, either following or developing a "poetic." In our own time, American poets have made free use of all sorts of technical terms, whereas French poets have refused to allow such terms into their work. The point of the example is not that all American poets write a language, but that to the extent that French poets fend off all technical terms *they* are writing a diction. Such terms have been branded "unpoetic" and have been deliberately excluded. Davie cites Goldsmith on Homer to illustrate a similar difference in point of view:

> Homer has been blamed for the bad choice of his similes on some particular occasions. He compares Ajax to an ass, in the *Iliad,* and Ulysses to a steak broiling on the coals, in the *Odyssey.* His admirers have endeavored to excuse him, by reminding us of the simplicity of the age in which he wrote; but they have not been able to prove that any ideas of dignity or importance were, even in those days, affixed to the character of an ass, or the quality of a beef collop; therefore they were very improper illustrations for any situation in which a hero ought to be represented.

If one agrees with Goldsmith on what is dignified and important, one must agree with his censure of Homer. One must not miss the point, however, that diction is more than a matter of stylish word choices. A man's diction involves the whole of his attitude toward himself and toward everything else. Cleanth Brooks, in his *Modern Poetry and the Tradition,* makes nearly the same distinction when he speaks of the *poets of wit* as opposed to the *poets of high seriousness.* The *poets of wit* (John Donne will do as an example) strive toward a language and welcome into their poems the rush of every sort of experience. The *poets of high seriousness* (William Wordsworth will do as an example) strive toward a diction and exclude all that is not "dignified and important."

Quite clearly most poets, especially the American and English poets of the eighteenth and nineteenth centuries, wrote a diction. And a diction is certainly a lesser thing than a language. On the other hand a poet who practices a diction, Alexander Pope for example, may achieve what he achieves not in spite of his diction, but because of it. Poetry remains large enough to be all things to all who care to read. Even as considerable a poet as Milton wrote essentially a diction. One would certainly have no trouble imagining good English words that Milton would not have accepted. Like Goldsmith, he will allow no beefsteaks in Eden. And he will not allow them precisely because he has excluded from the Eden of his poetic imagination those concepts which such excluded words express.

Finally, it seems to be true that poets who write in a diction tend to be more ornamental, and poets who write in a language to be more direct. Once again, no judgment for or against is implied in pointing out this difference. The aim is to identify. Poetry is the one, the other, and both together. Hamlet's "So I have heard and do, in part, believe" is an example of the direct, unornamented line. Tennyson's "The mellow ousel fluted in the elm," is an example of the richly ornamented line.

There are real pleasures in either manner, but the highest effects of passionately moving speech seem to occur in the simplicity of poetic language as distinct from diction. The more passionate the statement the more simple the form it tends to take.

Perhaps the best example of this difference in a single passage is the speech Dante puts into the mouth of Pier delle Vigne on the journey through Hell. Since it occurs in a complicated context, a little advance explanation will assist the reading.

The spirit of Pier delle Vigne is condemned among the suicides. Since these are sinners who destroyed their own bodies, they are denied a bodily form and grow as trees in a dark wood of Hell. Thus the reference to the "trunk" and the oath "by the new roots of this tree" (delle Vigne has been dead only a short time). In life, delle Vigne was the powerful minister of Frederick II until he was accused of treachery, imprisoned, and blinded. It was to escape further torture that he killed himself. (The "Caesar" of line 10 is a generic term for "Emperor.")

Pier delle Vigne was also famous for his eloquence and for his mastery of the ornate and intricate poetry of the Provençal-inspired Sicilian School. He was an embroiderer of words. It may help to think of him as a slightly more elegant but equally pompous Polonius.

Thus as he begins to speak, he carefully announces that he will wind up slowly (line 3). He then proceeds through a series of little rhetorical exercises, such as the balanced construction of line 5, and the double and triple repetitions of key words in the passage that follows. In the middle of line 18, however, the elaborate courtly prologue ends abruptly, and in a sudden rush of language (as distinct from diction), he speaks his grief from the heart, simply and passionately.

Pier delle Vigne

Dante Alighieri

Translated by John Ciardi

And the trunk: "So sweet those words to me that I
   cannot be still, and may it not annoy you
   if I seem somewhat lengthy in reply.

I am he who held both keys to Frederick's heart,
   locking, unlocking with so deft a touch
   that scarce another soul had any part

in his most secret thoughts. Through every strife
   I was so faithful to my glorious office
   that for it I gave up both sleep and life.

That harlot, Envy, who on Caesar's face
   keeps fixed forever her adulterous stare,
   the common plague and vice of court and palace,

inflamed all minds against me. These inflamed
   so inflamed him that all my happy honors
   were changed to mourning. Then, unjustly blamed,

my soul in scorn, and thinking to be free
   of scorn in death, made me at last, though just,
   unjust to myself. By the new roots of this tree

I swear to you that never in word or spirit
   did I break faith to my lord and emperor
   who was so worthy of honor in his merit.

If ever you regain the world, speak for me,
   to vindicate in the memory of men
   one who lies prostrate from the blows of Envy."

In case the distinction is not wholly clear, imagine how different the
effect of this passage would have been had delle Vigne continued his
elaborate rhetoric to the end, as for example:

By the firm root of this tree

I firmly swear my faith was ever firm
   to him who was my lord, as to the Lord
   who was our Lord alike. If at the term

of your dark way you make your way to light
   I pray you lighten the dark memory
   Envy's brief day cast to eternal night.

3. A poem is a context for making choices.   A poet who writes in a diction is constantly making one sort of choice; a poet who writes in a language is constantly making another. A poem may well be conceived as a context for making choices. At any given point in the poem, the poet must select the next thing to do. He must choose a word, an idea, an image—all these together. He must decide to add ornamentation or to thrust for the statement and center of his feeling. If nothing else, he must choose from the total language one word and not another.

Keats' "Epistle to Charles Cowden Clarke" is an early poem. Clarke had been instrumental in turning Keats to the pleasures of poetry. Among other things, Clarke had introduced Keats to Spenser's poetry. Keats responded with a sense of uncontainable and joyous excitement at such discoveries. Keats writes to thank Clarke for having taught him:

> all the sweets of song:
> The grand, the sweet, the terse, the free, the fine;
> What swelled with pathos, and what right divine:
> Spenserian vowels that . . .

That what? What will his choice be? Having equated Spenser's verse to vowels, what shall he say about it? He has a new rhyme at his disposal (the "Epistle" is written in couplets) and is therefore free of rhyme demand. Shall he say

> Spenserian vowels, that divinely lilt?

or:

> Spenserian vowels, delicate and light?

He wrote instead:

> Spenserian vowels that elope with ease.

And what a magnificent choice "elope" is in this context! "Divinely lilt" could not be objected to. Nor could "delicate and light." But nothing distinguishes them; one could easily improvise choices that good. These, in fact, were improvised on the typewriter. But "elope" contains that shiver of real poetry that Emily Dickinson had in mind when she spoke of "the desirable gooseflesh which is poetry." And at least three reasons can be pointed out for the rush of pleasure that arises from this source. First, the word is *both surprising and surprisingly right*. One could not have foreseen it, but he is immediately convinced by it; he has made a happy discovery. Second, the sound of "elope" exactly illustrates the Spenserian vowel: *the thing itself echoes through the word*. Third, the overtone of "elope" is delicate, light, and divinely lilting. All that the adjectives of the lesser choices labor to say, the exactly right choice releases, seemingly without labor, and directly into our sensations. Moreover, one knows, from having read Keats' later poems, that the overtone is exactly right to Keats' own deepest point of view—a romantic, light, incomplete, and loving action. What the lovers on the Grecian Urn are yearning to (p. 158) and what Porphyro and Madeline dramatize in an actual elopement at the end of "The Eve of St. Agnes" (p. 82) is already germinally in this loving usage of "Elope."

As Keats himself later described this quality of poetry, it "should surprise with a fine excess, and not by singularity; it should strike the reader as a wording of his own thoughts, and appear almost a remembrance."

Whether a poet writes in a language or a diction (and hereafter unless one or the other is specified it should be assumed that the discussion applies to both) this "fine excess" is inseparable from the richness and muscular stir of good poetry. A good poem is always better than one could have expected. Even on rereading, and even on many rereadings, the truly achieved poem stays richer than one's best memory of it.

Here, for example, is Hamlet's familiar soliloquy from Act IV, scene iv. Hamlet has just seen Fortinbras lead his army away to battle for a plot of ground worthless in itself but involving a small point of honor. This grand tossing of life and death for such minute reasons is the occasion that informs against Hamlet, damning him in his own eyes for having hesitated so long in the much greater cause of avenging his father:

> How all occasions do inform against me,
> And spur my dull revenge! What is a man
> If his chief good and market of his time
> Be but to sleep and feed? a beast, no more.
> Sure, he that made us with such large discourse
> Looking before and after, gave us not
> The capability of god-like reason
> To fust in us unused. Now, whether it be
> Bestial oblivion, or some craven scruple
> Of thinking too precisely on the event—
> A thought which, quartered, hath but one part wisdom,
> And ever three parts coward—I do not know
> Why yet I live to say "This thing's to do,"
> Sith I have cause, and will, and strength, and means
> To do't. Examples gross as earth exhort me:
> Witness this army of such mass and charge,
> Led by a delicate and tender prince,
> Whose spirit, with divine ambition puffed,
> Makes mouths at the invisible event,
> Exposing what is mortal and unsure
> To all that fortune, death, and danger dare,
> Even for an eggshell. Rightly to be great
> Is not to stir without great argument,
> But greatly to find quarrel in a straw
> When honor's at the stake. How stand I then
> That have a father killed, a mother stained,
> Excitements of my reason and my blood,

> And let all sleep? while to my shame I see
> The imminent death of twenty thousand men,
> That for a fantasy and trick of fame
> Go to their graves like beds, fight for a plot
> Whereon the numbers cannot try the cause,
> Which is not tomb enough and continent
> To hide the slain? O, from this time forth
> My thoughts be bloody, or be nothing worth.

The total effect of such a passage cannot, certainly, be said to spring simply from its word choices. The rhythms and the dramatic pauses and contrasts determine its pace. Hamlet's narrative situation helps create an identity with him (empathy). And the whirl of many images glimpsed and gone (the sharpness of "spur," the sleeping beast, the heraldic suggestion of "quartered," as if Hamlet were thinking of an escutcheon for his state of mind) populates the mind's eye. Still, considered simply as a series of word choices delivering each thought (denotation) wrapped in the aura of its precisely felt and precisely suggestive overtone, the passage certainly gives off a sense that English cannot be better selected than this. Let it stand as a high example of that kind of poetry which is written in a *language* as distinct from a *diction* and with the impulse toward passionate simplicity rather than toward ornamentation. What are some of its characteristics? How does one measure the firmness of its selection?

Marie Gilchrist offers one measure that should never be lost sight of:

> Verbs and words derived from verbs are of great importance. When you say that your object does something, rather than that it is something or like something else, you give it life and movement. Nouns stand for ideas, names, and things. Each noun is a complete picture. Nouns and verbs are almost pure metal. Adjectives are cheaper ore; they have less strength of meaning, since they stand for just one aspect of a thing, one characteristic, and do not represent it in its entirety.*

Adjectives, then, may be said to be relatively inactive. And with this in mind one may formulate a valuable principle:

4. *The language of good poetry is active.* No all-encompassing rules work in poetry, yet here is one which, used with discretion, can offer a simple, tangible, and still basically sound measure of the quality of a poem's language: count the adjectives and the verbs; good writing (*active* writing) will almost invariably have more verbs.

There seems always to be some difference of opinion on the adjective count. Should "quartered" (line 11), for example, be argued as an adjective ("a quartered thought") or as a verb ("quarter the thought and you will see")? As it falls in the text, it certainly is presented as a

---

* Marie Gilchrist, *Writing Poetry* (Boston: Houghton Mifflin, 1932).

verb. And still its force could be argued to be adjectival. The point at issue, however, does not require any real concern with such hairsplitting. When in doubt let it count as an adjective. The Hamlet passage will still turn up a count of approximately two verbs per adjective: forty-six verbs to twenty-four adjectives.

The nearly two-to-one ratio is not exorbitant (as a count through the poems in this volume will demonstrate) and it seems to be a general rule that passages of poetry (one must, of course, assume a passage of sufficient length to be representative) that have generally been agreed upon as good English poetry by critics of various ages of taste, always seem to hit toward this ratio.

Note, too, that the rule (as a simplification) has been restricted to verbs and adjectives. Were adverbs to be added to the adjective count and nouns to the verb count, the ratio would mount sharply in favor of nouns and verbs. (Suggestion: Count the adverbs and the nouns in the Hamlet passage and add that count to the adjective-verb ratio of twenty-four to forty-six. What is the new ratio?)

The idea of such a count is not to show that adjectives cannot be well used in poetry, but rather to underline the fact that they *must* be well used, or not at all. Chaucer, in summarizing his description of the Knight in the General Prologue to the *Canterbury Tales*, makes memorable use of piled-on adjectives:

> He was a verray, parfit, gentil Knyght.

It must be remembered, however, that Chaucer piled on his adjectives only after twenty-eight lines of detailed description at the end of which the three adjectives precisely sum up the merit of the Knight and are conferred upon him almost as a title. And it is worth noting, too, that though the passage from which this line is taken is one of introductory physical description rather than one of narrated action or of reinvoked experience, there are still in the preceding twenty-eight lines twenty-four verbs to seventeen adjectives. In the description of a person's appearance a writer will find it all but impossible to avoid some more than normal inflow of adjectives. Aside from passages of such introductory description, and aside from those least interesting passages of Chaucer where he piles elaboration upon elaboration with a medieval gusto for brocading, the verb-adjective ratio of Chaucer's language will mount sharply in favor of the verbs. In any case a diction in which every noun is propped up by an adjective may almost flatly be said to be a bad one.

A second and indispensable characteristic of an active poetic language derives from the basic characteristics of a good English sentence. Reduced to its essence, a *good English sentence* is "a statement (in idiomatic word order) that an agent (the subject of the sentence) performed an action (the verb) upon something (the object)." However complex the demands and resources of language, that norm must not long be lost: *active voice, idiomatic word order,* and *agent-action-object order.*

"The odor of cooking cabbage was wafted to my nostrils" is a bad way of saying "I smelled cabbage cooking." In the inert passive voice it seems to be the "odor of cooking cabbage" which is the agent of the action. No such thing. The agent is "I." Good prose, as Coleridge pointed out, is words in their best order and good poetry is the best words in the best order. The idiom of English, whether in poetry or in prose, establishes a sense of sequence and that sense is basically keyed to statement in the active voice, with the passive voice serving not as a ready and elegant substitute for all occasions, but rather standing by to be used for special purposes. Imagine, if you will, how Hamlet's speech might have run had it been keyed to the passive voice and had the agent of the action consistently been obscured:

> How I am informed against by all,
> Till my revenge do spur me. What is a man
> If sleep and food together constitute
> His time's chief good and mart? a beast, no more.
> Sure, made as we have been, such large discourse
> Looking before and after, given us . . .

But enough of that. The point of such vandalism is not to make Shakespeare sound like Browning in one of his worst moments, but to reemphasize what must not be lost sight of even at the cost of redundancy: the norm of good language is the *active voice*. The norm of a good sentence is a subject that appears *first* in the sentence.

It may be argued perhaps that all of the Hamlet passage can be reduced to the last line and a half:

> O, from this time forth
> My thoughts be bloody or be nothing worth!

A good muscular exclamation, and one that states the essence of Hamlet's determination. But how could one *feel* Hamlet's situation in the last line and a half, without the preceding lines as a preparation? The communication of a poem is an involvement. The reader must be made to enter Hamlet's state of mind in telling detail. In this sense then, the irreducibility of a passage of poetry may be seen as the long way round, but always as the most direct line to our involvement. What must be cut away from the poem is not words, but those parts of the poem, if any, that do not serve to involve us. The best conductor is not the man who can lead the orchestra through a Mozart symphony in the shortest elapsed time, but the one who can bring the orchestra to the fullest involvement in the music and to its fullest suggestion. It is the density of the suggestion that counts. Suppose, for example, that Shakespeare had inserted after the first half of line twenty-one, some such lines as:

> I have heard
> Saints and philosophers aver alike
> That greatness is the measure of the will
> Not of the object sought, its formal cause

Being but the vessel that the spirit fills,
Costly or worthless. Rightly to be great
Is not to stir . . . etc. . . . .

Quite obviously the intrusive lines are worthless, but even assuming by some large effort of the imagination that they are worthy of Shakespeare, they certainly could serve only to delay the passage. The irreducibility of the poem must be seen not as the shortest verbal line between two points, but as the shortest completely involving line.

Read the following two poems with an eye to the ways in which the poets have employed verbs, nouns, and adjectives. (It is interesting to note here that "employ" in its Latin roots *im* and *plicare* means both "to fold into" and "to imply.") Check the number of adjectives against the number of nouns in each of the poems, and see if you can justify the introduction of the adjective in each case. Does the adjective "fold into" the line without too much resistance, so that it seems at home there, and does it shift the import of the noun sufficiently to tell us something significant about the noun that we might not have known otherwise?

Mr Bleaney

Philip Larkin

"This was Mr Bleaney's room. He stayed
The whole time he was at the Bodies, till
They moved him." Flowered curtains, thin and frayed,
Fall to within five inches of the sill,

Whose window shows a strip of building land,
Tussocky, littered "Mr. Bleaney took
My bit of garden properly in hand."
Bed, upright chair, sixty-watt bulb, no hook

Behind the door, no room for books or bags—
"I'll take it." So it happens that I lie
Where Mr Bleaney lay, and stub my fags
On the same saucer-souvenir, and try

Stuffing my ears with cotton-wool, to drown
The jabbering set he egged her on to buy.
I know his habits—what time he came down,
His preference for sauce to gravy, why

He kept on plugging at the four aways—
Likewise their yearly frame: the Frinton folk
Who put him up for summer holidays,
And Christmas at his sister's house in Stoke.

But if he stood and watched the frigid wind
Tousling the clouds, lay on the fusty bed

Telling himself that this was home, and grinned,
And shivered, without shaking off the dread

That how we live measures our own nature,
And at his age having no more to show
Than one hired box should make him pretty sure
He warranted no better, I don't know.

The Farmer's Wife

Anne Sexton

From the hodge porridge
of their country lust,
their local life in Illinois,
where all their acres look
like a sprouting broom factory,
they name just ten years now
that she has been his habit;
as again tonight he'll say
honey bunch let's go
and she will not say how there
must be more to living
than this brief bright bridge
of the raucous bed or even
the slow braille touch of him
like a heavy god grown light,
that old pantomime of love
that she wants although
it leaves her still alone,
built back again at last,
mind's apart from him, living
her own self in her own words
and hating the sweat of the house
they keep when they finally lie
each in separate dreams
and then how she watches him,
still strong in the blowzy bag
of his usual sleep while
her young years bungle past
their same marriage bed
and she wishes him cripple, or poet,
or even lonely, or sometimes,
better, my lover, dead.

The following two poems by Robert Frost express much the same
dark vision. Note the relative presence of adjectives (and adverbs) in
each of the poems, and apply the same test as was applied to the

modifiers in the previous poems. Does the relative abundance of modifiers in the first poem have any influence upon the effectiveness of the poem?

Notice the complete lack of adjectives in the first stanza of "The Draft Horse" as the speaker's voice shifts from the dramatic telling of the incident to the resigned, fatalistic conclusion, without any use for the verbal trappings of romance and a somber grandeur.

The Draft Horse

Robert Frost

With a lantern that wouldn't burn
In too frail a buggy we drove
Behind too heavy a horse
Through a pitch-dark limitless grove.

And a man came out of the trees
And took our horse by the head
And reaching back to his ribs
Deliberately stabbed him dead.

The ponderous beast went down
With a crack of a broken shaft.
And the night drew through the trees
In one long invidious draft.

The most unquestioning pair
That ever accepted fate
And the least disposed to ascribe
Any more than we had to to hate,

We assumed that the man himself
Or someone he had to obey
Wanted us to get down
And walk the rest of the way.

The Impulse

Robert Frost

It was too lonely for her there,
    And too wild,
And since there were but two of them,
    And no child,

And work was little in the house,
  She was free,
And followed where he furrowed field,
  Or felled tree.

She rested on a log and tossed
  The fresh chips,
With a song only to herself
  On her lips.

And once she went to break a bough
  Of black alder.
She strayed so far she scarcely heard
  When he called her—

And didn't answer—didn't speak—
  Or return.
She stood, and then she ran and hid
  In the fern.

He never found her, though he looked
  Everywhere,
And he asked at her mother's house
  Was she there.

Sudden and swift and light as that
  The ties gave,
And he learned of finalities
  Besides the grave.

A poet may alter and sharpen the impression a reader gets from a word or a situation not only by the use of adjectives and adverbs to describe the qualities of a thing directly, but also by the use of simile and metaphor to tell the reader what a thing is like. Metaphor allows the poet to specify qualities without letting a glut of modifying words deaden the sense of a poem's "activeness." At the same time, a simile or metaphor is a means of comparison that acts on the reader's physical senses and so tends to heighten the reader's involvement.

Simile and metaphor will be considered more fully in Chapter Six. For now it will be helpful to look at a poem in which comparison often takes the place of the adjective. Read "The Fish," paying particular attention to the comparisons. (To say as in lines 37–38 that the eyes of the fish are "backed and packed/with tarnished tinfoil" is to make a comparison, to say that it is *as if they were* that way.) Then write the poem out with each comparison replaced by the freshest appropriate adverb or adjective you can come up with. The modifier you introduce should as nearly as possible tell the reader the same thing the comparison told him about the noun or verb or situation involved. What happens to the energy level and the sense of forward thrust of the poem?

The Fish

Elizabeth Bishop

I caught a tremendous fish
and held him beside the boat
half out of water, with my hook
fast in a corner of his mouth.
He didn't fight.
He hadn't fought at all.
He hung a grunting weight,
battered and venerable
and homely. Here and there
his brown skin hung in strips
like ancient wallpaper,
and its pattern of darker brown
was like wallpaper:
shapes like full-blown roses
stained and lost through age.
He was speckled with barnacles,
fine rosettes of lime,
and infested
with tiny white sea-lice,
and underneath two or three
rags of green weed hung down.
While his gills were breathing in
the terrible oxygen
—the frightening gills,
fresh and crisp with blood,
that can cut so badly—
I thought of the coarse white flesh
packed in like feathers,
the big bones and the little bones,
the dramatic reds and blacks
of his shiny entrails,
and the pink swim-bladder
like a big peony.
I looked into his eyes
which were far larger than mine
but shallower, and yellowed,
the irises backed and packed
with tarnished tinfoil
seen through the lenses
of old scratched isinglass.
They shifted a little, but not
to return my stare.
—It was more like the tipping
of an object toward the light.
I admired his sullen face,
the mechanism of his jaw,

and then I saw
that from his lower lip
—if you could call it a lip—
grim, wet, and weaponlike,
hung five old pieces of fish-line,
or four and a wire leader
with the swivel still attached,
with all their five big hooks
grown firmly in his mouth.
A green line, frayed at the end
where he broke it, two heavier lines,
and a fine black thread
still crimped from the strain and snap
when it broke and he got away.
Like medals with their ribbons
frayed and wavering,
a five-haired beard of wisdom
trailing from his aching jaw.
I stared and stared
and victory filled up
the little rented boat,
from the pool of bilge
where oil had spread a rainbow
around the rusted engine
to the bailer rusted orange,
the sun-cracked thwarts,
the oarlocks on their strings,
the gunnels—until everything
was rainbow, rainbow, rainbow!
And I let the fish go.

5. *The language of good poetry is exact.* When Milton speaks of locusts "warping" on the Eastern wind, nothing spectacular has happened, to be sure, but the word is obviously being used in a precise way. There is a quality of motion involved in the verb "to warp" which is not available in any other single word of English, and that quality is exactly the one Milton sought. "Weaving," for example, is close to "warping" in some ways, but it is still not exactly right for the motion Milton intended.

The only other way in which Milton could have achieved exactly that shade of meaning would have been to use a less specific verb ("moving" or "progressing" or "advancing," for example) followed by a string of modifiers. Thus, he might have spoken of "locusts advancing on the Eastern wind with a motion that . . . ," And he would then have been committed to adding something like the dictionary definition of "to warp"—a necessarily laborious and necessarily forceless way of writing.

A minimum qualification of good poetic language is the ability to find the word that is exactly right to the physical fact. "Waddle," "sidle," "lurch," "march," "stumble," are all verbs of motion and each locates a specific kind of motion. The least that one can expect of language well used is the precision of such choices. The examples above have all been verbs, but true precision must obviously extend to all parts of speech. One can scarcely admire, for example, a writer who finds it necessary to write "He was a man who amassed wealth simply for the joy of possession rather than for the good things of life that it could bring him" when the same idea might as well be rendered simply "He was a miser."

Often, however, the poets have found that the words they seek do not exist ready-made, and they have forced words to perform duties not normally expected of them. Thus Shakespeare refers to a flag across the water "lackeying the tide." "Lackeying" is of course from "lackey" and implies a servile bowing and fluttering. Its intent obviously is not only to catch the exact motion but to couple it with a precise overtone. Suppose for example that Shakespeare had spoken of the flag as "sweeping the tide." There would still be a sense of the back and forth fluttering motion, but the overtone of servility would have disappeared.

There is, of course, the fact that such wrenchings of one part of speech into another can seem forced and thereby call attention to themselves rather than to their communication. Shakespeare's use of "lackeying" is not an especially offensive example, and yet it might reasonably be argued that it does seem strained. When, on the other hand, Emily Dickinson says of a snake "it wrinkled and was gone," "wrinkled" comes not only as a delightful surprise but seems to enter the line with no resistance whatever from the language. The doubt one may have about "lackeying" is from the opposite source; there is a sense that English resists making "lackey" into a verb, perhaps only because "lackeying" is difficult to say.

One asks of the language of good poetry, then, *exactness without strain*. If that exactness may be said to begin with exactness of denotation, it must also be seen to carry over to a point at which denotation is all but irrelevant. Hamlet's use of "puffed" in line 18 is worth careful attention.

> Led by a delicate and tender prince
> Whose spirit with divine ambition puffed,
> Makes mouths at the invisible event

Hamlet might have said, for example, "swelled" instead of "puffed." But "swelled" has an overtone of heaviness, of being "swollen" as in a bruise; whereas "puffed" is lighter and airier. Fortinbras, Hamlet has seen, is staking everything "even for an eggshell." He and his men go to their deaths for a "fantasy and trick of fame." Obviously the lightness of "puffed" is better keyed to "eggshell" to "fantasy" and to "trick" than would have been the weightier "swelled."

Note, however, that it is relatively difficult to fix an exact denotation for "puffed." Some sort of inflation of the spirit, yes. But certainly nothing that can be fixed with the physical exactness of "warping."

By the very nature of language in general, and of the language of poetry in particular, words and phrases may be used with what seems to be no denotation at all. "Wet sea," for example, presents a problem of redundancy but none of denotation. What happens, however, when someone speaks of a "dry sea"? Milton comes very close to doing so when he speaks of Satan pacing up and down on a "windy sea of land":

> As when a vulture on Imaus bred,
> Whose snowy ridge the roving Tartar bounds,
> Dislodging from a region of scarce prey
> To gorge the flesh of lambs or yearling kids
> On hills where flocks are fed, flies toward the springs
> Of Ganges or Hydaspes, Indian streams;
> But on his way lights on the barren plains
> Of Sericana where Chineses drive
> With sails and wind their cany wagons light:
> So on this windy sea of land, the Fiend
> Walked up and down alone, bent on his prey,
> Alone for other creatures in this place,
> Living or lifeless, to be found was none.

Here, of course, Milton is using the language of *as if*: the endless stretch of the high plateau is land, to be sure, but it presents itself to the eye "as if" it were a sea, an "as if" already suggested by the fantastic image of lightly built wagons moved by sail, as if they were boats. In Milton's description of Satan's fall, however, there is no such "as if":

> Him the Almighty Power
> Hurled headlong flaming from the ethereal sky
> With hideous ruin and combustion down
> To bottomless perdition.

And while no word can be wholly free of some element of denotation, it certainly seems to be true in such a line as "With hideous ruin and combustion down" that the words are being selected for their large suggestiveness and sound rather than for their denotation. They are, that is, being *exact to the feeling rather than to the physical detail* of the scene.

Milton, in fact, made such considerable use of this sort of word choice that this quality of his style has been labeled "the Miltonic vague." In the line cited, for example, "ruin" is a conceptual word. As such, it has relatively little denotation. And "combustion" is certainly the most abstract of possible words to denote "kinds of burning." Any number of more specific kinds of combustion suggest themselves: "flaming," "fire-spewing," "blazing," "incandescence." "Combustion" is the one word that includes them all, and it can do so only by being the least specific. The line, then, is built on a concept and an abstraction. And it is modified by another concept, "hideous."

Poetry generally strives for more specific effect than this, but Milton's principle of selection remains firm. The "big" sound of the line is obviously part of what Milton intended. One cannot, moreover, be specific in dealing with the primal: ultimate good and evil defy exact definition. Milton chose exactly for the effect of the necessary feeling.

Thus, poetry may achieve high effect by the power of suggestion (overtone) rather than by its specific identification (denotation). John William Burgon, an English poet of the nineteenth century, wrote many poems but survives only as the author of one line describing the Trans-Jordan city of Petra:

> A rose-red city half as old as time.

The "rose-red" is clearly intended to convey the color of the sandstone from which the city is built. In another context it might suggest the sunset stain on white walls. In either case the effect is denotative. But the truly memorable quality of the line certainly rests in "half as old as time," a phrase about as far from denotation as language seems able to go this side of nonsense syllables.

6. *The language of good poetry is true to its own roots and distinctions.* Every student, at one time or another, has had pointed out to him the precision of the distinction Edgar Allan Poe locates in

> The glory that was Greece
> And the grandeur that was Rome.

In common speech one tends to ignore such distinctions. When the newspapers haul out their standard banner heads on "The grand and glorious Fourth," "grand" and "glorious" seem to blur together into one thing. Poe saves the distinction by putting it into such a context that one is reminded of the quality and force of each word. At once and without strain, one understands what he had always known but had tended to forget, that "glory" is a spiritual achievement and "grandeur" a material one. By the exactness of good poetic usage, that is to say, the language is made new. It is one of the functions of the poet, wrote the French critic Paul Valéry, to "purify the language of the tribe."

Thus, in the seventeenth century Beaumont wrote in praise of Ben Jonson's language that it quickened the speech of the whole succeeding age:

> His wit and language still remain the same
> In all men's mouths; grave preachers did it use
> As golden pills, by which they might infuse
> Their heavenly physic; ministers of state
> Their grave dispatches in his language wrate;
> Ladies made curt'sies in it, courtiers legs,
> Physicians bills;—perhaps, some pedant begs
> He may not use it, for he hears 'tis such

Legs: to make a leg; to make a formal bow (in this context, to bow while delivering a complimentary phrase).

> As in few words a man may utter much.
> Could I have spoken in his language too,
> I had not said as much, as now I do,
> To whose clear memory I this tribute send,
> Who dead's my Wonder, living was my Friend.

Beaumont here makes the essential connection between economy and precision. The exact placement of one shade of meaning against another certainly makes for an irreducible kind of saying. One has only to attempt to state Poe's distinction without the precise counterbalancing of "glory" against "grandeur," to realize with Beaumont that:

> Could I have spoken in his language too,
> I had not said as much as now I do.

A superb example of this power of exact selection occurs in Denham's lines on Cowley:

> To him no author was unknown,
> Yet what he wrote was all his own;
> Horace's wit and Virgil's state,
> He did not steal, but emulate!
> And when he would like them appear,
> Their garb, but not their cloaths, did wear.

As one comes on the turn of "he did not steal, but emulate" there can certainly be no doubt that language is being well and irreducibly used here. The kind of "taking" that is involved in "steal" and the kind that is involved in "emulate" seem precisely played, one against the other. But it is in the distinction between "garb" and "clothes" that the language truly arrives to us refreshed. As in the case of the "grand and glorious Fourth," the level of ordinary attention tends to run these words one into the other. Before reading Denham, one would probably have used "garb" and "clothes" as synonyms. With Denham's awakening of the exact possibilities of these two words, however, their root suggestion is precisely purified. "Clothes," of course, derives from "cloth" and, strictly speaking, our clothes are the actual physical tissues we have on. "Garb," however, derives from the Italian *garbo* meaning "grace" and has come to mean by extension "bearing, manner, fashion, style." "Garb" is not the cloth but the cut. So Cowley is no rag picker, but an emulator of grace. It seems impossible to find a better example of the poet finding his delight in "hanging around words" to overhear them talking to one another:

Thus Hamlet in:

> How all occasions do inform against me
> And spur my dull revenge

is obviously displaying Shakespeare's relish in placing "spur" against "dull." Thus, too, in a line much quoted since the British critic F. R. Leavis drew special attention to it, Samuel Johnson wrote (italics mine):

I had not said: I would not have said. **As much:** as many words as.

The festal blazes, the triumphant show,
The ravished standard and the captive foe,
The senate's thanks, the gazette's pompous tale,
With force resistless o'er the brave prevail.
Such bribes the rapid Greek o'er Asia whirled,
For such the steady Romans shook the world.

One does not normally think of being shaken by that which is steady: the line arrives first in an instant of surprise. "Shook the world," moreover, is certainly a cliché. But the presence of that "steady" lifts it away from vague stereotype. Consider in how many ways the Roman Legions could be called "steady." Certainly, in this context, the steady tread of their marching feet is the first effect to suggest itself. Consider, too, the precise relation of the line to the physical phenomenon known as "resonance." A rhythmic repetition of blows can often cause a wave effect that may result in a constant increase of vibration. Thus columns of foot soldiers marching across a weak bridge break step, since the rhythmic falling of thousands of feet may build up a wave of resonance that could topple the bridge. It is such a combination of surprising rightnesses that offers the reader his reward. One's very expectation of what language can accomplish is enlarged in the process of seeing it so well used.

7. The language of good poetry echoes itself. Man has always been taken with the patterns through which the things of this world move. The scientist's concern with pattern is reflected, for example, in the periodic table of elements that hangs from the wall of virtually every chemistry lecture room. The poet addresses his work to man's sense of the nature of things by moving his language through patterns.

Pattern is not the professional poet's invention: language moves through patterns for anyone who says "willy-nilly" or "See ya later, alligator," or who joins in most any football yell, or who repeats any of a number of good political slogans.

The poet simply gives close attention to this movement of language through patterns, as he gives close attention to every aspect of language, and he draws upon the joy we naturally take in responding to pattern, using it to heighten the experience we come to inside the poem.

The movement of language through a pattern of sound variation produces rhyme and rhythm: rhyme is produced by the movement of language through a pattern of variation in sound quality; rhythm is produced by movement through a pattern of variation in sound intensity.

The traditional rhyme of English poetry is *syllabic,* which is to say it matches the final syllable of the rhyme pair except for the introductory consonant (fit/bit). *Assonance,* much used in French poetry but seldom in English, rhymes only the vowels of the paired words with the further provision that the rhymed vowels must be accented (say/male, but not parley/away). *Consonance* rhymes the consonants fore and aft in the

the rapid Greek: Alexander the Great.

rhyme syllable but varies the vowel (fit/fat). *Approximate* or *slant rhyme* pairs words whose sounds noticeably approximate one another without meeting all the requirements of any of the preceding sorts of rhyme (domestic/plastic, flex/fix, summer/somewhere, ruin/strewn).

If the rhyme ends in an accented syllable (sail/whale, defer/incur) it is called *masculine.* If it ends in an unstressed syllable (laden/maiden; sailor/whaler), it is called *feminine.* If it ends in two unstressed syllables (stupidity/avidity) it is called *double feminine.*

Depending on the number of sounds being matched a rhyme may be single, double, triple (intellectual/henpecked you-all), or even quadruple (Mephistopheles/with the most awful ease). It is well to note, however, that triple and quadruple rhymes so obviously call attention to their own cleverness that English poets have used them almost exclusively in light verse. Poems of deep feeling, if they rhyme at all, tend to rhyme on the simplest one-syllable rhymes with two-syllable feminine rhymes as the one variation.

Rhythm is much more complex than rhyme in its problems and possibilities, and merits the special attention it receives in Chapter Seven, where rhyme is considered especially for the way it affects the pacing of a line. For now it will be useful to take a general look at how the sounds of words can echo each other, and how poets can use this echo.

There are two important qualifications to be noted here. One is that while regular variation in the intensity of a poem's sounds—rhythm—is a *sine qua non* of poetry, regular echoes in the quality of sounds—rhyme— are not at all necessary. Blank verse, the pattern in which Shakespeare wrote his plays and Milton wrote *Paradise Lost,* does not employ rhyme, and so-called "free verse" employs rhyme, when it does so at all, scattered apparently at random through the poem.

The other qualification is that not all echoes in the quality of sounds follow a sustained pattern; the echoes may appear quite simply as *alliteration,* syllables close to each other echoing their initial consonants.

Echoes in the quality of sounds may play a vital role in a poem, or play virtually none, but their presence or absence will affect the texture of a poem, and if he chooses not to employ them, the poet must take their absence into account and compensate for it by the use of other devices or allow the poem to move toward the less controlled and more casual artifact of prose.

The four following poems show different means of using the sounds of words in a poem. The first, which may seem at a glance to make little use of sound qualities, actually is filled with strong echoes occurring close together (though not at regular intervals). The second is regularly rhymed, but the rhymes are not on every line. The third has every line rhymed, but only slant rhymes are used. The fourth has, as required by the villanelle form in which it is written, not only six rhymes for the same sound, but three repetitions of the same two lines, for an echo even stronger than rhyme.

The Second Coming

John William Corrington

it said WELCOME
right in the middle as if a
   hollow finger
       joined to an
  indigo sac
  had writ
       and then moved
  on
    and the magistrates
      wagging their troubled
      scruffs
      adjusting their
       trusses
   counting their getaway
     cash
were torn between
         reprisal and
      sacrifice
  while
    the common folk
      shuddering when their
       betters shuddered
   gaping and whistling
asked about auguries and signs and
one old doll keened dark portents
till a soldier cut her down

  and it hardened
bright and blue there on the
     temple floor
        where
  nothing could budge a stroke
   of it
    and breeding
    and commonality
  resolved in a single amaze
    looking for god knows
   how long
      at the place where
it said WELCOME
      at the end of the
   scarlet carpet
     and wondered
  what would come next

"Not Marble nor the Gilded Monuments"
For Adele

Archibald MacLeish

The praisers of women in their proud and beautiful poems,
Naming the grave mouth and the hair and the eyes,
Boasted those they loved should be forever remembered:
These were lies.

The words sound but the face in the Istrian sun is forgotten.
The poet speaks but to her dead ears no more.
The sleek throat is gone—and the breast that was troubled to
   listen:
Shadow from door.

Therefore I will not praise your knees nor your fine walking
Telling you men shall remember your name as long
As lips move or breath is spent or the iron of English
Rings from a tongue.

I shall say you were young, and your arms straight, and your
   mouth scarlet:
I shall say you will die and none will remember you:
Your arms change, and none remember the swish of your
   garments,
Nor the click of your shoe.

Not with my hand's strength, not with difficult labor
Springing the obstinate words to the bones of your breast
And the stubborn line to your young stride and the breath to
   your breathing
And the beat to your haste
Shall I prevail on the hearts of unborn men to remember.

(What is a dead girl but a shadowy ghost
Or a dead man's voice but a distant and vain affirmation
Like dream words most)

Therefore I will not speak of the undying glory of women.
I will say you were young and straight and your skin fair
And you stood in the door and the sun was a shadow of leaves
   on your shoulders
And a leaf on your hair—

I will not speak of the famous beauty of dead women:
I will say the shape of a leaf lay once on your hair.
Till the world ends and the eyes are out and the mouths
   broken
Look! It is there!

Strange Meeting

Wilfred Owen

It seemed that out of battle I escaped
Down some profound dull tunnel, long since scooped
Through granites which titanic wars had groined.
Yet also there encumbered sleepers groaned,
Too fast in thought or death to be bestirred.
Then, as I probed them, one sprang up, and stared
With piteous recognition in fixed eyes,
Lifting distressful hands as if to bless.
And by his smile, I knew that sullen hall,
By his dead smile I knew we stood in Hell.
With a thousand pains that vision's face was grained;
Yet no blood reached there from the upper ground,
And no guns thumped, or down the flues made moan.
"Strange friend," I said, "here is no cause to mourn."
"None," said that other, "save the undone years,
The hopelessness. Whatever hope is yours,
Was my life also; I went hunting wild
After the wildest beauty in the world,
Which lies not calm in eyes, or braided hair,
But mocks the steady running of the hour,
And if it grieves, grieves richlier than here.
For of my glee might many men have laughed,
And of my weeping something had been left,
Which must die now. I mean the truth untold,
The pity of war, the pity war distilled.
Now men will go content with what we spoiled,
Or, discontent, boil bloody, and be spilled.
They will be swift with swiftness of the tigress.
None will break ranks, though nations trek from progress.
Courage was mine, and I had mystery,
Wisdom was mine, and I had mastery:
To miss the march of this retreating world
Into vain citadels that are not walled.
Then, when much blood had clogged their chariot-wheels,
I would go up and wash them from sweet wells,
Even with truths that lie too deep for taint.
I would have poured my spirit without stint
But not through wounds; not on the cess of war.
Foreheads of men have bled where no wounds were.
I am the enemy you killed, my friend.
I knew you in this dark: for so you frowned
Yesterday through me as you jabbed and killed.
I parried; but my hands were loath and cold.
Let us sleep now. . . ."

Do Not Go Gentle into That Good Night

Dylan Thomas

Do not go gentle into that good night,
Old age should burn and rave at close of day;
Rage, rage against the dying of the light.

Though wise men at their end know dark is right,
Because their words had forked no lightning they
Do not go gentle into that good night.

Good men, the last wave by, crying how bright
Their frail deeds might have danced in a green bay,
Rage, rage against the dying of the light.

Wild men who caught and sang the sun in flight,
And learn, too late, they grieved it on its way,
Do not go gentle into that good night.

Grave men, near death, who see with blinding sight
Blind eyes could blaze like meteors and be gay,
Rage, rage against the dying of the light.

And you, my father, there on the sad height,
Curse, bless, me now with your fierce tears, I pray.
Do not go gentle into that good night.
Rage, rage against the dying of the light.

Read each of the following poems with an ear especially tuned to
rhyme and alliteration. Note the way in which a rhyme scheme helps to
assert the formal integrity of a poem, and how the type of rhyme helps
to determine the feel (the texture) of a poem.

The Couple Overhead

William Meredith

They don't get anywhere,
The couple overhead;
They wrangle like the damned
In the bed above my bed,
But the harm has all been done.
And this is a short despair:
Count Ugolino dead
Was endlessly condemned
To gnaw the archbishop's head
Where the nape and the skull are one.

Not so, these secular drunks.
Dante would find their treason
Too spiritless to keep;
Like children stealing raisins
They eat each other's eyes;
The ice that grips their flanks
Is something they have frozen.
After a while they sleep;
And the punishment they've chosen,
After a while it dies.

Pied Beauty

Gerard Manley Hopkins

Glory be to God for dappled things—
   For skies of couple-colour as a brinded cow;
     For rose-moles all in stipple upon trout that swim;
Fresh-firecoal chestnut-falls; finches' wings;
    Landscape plotted and pieced—fold, fallow, and plough;
    And áll trádes, their gear and tackle and trim.

All things counter, original, spare, strange;
   Whatever is fickle, freckled (who knows how?)
    With swift, slow; sweet, sour; adazzle, dim;
He fathers-forth whose beauty is past change:
       Praise him.

Pictures of the Gone World #10

Lawrence Ferlinghetti

       Terrible

          a horse at night

    standing hitched alone

         in the still street

     and whinnying

       as if some sad nude astride him

had gripped hot legs on him

      and sung

        a sweet high hungry

    single syllable

An Emblem of Two Foxes

Barry Spacks

Simply to breathe
can make him bleed,
the fox whose leg
is trapped, whose will
awaits the kill.
Why should he flail?
Moving hurts,
so he lies still.

Around him walks
a prouder fox,
his severed leg
a homily
on going free,
as if to say
it hurts, it hurts
either way.

We Real Cool
The Pool Players.
Seven at the Golden Shovel.

Gwendolyn Brooks

We real cool. We
Left school. We

Lurk late. We
Strike straight. We

Sing sin. We
Thin gin. We

Jazz June. We
Die soon.

Love and Death

John Nims

And yet a kiss (like blubber) 'd blur and slip,
Without the assuring skull beneath the lip.

Two

Robert Canzoneri

Both were so shy
Their only tie
Was bedded, hooded dark delight.

Pity their plight
And curse the night
She wept and could not tell him why.

Poem to Be Read at 3 A.M.

Donald Justice

Excepting the diner
On the outskirts
The town of Ladora
At 3 A.M.
Was dark but
For my headlights
And up in
One second-story room
A single light
Where someone
Was sick or
Perhaps reading
As I drove past
At seventy
Not thinking
This poem
Is for whoever
Had the light on

Reincarnation (I)

James Dickey

Still, passed through the spokes of an old wheel, on and
    around
The hub's furry rust in the weeds and shadows of the
    riverbank,
This one is feeling his life as a man move slowly away.
Fallen from that estate, he has gone down on his knees
And beyond, disappearing into the egg buried under the sand

And wakened to the low world being born, consisting now
Of the wheel on its side not turning, but leaning to rot away

In the sun a few feet farther off than it is for any man.
The roots bulge quietly under the earth beneath him;
With his tongue he can hear them in their concerted effort

To raise something, anything, out of the dark of the ground.
He has come by gliding, by inserting the head between stems.
Everything follows that as naturally as the creation
Of the world, leaving behind arms and legs, leaving behind
The intervals between tracks, leaving one long wavering step

In sand and none in grass: he moves through, moving
     nothing,
And the grass stands as never entered. It is in the new
Life of resurrection that one can come in one's own time
To a place like a rotting wheel, the white paint flaking from
     it,
Rust slowly emerging, and coil halfway through it, stopped

By a just administration of light and dark over the diamonds
Of the body. Here, also naturally growing, is a flat leaf
To rest the new head upon. The stem bends but knows the
     weight
And does not touch the ground, holding the snub, patterned
     face
Swaying with the roots of things. Inside the jaws, saliva

Has turned ice cold, drawn from bird eggs and thunderstruck
     rodents,
Dusty pine needles, blunt stones, horse dung, leaf mold,
But mainly, now, from waiting—all the time a symbol of evil—
Not for food, but for the first man to walk by the gentle
     river:
Minute by minute the head becomes more poisonous and
     poised.

Here in the wheel is the place to wait, with the eyes
     unclosable,
Unanswerable, the tongue occasionally listening, this time
No place in the body desiring to burn the tail away or to
     warn,
But only to pass on, handless, what yet may be transferred
In a sudden giving-withdrawing move, like a county judge
     striking a match.

8. *The language of good poetry tends to be double language.*   According to
Amy Lowell, the role of poetry is "to excite the consciousness." This
may seem a bit categorical, but certainly poetry works in great part by
throwing the imagination into action and involving through the imagi-
nation the *participation* of the reader. The intellect and the emotions,
inasmuch as they can be distinguished from the imagination, follow a

little behind. So if a poet is to involve the reader in a poem, he has first to help the reader feel that what is not necessarily so might be so, and that what has not been said has been suggested.

One of the most effective means to this excitement of the conscious- ness is the use of ambiguity, the exploitation of a word's two or more meanings, the insinuation into the poem of a second vision, an other meaning—or better, an "under-meaning," because whatever is sug- gested by the second and third sense of a word must seem to rise from below the same surface the word first presents, and be consistent with the central import of the poem.

Following are some poems in which "double language" is notably at work. In which of them does the ambiguity of the language seem best to serve the statement? Does your answer have anything to do with the ease with which you see the under-meanings? Does it have anything to do with the natural relationship between the immediate meaning of the poem as a whole, and the meaning that begins to grow with the recog- nition of the secondary senses of the words?

Fire and Ice

Robert Frost

Some say the world will end in fire,
Some say in ice.
From what I've tasted of desire
I hold with those who favor fire.
But if it had to perish twice,
I think I know enough of hate
To say that for destruction ice
Is also great
And would suffice.

Cross Ties

X. J. Kennedy

Out walking ties left over from a track
Where nothing travels now but rust and grass,
I could take stock in something that would pass
Bearing down Hell-bent from behind my back:
A think to sidestep or go down before,
Far-off, indifferent as that curfew's wail
The evening wind flings like a sack of mail
Or close up as the moon whose headbeam stirs
A flock of cloud to make tracks. Down to strafe
The bristled grass a hawk falls—there's a screech
Like steel wrenched taut till severed. Out of reach

Or else beneath desiring, I go safe,
Walk on, tensed for a leap, unreconciled
To a dark void all kindness.
                    When I spill
The salt I throw the Devil some and, still,
I let them sprinkle water on my child.

I Hope I Don't Have You Next Semester, But

Edwin Godsey

before you step out
Aphrodite
honey
hold your ear down close to the conch
and see can you make out
any
noises.

Remembering the story of the birth of Aphrodite (Venus), and taking the poem as addressed to a student by her instructor, see how many words and phrases you can find in the poem which suggest both the classical goddess of love and the contemporary love goddess, the campus honey pot. Does the word "honey" itself have ancient implications that would serve the poem? What does the poet mean when he suggests that she might hear something in the conch? Why "noises"?

Still, Citizen Sparrow

Richard Wilbur

Still, citizen sparrow, this vulture which
    you call
Unnatural, let him but lumber again to air
Over the rotten office, let him bear
The carrion ballast up, and at the tall

Tip of the sky lie cruising. Then you'll see
That no more beautiful bird is in heaven's
    height,
No wider more placid wings, no watchfuller
    flight;
He shoulders nature there, the frightfully
    free,

The naked-headed one. Pardon him, you
Who dart in the orchard aisles, for it is he

Devours death, mocks mutability,
Has heart to make an end, keeps nature
  new.

Thinking of Noah, childheart, try to forget
How for so many bedlam hours his saw
Soured the song of birds with its wheezy
  gnaw,
And the slam of his hammer all the day
  beset

The people's ears. Forget that he could bear
To see the towns like coral under the keel,
And the fields so dismal deep. Try rather
  to feel
How high and weary it was, on the waters
  where

He rocked his only world, and everyone's.
Forgive the hero, you who would have died
Gladly with all you knew; he rode that tide
To Ararat; all men are Noah's sons.

Richard Wilbur makes a comparison between Noah, sailing the ark far above the flooded land, and the vulture, sailing on the air high over the heads of less heroic creatures. Much of the effectiveness of the poem lies in the ironic vision of the vulture as hero, but it owes part of its success to the skillful use of double language. Taking the first three stanzas as consideration of the vulture, and the last three as considera- tion of Noah and the ark, how many terms can you recognize in the bird stanzas that suggest the ark? How many terms are there in the ark stanzas that suggest a bird? Why do you suppose the poet throught it more important to anticipate in the first half of the poem than to look back in the last half?

9. Some notes on adjectives. Adjectives and, to a lesser extent, adverbs are the points at which the weakness of a weak diction are likely to be most apparent. It is still true, however, that adjectives may be the source of major effect. Poetry will suffer no absolute rules. Short of the absolute, however, and assuming some discretion on the part of the reader, one may still defend a few useful rules of thumb. It is at least possible to distinguish kinds of adjectives and to observe that some kinds are more likely to occur in bad writing than in good.

A useful first distinction can be made by dividing all adjectives (and by extension, all modifiers) into those that present *evidence* and those that present *judgments.*

When one speaks of "the blonde girl," the adjective "blonde" offers evidence that helps to identify the girl. When one speaks of "the bad girl," however, "bad" does not help identify the girl unless one knows the speaker well enough to have some notion of his ideas of good and bad. "Blonde" is evidence; "bad" is a judgment. One can see the blondeness for himself; he cannot meaningfully see the "badness" until it is located in some observable characteristic.

The speaker himself, before he could reasonably judge the girl to be bad, must have observed some evidence on which to base his judgment. He may even be of the school that believes lipstick to be the mark of a lost woman. For him, then, "bad girl" may mean no more than "girl wearing lipstick." Had he presented such evidence for his judgment one would have a clear basis for rejecting it. If, on the other hand, he had mentioned that there was an automatic in her purse and that her picture was on the post office wall, one might reasonably conclude that the girl was something less than wholly virtuous. The point is that the reader could then reach his own judgment. In general it is much better to let the reader reach his own judgments than to make them for him. "The armed and wanted girl" or "the girl wearing lipstick" are more self-evident phrases than "the bad girl."

Good writing tends to present evidence rather than judgments. When the evidence is well presented, the reader's judgments will agree with those implicit in the writing. But nothing is more disastrous to the communication between writer and reader than a series of implicit judgments with which the reader cannot agree, or which he finds to be simply silly (see "My Garden," p. 170, and "Threnody," p. 171), or for which he is given no evidence he can respect.

It follows that poems in which judgment adjectives appear with any sort of regularity are reasonably suspect as bad poems unless some special principle of selection is operating to achieve a special effect. And barring such special intent, a good starting orientation is the assumption that adjectives presenting evidence are better than adjectives asserting unsupported judgments.

Nevertheless it remains difficult at times to distinguish adjectives of evidence from those of judgments. "Serene twilight" is a cliché, to be sure, and the fact is that the root meaning of "serene" already includes the idea of twilight, whereby a certain amount of objectionable redundancy (consult the dictionary for the root meanings of "serene") calls the whole phrasing into question. Nevertheless we may fairly ask: is "serene" a judgment or a statement of physical characteristics? The answer will have to be left to the individual's own search of the dictionary and to his own assessment of the root implications of the word.

Or in the case of Milton's "With hideous ruin and combustion down," is "hideous" an adjective of judgment or of evidence? Once more the question is more important than the answer. One might ask, what makes it "hideous" and argue that no denotation can be found as evidence of the hideousness of the ruin and combustion. Or one might argue that the whole ringing overtone of the word amply suggests the idea of the hideous, whereby the asserted judgment and the active suggestion of the word fuse into one. But the pro and con has point only as it opens both sides to view. Each case must determine itself.

One category of judgment adjectives, however, seems particularly defensible. Thus Ben Jonson speaks of the "spacious theater" and Richard Wilbur speaks of "beasts in their major freedom." "Spacious" and "major" deserve a separate category as "philosophical" or "think-ing" adjectives. It is not the physical dimensions of the theater that "spacious" calls forth, but its intellectual dimension. The theater is spacious because its illusion can reach into all dimensions of space and time. The stage is a space in which anything can be imagined. Thus "spacious" manages to summarize the whole idea of the theater and the reader welcomes it as an expansion of his own concept of the theater. It *thinks,* and thought is always welcome in poetry. As Kant observed: "Art without mind is horrid." And as Frost stated the corol-lary:

> No one knows how glad I am to find
> On any sheet the least display of mind.

Richard Wilbur's use of "major" responds to the same criteria. To speak of "beasts in their major freedom" does not seem to identify the freedom so much as to judge it. But if the freedom of beasts is major, there must also be a minor freedom, and that must be man's freedom. Any number of ways in which this implicit distinction is valid im-mediately suggest themselves.

We may go a step further then and speculate that what is really required of a modifier is *a principle of selection that displays both integrity and imagination.* We may summarize some rules of thumb:

Adjectives that present evidence may generally be judged by their freshness, by their responsiveness to the actuality of the thing modified, and by their ability to sharpen our perceptions. Some exam-ples of single phrases that present this power of the well-selected adjec-tive are: "the tiger moth's deep-damasked wing," "vertical New York," "the stucco faces" (of people glaring in the sun), "the running fuse of surf" (the running-fuse surf).

Adjectives that present judgments rather than physical or sensory evidence may generally be judged on the basis of how much emotional or philosophical depth speaks from their selection.

One last class of adjectives may be called "redundant" and may almost categorically be taken as an evidence of language poorly selected. A redundant adjective is one that asserts a quality already implicit in the noun it modifies. Thus, "green grass," "strong steel," "the hushed calm of evening," "distant sunset," and "blue sky."

Grass may of course be brown, or it may conceivably be stained by chemicals from a nearby factory. In one way or another a case can be made for almost any possibility. The fact remains that unmodified "grass" is automatically green, and that unless one is distinguishing a field of burned grass from a field of (perhaps irrigated) green grass, "green" has no function. Similarly, it may be argued that certain kinds of steel, depending upon their alloys and preparations, are "stronger" than other kinds. A technical manual on the strength of materials must certainly consider such differences carefully. It would be simply silly, however, to argue that "steel" in poetry is anything but strong. The case is even simpler for "hushed calm" and "distant sunset": one need only try to imagine an *unhushed* calm or a *nearby* sunset, to realize that such adjectives must tend above all else to indicate the incompetence of the writer. The least one should expect of poetry is that it find for itself a language (or a diction) better than the reader could improvise.

Poems for Study: The Word Choice

Burning the Letters

Gwendolyn Grew

One flutter of memory, then all becomes
First blaze, then char. A Fall of after-thought,
And leaf by leaf, a slant wind numbs
Summer from the bone-tree. "Nothing is not

Something," she thinks. And it is nothing now
To send a season blazing. Day by day
What greened, a sun-machine upon its bough,
Unsuns, ungreens, discolors toward decay.

Up from the bed now she can see the pale
Last glow of paper X-rayed by the bright
Underglow of the flame. A becalmed sail
It stirs, uncertain. Then it bursts a-light.

Like leaf-veins, the black lines stand in relief
As fire travels them clean. Then a black bloat
Riffles the page. Footless as a night-thief
The fire draft stirs them then, sets them afloat

And sucks them up to darkness, each a bat.
Till the last line has swollen and gone out
With its black mouse-bird. "How long have I sat
Here in self-pity?" she begins to doubt.

And still she kneels, and with a poker stirs
A last bird from the blaze, loving its flight.
Nursing the not-much hurt. But it is hers,
And nurse it she will through one more acted night.

QUESTIONS

The words of poetry do not needlessly repeat what has already been established. It is sometimes difficult, however, to decide what is "needless" repetition. Line 8 offers a fair test case. What is the function of "discolors"? Could it be argued that "Unsuns" and "ungreens" have already, in effect, "discolored" the leaf? Which of the three words most meaningfully suggests "discoloration"?

In the same line, can "decay" be justified? Can a leaf "discolor" toward anything but "decay"?

It is dangerous to rhyme on an adjective, for if it is less than brilliantly chosen it will seem that the poet selected that adjective not in faithfulness to the experience he is presenting, but only to pad out the rhyme. In line 9, could "pale" be considered rhyme forced? Is the paper on which one writes love letters likely to be anything but "pale"? If it is "X-rayed by the bright underglow," can it still be "pale"?

In the same line, how apt a choice is "X-rayed"? Is it physically accurate? Physically wrong? Is it a natural-seeming word choice?

In stanzas 4 and 5 we are told that a "night-thief" does several things to the papers: he "stirs" them; he "sets them afloat"; he "sucks them up to darkness." Do these three specific actions seem natural to the work of a "night-thief"?

Other words and phrases that might well be closely considered are: line 3, "slant"; line 11, "travels them clean"; line 12, "riffles" and "footless"; line 18, "swollen"; line 19, "black mouse-bird"; line 24, "acted."

Burning Love Letters

Howard Moss

I

Fire that cancels all that is
Devours paper and pen,
And makes of the heart's histories
A cold hearth warm again.
It could as well consume a branch,
Blank paper or black coal
That now in ashy avalanche,
Scatters the heart whole.

II

What words led to the end of words?
Coldly, all separate sighs
Shiver in flame, flying upwards,
Merged into burnt lies.
In somersaults of light, words burn
To nothingness, then roll
In dead scrolls, delicate as fern,
Or hiss like a waterfall.

III

From partial feast to total fast
From object to mirage
An animal that cannot last
Appears in fire's cage:

Love's crazy dog in a cold sweat
Far from its neighborhood,
Circles the puzzle of regret,
On fire in the wood.

IV

Love's ashes lie and will not rise
As fire dies to a black sun
And makes of the heart's histories
A warm hearth cold again.
Cremation's scattered dust confronts
Dead vision, and in these
Ashes I write your name once,
Bending on cold knees.

QUESTIONS

Stanza II is a physical description of paper in a fire. The last four
stanzas of Gwendolyn Grew's "Burning the Letters" offer a description
of the same physical experience. Which seems more convincingly fiery?

Can "pen" (line 2) be justified? Does the fire that consumes love letters
consume the pen? Or is the poem opening with a general statement
that fire consumes all? If so, is it an acceptable general statement?

What sort of adjective is "black" in line six? Would anything be lost
from the poem (leaving rhythm out of consideration) if "black" were
omitted? Is it fair to argue that "coal" already contains the idea "black"?

Lines 7 and 8 speak of an avalanche as "scattering." Suppose line 8 had
read "Bury the heart whole." What would the difference be? Is an
avalanche a "scattering" phenomenon?

What is the effect of "partial" in line 1 of Stanza III? What may have
dictated the author's choice of "partial"?

A Narrow Fellow in the Grass

Emily Dickinson

A narrow fellow in the grass
Occasionally rides;
You may have met him—did you not?
His notice sudden is.

The grass divides as with a comb,
A spotted shaft is seen;
And then it closes at your feet
And opens further on.

He likes a boggy acre,
A floor too cool for corn.

Yet when a boy, and barefoot,
I more than once, at morn,

Have passed, I thought, a whip lash
Unbraiding in the sun,—
When, stooping to secure it,
It wrinkled, and was gone.

Several of nature's people
I know, and they know me;
I feel for them a transport
Of cordiality;

But never met this fellow,
Attended or alone,
Without a tighter breathing,
And Zero at the Bone.

QUESTIONS

What is the effect of calling a snake "a narrow fellow"? Does the phrasing seem more nearly direct and felt or artful and coy?

Suppose similarly (disregarding consideration of rhyme) that the last line had read not "And Zero at the Bone" but "And a shudder deep inside." Which would be the more forceful? Why?

In earlier drafts Emily Dickinson wrote the fourth line, "His notice instant is." Is "instant" better or worse than "sudden" in this context?

Line 11 appears in some worksheets as "But when a boy, and barefoot." Is there any reason for the poet to have hesitated between "Yet" and "But"? Having so hesitated, is there any reason for the poet to decide on "Yet"?

Snake

D. H. Lawrence

A snake came to my water-trough
On a hot, hot day, and I in pyjamas for the heat,
To drink there.

In the deep, strange-scented shade of the great dark carob-tree
I came down the steps with my pitcher
And must wait, must stand and wait, for there he was at the trough
    before me.

He reached down from a fissure in the earth-wall in the gloom
And trailed his yellow-brown slackness soft-bellied down, over the
    edge of the stone trough
And rested his throat upon the stone bottom,

And where the water had dripped from the tap, in a small clearness,
He sipped with his straight mouth,
Softly drank through his straight gums, into his slack long body,
Silently.

Someone was before me at my water-trough,
And I, like a second comer, waiting.

He lifted his head from his drinking, as cattle do,
And looked at me vaguely, as drinking cattle do,
And flickered his two-forked tongue from his lips, and mused a
    moment,
And stooped and drank a little more,
Being earth brown, earth golden from the burning burning bowels of
    the earth
On the day of Sicilian July, with Etna smoking.

The voice of my education said to me
He must be killed
For in Sicily the black, black snakes are innocent, the gold are
    venomous.

And voices in me said, If you were a man
You would take a stick and break him now, and finish him off.

But I must confess how I liked him,
How glad I was he had come like a guest in quiet, to drink at my
    water-trough
And departed peaceful, pacified, and thankless,
Into the burning bowels of the earth.

Was it cowardice, that I dared not kill him?
Was it perversity, that I longed to talk to him?
Was it humility, to feel so honoured?
I felt so honoured.

And yet those voices:
If you were not afraid, you would kill him!

And truly I was afraid, I was most afraid,
But even so, honoured still more
That he should seek my hospitality
From out the dark door of the secret earth.

He drank enough
And lifted his head, dreamily, as one who has drunken.

And flickered his tongue like a forked night on the air, so black,
Seeming to lick his lips,
And looked around like a god, unseeing, into the air,

And slowly turned his head,
And slowly, very slowly, as if thrice adream,
Proceeded to draw his slow length curving round
And climb again the broken bank of my wall-face.

And as he put his head into that dreadful hole,
And as he slowly drew up, snake-easing his shoulders, and entered
farther,
A sort of horror, a sort of protest against his withdrawing into that
horrid black hole,
Deliberately going into the blackness, and slowly drawing himself
after,
Overcame me now his back was turned.

I looked round, I put down my pitcher,
I picked up a clumsy log
And threw it at the water-trough with a clatter.

I think it did not hit him,
But suddenly that part of him that was left behind convulsed in
undignified haste,
Writhed like lightning, and was gone
Into the black hole, the earth lipped fissure in the wall-front,
At which, in the intense still noon, I stared with fascination.

And immediately I regretted it.
I thought how paltry, how vulgar, what a mean act!
I despised myself and the voices of my accursed human education.

And I thought of the albatross,
And I wished he would come back, my snake.

For he seemed to me again like a king,
Like a king in exile, uncrowned in the underworld,
Now due to be crowned again.

And so I missed my chance with one of the lords
Of life.
And I had something to expiate;
A pettiness.

QUESTIONS

Compare this treatment of the snake with Emily Dickinson's. Certainly
some of the difference in the two poems comes from the relative
lengthiness of the one by Lawrence, but it is at least equally important
that while Lawrence keeps his statement to a kind of primitive simplic-
ity, Emily Dickinson carefully jewels her phrasing. What difference of
feeling results? Which poem reacts more profoundly to the earth trace
of the snake? Which, to put it another way, has its "zero deeper in the
bone"?

Lawrence seems so wholly taken with the presence of the snake that even clichés are admitted into the poem ("undignified haste," "writhed like lightning," "stared with fascination"). Can such phrasing be admitted as part of the merit of the poem, or should the poem be said to succeed in spite of such phrasing?

Underline each adjective Lawrence uses and consider it as presenting evidence or a judgment, as essential or inessential. Can the language of this poem be said to be even throughout? Compare the description of the snake's arrival (lines 7–10) with the description of the snake's departure (lines 50–55). What differences, if any, are observable?

Which of these two poems seems written in a diction; which in a language?

Lines 9–10: "straight mouth . . . straight gums . . . slack long body." Is "straight" a good adjective choice? Note its play against "slack long body."

Compare the snake's sudden motion in lines 59–60 with Emily Dickinson's "It wrinkled, and was gone."

Ode on a Grecian Urn

John Keats

I

Thou still unravished bride of quietness,
   Thou foster-child of silence and slow time,
Sylvan historian, who canst thus express
   A flowery tale more sweetly than our rhyme:
What leaf-fringed legend haunts about thy shape
   Of deities or mortals, or of both,
     In Tempe or the dales of Arcady?
   What men or gods are these? What maidens loth?
What mad pursuit? What struggle to escape?
     What pipes and timbrels? What wild ecstacy?

II

Heard melodies are sweet, but those unheard
   Are sweeter; therefore, ye soft pipes, play on;
Not to the sensual ear, but, more endeared,
   Pipe to the spirit ditties of no tone:
Fair youth, beneath the trees, thou canst not leave
   Thy song, nor ever can those trees be bare;
     Bold Lover, never, never, canst thou kiss,
Though winning near the goal—yet, do not grieve;
   She cannot fade, though thou hast not thy bliss,
     For ever wilt thou love, and she be fair!

III

Ah, happy, happy boughs! that cannot shed
　　Your leaves, nor ever bid the Spring adieu;
And, happy melodist, unwearied,
　　For ever piping songs forever new;
More happy love! more happy, happy love!
　　For ever warm and still to be enjoyed,
　　　　For ever panting, and for ever young;
All breathing human passion far above,
　　That leaves a heart high-sorrowful and cloyed,
　　　　A burning forehead, and a parching tongue.

IV

Who are these coming to the sacrifice?
　　To what green altar, O mysterious priest,
Lead'st thou that heifer lowing at the skies,
　　And all her silken flanks with garlands drest?
What little town by river or sea shore,
　　Or mountain-built with peaceful citadel,
　　　　Is emptied of this folk, this pious morn?
And, little town, thy streets for evermore
　　Will silent be; and not a soul to tell
　　　　Why thou art desolate, can e'er return.

V

O Attic shape! Fair attitude, with brede
　　Of marble men and maidens overwrought,
With forest branches and the trodden weed;
　　Thou, silent form, dost tease us out of thought
As doth eternity: Cold Pastoral!
　　When old age shall this generation waste,
　　　　Thou shalt remain, in midst of other woe
Than ours, a friend to man, to whom thou say'st,
　　"Beauty is truth, truth beauty,"—that is all
　　　　Ye know on earth and all ye need to know.

QUESTIONS

There are more adjectives than verbs in this poem. "Happy," for exam-
ple, occurs six times in five lines of stanza three. What reasons suggest
themselves for Keats' profusion of adjectives? The two stanzas in
which the adjectives outnumber the verbs are one and three. Note that
stanza one is built on an extended parallel construction in which the
verbs are implicit rather than stated. For example:

What men or gods are these? What maidens loth [are these]?
What mad pursuit [is this]?

What would happen to the adjective-verb count if these implicit verbs were counted? Note that stanza three is an invocation. What special situation does that involve that might affect the number of verbs?

The exact word: in line 5 of stanza one Keats uses "haunt." He might have used "wreathes" or "surrounds" (omitting considerations of rhythm). What special overtone makes "haunt" the exactly right choice? In line 4 of stanza four Keats originally wrote "sides" and later changed it to "flanks." Why? Line 9 of stanza one originally read: "What love? what dance? what struggle to escape?" and was revised to "What mad pursuit? What struggle to escape?" Before the revision was there anything to "escape" from?

One of the basic themes of this poem is the idea of the still serenity of eternally arrested motion. How many words can you locate in it whose overtones contribute directly to this theme?

Medusa

Louise Bogan

I had come to the house, in a cave of trees,
Facing a sheer sky.
Everything moved,—a bell hung ready to strike,
Sun and reflection wheeled by.

When the bare eyes were before me
And the hissing hair,
Held up at a window, seen through a door.
The stiff bald eyes, the serpents on the forehead
Formed in the air.

This is a dead scene forever now.
Nothing will ever stir.
The end will never brighten it more than this,
Nor the rain blur.

The water will always fall, and will not fall,
And the tipped bell make no sound.
The grass will always be growing for hay
Deep on the ground.

And I shall stand here like a shadow
Under the great balanced day,
My eyes on the yellow dust, that was lifting in the wind,
And does not drift away.

QUESTIONS

This poem, like "Ode on a Grecian Urn," is built about a kind of arrested motion. Keats however centered his impression in the serenity of a Grecian urn. Louise Bogan centers hers about the terrible image of the snake-headed Medusa whose look changed men to stones. Accordingly there is one moment of motion (in the first stanza)—the moment of the change; then all is frozen.

"Bare eyes" and "stiff bald eyes" are strikingly strange usages, as is "hissing hair." "Hissing," of course, is a direct reference to the fact that Medusa's hair is made of snakes. What is the force of "bare" and "stiff bald" when applied to Medusa?

Why are the snakes said to be "formed" in the air?

Why is the bell "tipped"? Is there any connection between "tipped" bell and "balanced" day?

Howard Nemerov's poem "Lot Later" retells the biblical story of Lot. Following are both the story from the Bible and the poem. How much of the modernizing of the second version depends upon the poet's choice of words, and how much upon the use of a more casual, conversational sentence structure than is found in the Bible? Note in Nemerov's poem those lines that might have been found in the biblical story, and tell why each of the other lines would not have belonged.

Genesis 19

And there came two angels to Sodom at even; and Lot sat in the gate of Sodom: and Lot seeing *them,* rose up to meet them; and he bowed himself with his face toward the ground;

2 And he said, Behold now, my lords, turn in, I pray you, into your servant's house, and tarry all night, and wash your feet; and ye shall rise up early, and go on your ways. And they said, Nay; but we will abide in the street all night.

3 And he pressed upon them greatly; and they turned in unto him, and entered into his house; and he made them a feast, and did bake unleavened bread, and they did eat.

4 But before they lay down, the men of the city, *even* the men of Sodom compassed the house round, both old and young, all the people from every quarter:

5 And they called unto Lot, and said unto him, Where *are* the men which came in to thee this night? bring them out unto us, that we may know them.

6 And Lot went out at the door unto them, and shut the door after him;

7 And said, I pray you, brethren, do not so wickedly.

8 Behold now, I have two daughters which have not known man; let me, I pray you, bring them out unto you, and do ye to them as *is* good in your eyes: only unto these men do nothing; for therefore came they under the shadow of my roof.

9 And they said, Stand back. And they said *again,* This one *fellow* came in to sojourn, and he will needs be a judge: now will we deal worse with thee than with them. And they pressed sore upon the man, *even* Lot, and came near to break the door.

10 But the men put forth their hand, and pulled Lot into the house to them, and shut to the door.

11 And they smote the men that *were* at the door of the house, with blindness, both small and great; so that they wearied themselves to find the door.

12 And the men said unto Lot, Hast thou here any besides? son in law, and thy sons, and thy daughters, and whatsoever thou hast in the city, bring *them* out of this place:

13 For we will destroy this place, because the cry of them is waxen great before the face of the LORD; and the LORD hath sent us to destroy it.

14 And Lot went out, and spake unto his sons in law, which married his daughters, and said, Up, get you out of this place; for the LORD will destroy this city. But he seemed as one that mocked unto his sons in law.

15 And when the morning arose, then the angels hastened Lot, saying, Arise, take thy wife, and thy two daughters, which are here; lest thou be consumed in the iniquity of the city.

16 And while he lingered, the men laid hold upon his hand, and upon the hand of his wife, and upon the hand of his two daughters; the LORD being merciful unto him: and they brought him forth, and set him without the city.

17 And it came to pass, when they had brought them forth abroad, that he said, Escape for thy life; look not behind thee, neither stay thou in all the plain; escape to the mountain, lest thou be consumed.

18 And Lot said unto them, Oh, not so, my Lord:

19 Behold now, thy servant hath found grace in thy sight, and thou hast magnified thy mercy, which thou hast shewed unto me in saving my life; and I cannot escape to the mountain, lest some evil take me, and I die:

20 Behold now, this city *is* near to flee unto, and it *is* a little one. Oh, let me escape thither, (*is* it not a little one?) and my soul shall live.

21 And he said unto him, See, I have accepted thee concerning this thing also, that I will not overthrow this city, for the which thou hast spoken.

22 Haste thee, escape thither; for I cannot do any thing till thou be come thither. Therefore the name of the city was called Zoar.

23 The sun was risen upon the earth when Lot entered into Zoar.

24 Then the LORD rained upon Sodom and upon Gomorrah, brimstone and fire from the LORD out of heaven;

25 And he overthrew those cities, and all the plain, and all the inhabitants of the cities, and that which grew upon the ground.

26 But his wife looked back from behind him, and she became a pillar of salt.

27 And Abraham gat up early in the morning to the place where he stood before the LORD:

28 And he looked toward Sodom and Gomorrah, and toward all the land of the plain, and beheld, and, lo, the smoke of the country went up as the smoke of a furnace.

29 And it came to pass, when God destroyed the cities of the

plain, that God remembered Abraham, and sent Lot out of the midst of the overthrow, when he overthrew the cities in the which Lot dwelt.

30 And Lot went up out of Zoar, and dwelt in the mountain, and his two daughters with him; for he feared to dwell in Zoar: and he dwelt in a cave, he and his two daughters.

31 And the firstborn said unto the younger, Our father *is* old, and *there is* not a man in the earth to come in unto us after the manner of all the earth:

32 Come, let us make our father drink wine, and we will lie with him, that we may preserve seed of our father.

33 And they made their father drink wine that night: and the firstborn went in, and lay with her father; and he perceived not when she lay down, nor when she arose.

34 And it came to pass on the morrow, that the firstborn said unto the younger, Behold, I lay yesternight with my father: let us make him drink wine this night also; and go thou in, *and* lie with him, that we may preserve seed of our father.

35 And they made their father drink wine that night also: and the younger arose, and lay with him; and he perceived not when she lay down, nor when she arose.

36 Thus were both the daughters of Lot with child by their father.

37 And the firstborn bare a son, and called his name Moab: the same *is* the father of the Moabites unto this day.

38 And the younger, she also bare a son, and called his name Benammi: the same *is* the father of the children of Ammon unto this day.

Lot Later
Vaudeville for George Finckel

Howard Nemerov

It seems now far off and foolish, a memory
Torn at the hem from the fabric of a dream
In drunken sleep, but why was I the one?
God knows, there were no fifty righteous, nor
Ten righteous, in town just at that very moment;
Gone south for the winter, maybe. And moreover,
I wouldn't have been one of the ten or fifty
Or whatever, if there had been. Abraham
Stood up to Him, but not for me—more likely
For the principle of the thing. I've always been
Honest enough for this world, and respected
In this town—but to be taken by the hair
Like that and lifted into that insane story,
Then to be dropped when it was done with me . . .

I tell you, I felt *used.*
                     In the first place,
I never knew the two of them were angels:
No wings, no radiance. I thought they might be students
Going from town to town, seeing the country.
I said "Come in the house, we'll have a drink,
Some supper, why not stay the night?" They did.
The only oddity was they didn't bother
With evening prayers, and that made me suspect
They might be Somebody. But in my home town
It doesn't take much; before I thought it out
People were coming round beating the door:
"Who you got in the house, let's have a party."
It was a pretty nice town in those days,
With always something going on, a dance
Or a big drunk with free women, or boys
For those who wanted boys, in the good weather
We used to play strip poker in the yard.
But just then, when I looked at those young gents,
I had a notion it was not the time,
And shouted through the door, "Go home, we're tired."
Nobody went. But all these drunks began
To pound the door and throw rocks at the windows
And make suggestions as to what they might do
When they got hold of the two pretty young men.
Matters were getting fairly desperate
By this time, and I said to those outside,
"Look, I got here my two daughters, virgins
Who never been there yet. I send them out,
Only my guests should have a peaceful night."
That's how serious the situation was.
Of course it wasn't the truth about the kids,
Who were both married, and, as a matter of fact,
Not much better than whores, and both the husbands
Knocking their horns against the chandeliers
Of my own house—but still, it's what I said.
It got a big laugh out there, and remarks,
Till the two young men gave me a nice smile
And stretched out one hand each, and suddenly
It got pitch dark outside, people began
Bumping into each other and swearing; then
They cleared away and everything was quiet.
So one young man opens his mouth, he says,
"You've got till sunrise, take the wife and kids
And the kids' husbands, and go. Go up to the hills."
The other says, "The Lord hath sent us to
Destroy this place" and so forth and so forth.
You can imagine how I felt. I said,
"Now look, now after all . . ." and my wife said,

"Give me a few days till I pack our things,"
And one of them looked at his watch and said,
"It's orders, lady, sorry, you've got till dawn."
I said, "Respectfully, gentlemen, but who
Lives in the hills? I've got to go, so why
Shouldn't I go to Zoar, which is a nice
Town with a country club which doesn't exclude
Jews?" "So go to Zoar if you want," they said.
"Whatever you do, you shouldn't look back here."
We argued all night long. First this, then that.
My son-in-laws got into the act: "You're kidding,
Things of this nature simply do not happen
To people like us." The pair of them said, "We'll stay,
Only deed us the house and furniture."
"I wouldn't deed you a dead fish," I said,
"Besides, I'm going to take the girls along."
"So take," they said, "they weren't such a bargain."
The two visitors all this time said nothing,
They might as well not have been there. But I
Believed what I was told, and this, I think,
Makes all the difference—between life and death,
I mean—to feel sincerely that there's truth
In something, even if it's God knows what.
My poor old woman felt it too, that night,
She only couldn't hold it to the end.
The girls just packed their biggest pocketbooks
With candy and perfume; they'd be at home
Most anywhere, even in a hill.
                    At last
I knelt down and I spoke to my God as follows:
"Dear Sir," I said, "I do not understand
Why you are doing this to my community,
And I do not understand why, doing it,
You let me out. There's only this one thing,
So help me, that with all my faults I do
Believe you are able to do whatever you say
You plan to do. Myself, I don't belong
In any operation on this scale.
I've always been known here as a nice fellow,
Which is low enough to be or want to be:
Respectfully I ask to be let go
To live out my declining years at peace
In Zoar with my wife and the two kids
Such as they are. A small house will do.
Only I shouldn't be part of history."
Of course no one answered. One of them said:
"If you're about through, please get on your feet,
It's time to go." My daughters' gorgeous husbands
Were drinking on the porch before we left.

II

My relative Abraham saw it happen: the whole
Outfit went up in smoke, he said. One minute
There was the town, with banks and bars and grills
And the new sewage disposal plant, all looking
(he said) terribly innocent in the first light;
Then it ignited. It went. All those old pals
Gone up, or maybe down. I am his nephew,
Maybe you know, he had troubles himself,
With the maid, and his own son. That's neither here
Nor there. We'd been forbidden to look, of course,
But equally of course my old girl had to look.
She turned around, and in one minute there
She was, a road sign or a mileage marker.
By this time, though, I knew that what we were in
Was very big, and I told the kids Come on.
We didn't stop to cry, even. Also
We never went to Zoar. I began to think
How real estate was high, how I'd been told
To go up in the hills, and how I'd always
Wanted to live in the country, a gentleman
Like Abraham, maybe, and have my flocks
Or whatever you call them—herds. Well, I found out.
A cave, we lived in, a real cave, out of rock.
I envied those bums my son-in-laws, until
I remembered they were dead. And the two girls,
My nutsy kids, getting the odd idea
That the whole human race had been destroyed
Except for us, conceived—this word I love,
Conceived—the notion that they should be known
In carnal union by their poppa. Me.
Poor dear old Dad. Most any man might dream
About his daughters; darling and stupid chicks
As these ones were, I'd dreamed, even in daytime,
Such brilliant dreams. But they? They bought some booze,
Having remembered to bring money along,
Something I never thought of, considering
I was in the hand of God, and got me boiled.
And then—I'm told—on two successive nights
Arrived on my plain stone couch and—what shall I say?
Had me? I was completely gone at the time,
And have no recollection. But there they were,
The pair of them, at the next moon, knocked up,
And properly, and by their Dad. The kids
Turned out to be boys, Moab and Ben-Ammi
By name. I have been given to understand
On competent authority that they will father
A couple of peoples known as Moabites

And Ammonites, distinguished chiefly by
Heathenish ways and ignorance of the Law.
And I did this? Or this was done to me,
A foolish man who lived in the grand dream
One instant, at the fuse of miracle and
The flare of light, a man no better than most,
Who loves the Lord and does not know His ways,
Neither permitted the pleasure of his sins
Nor punished for them, and whose aging daughters
Bring him his supper nights, and clean the cave.

The following poem, like Nemerov's "Lot Later" and X. J. Kennedy's "In a Prominent Bar in Secaucus One Day," is written *after the fashion* of an earlier time. In this case the poet has reminded us by his rhythms, attitudes, and treatment of characters somewhat of the *Canterbury Tales* of Chaucer. But like the other two poets, Whitehead in his sestina lets the reader know by certain turns of language that the story is not old at all. Note those words or phrases in "The Narrative Hooper" that could have not been written before the mid-twentieth century, and those words or phrases that one would expect in a poem from an earlier time. Does the poet keep his balance all the way through the poem? Does the poet gain anything by the ancient flavor he lends to the poem, or would the poem have essentially the same import if it had been written in a wholly modern mood? In which of the three poems does the ancient flavor seem most essential to the effect of the poem?

The Narrative Hooper and L.D.O.*
Sestina with a Long Last Line

James Whitehead

One fall not far from Ozark, Arkansas
A gentle sheriff saw a hairy man
Upon the berm—hairy in the extreme
This man was, but kindly from his bearded face.
He hunkered there upon the fading grass
And to the sheriff seemed entirely at peace.

It's wonderful to see a boy at peace
So much he seems to love our Arkansas,
Even if he's vagrant on the grass
The sheriff thought, who was a decent man,
Although not one to wear a bearded face,
Which faces were to him at least a bit extreme.

---

* **Hooper** and **L.D.O.**: corruptions of "hippie" and "L.S.D."; overheard as spoken by a sheriff.

Could be this boy is real extreme,
A hooper flipped on dope and not at peace
At all with Arkansas—he'd have to face
This hairy one near Ozark, Arkansas
To prove the Law is not the Lesser Man
Than one who is so fearless in the autumn grass.

And so the sheriff stopped his car, on the grass
And on the berm, in a state of mind extreme
For such a gentle man
Who lived in fact essentially at peace
With every normal man in Arkansas.
He parked, but showed some fear upon his razored face.

It was a moment all good men will face
In time, and man to man on God's own grass—
We all must be in Ozark, Arkansas
Or somewhere just the same and as extreme
Some time, attempting to maintain the peace,
As honest sheriff or as gentle hairy man.

And so it was with our two friends. The man
Who had the hair on said, "Sheriff, your face
Suggests I've done some thing to break the peace
While taking of my ease upon the grass."
"I'm not exactly sure it's that extreme . . .
Are you a hooper?" the sheriff mumbled, then clearly saw

His man was nervous. "Boy, are you on grass
Or L.D.O.!" His face was now extreme.
"Peace, Sheriff," said the hairy man, "I'm no hooper—I'm
    from Dumas, Arkansas."

Poems for Study: "Hard" and "Soft" Diction

Cards and Kisses

John Lyly

Cupid and my Campaspe played
At cards for kisses—Cupid paid:
He stakes his quiver, bow, and arrows,
His mother's doves, and team of sparrows;
Loses them too; then down he throws
The coral of his lips, the rose
Growing on's cheek (but none knows how);
With these, the crystal of his brow,

And then the dimple of his chin:
All these did my Campaspe win.
At last he set her both his eyes—
She won, and Cupid blind did rise.
    O Love! hath she done this to thee?
    What shall, alas! become of me?

Sonnet CXXX

William Shakespeare

My mistress' eyes are nothing like the sun;
Coral is far more red than her lips' red:
If snow be white, why then her breasts are dun;
If hairs be wires, black wires grow on her head.
I have seen roses damasked, red and white,
But no such roses see I in her cheeks;
And in some perfumes is there more delight
Than in the breath that from my mistress reeks.
I love to hear her speak—yet well I know
That music hath a far more pleasing sound;
I grant I never saw a goddess go—
My mistress, when she walks, treads on the ground.
    And yet, by heaven, I think my love as rare
    As any she belied with false compare.

QUESTIONS

"Cards and Kisses" is an elaborate rhymed compliment to the poet's lady, a compliment so fulsome that it is saved only by its own graceful playfulness. Lyly is clearly playing a game of compliments and having fun doing so. Such rhymed compliments were traditional among Elizabethan poets. It should not be hard to imagine that the game if taken too seriously by a poet less graceful than Lyly might well become cloying.

It was in reaction to the second sort of false praise that Shakespeare wrote Sonnet CXXX. The sonnet may be taken in fact as a short catalogue of the most familiarly trite and familiarly false ways of detailing the ladies' beauty. Eyes like suns, coral lips, snow-white breasts, hairs like golden wires, and so forth ran without end through the flutter of bad poems. Shakespeare deliberately set himself to argue against the falseness of this tradition, puncturing its pretty and false compliments one by one. Underline in Sonnet CXXX the phrases that paraphrase the compliments Shakespeare is satirizing and then bracket the phrases in which Shakespeare describes his own mistress. What can be said of the difference between the words so underlined and the words so bracketed? Note particularly "dun" and "reeks." Why did Shakespeare settle on such "strong" words?

Mowing

Robert Frost

There was never a sound beside the wood but one,
And that was my long scythe whispering to the ground.
What was it it whispered? I knew not well myself;
Perhaps it was something about the heat of the sun,
Something, perhaps, about the lack of sound—
And that was why it whispered and did not speak.
It was no dream of the gift of idle hours,
Or easy gold at the hand of fay or elf:
Anything more than the truth would have seemed too weak
To the earnest love that laid the swale in rows,
Not without feeble-pointed spikes of flowers
(Pale orchises), and scared a bright green snake.
The fact is the sweetest dream the labor knows.
My long scythe whispered and left the hay to make.

QUESTIONS

Robert Frost would have agreed with Shakespeare's impulse in Sonnet
CXXX. What Shakespeare says about his refusal to "belie with false
compare" Frost says in a different way in the lines "Anything more
than the truth would have seemed too weak" and "The fact is the
sweetest dream the labor knows." Both poems are declarations of the
poets' mortal intention to speak the fact of the world in the most faith-
ful rather than the most elaborate terms.

In the two poems that follow immediately mark any phrase that you
believe Frost might have taken to be "more than the truth" or that
Shakespeare might have suspected of "belying with false compare."
What can be said of the quality of the diction of those phrases?

My Garden

Janice Appleby Succorsa

There's a faerie at the bottom of my garden.
  I see her when the dew is on the rose,
And the bumble bee is bumbling, "Oops! Beg pardon"
  As he bumps along the shining iris-rows.

Oh, of course, it's only sunlight if you say so
  Making spangled stars when it begins to rise
And shine on all my dew-drenched pretty flower show;
  But I can tell the shine's my faerie's eyes.

And oh, the happy hours we've shared together!
  And oh, the happy garden paths we've trod!
Year in, year out, in every sort of weather,
  Finding our way to Beauty—and to God!

Threnody

I. O. Scherzo

Truth is a golden sunset far away
Above the misty hills. Its burning eye
Lights all the fading world. A bird flies by
Alive and singing on the dying day.
Oh mystic world, what shall the proud heart say
When beauty flies on beauty beautifully
While blue-gold hills look down to watch it die
Into the falling miracle of clay?

Say: "I have seen the wing of sunset lift
Into the golden vision of the hills
And truth come flooding proud through the cloud rift,
And known that souls survive their mortal ills."
Say: "Having seen such beauty in the air,
I have seen truth and will no more despair."

Compare the approach to "truth" in the following poem with the
assault on "truth" made by the author of "Threnody," and judge how
much of the difference in the two poems is a matter of diction. Begin by
listing from each poem those words which the author of the other
probably would not have used even if they had occurred to him.

Truth

Howard Nemerov

Around, above my bed, the pitch-dark fly
Buzzed in the darkness till in my mind's eye
His blue sound made the image of my thought
An image that his resonance had brought
Out of a common midden of the sun—
A garbage pit, and pile where glittering tin
Cans turned the ragged edges of their eyes
In a mean blindness on mine, where the loud flies
Would blur the summer afternoons out back
Beyond the house. Sleepy, insomniac, black
Remainder of a dream, what house? and when?
Listening now, I knew never again
That winged image as in amber kept
Might come, summoned from darkness where it slept
The common sleep of all such sunken things
By the fly's loud buzzing and his dreaming wings.

I listened in an angry wakefulness;
The fly was bitter. Between dream and guess
About a foundered world, about a wrong
The mind refused, I waited long, long,

And then that humming of the garbage heap
I drew beneath the surface of my sleep
Until I saw the helmet of the king
Of Nineveh, pale gold and glittering
On the king's brow, yet sleeping knew that I
But thought the deepening blue thought of the fly.

A Sort of a Song

William Carlos Williams

Let the snake wait under
his weed
and the writing
be of words, slow and quick, sharp
to strike, quiet to wait,
sleepless

—through metaphor to reconcile
the people and the stones.
Compose. (No ideas
but in things) Invent!
Saxifrage is my flower that splits
the rocks.

The Lyric Pulse
a paraphrase of "A Sort of a Song"

Let the serpent bide under
his frond
and the vision
be of words, languid and lithe, tempered
to thrust, silent to bide,
undreaming

—through fantasy to harmonize
spiritual and material.
Create! (No dream
but in being) Give form!
Saxifrage is my bloom that cleaves
the crags.

QUESTIONS

"The Lyric Pulse" was written in an effort to "soften" Williams'
"hard" diction in "A Sort of a Song." Wherever possible the editor has
substituted for Williams' words others with larger, vaguer, or more

specifically literary connotations. Where no such words offered readily, he tried for the most lifeless possible equivalent. Compare the diction of the two poems word for word, applying the criteria already discussed. Which words would Shakespeare and Robert Frost have preferred? Which would Succorsa and Scherzo have preferred?

The Lover Showeth How He Is Forsaken of Such as He Sometime Enjoyed

Sir Thomas Wyatt

They flee from me, that sometime did me seek,
With naked foot stalking within my chamber.
Once have I seen them gentle, tame, and meek,
That now are wild, and do not once remember
That sometime they have put themselves in danger
To take bread at my hand; and now they range,
Busily seeking in continual change.

Thanked be fortune it hath been otherwise,
Twenty times better; but once especial,
In thin array, after a pleasant guise,
When her loose gown did from her shoulders fall,
And she me caught in her arms long and small,
And therewithal so sweetly did me kiss
And softly said, Dear heart, how like you this?

It was no dream, for I lay broad awaking.
But all is turned now, through my gentleness,
Into a bitter fashion of forsaking;
And I have leave to go of her goodness,
And she also to use newfangleness.
But since that I unkindly so am served,
How like you this? what hath she now deserved?

The Frailty and Hurtfulness of Beauty

Henry Howard, Earl of Surrey

Brittle beauty that nature made so frail,
Whereof the gift is small, and short the season,
Flowering today, tomorrow apt to fail,
Tickle treasure, abhorred of reason,
Dangerous to deal with, vain, of none avail,
Costly in keeping, past not worth two peason,
Slipper in sliding as an eelës tail,
Hard to attain, once gotten not geason,

Tickle: delicate. **slipper:** slippery. **eelës:** eel's. **geason:** rare.

Jewel of jeopardy that peril doth assail,
False and untrue, enticëd oft to treason,
En'my to youth (that most may I bewail!),
Ah, bitter sweet! infecting as the poison,
Thou farest as fruit that with the frost is taken:
Today ready ripe, tomorrow all to-shaken.

QUESTION

The two preceding poems were written during the earlier half of the sixteenth century. Most critics since that time have thought of Surrey's poem as a dull poetic exercise and of Wyatt's as a moving capture of a sincere emotion. Analyze the diction of the poems, and basing the discussion upon that analysis, do you agree or disagree with the general verdict of the critics?

To Helen

Edgar Allan Poe

Helen, thy beauty is to me
    Like those Nicaean barks of yore,
That gently o'er the perfumed sea,
    The weary, wayworn wanderer bore
    To his own native shore.

On desperate seas long wont to roam,
    Thy hyacinth hair, thy classic face,
Thy Naiad airs have brought me home
    To the glory that was Greece
    And the grandeur that was Rome.

Lo! in yon brilliant window-niche
    How statue-like I see thee stand,
The agate lamp within thy hand!
    Ah, Psyche, from the regions which
    Are Holy Land.

---

to-shaken: shaken apart; compare German use of prefix *ver* as in *spielen*, "to play"; *verspielen*, "to play away," to lose in gambling.

Nicaean: Nicaea was the ancient name of modern Nice. **Nicaean barks** probably meant the ships of the Greeks (perhaps of Ulysses) sailing past Nicaea. The classic seas of such a voyage ("perfumed sea") are powerfully contrasted with the "desperate seas" (of Poe's life? of his times?), in which the author finds himself astray and from which he is brought to his classic peace by Helen's virtue and beauty. **hyacinth hair:** borrowed from Homer. **Naiad:** a Greek water nymph. **Psyche:** the classic personification of the soul. She was loved by Cupid, who came to her only in darkness so that she might not see him, until one night, while he slept, she stood above him with a lamp and discovered how beautiful he was. Hence "the agate lamp." Note that all these references are to the classic, "the perfumed sea." Only the one reference to "desperate seas" gives us Poe's distance from his wish.

Love Poem

John Frederick Nims

My clumsiest dear, whose hands shipwreck vases,
At whose quick touch all glasses chip and ring,
Whose palms are bulls in china, burs in linen,
And have no cunning with any soft thing

Except all ill at ease fidgeting people:
The refugee uncertain at the door
You make at home; deftly you steady
The drunk clambering on his undulant floor.

Unpredictable dear, the taxi drivers' terror,
Shrinking from far headlights pale as a dime
Yet leaping before red apoplectic streetcars—
Misfit in any space. And never on time.

A wrench in clocks and the solar system. Only
With words and people and love you move at ease.
In traffic of wit expertly manoeuvre
And keep us, all devotion, at your knees.

Forgetting your coffee spreading on our flannel,
Your lipstick grinning on our coat,
So gayly in love's unbreakable heaven
Our souls on glory of spilt bourbon float.

Be with me darling early and late. Smash glasses—
I will study wry music for your sake.
For should your hands drop white and empty
All the toys of the world would break.

QUESTIONS

Poe and Nims both seem to have written love poems, but Poe has idealized his love into a single emotion of passionate yearning, and Nims has taken an emotional position closer to that of everyday love. Poe worships from afar in total seriousness. Nims pokes gentle but loving fun. With no suggestion that one poem need be better than the other, which seems closer to your own sense of things? How does the diction reflect this difference? Which poem is more nearly written in a diction, and which more nearly in a language? Is Poe's poem really about love?

Because the two elegies that follow are long, it may be well to set a few directions before rather than after the reading. Both poems were written by poets on the deaths of fellow poets. Shelley did not know Keats intimately; nor did Auden, Yeats. Both poems are more nearly motivated by an idea of what a life value should be than by an intense personal grief.

Even upon a glancing reading, however, it should be clear that Auden's view is very different from Shelley's. Shelley writes as if he were personally grief stricken, as if nature itself has been impoverished by Keats' death, as if nature itself wept for Keats' passing. Auden very carefully refuses to indulge any such "as if's." One cannot fail to note, in fact, that "In Memory of W. B. Yeats" is not only a thoughtful statement of what a poet's life and death finally mean, but that it is in part a poem written against "Adonais." Nor need that additional motive imply that Auden believes "Adonais" is a bad poem. "Adonais" was written in another age, in a different literary tradition, with a different view of human destiny. Inevitably its tone is set by that complex. As Auden's tone is set by the complex of his own human position in time.

QUESTIONS

How would you describe Shelley's tone? How does the diction release that tone? How, similarly, would you describe Auden's tone and what part does the diction play in establishing it? How would the diction of the two poems measure against Frost's statement that anything more than the truth would be too weak?

What other devices of the two poems contribute notably to the tone? (Imagery? rhythm? form? grammatical structure?)

Adonais

Percy Bysshe Shelley

I weep for Adonais—he is dead!
Oh, weep for Adonais! though our tears
Thaw not the frost which binds so dear a head!
And thou, sad Hour, selected from all years
To mourn our loss, rouse thy obscure compeers,
And teach them thine own sorrow! Say: "With me
Died Adonais; till the Future dares
Forget the Past, his fate and fame shall be
An echo and a light unto eternity."

Where wert thou, mighty Mother, when he lay,
When thy son lay, pierced by the shaft which flies
In darkness? Where was lorn Urania
When Adonais died? With veiled eyes,
'Mid listening Echoes, in her Paradise
She sate, while one, with soft enamored breath,
Rekindled all the fading melodies.
With which, like flowers that mock the corse beneath,
He had adorned and hid the coming bulk of death.

Oh, weep for Adonais—he is dead!
Wake, melancholy Mother, wake and weep!
Yet wherefore? Quench within their burning bed
Thy fiery tears, and let thy loud heart keep,
Like his, a mute and uncomplaining sleep;
For he is gone, where all things wise and fair
Descend—oh, dream not that the amorous Deep
Will yet restore him to the vital air;
Death feeds on his mute voice, and laughs at our despair.

Most musical of mourners, weep again!
Lament anew, Urania!—He died—
Who was the Sire of an immortal strain,
Blind, old, and lonely, when his country's pride,
The priest, the slave, and the liberticide,
Trampled and mocked with many a loathed rite
Of lust and blood; he went, unterrified,
Into the gulf of death; but his clear Sprite
Yet reigns o'er earth—the third among the sons of light.

Most musical of mourners, weep anew!
Not all to that bright station dared to climb;
And happier they their happiness who knew,
Whose tapers yet burn through that night of time
In which suns perished; others more sublime,
Struck by the envious wrath of man or god,
Have sunk, extinct in their refulgent prime;
And some yet live, treading the thorny road,
Which leads, through toil and hate, to Fame's serene abode.

But now, thy youngest, dearest one has perished,
The nursling of thy widowhood, who grew,
Like a pale flower by some sad maiden cherished,
And fed with true-love tears, instead of dew;
Most musical of mourners, weep anew!
Thy extreme hope, the loveliest and the last,
The bloom, whose petals, nipped before they blew,
Died on the promise of the fruit, is waste;
The broken lily lies—the storm is overpast.

To that high Capital, where kingly Death
Keeps his pale court in beauty and decay,
He came; and bought, with price of purest breath,
A grave among the eternal.—Come away!
Haste, while the vault of blue Italian day
Is yet his fitting charnel-roof! while still
He lies, as if in dewy sleep he lay;
Awake him not! surely he takes his fill
Of deep and liquid rest, forgetful of all ill.

He will awake no more, oh, never more!—
Within the twilight chamber spreads apace
The shadow of white Death, and at the door
Invisible Corruption waits to trace
His extreme way to her dim dwelling-place;
The eternal Hunger sits, but pity and awe
Soothe her pale rage, nor dares she to deface
So fair a prey, till darkness and the law
Of change shall o'er his sleep the mortal curtain draw.

Oh, weep for Adonais!—The quick Dreams,
The passion-winged Ministers of thought,
Who were his flocks, whom near the living streams
Of his young spirit he fed, and whom he taught
The love which was its music, wander not—
Wander no more, from kindling brain to brain,
But droop there, whence they sprung; and mourn their lot
Round the cold heart, where, after their sweet pain,
They ne'er will gather strength, or find a home again.

And one with trembling hands clasps his cold head,
And fans him with her moonlight wings, and cries:
"Our love, our hope, our sorrow, is not dead;
See, on the silken fringe of his faint eyes,
Like dew upon a sleeping flower, there lies
A tear some Dream has loosened from his brain."
Lost Angel of a ruined Paradise!
She knew not 'twas her own; as with no stain
She faded, like a cloud which had outwept its rain.

One from a lucid urn of starry dew
Washed his light limbs as if embalming them;
Another clipped her profuse locks, and threw
The wreath upon him, like an anadem,
Which frozen tears instead of pearls begem;
Another in her willful grief would break
Her bow and winged reeds, as if to stem
A greater loss with one which was more weak;
And dull the barbed fire against his frozen cheek.

Another Splendor on his mouth alit,
That mouth, whence it was wont to draw the breath
Which gave it strength to pierce the guarded wit,
And pass into the panting heart beneath
With lightning and with music; the damp death
Quenched its caress upon his icy lips;
And, as a dying meteor stains a wreath
Of moonlight vapor, which the cold night clips,
It flushed through his pale limbs, and passed to its eclipse.

And others came—Desires and Adorations,
Winged Persuasions and veiled Destinies,
Splendors, and Glooms, and glimmering Incarnations
Of hopes and fears, and twilight Phantasies;
And Sorrow, with her family of Sighs,
And Pleasure, blind with tears, led by the gleam
Of her own dying smile instead of eyes,
Came in slow pomp—the moving pomp might seem
Like pageantry of mist on an autumnal stream.

All he had loved, and molded into thought
From shape, and hue, and odor, and sweet sound,
Lamented Adonais. Morning sought
Her eastern watchtower, and her hair unbound,
Wet with the tears which should adorn the ground,
Dimmed the aërial eyes that kindle day;
Afar the melancholy thunder moaned,
Pale Ocean in unquiet slumber lay,
And the wild winds flew round, sobbing in their dismay.

Lost Echo sits amid the voiceless mountains,
And feeds her grief with his remembered lay,
And will no more reply to winds or fountains,
Or amorous birds perched on the young green spray,
Or herdsman's horn, or bell at closing day;
Since she can mimic not his lips, more dear
Than those for whose disdain she pined away
Into a shadow of all sounds—a drear
Murmur, between their songs, is all the woodmen hear.

Grief made the young Spring wild, and she threw down
Her kindling buds, as if she Autumn were,
Or they dead leaves; since her delight is flown,
For whom should she have waked the sullen year?
To Phoebus was not Hyacinth so dear
Nor to himself Narcissus, as to both
Thou, Adonais. Wan they stand and sere
Amid the faint companions of their youth,
With dew all turned to tears; odor, to sighing ruth.

Thy spirit's sister, the lorn nightingale,
Mourns not her mate with such melodious pain;
Not so the eagle, who like thee could scale
Heaven, and could nourish the sun's domain
Her mighty youth with morning, doth complain,
Soaring and screaming round her empty nest,
As Albion wails for thee. The curse of Cain
Light on his head who pierced thy innocent breast,
And scared the angel soul that was its earthly guest!

Ah, woe is me! Winter is come and gone,
But grief returns with the revolving year;
The airs and streams renew their joyous tone;
The ants, the bees, the swallows reappear;
Fresh leaves and flowers deck the dead Seasons' bier;
The amorous birds now pair in every brake,
And build their mossy homes in field and brere;
And the green lizard, and the golden snake,
Like unimprisoned flames, out of their trance awake.

Through wood and stream and field and hill and ocean
A quickening life from the earth's heart has burst,
As it has ever done, with change and motion,
From the great morning of the world when first
God dawned on Chaos; in its stream immersed,
The lamps of heaven flash with a softer light;
All baser things pant with life's sacred thirst,
Diffuse themselves, and spend in love's delight
The beauty and the joy of their renewèd might.

The leprous corpse, touched by this spirit tender,
Exhales itself in flowers of gentle breath;
Like incarnations of the stars, when splendor
Is changed to fragrance, they illumine death
And mock the merry worm that wakes beneath;
Naught we know, dies. Shall that alone which knows
Be as a sword consumed before the sheath
By sightless lightning?—the intense atom glows
A moment, then is quenched in a most cold repose.

Alas! that all we loved of him should be,
But for our grief, as if it had not been,
And grief itself be mortal! Woe is me!
Whence are we, and why are we? Of what scene
The actors or spectators? Great and mean
Meet massed in death, who lends what life must borrow.
As long as skies are blue, and fields are green,
Evening must usher night, night urge the morrow,
Month follow month with woe, and year wake year to sorrow.

He will awake no more, oh, never more!
"Wake thou," cried Misery, "childless Mother, rise
Out of thy sleep, and slake, in thy heart's core,
A wound more fierce than his with tears and sighs."
And all the Dreams that watched Urania's eyes,
And all the Echoes whom their sister's song
Had held in holy silence, cried: "Arise!"
Swift as a Thought by the snake Memory stung,
From her ambrosial rest the fading Splendor sprung.

She rose like an autumnal Night, that springs
Out of the East, and follows wild and drear
The golden Day, which, on eternal wings,
Even as a ghost abandoning a bier,
Had left the earth a corpse. Sorrow and fear
So struck, so roused, so rapt Urania;
So saddened round her like an atmosphere
Of stormy mist; so swept her on her way
Even to the mournful place where Adonais lay.

Out of her secret Paradise she sped,
Through camps and cities rough with stone, and steel,
And human hearts, which to her aëry tread
Yielding not, wounded the invisible
Palms of her tender feet where'er they fell;
And barbed tongues, and thoughts more sharp than they,
Rent the soft Form they never could repel,
Whose sacred blood, like the young tears of May,
Paved with eternal flowers that undeserving way.

In the death chamber for a moment Death,
Shamed by the presence of that living Might,
Blushed to annihilation, and the breath
Revisited those lips, and life's pale light
Flashed through those limbs, so late her dear delight.
"Leave me not wild and drear and comfortless,
As silent lightning leaves the starless night!
Leave me not!" cried Urania. Her distress
Roused Death; Death rose and smiled, and met her vain caress.

"Stay yet awhile! speak to me once again;
Kiss me, so long but as a kiss may live;
And in my heartless breast and burning brain
That word, that kiss, shall all thoughts else survive.
With food of saddest memory kept alive,
Now thou art dead, as if it were a part
Of thee, my Adonais! I would give
All that I am to be as thou now art!
But I am chained to Time, and cannot thence depart!

"O gentle child, beautiful as thou wert,
Why didst thou leave the trodden paths of men
Too soon, and with weak hands though mighty heart
Dare the unpastured dragon in his den?
Defenseless as thou wert, oh, where was then
Wisdom the mirrored shield, or scorn the spear?
Or hadst thou waited the full cycle, when
Thy spirit should have filled its crescent sphere,
The monsters of life's waste had fled from thee like deer.

"The herded wolves, bold only to pursue;
The obscene ravens, clamorous o'er the dead;
The vultures to the conqueror's banner true,
Who feed where Desolation first has fed,
And whose wings rain contagion—how they fled,
When like Apollo, from his golden bow,
The Pythian of the age, one arrow sped
And smiled!—The spoilers tempt no second blow;
They fawn on the proud feet that spurn them lying low.

"The Sun comes forth, and many reptiles spawn;
He sets, and each ephemeral insect then
Is gathered into death without a dawn,
And the immortal stars awake again;
So is it in the world of living men:
A godlike mind soars forth, in its delight
Making earth bare and veiling heaven, and when
It sinks, the swarms that dimmed or shared its light
Leave to its kindred lamps the spirit's awful night."

Thus ceased she; and the mountain shepherds came,
Their garlands sere, their magic mantles rent;
The Pilgrim of Eternity, whose fame
Over his living head like heaven is bent,
An early but enduring monument,
Came, veiling all the lightnings of his song
In sorrow; from her wilds Ierne sent
The sweetest lyrist of her saddest wrong,
And love taught grief to fall like music from his tongue.

Midst others of less note, came one frail Form,
A phantom among men, companionless
As the last cloud of an expiring storm
Whose thunder is its knell; he, as I guess,
Had gazed on Nature's naked loveliness,
Actaeon-like, and now he fled astray
With feeble steps o'er the world's wilderness,
And his own thoughts, along that rugged way,
Pursued, like raging hounds, their father and their prey.

A pardlike Spirit beautiful and swift—
A Love in desolation masked—a Power
Girt round with weaknesses:—it can scarce uplift
The weight of the superincumbent hour;
It is a dying lamp, a falling shower,
A breaking billow—even whilst we speak

The Pythian of the age: Byron. As Apollo struck down the Python, so Byron struck down
the critics. **The Pilgrim of Eternity:** Byron. **Ierne:** Ireland. **The sweetest lyrist:** Thomas
Moore. **one frail Form:** Shelley himself.

Is it not broken? On the withering flower
The killing sun smiles brightly; on a cheek
The life can burn in blood, even while the heart may break.

His head was bound with pansies overblown,
And faded violets, white, and pied, and blue;
And a light spear topped with a cypress cone,
Round whose rude shaft dark ivy-tresses grew
Yet dripping with the forest's noonday dew,
Vibrated, as the ever-beating heart
Shook the weak hand that grasped it; of that crew
He came the last, neglected and apart;
A herd-abandoned deer, struck by the hunter's dart.

All stood aloof, and at his partial moan
Smiled through their tears; well knew that gentle band
Who in another's fate now wept his own;
As, in the accents of an unknown land,
He sung new sorrow; sad Urania scanned ·
The Stranger's mien, and murmured, "Who art thou?"
He answered not, but with a sudden hand
Made bare his branded and ensanguined brow,
Which was like Cain's or Christ's—Oh! that it should be so!

What softer voice is hushed over the dead?
Athwart what brow is that dark mantle thrown?
What form leans sadly o'er the white deathbed,
In mockery of monumental stone,
The heavy heart heaving without a moan?
If it be He, who, gentlest of the wise,
Taught, soothed, loved, honored the departed one,
Let me not vex with inharmonious sighs
The silence of that heart's accepted sacrifice.

Our Adonais has drunk poison—oh!
What deaf and viperous murderer could crown
Life's early cup with such a draught of woe?
The nameless worm would now itself disown.
It felt, yet could escape, the magic tone
Whose prelude held all envy, hate, and wrong,
But what was howling in one breast alone,
Silent with expectation of the song,
Whose master's hand is cold, whose silver lyre unstrung.

Live thou, whose infamy is not thy fame!
Live! fear no heavier chastisement from me,
Thou noteless blot on a remembered name!
But be thyself, and know thyself to be!

The nameless worm: Shelley (falsely) attributed Keats' death to a vicious unsigned review
of Keats' *Endymion*.

And ever at thy season be thou free
To spill the venom when thy fangs o'erflow.
Remorse and self-contempt shall cling to thee;
Hot shame shall burn upon thy secret brow,
And like a beaten hound tremble thou shalt—as now.

Nor let us weep that our delight is fled
Far from these carrion kites that scream below;
He wakes or sleeps with the enduring dead;
Thou canst not soar where he is sitting now.—
Dust to the dust! but the pure spirit shall flow
Back to the burning fountain whence it came,
A portion of the Eternal, which must glow
Through time and change, unquenchably the same,
Whilst thy cold embers choke the sordid hearth of shame.

Peace, peace! he is not dead, he doth not sleep—
He hath awakened from the dream of life—
'Tis we who, lost in stormy visions, keep
With phantoms an unprofitable strife,
And in mad trance strike with our spirit's knife
Invulnerable nothings.—*We* decay
Like corpses in a charnel; fear and grief
Convulse us and consume us day by day,
And cold hopes swarm like worms within our living clay.

He has outsoared the shadow of our night;
Envy and calumny and hate and pain,
And that unrest which men miscall delight,
Can touch him not and torture not again;
From the contagion of the world's slow stain
He is secure, and now can never mourn
A heart grown cold, a head grown gray in vain;
Nor, when the spirit's self has ceased to burn,
With sparkless ashes load an unlamented urn.

He lives, he wakes—'tis Death is dead, not he;
Mourn not for Adonais.—Thou young Dawn,
Turn all thy dew to splendor, for from thee
The spirit thou lamentest is not gone;
Ye caverns and ye forests, cease to moan!
Cease, ye faint flowers and fountains, and thou Air,
Which like a mourning veil thy scarf hadst thrown
O'er the abandoned Earth, now leave it bare
Even to the joyous stars which smile on its despair!

He is made one with Nature; there is heard
His voice in all her music, from the moan
Of thunder, to the song of night's sweet bird;
He is a presence to be felt and known
In darkness and in light, from herb and stone,

Spreading itself where'er that Power may move
Which has withdrawn his being to its own;
Which wields the world with never-wearied love,
Sustains it from beneath, and kindles it above.

He is a portion of the loveliness
Which once he made more lovely; he doth bear
His part, while the one Spirit's plastic stress
Sweeps through the dull, dense world, compelling there
All new successions to the forms they wear;
Torturing th' unwilling dross that checks its flight
To its own likeness, as each mass may bear;
And bursting in its beauty and its might
From trees and beasts and men into the Heaven's light.

The splendors of the firmament of time
May be eclipsed, but are extinguished not;
Like stars to their appointed height they climb
And death is a low mist which cannot blot
The brightness it may veil. When lofty thought
Lifts a young heart above its mortal lair,
And love and life contend in it for what
Shall be its earthly doom, the dead live there
And move like winds of light on dark and stormy air.

The inheritors of unfulfilled renown
Rose from their thrones, built beyond mortal thought,
Far in the Unapparent. Chatterton
Rose pale; his solemn agony had not
Yet faded from him. Sidney, as he fought
And as he fell and as he lived and loved,
Sublimely mild, a Spirit without spot,
Arose. And Lucan, by his death approved—
Oblivion, as they rose, shrank like a thing reproved.

And many more, whose names on earth are dark
But whose transmitted effluence cannot die
So long as fire outlives the parent spark,
Rose, robed in dazzling immortality.
"Thou art become as one of us," they cry,
"It was for thee yon kingless sphere has long
Swung blind in unascended majesty,
Silent alone amid an Heaven of Song.
Assume thy winged throne, thou Vesper of our throng!"

Who mourns for Adonais? oh, come forth,
Fond wretch! and know thyself and him aright.
Clasp with thy panting soul the pendulous Earth;
As from a center, dart thy spirit's light
Beyond all worlds, until its spacious might

Satiate the void circumference. Then shrink
Even to a point within our day and night;
And keep thy heart light, lest it make thee sink,
When hope has kindled hope, and lured thee to the brink.

Or go to Rome, which is the sepulchre,
Oh, not of him, but of our joy; 'tis naught
That ages, empires, and religions there
Lie buried in the ravage they have wrought;
For such as he can lend—they borrow not
Glory from those who made the world their prey;
And he is gathered to the kings of thought
Who waged contention with their time's decay,
And of the past are all that cannot pass away.

Go thou to Rome—at once the Paradise,
The grave, the city, and the wilderness;
And where its wrecks like shattered mountains rise,
And flowering weeds and fragrant copses dress
The bones of Desolation's nakedness,
Pass, till the Spirit of the spot shall lead
Thy footsteps to a slope of green access
Where, like an infant's smile, over the dead
A light of laughing flowers along the grass is spread.

And gray walls molder round, on which dull Time
Feeds, like slow fire upon a hoary brand;
And one keen pyramid with wedge sublime,
Pavilioning the dust of him who planned
This refuge for his memory, doth stand
Like flame transformed to marble; and beneath,
A field is spread, on which a newer band
Have pitched in Heaven's smile their camp of death,
Welcoming him we lose with scarce extinguished breath.

Here pause. These graves are all too young as yet
To have outgrown the sorrow which consigned
Its charge to each; and if the seal is set,
Here, on one fountain of a mourning mind,
Break it not thou! too surely shalt thou find
Thine own well full, if thou returnest home,
Of tears and gall. From the world's bitter wind
Seek shelter in the shadow of the tomb.
What Adonais is, why fear we to become?

The One remains, the many change and pass;
Heaven's light forever shines, earth's shadows fly;
Life, like a dome of many-colored glass,
Stains the white radiance of Eternity,
Until Death tramples it to fragments.—Die,

If thou wouldst be with that which thou dost seek!
Follow where all is fled!—Rome's azure sky,
Flowers, ruins, statues, music, words, are weak
The glory they transfuse with fitting truth to speak.

Why linger, why turn back, why shrink, my Heart?
Thy hopes are gone before; from all things here
They have departed; thou shouldst now depart!
A light is past from the revolving year,
And man, and woman; and what still is dear
Attracts to crush, repels to make thee wither.
The soft sky smiles—the low wind whispers near;
'Tis Adonais calls! oh, hasten thither,
No more let Life divide what Death can join together.

That Light whose smile kindles the universe,
That Beauty in which all things work and move,
That Benediction which the eclipsing Curse
Of birth can quench not, that sustaining Love
Which, through the web of being blindly wove
By man and beast and earth and air and sea,
Burns bright or dim, as each are mirrors of
The fire for which all thirst, now beams on me,
Consuming the last clouds of cold mortality.

The breath whose might I have invoked in song
Descends on me; my spirit's bark is driven
Far from the shore, far from the trembling throng
Whose sails were never to the tempest given;
The massy earth and spherèd skies are riven!
I am borne darkly, fearfully, afar;
Whilst, burning through the inmost veil of Heaven,
The soul of Adonais, like a star,
Beacons from the abode where the Eternal are.

In Memory of W. B. Yeats

W. H. Auden

I

He disappeared in the dead of winter:
The brooks were frozen, the air-ports almost deserted,
And snow disfigured the public statues;
The mercury sank in the mouth of the dying day.
O all the instruments agree
The day of his death was a dark cold day.

Far from his illness
The wolves ran on through the evergreen forests,

The peasant river was untempted by the fashionable quays;
By mourning tongues
The death of the poet was kept from his poems.

But for him it was his last afternoon as himself,
An afternoon of nurses and rumours;
The provinces of his body revolted,
The squares of his mind were empty,
Silence invaded the suburbs,
The current of his feeling failed: he became his admirers.

Now he is scattered among a hundred cities
And wholly given over to unfamiliar affections;
To find his happiness in another kind of wood
And be punished under a foreign code of conscience.
The words of a dead man
Are modified in the guts of the living.

But in the importance and noise of to-morrow
When the brokers are roaring like beasts on the floor of the Bourse.
And the poor have the sufferings to which they are fairly accustomed,
And each in the cell of himself is almost convinced of his freedom;
A few thousand will think of this day
As one thinks of a day when one did something slightly unusual.

O all the instruments agree
The day of his death was a dark cold day.

II

You were silly like us: your gift survived it all;
The parish of rich women, physical decay,
Yourself; mad Ireland hurt you into poetry.
Now Ireland has her madness and her weather still,
For poetry makes nothing happen: it survives
In the valley of its saying where executives
Would never want to tamper; it flows south
From ranches of isolation and the busy griefs,
Raw towns that we believe and die in; it survives,
A way of happening, a mouth.

III

Earth receive an honored guest;
William Yeats is laid to rest:
Let the Irish vessel lie
Emptied of its poetry.

Time that is intolerant
Of the brave and innocent,
And indifferent in a week
To a beautiful physique,

Worships language and forgives
Everyone by whom it lives;
Pardons cowardice, conceit,
Lays its honours at their feet.

Time that with this strange excuse
Pardoned Kipling and his views,
And will pardon Paul Claudel,
Pardons him for writing well.

In the nightmare of the dark
All the dogs of Europe bark,
And the living nations wait,
Each sequestered in its hate;

Intellectual disgrace
Stares from every human face,
And the seas of pity lie
Locked and frozen in each eye.

Follow, poet, follow right
To the bottom of the night,
With your unconstraining voice
Still persuade us to rejoice;

With the farming of a verse
Make a vineyard of the curse,
Sing of human unsuccess
In a rapture of distress;

In the deserts of the heart
Let the healing fountain start,
In the prison of his days
Teach the free man how to praise.

The following two poems are about the horrors of war (specifically, Word War One) and were written at approximately the same time by men of the same generation. Compare the language and diction each poet felt was appropriate to his purpose. Do you, as a reader, feel that one vocabulary is more effective than the other? If so, which vocabulary do you prefer, and why?

Dulce Et Decorum Est

Wilfred Owen

Bent double, like old beggars under sacks,
Knock-kneed, coughing like hags, we cursed through sludge,
Till on the haunting flares we turned our backs

And towards our distant rest began to trudge.
Men marched asleep. Many had lost their boots
But limped on, blood-shod. All went lame; all blind;
Drunk with fatigue; deaf even to the hoots
Of tired, outstripped Five-Nines that dropped behind.

Gas! Gas! Quick boys!—An ecstacy of fumbling,
Fitting the clumsy helmets just in time;
But someone still was yelling out and stumbling
And flound'ring like a man in fire or lime . . .
Dim, through the misty panes and thick green light,
As under a green sea, I saw him drowning.
In all my dreams, before my helpless sight,
He plunges at me, guttering, choking, drowning.

If in some smothering dreams you too could pace
Behind the wagon that we flung him in,
And watch the white eyes writhing in his face,
His hanging face, like a devil's sick of sin;
If you could hear, at every jolt, the blood
Come gargling from the froth-corrupted lungs,
Obscene as cancer, bitter as the cud
Of vile, incurable sores on innocent tongues,—
My friend, you would not tell with such high zest
To children ardent for some desperate glory,
The old Lie: Dulce et decorum est
Pro patria mori.

Motley

Walter de la Mare

Come, Death, I'd have a word with thee;
And thou, poor Innocency;
And Love—a lad with broken wing;
And Pity, too:
The Fool shall sing to you,
As Fools will sing.

Ay, music hath small sense,
And a tune's soon told,
And Earth is old,
And my poor wits are dense;
Yet have I secrets,—dark, my dear,
To breathe you all. Come near.
And lest some hideous listener tells,
I'll ring my bells.

They are all at war!—
Yes, yes, their bodies go
'Neath burning sun and icy star
To chaunted songs of woe,
Dragging cold cannon through a mire
Of rain and blood and spouting fire,
The new moon glinting hard on eyes
Wide with insanities!

Hush! . . . I use words
I hardly know the meaning of;
And the mute birds
Are glancing at Love
From out their shade of leaf and flower,
Trembling at treacheries
Which even in noonday cower.
Heed, heed not what I said
Of frenzied hosts of men,
More fools than I,
On envy, hatred fed,
Who kill, and die—
Spake I not plainly, then?
Yet Pity whispered, 'Why?'

Thou silly thing, off to thy daisies go.
Mine was not news for child to know,
And Death—no ears hath. He hath supped where creep
Eyeless worms in hush of sleep;
Yet, when he smiles, the hand he draws
Athwart his grinning jaws—
Faintly the thin bones rattle, and—there, there!
Hearken how my bells in the air
Drive away care! . . .

Nay, but a dream I had
Of a world all mad.
Not simply happy mad like me,
Who am mad like an empty scene
Of water and willow tree,
Where the wind hath been;
But that foul Satan-mad,
Who rots in his own head,
And counts the dead,
Not honest one—and two—
But for the ghosts they were,
Brave, faithful, true,
When, head in air,
In Earth's clear green and blue

Heaven they did share
With beauty who bade them there. . . .

There, now! Death goes—
Mayhap I've wearied him.
Ay, and the light doth dim,
And asleep's the rose,
And tired Innocence
In dreams is hence. . . .
Come, Love, my lad,
Nodding that drowsy head,
'Tis time thy prayers were said!

Poems for Study: Interrelation of Overtones

Naming of Parts

Henry Reed

Today we have naming of parts. Yesterday,
We had daily cleaning. And tomorrow morning,
We shall have what to do after firing. But today,
Today we have naming of parts. Japonica
Glistens like coral in all of the neighbouring gardens,
　　And today we have naming of parts.

This is the lower sling swivel. And this
Is the upper sling swivel, whose use you will see,
When you are given your slings. And this is the piling swivel,
Which in your case you have not got. The branches
Hold in the gardens their silent, eloquent gestures,
　　Which in our case we have not got.

This is the safety-catch, which is always released
With an easy flick of the thumb. And please do not let me
See anyone using his finger. You can do it quite easy
If you have any strength in your thumb. The blossoms
Are fragile and motionless, never letting anyone see
　　Any of them using their finger.

And this you can see is the bolt. The purpose of this
Is to open the breech, as you see. We can slide it
Rapidly backwards and forwards: we call this
Easing the spring. And rapidly backwards and forwards
The early bees are assaulting and fumbling the flowers:
　　They call it easing the Spring.

They call it easing the Spring: it is perfectly easy
If you have any strength in your thumb: like the bolt,
And the breech, and the cocking-piece, and the point of balance,

Which in our case we have not got; and the almond-blossom
Silent in all of the gardens and the bees going backwards and
    forwards,
    For today we have naming of parts.

QUESTIONS

"Naming of Parts" describes a young soldier's reaction to his basic
training in the manual of arms. He stands rifle in hand in the full hour
of spring caught between two voices, one the army's, the other
spring's. What is the quality of the diction in the voice of the army? In
the voice of the spring? One of the special successes of this poem is in
its ability to slide one voice into the other in a series of puns and near
puns (as in "easing the spring"). How many other phrases in the poem
have double meanings and what part do the two basically opposed
overtone themes have in making these double meanings function?

Polo Grounds

    Rolfe Humphries

Time is of the essence. This is a highly skilled
And beautiful mystery. Three or four seconds only
From the time that Riggs connects till he reaches first,
And in those seconds Jurges goes to his right,
Comes up with the ball, tosses to Witek at second
For the force on Reese, Witek to Mize at first,
In time for the out—a double play.

(Red Barber crescendo. Crowd noises, obbligato;
Scattered staccatos from the peanut boys,
Loud in the lull, as the teams are changing sides) . . .
Hubbell takes the sign, nods, pumps, delivers—
A foul into the stands. Dunn takes a new ball out,
Hands it to Danning, who throws it down to Werber;
Werber takes off his glove, rubs the ball briefly,
Tosses it over to Hub, who goes to the rosin bag,
Takes the sign from Danning, pumps, delivers—
Low, outside, ball three. Danning goes to the mound,
Says something to Hub, Dunn brushes off the plate,
Adams starts throwing in the Giant bullpen,
Hub takes the sign from Danning, pumps, delivers,
Camilli gets hold of it, a *long* fly to the outfield,
Ott goes back, back, back, against the wall, gets under it,
Pounds his glove, and takes it for the out.
That's all for the Dodgers. . . .

Time is of the essence. The rhythms break,
More varied and subtle than any kind of dance,
Movement speeds up or lags. The ball goes out

In sharp and angular drives, or long, slow arcs,
Comes in again controlled and under aim;
The players wheel or spurt, race, stoop, slide, halt,
Shift imperceptibly to new positions,
Watching the signs, according to the batter,
The score, the inning. Time is of the essence.

Time is of the essence. Remember Terry?
Remember Stonewall Jackson, Lindstrom, Frisch,
When they were good? Remember Long George Kelly?
Remember John McGraw and Benny Kauff?
Remember Bridwell, Tenney, Merkel, Youngs,
Chief Meyers, Big Jeff Tesreau, Shufflin' Phil?
Remember Matthewson, and Ames, and Donlin,
Buck Ewing, Rusie, Smiling Mickey Welch?
Remember a left-handed catcher named Jack Humphries,
Who sometimes played the outfield, in '83?

Time is of the essence. The shadow moves
From the plate to the box, from the box to second base,
From second to the outfield, to the bleachers.

Time is of the essence. The crowd and players
Are the same age always, but the man in the crowd
Is older every season. Come on, play ball!

QUESTIONS

"Polo Grounds," like "Naming of Parts," is a poem basically contrived
of two voices playing against one another. One voice sets itself to
capture the tone of the radio announcer who describes the action of the
baseball game taking place at the Polo Grounds. The second voice is
that of the writer commenting upon the action. There is a further com-
plication in the fact that the second voice divides again into two kinds
of voices. In one of his personal voices the writer takes on the role of an
enthusiastic fan relishing not only what he sees but what he remembers
of the game. In stanza five, the author summons this voice to think
back over the history of baseball, naming a long list of past players and
ending with one Jack Humphries whose climactic place in the series
would suggest that he is the author's father. In the second of his per-
sonal voices, the writer speaks not so much as a baseball fan but as an
aesthete: in this voice he runs to such terms as "beautiful mystery,"
"crescendo," "obbligato."

What is the effect of combing these tones? What motivates the author in
mixing "rhythms more varied and subtle than any kind of dance" (is
that a reasonable claim to make for baseball? Might a professional
choreographer agree or disagree?) with such tough-lunged "regular
talk" as "Come on, play ball!"?

What evidence can you find of still a third personal voice?

What is the effect of the frequent repetition of "Time is of the essence"? In what voice is that phrase spoken? The phrase itself is clearly a cliché: does it justify itself in the course of the poem, or must it be put down as a device that failed?

When all of the author's personal voices are put together into the composite second voice, what principle or principles of selection manifest themselves?

Dover Beach

Matthew Arnold

The sea is calm to-night.
The tide is full, the moon lies fair
Upon the straits;—on the French coast the light
Gleams and is gone; the cliffs of England stand,
Glimmering and vast, out in the tranquil bay.
Come to the window, sweet is the night-air!
Only, from the long line of spray
Where the sea meets the moon-blanched land,
Listen! you hear the grating roar
Of pebbles which the waves draw back, and fling,
At their return, up the high strand,
Begin, and cease, and then again begin,
With tremulous cadence slow, and bring
The eternal note of sadness in.

Sophocles long ago
Heard it on the Ægean, and it brought
Into his mind the turbid ebb and flow
Of human misery; we
Find also in the sound a thought,
Hearing it by this distant northern sea.
The Sea of Faith
Was once, too, at the full, and round earth's shore
Lay like the folds of a bright girdle furled.
But now I only hear
Its melancholy, long, withdrawing roar,
Retreating, to the breath
Of the night-wind, down the vast edges drear
And naked shingles of the world.

Ah, love, let us be true
To one another! for the world, which seems
To lie before us like a land of dreams,
So various, so beautiful, so new,
Hath really neither joy, nor love, nor light,
Nor certitude, nor peace, nor help for pain;

And we are here as on a darkling plain
Swept with confused alarms of struggle and flight,
Where ignorant armies clash by night.

QUESTIONS

Assume "the eternal note of sadness" to be a key statement of this poem. How many of the words and phrases of the poem are keyed to the same overtone of sad and everlasting things?

Note that after a major division following stanza two, the poem pursues a very different tone. What is the difference in tone of the two parts of the poem?

Assume "confused alarms of struggle and flight" to be a key statement of part two. How many of the other words and phrases in this part have the same overtone of meaningless and ephemeral things?

Love, on the other hand, tries to imagine a land of dreams and certitude. Which words and phrases in the second part are keyed to this overtone? How does this overtone relate to the other two? It is obviously in opposition to "meaningless and ephemeral." Is it the same thing as "sad and everlasting"? Or is it truly a third theme lost to both the others?

The Coming of Dusk Upon a Village in Haiti

Henry Rago

The island that had flowered to the sun
Folded the night into its dark hills. Slow
Gestures of wind signed over it with sleep.
A dust of silver weighed upon the leaves
And touched the village roofs half into air.

Soft, soft, the air insisted: all things now
Be muted to the night, be drugged, be dumb,
Like that brown girl and boy who gravely move,
Sleepwalking, toward each other; like these leaves,
Huge in a dream, luxurious with fatigue.

And darkness, subtle as an undersea,
Became the secret touch upon the ferns,
Smothered the burning poinciana, quenched
All but the deepest red. All that could live
Lived only in one swollen influence.

O from the sea of jasmine, where no word
Could find its breath, and tambours from the hills
Spoke to the night, the helpless mind turned still

Its pale look upward, so the heart, that last
Bloom of conspiracy, would not be lost!

QUESTIONS

"Gravely move" in line 8 and "sleepwalking" in line 9 both describe the
motion of the young people. Is the poet justified in describing the same
motion twice? Is "sleepwalking," per se, a "grave motion"? (If the
answer is yes, one must conclude that "grave motion" is wasted in
redundancy. If the answer is no, he must decide how one description
assists the other or contributes to the total effect of the poem.)

What is the modern meaning of "influence" (line 15)? What is its root
meaning? Assume (what seems clear enough) that Rago meant both
meanings to function at once. What does such a double sense contrib-
ute to the poem's performance?

Take "slow gestures" to be a key phrase. How many of the words and
phrases have overtones that relate to "slow gestures"?

Placing "Dover Beach" and "The Coming of Dusk Upon a Village in
Haiti" in comparison as two poems that attempt to capture the mood
of descending night and melancholy for the reader, which do you feel
more effectively does this? As well as you can, as a learning critic,
explain why you believe one poem is better than the other? Turn back
to this section after you have finished the book, and see if you still make
the same judgment, and if you are better able to defend whatever
judgment you make.

A Long-Tail Simile
from The Faerie Queene

Edmund Spenser

Like as the tide that comes from th' Ocean main,
  Flows up the Shenan with *contrary force,*
  And *overruling* him in his own *rayne,*
  Drives back the current of his kindly course,
  And makes it seem to have some other source:
  But when the flood is spent, then back again
  His borrowed waters *forced to redisbourse,*
  He sends the sea his own with double gain,
  And *tribute* eke withal, as to his *Souveraine.*

Thus did the battle vary to and fro . . .

QUESTIONS

What do the words we have italicized have in common? Compare the
metaphor implied in their connotations with that of stanza three of

Auden's "In Memory of W. B. Yeats." To what is Yeats' death compared by implication? How does the diction release that implication?

The Heart

Harvey Shapiro

In the midst of words your wordless image
Marches through the precincts of my night
And all the structures of my language lie undone:
The bright cathedrals clatter, and the moon-
Topped spires break their stalks.
Sprawled before that raid, I watch the towns
Go under. And in the waiting dark, I loose
Like marbles spinning from a child
The crazed and hooded creatures of the heart.

QUESTIONS

"The Heart," like "A Long-Tail Simile," is based on a single comparison. The image of the loved one moves through the lover's midnight like a military raid.

Underline every word and phrase that could be taken as a literal description of a military raid. Note that the raid is presented not as an air raid but as one that comes marching (line 2); a foray. What causes the bright cathedrals to "clatter"? (clatter down?) the spires to "break their stalks"?

Is it possible that the poet is confused and that he is describing air raid damage in connection with a raid that comes marching? Or are his choices coherent and defensible?

Upon Julia's Clothes

Robert Herrick

Whenas in silks my Julia goes,

Then, then, methinks, how sweetly flows

    [slip and rustle]
The liquefaction of her clothes.
    [soft cascading]

Next when I cast mine eyes, and see

    [disturbance]
That brave vibration each way free,
    [meander]

O, how that glittering taketh me!

QUESTION

In what way do the alternate readings above and below the original words trouble the diction with unwelcome suggestions?

Simplex Munditiis
("In Simple Elegance")

Ben Jonson

Still to be neat, still to be dressed,

As you were going to a feast;

Still to be powdered, still perfumed:

Lady, it is to be presumed,

Though art's hid causes are not found,

All is not sweet, all is not sound.

Give me a look, give me a face,

         [sweet innocence]
That makes simplicity a grace;
         [of naturalness]

Robes loosely flowing, hair as free:

Such sweet neglect more taketh me

         [counterfeits]
Than all th' adulteries of art;
         [appearances]

They strike mine eyes, but not my heart.
    [touch]

QUESTION

In each case the original phrasing is that printed in the line itself. Compare the original with the alternate phrasings and attack or defend the original compared to the alternate choices. Why do you believe that one or the other is better?

Elegy Written in a Country Churchyard

Thomas Gray

The curfew tolls the knell of parting day,
The lowing herd wind slowly o'er the lea,
The ploughman homeward plods his weary way,
And leaves the world to darkness and to me.

Now fades the glimmering landscape on the sight,
And all the air a solemn stillness holds,
Save where the beetle wheels his droning flight,
And drowsy tinklings lull the distant folds:

Save where from yonder ivy-mantled tower
The moping owl does to the moon complain
Of such as, wandering near her secret bower,
Molest her ancient solitary reign.

Beneath those rugged elms, that yew-tree's shade
Where heaves the turf in many a moldering heap,
Each in his narrow cell for ever laid,
The rude forefathers of the hamlet sleep.

The breezy call of incense-breathing morn,
The swallow twittering from the straw-built shed,
The cock's shrill clarion, or the echoing horn,
No more shall rouse them from their lowly bed.

For them no more the blazing hearth shall burn,
Or busy housewife ply her evening care:
No children run to lisp their sire's return,
Or climb his knees the envied kiss to share.

Oft did the harvest to their sickle yield,
Their furrow oft the stubborn glebe has broke;
How jocund did they drive their team afield!
How bowed the woods beneath their sturdy stroke!

Let not ambition mock their useful toil,
Their homely joys, and destiny obscure;
Nor grandeur hear with a disdainful smile
The short and simple annals of the poor.

The boast of heraldry, the pomp of power,
And all that beauty, all that wealth e'er gave
Awaits alike th' inevitable hour:—
The paths of glory lead but to the grave.

Nor you, ye proud, impute to these the fault,
If memory o'er their tomb no trophies raise,
Where through the long-drawn aisle and fretted vault
The pealing anthem swells the note of praise.

Can storied urn or animated bust
Back to its mansion call the fleeting breath?
Can honor's voice provoke the silent dust,
Or flattery soothe the dull, cold ear of death?

Perhaps in this neglected spot is laid
Some heart once pregnant with celestial fire,
Hands, that the rod of empire might have swayed,
Or waked to ecstasy the living lyre.

But knowledge to their eyes her ample page,
Rich with the spoils of time, did ne'er unroll;
Chill penury repressed their noble rage,
And froze the genial current of the soul.

Full many a gem of purest ray serene
The dark unfathomed caves of ocean bear:
Full many a flower is born to blush unseen,
And waste its sweetness on the desert air.

Some village-Hampden, that with dauntless breast
The little tyrant of his fields withstood;
Some mute inglorious Milton here may rest,
Some Cromwell, guiltless of his country's blood.

Th' applause of listening senates to command,
The threats of pain and ruin to despise,
To scatter plenty o'er a smiling land,
And read their history in a nation's eyes,

Their lot forbade: nor circumscribed alone
Their growing virtues, but their crimes confined;
Forbade to wade through slaughter to a throne,
And shut the gates of mercy on mankind;

The struggling pangs of conscious truth to hide,
To quench the blushes of ingenuous shame,
Or heap the shrine of luxury and pride
With incense kindled at the Muse's flame.

Far from the madding crowd's ignoble strife,
Their sober wishes never learned to stray;
Along the cool sequestered vale of life
They kept the noiseless tenor of their way.

Yet e'en these bones from insult to protect
Some frail memorial still erected nigh,
With uncouth rhymes and shapeless sculpture decked
Implores the passing tribute of a sigh.

Their name, their years, spelt by th' unlettered Mūse,
The place of fame and elegy supply:
And many a holy text around she strews,
That teach the rustic moralist to die.

Hampden: soldier and statesman, a great leader in the English Civil War.

For who, to dumb forgetfulness a prey,
This pleasing anxious being e'er resigned,
Left the warm precincts of the cheerful day,
Nor cast one longing, lingering look behind?

On some fond breast the parting soul relies,
Some pious drops the closing eye requires;
E'en from the tomb the voice of Nature cries,
E'en in our ashes live their wonted fires.

For thee, who, mindful of th' unhonored dead,
Dost in these lines their artless tale relate;
If chance, by lonely contemplation led,
Some kindred spirit shall enquire thy fate,—

Haply some hoary-headed swain may say,
"Oft have we seen him at the peep of dawn
Brushing with hasty steps the dews away,
To meet the sun upon the upland lawn;

"There at the foot of yonder nodding beech
That wreathe its old fantastic roots so high,
His listless length at noon-tide would he stretch,
And pore upon the brook that babbles by.

"Hard by yon wood, now smiling as in scorn,
Muttering his wayward fancies he would rove;
Now drooping, woeful-wan, like one forlorn,
Or crazed with care, or crossed in hopeless love.

"One morn I missed him on the customed hill,
Along the heath, and near his favorite tree;
Another came; nor yet beside the rill,
Nor up the lawn, nor at the wood was he;

"The next, with dirges due in sad array
Slow through the church-way path we saw him borne—
Approach and read (for thou canst read) the lay
Graved on the stone beneath yon aged thorn."

THE EPITAPH

Here rests his head upon the lap of earth
A youth, to fortune and to fame unknown;
Fair science frowned not on his humble birth
And melancholy marked him for her own.

Large was his bounty, and his soul sincere;
Heaven did a recompense as largely send:

For thee: addressed to Richard West, a friend.

He gave to misery all he had, a tear;
He gained from heaven ('twas all he wished) a friend.

No farther seek his merits to disclose,
Or draw his frailties from their dread abode
(There they alike in trembling hope repose),
The bosom of his Father and his God.

QUESTIONS

"Elegy Written in a Country Churchyard" is said to be the most perfect long poem in the English language, measured by its rhyme and meter alone. Do the regularity of the meter and the near perfection of the rhyme distract from the experience of the poem, or add to it, or are these considerations irrelevant to a good reading of the poem?

Is the poem written in a language or a diction? Would the peasants of the poem have understood it? Should the author have been concerned about such a question?

Compare "Elegy Written in a Country Churchyard" with the following poem. Which poem employs the more moving and suggestive language?

In which poem do you find the handling of rhyme and meter more pleasing? Why?

The Jewish Cemetery at Newport

Henry Wadsworth Longfellow

How strange it seems! These Hebrews in their graves,
    Close by the street of this fair seaport town,
Silent beside the never-silent waves,
    At rest in all this moving up and down!

The trees are white with dust, that o'er their sleep
    Wave their broad curtains in the southwind's breath,
While underneath these leafy tents they keep
    The long, mysterious Exodus of Death.

And these sepulchral stones, so old and brown,
    That pave with level flags their burial-place,
Seem like the tablets of the Law, thrown down
    And broken by Moses at the mountain's base.

The very names recorded here are strange,
    Of foreign accent, and of different climes;
Alvares and Rivera interchange
    With Abraham and Jacob of old times.

"Blessed be God, for he created Death!"
    The mourners said, "and Death is rest and peace";

Then added, in the certainty of faith,
"And giveth Life that nevermore shall cease."

Closed are the portals of their Synagogue,
No Psalms of David now the silence break,
No Rabbi reads the ancient Decalogue
In the grand dialect the Prophets spake.

Gone are the living, but the dead remain,
And not neglected; for a hand unseen,
Scattering its bounty, like a summer rain,
Still keeps their graves and their remembrance green.

How came they here? What burst of Christian hate,
What persecution, merciless and blind,
Drove o'er the sea—that desert desolate—
These Ishmaels and Hagars of mankind?

They lived in narrow streets and lanes obscure,
Ghetto and Judenstrass, in mirk and mire;
Taught in the school of patience to endure
The life of anguish and the death of fire.

All their lives long, with the unleavened bread
And bitter herbs of exile and its fears,
The wasting famine of the heart they fed,
And slaked its thirst with marah of their tears.

Anathema maranatha! was the cry
That rang from town to town, from street to street:
At every gate the accursed Mordecai
Was mocked and jeered, and spurned by Christian feet.

Pride and humiliation hand in hand
Walked with them through the world where'er they went;
Trampled and beaten were they as the sand,
And yet unshaken as the continent.

For in the background figures vague and vast
Of patriarchs and of prophets rose sublime,
And all the great traditions of the Past
They saw reflected in the coming time.

And thus forever with reverted look
The mystic volume of the world they read,
Spelling it backward, like a Hebrew book,
Till life became a Legend of the Dead.

But ah! what once has been shall be no more!
The groaning earth in travail and in pain
Brings forth its races, but does not restore,
And the dead nations never rise again.

CHAPTER FIVE

THE SYMPATHETIC CONTRACT

Every poem makes some demand upon the reader's sympathies. In addressing his subject, the poet takes an attitude toward it and adopts a tone he believes to be appropriate. His sense of what is appropriate, either in tone or in attitude, is of course a question of values. As such, it is obviously basic to the effect of the poem upon the reader. The reader may be right or wrong in disagreeing with the poet's values, but once such disagreement has occurred, that poem has failed for that reader. It is a question, as Robert Frost once put it, of "the way the poet takes himself and the way the poet takes his subject."

That demand upon the reader's sympathies may be made implicitly or explicitly, but there can be no poem without some sort of sympathetic contract between poet and reader. If a poet writes, "O weep for me, for I am sick with love," he is clearly taking love as a matter of major consequence (so taking it, or pretending so to take it) and he is clearly taking himself (or pretending to) with a good round measure of self-pity. If the poem is to succeed with any given reader, that reader must be willing to sympathize with that attitude toward love and with that tone of self-pity.

But what of the reader who, far from being moved to weep, is inclined to think the poet silly and pretentious? For that reader at least, all is lost. It may be, of course, that "O weep for me" is simply a *convention*, which is to say, *a traditional form of poetic pretense.* In this case the "O weep for me" poet may be adopting the pastoral convention, common enough in English poetry, in which the poet pretends to the attitudes of an imaginary Greek shepherd. One must be careful to allow the poet his right to pretend an emotion for second purposes. Clearly, however, it can happen that a poet takes an attitude and strikes off on a tone with which the reader cannot sympathize.

Lewis Carroll's careful parodies of Southey (p. 16) and of Watts

(p. 18) certainly began with his deliberate refusal to take seriously what these poets had asked him to take seriously. Carroll would have felt a fool had he allowed himself to agree with that request. Finding himself compelled to refuse it, he inevitably felt that the poets who made it were the fools, and pompous and hypocritical fools at that. Another reader might have stopped there, but happily Carroll was moved to deflate their pretentiousness. He did so by pretending to preserve the heavily moral tone and by pretending to take seriously the patly moral subject while rearranging the details of the subject into an obvious absurdity. Carroll clearly felt that he was dealing with bad poetry. It should be obvious, however, that there is nothing technically bad about either of the parodied poems: Carroll, in fact, preserves intact the technical standards of the poems he is lampooning.

The badness of bad poetry can always and only be located in the quality of the sympathetic contract. A bad poem is, finally, a failure of aesthetic character. True, a poem may strike the reader as technically inadequate to its own aims. Yet it is impossible to demonstrate with any final conviction that any poem is bad for specific technical reasons. "This poem," one says, "is bad because the rhymes are forced," and it is true that forced rhymes are one sign of bad poetic practice, but what is one to say then of such a poet as Ogden Nash who deliberately uses forced rhymes and to excellent effect? "Well, it is bad because it is cliché-studded," one says. But what of such a poem as Lawrence's "Snake" (p. 155), which falls into cliché after cliché and still remains memorable though flawed? "Well, then, it is bad because the images are scattered all over the place and because the meter is uncertain." But what of John Donne's "A Valediction Forbidding Mourning" (p. 247) with its widely ranging images and with that typical metric that led Johnson to declare that Donne should have been hanged for "not keeping of accent"?

The fact is that no critic can find in any poem he means to condemn a technical device he could not also find in a poem he would have to praise. Nor need that fact subvert all attention from technical detail. An obviously derivative, cliché-studded, rhyme-forced poem in which the poet mangles his metaphors *without seeming to know what he is doing* may still be flatly declared to be a bad poem. But to say "without seeming to know what he is doing" is at once to raise the question of tone and attitude. To handle technical elements ineptly is to take an incompetent attitude toward the poem: the serious poet will have studied his form harder and will have learned to master his techniques.

It is still true, however, that the badness of bad poetry cannot conclusively be shown to exist in the technical handling alone. There are, moreover, any number of technically flawless poems that are certainly bad.

Invictus

William Ernest Henley

Out of the night that covers me,
  Black as the pit from pole to pole,

I thank whatever gods may be
For my unconquerable soul.

In the fell clutch of circumstance
    I have not winced nor cried aloud.
Under the blugeoning of Chance
    My head is bloody but unbowed.

Beyond this place of wrath and tears
    Looms but the Horror of the shade,
And yet the menace of the years
    Finds, and shall find, me unafraid.

It matters not how strait the gate,
    How charged with punishment the scroll.
I am the master of my fate;
    I am the captain of my soul.

"Invictus" ("Unconquered") is perhaps the most widely known bad poem in English, and certainly there is no trace in it of a technical flaw on which its badness could be blamed. Nor is the poem bad because of its subject matter. Hardy and Housman, among others, have written many poems that take as bleakly pessimistic an attitude toward life as does "Invictus." The success of many such poems is sufficient evidence that English and American readers can enter into a sympathetic contract to consider the world as some sort of unhappy pit. It is not in the way Henley takes his subject, but in the way he takes himself that the reader parts company with the poet. To take the world as one's subject and to take the attitude that it is nothing but a place of suffering is one thing; but to react by taking oneself with such chest-thumping heroics, is very much another. One feels that Henley is not really reacting from his own profoundest depths but that he is making some sort of overdramatic speech about pessimism. There is a failure of character in the tone he has assumed. The poet has presented himself as unflinchingly valiant. The reader cannot help but find him merely inflated and self-dramatizing.

Inevitably, therefore, the reader finds that he does not believe what the poet is saying. The reader tends to frown upon the poet, moreover, for pinning too many medals for moral valor on his own chest. Were the reader in charge of the presentation ceremony, the chances are that Henley would not emerge with quite so many citations for nobility of purpose. The poem has generated distrust and a touch of scorn, whereas it clearly intended to persuade the reader of the validity of Henley's moral pose. The reader must feel that there is something wrong with the values of a man who cannot distinguish between the truly persuasive and the merely mock heroic.

Thus, instead of being moved by the poem, one simply refuses to believe it. Does Henley honestly believe such a phrase as "this place of wrath and tears"? Isn't he, rather, being merely self-indulgent? One shrugs and turns the page, and there he finds this poem, by the same author and written within a year of "Invictus":

To A.D.

William Ernest Henley

The nightingale has a lyre of gold,
The lark's is a clarion call;
And the blackbird plays but a boxwood flute,
But I love him best of all.

For his song is all of the joy of life,
And we in the mad, spring weather,
We two have listened till he sang
Our hearts and lips together.

Despite the great, roaring rhetoric of "Invictus" there is after all, just as one suspected, something more than "wrath and tears" in "this place." The poet does, of course, have every right to change his attitude and his tone from poem to poem. But "Invictus" has given itself to absolute statements, and does one have the right to change his absolutes that readily? One ends by confirming what he had suspected from the first: that what "Invictus" offered as absolutes were not absolutes at all.

Interestingly, one is less inclined to call "To A.D." a bad poem, though it is technically inferior to "Invictus." Note that the grammar of the first two lines of "To A.D." has run away from Henley and has left him speaking of the "lark's lyre" having a "clarion [trumpet] call." To be sure, there is a sense in which "clarion" may be taken to mean "loud and shrill" and possibly there may be such a thing as a "loud, shrill lyre," but certainly "clarion" cannot help but suggest "trumpet" as its first meaning, and how can one permit a poet the idea of a lyre with a trumpet call? "To A.D." is a flawed poem, therefore, but it remains a happily-turned little poem. It does not, at least, call Henley's character into doubt.

But what is a reader doing when he asks this sort of question of the poem? Must one conclude, for example, that one must be a Roman Catholic in order to read Dante with pleasure? Or that he must agree with Milton's theology in order to read Milton's poetry? Not at all. One must pause to recognize that subject and attitude are not the same thing. Attitude is the way one takes the subject, not the subject itself. The stature of such a poet as Dante, for example, is set in part by the fact that though he saw his subject as profoundly a matter of Roman Catholic doctrine, one may yet find his attitude and his tone valid in terms very different from those of Roman Catholicism. Dante took the state of the souls in hell as examples of sin. A psychologist has only to receive the same details of the state of the damned as examples of behavioral flaws: Dante's tone and attitude remain equally apt to either interpretation. Whatever differences one may feel between himself and the poet in matters of detail, a good poem leaves us no quarrel with its sympathetic contract.

But assuming that the reader does refuse the sympathetic contract; is he within his rights in attacking the author's character? Let the question be asked in other terms: assume that Shakespeare had introduced into some play two characters, one of whom spoke the lines of "Invictus" and one of whom spoke the lines of "To A.D." Can one doubt that Shakespeare would have intended the first as a ridiculous figure—in somewhat the same way perhaps that Polonius is presented as a ridiculously pompous figure? (And what then, by the way, of the aesthetic situation of those very earnest student orators who annually declaim, as if it were high moral perception, Polonius's advice to Laertes—that passage ending "This above all to thine own self be true. . . ."—a passage Shakespeare certainly intended to document the narrowness and sententiousness of Polonius's character?)

The reader has every bit as much right to judge the character the poet invents for his poems as Shakespeare had to judge the characters he invented for his plays. For the character is, in fact, invented. The declaimer on the cosmic soap box of "Invictus" is no more William Ernest Henley than is the sweetly nostalgic lover with the slightly confused grammar: each poem is founded upon a role Henley tried on for himself. Every poem, that is to say, by its choice of tone and attitude is a mask the poet assumes. In one mask he may present himself as heroic. In another as flightily gay. In another as philosophically detached, or as wistful, or as torn two ways.

But whatever the mask, the poet must make the role resound winningly within the reader. Poetry is not an ornamental exercise. It is man's best means of perceiving most profoundly the action and the consequence of his own emotions. Every poem addresses in some way, however slight, the question: "What is a man?" The reader tries on the mask through which the poet addresses that question and wills himself vicariously into the role the poet is playing; but he must then feel that the role is well and meaningfully played, and he must resist any effort by the poet to win him to shoddy emotions. Such identification is the essence of the sympathetic contract. The poem asks the reader to "be someone," but it must be someone the reader can reach to by an ideal extension of his own sympathies. "Yes," he must conclude, "on these premises I can accept this way of taking the subject and myself as meaningful."

When, on the other hand, the poet becomes untrustworthy within his mask (and let "mask" be taken to mean "the total complex of tone and attitude"), then the reader has no choice but to look down on the poet.

Thus the badness of a bad poem must always be located in the fact that it misplaces its human sympathies; or, as in the case of gross technical incompetence, in the fact that the poet has not given enough devoted attention to the demands of his own form, a failure that is in itself a failure of character.

But if tone and attitude are the one certain location of poetic badness, they are also the everlasting charm of poetry's variety and richness. Whatever the subject, one can never exhaust its poetry because there is never an end to the ways in which a poet can take that subject, and to the ways in which he can take himself in speaking of it.

Poems for Study: Tone, Attitude, and the Sympathetic Contract

Of the following poems, those in the first group are all, in one way or another, about love. Read each poem with special attention to the way the poet takes his subject *(attitude)* and the way he sees himself in relation to that subject *(tone)*. Try to state as accurately as possible the quality of each poem's tone and attitude. The following questions should be asked of each poem:

QUESTIONS

Are the tone and attitude describable in the same terms, or does the poet take his subject more or less seriously than he takes himself?

Are the tone and attitude exactly what they profess to be or are they pretended for some second purpose?

Are the tone and attitude constant or does one or the other, or both, change in the course of the poem?

Are the tone and attitude single or does the author feel more than one way at the same time (ambivalence) about his subject and his relation to it?

What is the sympathetic contract? (That is, what does the poet ask the reader to agree with emotionally? to disagree with? which of his own details is the poet "for"? which, if any, is he "against"?) How willing should a good reader be to extend the sympathies the poet asks for? (The same question may be put as follows: To what extent should a good reader be willing to be "for" what the poet is "for" and "against" what the poet is "against"?)

Note: many other poems in this volume are also about love and may well be compared with those that follow.

The Good-Morrow

John Donne

I wonder by my troth, what thou, and I
Did, till we lov'd? were we not wean'd till then?
But suck'd on countrey pleasures, childishly?
Or snorted we in the seaven sleepers den?
T'was so; But this, all pleasures fancies bee.
If ever any beauty I did see,
Which I desir'd, and got, t'was but a dreame of thee.

And now good morrow to our waking soules,
Which watch not one another out of feare;
For love, all love of other sights controules,

And makes one little roome, an every where.
Let sea-discoverers to new worlds have gone,
Let Maps to other, worlds on worlds have showne,
Let us possesse one world, each hath one, and is one.

My face in thine eye, thine in mine appeares,
And true plaine hearts doe in the faces rest,
Where can we finde two better hemispheares
Without sharp North, without declining West?
What ever dyes, was not mixt equally;
If our two loves be one, or, thou and I
Love so alike, that none doe slacken, none can die.

Song

John Donne

Goe, and catche a falling starre,
    Get with child a mandrake roote,
Tell me, where all past yeares are,
    Or who cleft the Divels foot,
Teach me to heare Mermaides singing,
    Or to keep off envies stinging,
            And finde
            What winde
Serves to advance an honest minde.

If thou beest borne to strange sights,
    Things invisible to see,
Ride ten thousand daies and nights,
    Till age snow white haires on thee;
Thou, when thou retorn'st wilt tell mee
All strange wonders that befell thee,
            And sweare
            No where
Lives a woman true, and faire.

If thou findst one, let mee know,
    Such a Pilgrimage were sweet;
Yet doe not, I would not goe,
    Though at next doore wee might meet,
Though shee were true, when you met her,
And last, till you write your letter,
            Yet shee
            Will bee
False, ere I come, to two, or three.

When He Who Adores Thee

Thomas Moore

When he who adores thee has left but the name
  Of his fault and his sorrows behind,
Oh! say wilt thou weep, when they darken the fame
  Of a life that for thee was resign'd?
Yes, weep, and however my foes may condemn,
  Thy tears shall efface their decree;
For Heaven can witness, though guilty to them,
  I have been but too faithful to thee.

With thee were the dreams of my earliest love;
  Every thought of my reason was thine;
In my last humble prayer to the Spirit above,
  Thy name shall be mingled with mine.
Oh! blest are the lovers and friends who shall live
  The days of thy glory to see;
But the next dearest blessing that Heaven can give
  Is the pride of thus dying for thee.

The Time I've Lost in Wooing

Thomas Moore

The time I've lost in wooing,
In watching and pursuing
  The light that lies
  In woman's eyes,
Has been my heart's undoing.
Though Wisdom oft has sought me,
I scorn'd the lore she brought me,
  My only books
  Were woman's looks,
And folly's all they've taught me.

Her smile when Beauty granted,
I hung with gaze enchanted,
  Like him, the Sprite,
  Whom maids by night
Oft meet in glen that's haunted.
Like him, too, Beauty won me,
But while her eyes were on me:
  If once their ray
  Was turn'd away,
Oh, winds could not outrun me.

And are those follies going?
And is my proud heart growing
   Too cold or too wise
   For brilliant eyes
Again to set it glowing?
No, vain, alas! th' endeavor
From bonds so sweet to sever;
   Poor Wisdom's chance
   Against a glance
Is now as weak as ever.

Bright Be the Place of Thy Soul!

Lord Byron

Bright be the place of thy soul!
   No lovelier spirit than thine
E'er burst from its mortal control,
   In the orbs of the blessed to shine.

On earth thou wert all but divine,
   As thy soul shall immortally be;
And our sorrow may cease to repine
   When we know that thy God is with thee.

Light be the turf of thy tomb!
   May its verdure like emeralds be!
There should not be the shadow of gloom
   In aught that reminds us of thee.

Young flowers and an evergreen tree
   May spring from the spot of thy rest:
But nor cypress nor yew let us see;
   For why should we mourn for the blest?

When We Two Parted

Lord Byron

We we two parted
   In silence and tears,
Half broken-hearted
   To sever for years,
Pale grew thy cheek and cold,
   Colder thy kiss;
Truly that hour foretold
   Sorrow to this.

The Indian Serenade

Percy Bysshe Shelley

I arise from dreams of thee
  In the first sweet sleep of night,
When the winds are breathing low,
  And the stars are shining bright:
I arise from dreams of thee,
  And a spirit in my feet
Hath led me—who knows how?
  To thy chamber window, sweet!

The wandering airs, they faint
  On the dark, the silent stream;
The champak odors fail
  Like sweet thoughts in a dream;
The nightingale's complaint
  It dies upon her heart,
As I must die on thine,
  Oh, belovèd as thou art!

Oh, lift me from the grass!
  I die! I faint! I fail!
Let thy love in kisses rain
  On my lips and eyelids pale.
My cheek is cold and white, alas!
  My heart beats loud and fast;—
Oh! press it close to thine again,
  Where it will break at last.

Love's Philosophy

Percy Bysshe Shelley

The fountains mingle with the river
  And the rivers with the ocean;
The winds of heaven mix forever
  With a sweet emotion;
Nothing in the world is single;
  All things by a law divine
In one spirit meet and mingle.
  Why not I with thine?

See the mountains kiss high heaven,
  And the waves clasp one another;
No sister-flower would be forgiven
  If it disdained its brother;
And the sunlight clasps the earth,
  And the moonbeams kiss the sea;
What are all these kissings worth
  If thou kiss not me?

Rondeau

Leigh Hunt

Jenny kissed me when we met,
  Jumping from the chair she sat in;
Time, you thief, who love to get
  Sweets into your list, put that in:
Say I'm weary, say I'm sad,
  Say that health and wealth have missed me,
Say I'm growing old, but add,
  Jenny kissed me.

Rose Aylmer

Walter Savage Landor

Ah, what avails the sceptred race,
  Ah, what the form divine!
What every virtue, every grace!
  Rose Aylmer, all were thine.
Rose Aylmer, whom these wakeful eyes
  May weep, but never see,
A night of memories and of sighs
  I consecrate to thee.

To Electra

Robert Herrick

I dare not ask a kiss,
  I dare not beg a smile,
Lest having that, or this,
  I might grow proud the while.

No, no, the utmost share
  Of my desire shall be
Only to kiss that air
  That lately kissèd thee.

A Devout Lover

Thomas Randolph

I have a mistress, for perfections rare
In every eye, but in my thoughts most fair.
Like tapers on the altar shine her eyes;
Her breath is the perfume of sacrifice;

And wheresoe'er my fancy would begin,
Still her perfection lets religion in.
We sit and talk, and kiss away the hours
As chastely as the morning dews kiss flowers:
I touch her, like my beads, with devout care,
And come unto my courtship as my prayer.

To Amarantha, that She Would Dishevel Her Hair

Richard Lovelace

Amarantha sweet and fair,
Ah, braid no more that shining hair!
As my curious hand or eye
Hovering round thee, let it fly!

Let it fly as unconfined
As its calm ravisher, the wind,
Who hath left his darling, th' East,
To wanton o'er that spicy nest.

Every tress must be confest,
But neatly tangled at the best;
Like a clew of golden thread
Most excellently ravellèd.

Do not then wind up that light
In ribbands, and o'ercloud in night,
Like the Sun in's early ray;
But shake your head, and scatter day!

Ah, How Sweet It Is to Love!

John Dryden

Ah, how sweet it is to love!
　Ah, how gay is young Desire!
And what pleasing pains we prove
　When we first approach Love's fire!
Pains of love be sweeter far
Than all other pleasures are.

Sighs which are from lovers blown
　Do but gently heave the heart:
Ev'n the tears they shed alone
　Cure, like trickling balm, their smart:
Lovers, when they lose their breath,
Bleed away in easy death.

Love and Time with reverence use,
  Treat them like a parting friend;
Nor the golden gifts refuse
  Which in youth sincere they send:
For each year their price is more,
And they less simple than before.

Love, like spring-tides full and high,
  Swells in every youthful vein;
But each tide does less supply,
  Till they quite shrink in again:
If a flow in age appear,
'Tis but rain and runs not clear.

The Definition of Love

Andrew Marvell

My love is of a birth as rare
As 'tis for object strange and high:
It was begotten by Despair
Upon Impossibility.

Magnanimous Despair alone
Could show me so divine a thing,
Where feeble Hope could ne'er have flown
But vainly flapped its tinsel wing.

And yet I quickly might arrive
Where my extended soul is fixed,
But Fate does iron wedges drive,
And always crowds itself betwixt.

For Fate with jealous eye does see
Two perfect loves, nor lets them close:
Their union would her ruin be,
And her tyrannic power depose.

And therefore her decrees of steel
Us as the distant poles have placed,
(Though love's whole world on us doth wheel)
Not by themselves to be embraced,

Unless the giddy heaven fall,
And earth some new convulsion tear,
And, us to join, the world should all
Be cramped into a planisphere.

As lines, so loves oblique may well
Themselves in every angle greet;
But ours, so truly parallel,
Though infinite, can never meet.

Therefore the love which us doth bind,
But fate so enviously debars,
Is the conjunction of the mind,
And opposition of the stars.

I Knew a Woman

Theodore Roethke

I knew a woman, lovely in her bones,
When small birds sighed, she would sigh back at them;
Ah, when she moved, she moved more ways than one:
The shapes a bright container can contain!
Of her choice virtues only gods should speak,
Or English poets who grew up on Greek
(I'd have them sing in chorus, cheek to cheek).

How well her wishes went! She stroked my chin,
She taught me Turn, and Counter-turn, and Stand;
She taught me Touch, that undulant white skin;
I nibbled meekly from her proffered hand;
She was the sickle; I, poor I, the rake,
Coming behind her for her pretty sake
(But what prodigious mowing we did make).

Love likes a gander, and adores a goose:
Her full lips pursed, the errant note to seize;
She played it quick, she played it light and loose;
My eyes, they dazzled at her flowing knees;
Her several parts could keep a pure repose,
Or one hip quiver with a mobile nose
(She moved in circles, and those circles moved).

Let seed be grass, and grass turn into hay:
I'm martyr to a motion not my own;
What's freedom for? To know eternity.
I swear she cast a shadow white as stone.
But who would count eternity in days?
These old bones live to learn her wanton ways:
(I measure time by how a body sways).

Detroit Conference of Unity and Art
(For HRB)

Nikki Giovanni

We went there to confer
On the possibility of
Blackness
And the inevitability of
Revolution

We talked about
Black leaders
And
Black Love

We talked about
Women
And Black men

No doubt many important
Resolutions
Were passed
As we climbed Malcolm's ladder

But the most
Valid of them
All was that
Rap chose me

Romantic

George Garrett

I have heard some jealous women say
that if your skin were cut away
and tacked upon a public wall
it would not please the eyes at all.

They say your bones are no great prize,
that hanging in the neutral breeze,
your rig of ribs, your trim of thighs
would catch no fetching harmonies,

but tinkle like a running mouse
over piano keys. They hold
that, stripped, your shabby soul
would whimper like a vacant house

you are so haunted. "Ask
her," they say, "if she'll unmask.
Let her shed beauty like the trees.
Time will bring her to her knees."

Still, I must have you as you are,
all of a piece, beautiful and vain,
burning and freezing, near and far,
and all my joy and all my pain.

And if you live to scrub a floor
with prayer, to weep like a small ghost,
which of us will suffer more?
Who will be wounded most?

Thank You for the Valentine

Diane Wakoski

I leave my heart in the doorway
for you
or anyone
to trip over. This will not be Valentine
talk though,
            the lace of Chopin études that sprinkles over
my teeth, the velvet rag carnations I find whispering
suicide notes in the street.
                No, this is
to be a conversation of plasterers' dusty overalls,
and the gas meter reader's flashlight.

Look, I wear my heart on my sleeve, my arm rather,
cut in the shape of the letter "M."
Can you write a check for my rent?
Can you pay my dental bill?
Can you be a family man?
Can you give me the things I need?
You are not the man I want.
                I would have to climb a mountain in Tibet
                    to cash your checks.
                I would have to fill my teeth with pebbles.
                I would have to have paper children.
                You are six letters away from "M" in the
                    alphabet.
                You are not even the one who gave me this
                    Valentine.
And I want to thank you,
that is,
all my friends.

You's are as many as the facets of a fly's eye.
I wear my heart on my sleeve, sometimes a piece of it
lies sloppily in my doorway, and you gave me this Valentine,
loaned it, I should say,
a heart that is temporarily mine.
   Round
    or lumpy
or not decorative
or rusty
or full of slivers
this little tick-tock that slips through my throat
and taps under my arm pits

this clock that can be wound
only with a silver "M" shaped key.

After Work

  Gary Snyder

The shack and a few trees
float in the blowing fog

I pull out your blouse,
warm my cold hands
   on your breasts.
you laugh and shudder
peeling garlic by the
   hot iron stove.
bring in the axe, the rake,
the wood

we'll lean on the wall
against each other
stew simmering on the fire
as it grows dark
   drinking wine.

For Jane

  Charles Bukowski

225 days under grass
and you know more than I.

they have long taken your blood,
you are a dry stick in a basket.

is this how it works?

in this room
the hours of love
still make shadows.

when you left
you took almost
everything.

I kneel in the nights
before tigers
that will not let me be.

what you were
will not happen again.

the tigers have found me
and I do not care.

Style

Charles Bukowski

style is the answer to everything—
a fresh way to approach a dull or a
dangerous thing.
to do a dull thing with style
is preferable to doing a dangerous thing
without it.

Joan of Arc had style
John the Baptist
Christ
Socrates
Caesar,
Garcia Lorca.

style is the difference,
a way of doing,
a way of being done.

6 herons standing quietly in a pool of water
or you walking out of the bathroom naked
without seeing
me.

Short Order

Charles Bukowski

I took my girlfriend to your last poetry reading,
she said.
yes, yes? I asked.
she's young and pretty, she said.
and? I asked.
she hated your
guts.

then she stretched out on the couch
and pulled off her
boots.

I don't have very good legs,
she said.

all right, I thought, I don't have very good
poetry; she doesn't have very good
legs.

scramble two.

What Lips My Lips Have Kissed

Edna St. Vincent Millay

What lips my lips have kissed, and where, and why,
I have forgotten, and what arms have lain
Under my head till morning; but the rain
Is full of ghosts tonight, that tap and sigh
Upon the glass and listen for reply;
And in my heart there stirs a quiet pain
For unremembered lads that not again
Will turn to me at midnight with a cry.

Thus in the winter stands the lonely tree,
Nor knows what birds have vanished one by one,
Yet knows its boughs more silent than before:
I cannot say what loves have come and gone;
I only know that summer sang in me
A little while, that in me sings no more.

In studying the following groups of poems, with a special eye still to
the sympathetic contract, ask yourself in the case of each poem if it
"rings true." That is, do you believe the poet's feelings are what he says
they are? If there is much doubt, then it's important to look at the poem

and see why it seems less credible than another. If you do believe the poet's feelings are what he says they are (be sure you have not misread his own statement of his feelings), how intimately involved with the subject do those feelings seem to be? (What distance does the poet keep?)

Whether the tone is intimate or detached or something in between, does the poet view the subject as more worthy than his own voice, less worthy than his voice, or properly deserving of his voice?

Do you respond to the poem in such a way that you sympathize with the poet's feelings? Do you enter into the sympathetic contract?

Holy Sonnet XIV

John Donne

Batter my heart, three-personed God; for you
As yet but knock, breathe, shine, and seek to mend.
That I may rise and stand, o'erthrow me and bend
Your force to break, blow, burn, and make me new.
I, like an usurped town, to another due,
Labor to admit you, but, oh, to no end;
Reason, your viceroy in me, me should defend,
But is captived and proves weak or untrue.
Yet dearly I love you and would be lovèd fain,
But am betrothed unto your enemy:
Divorce me, untie or break that knot again,
Take me to you, imprison me, for I,
Except you enthrall me, never shall be free,
Nor ever chaste, except you ravish me.

Thou Art Indeed Just, Lord

Gerard Manley Hopkins

Thou art indeed just, Lord, if I contend
With thee; but, sir, so what I plead is just.
Why do sinners' ways prosper? and why must
Disappointment all I endeavour end?
Wert thou my enemy, O thou my friend,
How wouldst thou worse, I wonder, than thou dost
Defeat, thwart me? Oh, the sots and thralls of lust
Do in spare hours more thrive than I that spend,
Sir, life upon thy cause. See, banks and brakes
Now, leavèd how thick! lacèd they are again
With fretty chervil, look, and fresh wind shakes
Them; birds build—but not I build; no, but strain,
Time's eunuch, and not breed one work that wakes.
Mine, O thou lord of life, send my roots rain.

On Our Crucified Lord, Naked and Bloody

Richard Crashaw

They have left thee naked, Lord; O that they had!
This garment too I would they had denied.

Thee with thyself they have too richly clad,
Opening the purple wardrobe of thy side.

O never could be found garments too good
For thee to wear, but these, of thine own blood.

Love

George Herbert

I

Immortal Love, author of this great frame,
    Sprung from that beauty which can never fade;
    How hath man parcel'd out thy glorious name,
And thrown it on that dust which thou hast made,

While mortal love doth all the title gain!
    Which siding with invention, they together
    Bear all the sway, possessing heart and brain,
(Thy workmanship) and give thee share in neither.

Wit fancies beauty, beauty raiseth wit:
    The world is theirs; they two play out the game,
    Thou standing by: and though thy glorious name
Wrought our deliverance from th'infernal pit,

    Who sings thy praise? only a scarf or glove
    Doth warm our hands, and make them write of love.

II

Immortal Heat, O let thy greater flame
    Attract the lesser to it: let those fires,
    Which shall consume the world, first make it tame;
And kindle in our hearts such true desires,

As may consume our lusts, and make thee way.
    Then shall our hearts pant thee; then shall our brain
    All her invention on thine Altar lay,
And there in hymns send back thy fire again:

Our eyes shall see thee, which before saw dust;
    Dust blown by wit, till that they both were blinde:

Thou shalt recover all thy goods in kind,
Who were disseized by usurping lust:

All knees shall bow to thee; all wits shall rise,
And praise him who did make and mend our eyes.

A Prayer to the Father of Heaven

John Skelton

O radiant luminary of light interminable
   Celestial Father, potential God of might,
Of heaven and earth, O Lord incomparable,
   Of all perfections the essential most perfite!
   O maker of mankind, that formèd day and night,
Whose power imperial comprehendeth every place:
   Mine heart, my mind, my thought, my whole delight
Is after this life to see thy glorious face.

Whose magnificence is incomprehensible,
   All arguments of reason which far doth exceed,
Whose deity doubtless is indivisible,
   From whom all goodness and virtue doth proceed;
   Of thy support all creàtures have need:
Assist me, good Lord, and grant me thy grace
   To live to thy pleasure in word, thought, and deed,
And after this life to see thy glorious face.

For a Dead Lady

Edwin Arlington Robinson

No more with overflowing light
Shall fill the eyes that now are faded,
Nor shall another's fringe with night
Their woman-hidden world as they did.
No more shall quiver down the days
The flowing wonder of her ways,
Whereof no language may requite
The shifting and the many-shaded.

The grace, divine, definitive,
Clings only as a faint forestalling;
The laugh that love could not forgive
Is hushed, and answers to no calling;
The forehead and the little ears

Have gone where Saturn keeps the years;
The breast where roses could not live
Has done with rising and with falling.

The beauty, shattered by the laws
That have creation in their keeping,
No longer trembles at applause,
Or over children that are sleeping;
And we who delve in beauty's lore
Know all that we have known before
Of what inexorable cause
Makes Time so vicious in his reaping.

On My First Daughter

Ben Jonson

Here lies to each her parents' ruth,
Mary, the daughter of their youth:
Yet, all heaven's gifts, being heaven's due,
It makes the father, less, to rue.
At six months end, she parted hence
With safety of her innocence;
Whose soul heaven's Queen, (whose name she bears)
In comfort of her mother's tears,
Hath plac'd amongst her virgin-train:
Where, while that sever'd doth remain,
This grave partakes the fleshly birth,
Which cover lightly, gentle earth.

On My First Son

Ben Jonson

Farewell, thou child of my right hand, and joy;
My sin was too much hope of thee, loved boy.
Seven years thou wert lent to me, and I thee pay,
Exacted by thy fate, on the just day.
O, could I lose all father now. For why
Will man lament the state he should envy?
To have so soon 'scaped world's, and flesh's, rage,
And if no other misery, yet age?
Rest in soft peace, and, asked, say here doth lie
Ben Jonson, his best piece of poetry.
For whose sake, henceforth, all his vows be such,
As what he loves may never like too much.

Epitaph on S.P.,
a Child of Queen Elizabeth's Chapel

Ben Jonson

Weep with me, all you that read
   This little story;
And know, for whom a tear you shed
   Death's self is sorry.
'Twas a child that so did thrive
   In grace and feature,
As heaven and nature seemed to strive
   Which owned the creature.
Years he numbered scarce thirteen
   When fates turned cruel,
Yet three filled zodiacs had he been
   The stage's jewel;
And did act, what now we moan,
   Old men so duly,
As, sooth, the Parcæ thought him one,
   He played so truly.
So by error, to his fate
   They all consented;
But viewing him since, alas too late,
   They have repented,
And have sought, to give new birth,
   In baths to steep him;
But being so much too good for earth,
   Heaven vows to keep him.

Little Elegy
For a Child Who Skipped Rope

X. J. Kennedy

Here lies resting, out of breath,
Out of turns, Elizabeth
Whose quicksilver toes not quite
Cleared the whirring edge of night.

Earth whose circles round us skim
Till they catch the lightest limb,
Shelter now Elizabeth
And for her sake trip up Death.

On a Child Who Lived One Minute

X. J. Kennedy

Into a world where children shriek like suns
Sundered from other suns on their arrival,

She stared, and saw the waiting shape of evil,
But couldn't take its meaning in at once,
So fresh her understanding, and so fragile.

Her first breath drew a fragrance from the air
And put it back. However hard her agile
Heart danced, however full the surgeon's satchel
Of healing stuff, a blackness tiptoed in her
And snuffed the only candle of her castle.

Oh, let us do away with elegiac
Drivel! Who can restore a thing so brittle,
So new in any jingle? Still I marvel
That, making light of mountainloads of logic,
So much could stay a moment in so little.

Bells for John Whiteside's Daughter

John Crowe Ransom

There was such speed in her little body,
And such lightness in her footfall,
It is no wonder her brown study
Astonishes us all.

Her wars were bruited in our high window.
We looked among orchard trees and beyond
Where she took arms against her shadow,
Or harried unto the pond

The lazy geese, like a snow cloud
Dripping their snow on the green grass,
Tricking and stopping, sleepy and proud,
Who cried in goose, Alas,

For the tireless heart within the little
Lady with rod that made them rise
From their noon apple-dreams and scuttle
Goose-fashion under the skies!

But now go the bells, and we are ready,
In one house we are sternly stopped
To say we are vexed at her brown study,
Lying so primly propped.

December 24 and George McBride Is Dead

Richard Hugo

You a gentleman and I up from the grime—
now wind has shut your dark, dark eyes

and I am left to hate this Christmas eve.
Christ, they're playing carols. Some crap
never stops. You're dead and I'm without
one goddam Wagner record in the house
to play you up to what for some must be
behind the sky with solid orchestration.

Rest in your defeat, you stupid jerk,
so fat your heart gave out, so sweet
you couldn't help but hear the punks.
"One gulp. The whole quart, Mac." That town
you died in—so unlikely—vineyards,
sunny valleys, stark white missions
and the pale priest summoning
brown sinners from the olive grove.
I'll not know your grave, though I believe
our minds have music that can lead us
through the tangle to the lost stone of a friend.

I get along, write my poems. Essentially
a phony, I try my feelings now
and know I fail. George, it's Christmas eve
and bells are caroling. I'm in the kitchen,
fat and writing, drinking beer and shaking.

A Refusal to Mourn the Death, by Fire, of a Child in London

Dylan Thomas

Never until the mankind making
Bird beast and flower
Fathering and all humbling darkness
Tells with silence the last light breaking
And the still hour
Is come of the sea tumbling in harness

And I must enter again the round
Zion of the water bead
And the synagogue of the ear of corn
Shall I let pray the shadow of a sound
Or sow my salt seed
In the least valley of sackcloth to mourn

The majesty and burning of the child's death.
I shall not murder
The mankind of her going with a grave truth
Nor blaspheme down the stations of the breath
With any further
Elegy of innocence and youth.

Deep with the first dead lies London's daughter,
Robed in the long friends,
The grains beyond age, the dark veins of her mother,
Secret by the unmourning water
Of the riding Thames.
After the first death, there is no other.

Elegy for a Nature Poet

Howard Nemerov

It was in October, a favorite season,
He went for his last walk. The covered bridge,
Most natural of all the works of reason,
Received him, let him go. Along the hedge

He rattled his stick; observed the blackening bushes
In his familiar field; thought he espied
Late meadow larks; considered picking rushes
For a dry arrangement; returned home, and died

Of a catarrh caught in the autumn rains
And let go on uncared for. He was too rapt
In contemplation to recall that brains
Like his should not be kept too long uncapped

In the wet and cold weather. While we mourned,
We thought of his imprudence, and how Nature,
Whom he'd done so much for, had finally turned
Against her creature.

His gift was daily his delight, he peeled
The landscape back to show it was a story;
Any old bird or burning bush revealed
At his hands just another allegory.

Nothing too great, nothing too trivial
For him; from mountain range or humble vermin
He could extract the hidden parable—
If need be, crack the stone to get the sermon.

And now, poor man, he's gone. Without his name
The field reverts to wilderness again,
The rocks are silent, woods don't seem the same;
Demoralized small birds will fly insane.

Rude Nature, whom he loved to idealize
And would have wed, pretends she never heard
His voice at all, as, taken by surprise
At last, he goes to her without a word.

In the pair of poems making up the next group, W. B. Yeats and Francis Ledwidge have expressed very much the same feeling about World War One and a tenable attitude of a man fighting in it. Ask the same questions as you asked on reading the previous poems, bearing in mind that Yeats never saw combat during the war, while Ledwidge wrote in the trenches and was killed in action in 1917.

An Irish Airman Foresees His Death

W. B. Yeats

I know that I shall meet my fate
Somewhere among the clouds above;
Those that I fight I do not hate,
Those that I guard I do not love;
My country is Kiltartan Cross,
My countrymen Kiltartan's poor,
No likely end could bring them loss
Or leave them happier than before.
Nor law, nor duty bade me fight,
Nor public men, nor cheering crowds,
A lonely impulse of delight
Drove to this tumult in the clouds;
I balanced all, brought all to mind,
The years to come seemed waste of breath,
A waste of breath the years behind
In balance with this life, this death.

Soliloquy

Francis Ledwidge

When I was young I had a care
Lest I should cheat me of my share
Of that which makes it sweet to strive
For life, and dying still survive,
A name in sunshine written higher
Than lark or poet dare aspire.

But I grew weary doing well,
Besides, 'twas sweeter in that hell,
Down with the loud banditti people
Who robbed the orchards, climbed the steeple
For jackdaws' eggs and made the cock
Crow ere 'twas daylight on the clock.
I was so very bad the neighbours
Spoke of me at their daily labours.

And now I'm drinking wine in France,
The helpless child of circumstance.
Tomorrow will be loud with war,
How will I be accounted for?

It is too late now to retrieve
A fallen dream, too late to grieve
A name unmade, but not too late
To thank the gods for what is great;
A keen-edged sword, a soldier's heart,
Is greater than a poet's art.
And greater than a poet's fame
A little grave that has no name.

Do you feel that Ledwidge's involvement in the war helps his poem to ring more true than Yeats' poem? Does one poem seem to be more "sincere" than the other—that is, are you more likely in one poem than the other to believe that the poet's feelings are what he says they are? In which poem? In what specific lines or passages does one poem or the other seem more (or less) to be the poet's "real" feelings?

Aubade: N.Y.C.

Robert Wallace

it is morning darling look the sun
by the fire escape comes peeping
rose on our sheets how fresh how
still oh and the roaches are sleeping

The Roach

John Raven

A roach
came struttin
across my bedroom
floor,
like it was beyond
reproach,
or was
some sexy-lookin
whore,
and if I hadn't
snuffed it, had
left it
alive,

I know it would've
come right up
and gave me
five!

In the above two poems, the poets are reacting with some humor to essentially the same unpleasant fact, and yet the poems are quite different. Do the different levels of diction make one poem more honest than the other? Do they make one poem "better" than the other? Do you *like* one poem better than the other? If you do, can you give the reason for your preference?

For each of the following poems, write down your answers to the questions you have been asking about the poet's tone and attitude, and then write down what you feel your answers would have been in each case if the poet had not added the final line (disregarding if you can the truncation of formal stanzas). Try to put into words precisely how these lines change the poems.

Lying in a Hammock at William Duffy's Farm in Pine Island, Minnesota

James Wright

Over my head, I see the bronze butterfly,
Asleep on the black trunk,
Blowing like a leaf in green shadow.
Down the ravine behind the empty house,
The cowbells follow one another
Into the distances of the afternoon.
To my right,
In a field of sunlight between two pines,
The droppings of last year's horses
Blaze up into golden stones.
I lean back, as the evening darkens and comes on.
A chicken hawk floats over, looking for home.
I have wasted my life.

The Tragedy of the Leaves

Charles Bukowski

I awakened to dryness and the ferns were dead,
the potted plants yellow as corn.
My woman was gone and the
empty bottles like bled corpses
surrounded me with their uselessness;

the sun was still good, though,
and my landlady's note cracked in fine and
undemanding yellowness; what was needed now
was a good comedian, ancient style, a jester
with jokes upon absurd pain; pain is absurd
because it exists, nothing more;
I shaved carefully with an old razor,
the man who had once been young and
said to have genius; but
that's the tragedy of the leaves,
the dead ferns, the dead plants;
and I walked into the dark hall
where the landlady stood
execrating and final,
sending me to hell,
waving her fat sweaty arms
and screaming,
screaming for rent
because the world had failed us both.

Northwest Airlines
(My emergency instructions were in Chinese.)

Fred Chappell

And there I was. Not a dictionary
In that whole dumb sky. The plane fell
Apart; I grabbed the instructions. Impossible
As reading a woman's smile.
The stewardess drifted. "What now?"
I shrieked. She shrieked, "Ch'ing ki'ang kiaow."

The world splashed toward me. The Chinese,
I thought, have never lost a war.
And I thought, O God, please. Please!

The Place of Backs

W. S. Merwin

When what has helped us has helped us enough
it moves off and sits down
not looking our way

after that every time we call it
it takes away one of the answers it had given us

it sits laughing among its friends with wrong names
all of them nodding yes

if we stay there
they make fun of us
as we grow smaller because of the melting of our bones

The More Loving One

W. H. Auden

Looking up at the stars, I know quite well
That, for all they care, I can go to hell,
But on earth indifference is the least
We have to dread from man or beast.

How should we like it were stars to burn
With a passion for us we could not return?
If equal affection cannot be,
Let the more loving one be me.

Admirer as I think I am
Of stars that do not give a damn,
I cannot, now I see them, say
I missed one terribly all day.

Were all stars to disappear or die,
I should learn to look at an empty sky
And feel its total dark sublime,
Though this might take me a little time.

Woodchucks

Maxine Kumin

Gassing the woodchucks didn't turn out right.
The knockout bomb from the Feed and Grain Exchange
was featured as merciful, quick at the bone
and the case we had against them was airtight,
both exits shoehorned shut with puddingstone,
but they had a sub-sub-basement out of range.

Next morning they turned up again, no worse
for the cyanide than we for our cigarettes
and state-store Scotch, all of us up to scratch.
They brought down the marigolds as a matter of course
and then took over the vegetable patch
nipping the broccoli shoots, beheading the carrots.

The food from our mouths, I said, righteously thrilling
to the feel of the .22, the bullets' neat noses.
I, a lapsed pacifist fallen from grace
puffed with Darwinian pieties for killing,
now drew a bead on the littlest woodchuck's face.
He died down in the everbearing roses.

Ten minutes later I dropped the mother. She
flipflopped in the air and fell, her needle teeth
still hooked in a leaf of early Swiss chard.
Another baby next. O one-two-three
the murderer inside me rose up hard,
the hawkeye killer came on stage forthwith.

There's one chuck left. Old wily fellow, he keeps
me cocked and ready day after day after day.
All night I hunt his humped-up form. I dream
I sight along the barrel in my sleep.
If only they'd all consented to die unseen
gassed underground the quiet Nazi way.

CHAPTER SIX
THE IMAGE AND THE POEM

"Man," said the critic Kenneth Burke, "is the symbol-using animal." He might as well have said "Man is the metaphoric animal," for symbolism and metaphor are simply two aspects of the same process. Carried a step further, the statement might have been, "Thoughts are made of pictures."

For though there seems to be a general illusion that man "thinks in words," it should be obvious that "thoughts" go through our minds much more rapidly than we can phrase them. Many a writer has filled pages in trying to verbalize what went through his mind in a split second of heightened perception, a span of time in which he could not possibly have "thought" that many words.

One may readily experiment for himself. He has only to pause, make an effort to clear his mind, and then "think" some such central experience as "home for Christmas." Instantly many "thoughts" flash through one's mind. And clearly those thoughts are not words but "pictures" (and recollections of other sensory impressions such as sounds, smells, tastes). The "thought" in such a case is in fact many fragments of such images. Our consciousness may perhaps be best visualized as a kind of movie-strip photomontage, a sequence of many simultaneous impressions, mostly visual.

When the poet comes to verbalize that consciousness (as distinct from his original experience of it), he tends inevitably to metaphor. That is to say, he offers pictures to represent thoughts. When Archibald MacLeish writes in "Ars Poetica" (p. 281):

> For all the history of grief
> An empty doorway and a maple leaf

the concept "all the history of grief" is made equal to the picture "an empty doorway and a maple leaf."

The fact that such a "picture" can be offered as the equivalent of so large a concept is fundamental not only to the poetic method but to all thought. The fact that such a picture is conceptual rather than actually drawn can only serve to underline the power of such pictorial suggestion. It would seem to be impossible for man to think in any depth were he not able to "see pictures" in his mind's eye. The very words of human languages are images at root, and all written languages seem to have evolved from some form of drawing.

A process so fundamental to human thinking could provide material for endless analysis but the present discussion of imagery can be relatively brief. It can be so because the earlier discussion of symbolism has already introduced one special case of imagery. And it can be so even more because the basically pictorial nature of language makes it possible for much of what has been said about the words of poetry to be applied without significant change to the discussion of imagery.

Like words, images possess both denotation and connotation: they denote certain sensory (usually visual) identifications and they connote an emotional aura. Like words, therefore, images in a poem tend to fall into overtone themes united by either their denotations or their connotations. Thus, all images related to the sea may be taken as denotatively united, whereas all images suggesting a given emotional quality (as, for example, the harshness of such a chain of images as "rasp," "thong," "gnarled granite," "clawing winds") may be taken to be connotatively united.

Like words, too, images have histories. Images lack the philological histories of words whereby submerged former meanings can be played against more recently evolved meanings; as, for example, a poet may speak of "the aberration of the sea" and mean to imply to the sea both the evolved meaning of "derangement" (the sea as a madness of nature) and the root meaning of *ab* plus *errare*, "to wander away from," as the sea wanders off into distance. But though images lack this quality of words, they are like words in that they can become so possessed by the way they have been used in the past that they become stereotyped and degenerate into forceless clichés. Images, moreover, can become stereotyped quite apart from the way in which they are phrased.

The image of the "lance of Achilles" is an excellent example of how a fresh image can become dead. Achilles inherited from his father a lance that possessed magic qualities. A touch of its sharp end never failed to wound and a touch of the other end never failed to heal. Early in the thirteenth century an Italian poet writing a sonnet of courtly love to his lady came on an inspired moment and compared her eyes to the lance of Achilles: with one sharp look she never failed to wound, and with one soft look she never failed to heal.

The comparison was marvelously right for the mood of the courtly sonnet. It was learned, it was gallant, it was touched with the romantic suggestion of the golden past, and it implied that the lady possessed magical (hence more than earthly) powers: an extremely apt extravagance. It was so apt, in fact, that it was doomed. Before long, every eligible grocer's daughter in Italy had become the subject of a sonnet in which her eyes were compared to Achilles' lance. Or if not her eyes, then her lips (wounding with a frown, healing with a smile), or her tongue (wounding with a sharp word, healing with a soft one). Inevitably, the image lost all force, however elegantly it may have been rephrased. The first lady to be offered so gracious a comparison might well have been moved by it. The thousandth had every reason to feel that she was being offered shopworn daisies.

The reader, too, must be courted, and the good reader will be more demanding than the lady of the sonnets. He is ever willing to receive a true poetic effect into his feelings, but he must resist cheapening his feelings. He cannot allow himself to be moved by lifeless imitation, just as Shakespeare refused, in Sonnet CXXX, to cheapen his feelings by "false compare."

But though words and images have so much in common, there are a number of important ways in which images must be discussed in their own terms. Whether stereotyped or not, the image of Achilles' lance works exactly as does MacLeish's "empty doorway and a maple leaf." Both speak of one thing in terms of another.

But are they both, then, symbols? It was noted in Chapter Three that the distinction between a symbol and a metaphor cannot be rigidly drawn. But a symbol tends to stand for a more formal and more expansive area of meaning or of experience (the image of ripples on a pool again), whereas a metaphor tends to be more specific and rather more sensory than conceptual. What is basic to both is *the metaphoric sense.*

Nothing is more characteristic of poetry than this metaphoric sense. When the poet says, "Gather ye rosebuds while ye may," he is not telling the reader to go into the garden to cut roses. And when the poet says, "Make hay while the sun shines," he is not issuing a directive to get the hay in before it rains. Nor do the two statements mean the same thing. True, they have something in common. Both could be categorized as examples of the idea "Seize the day for it is fleeting." But to assume that because the two statements could be placed in the same category, they therefore are "the same thing" is to ignore all the connotative differences between the romantic delicacy of "rosebuds" and the more walloping lustiness of "make hay." The fact is that a man "making hay" is involved in a psychic state vastly different from that of a man "gathering rosebuds."

Literal-minded readers, the Gradgrinds of the world, are forever in difficulty with the metaphoric sense of poetic language. They want to know "what the poem is *about*," and they resist the essential duplicity whereby the poem is never entirely about what it *seems* to be about. Rupert Brooke's "Heaven" (p. 252), for example, purports to be about fish and is, of course, a satire on certain religious attitudes. Brooke is doubly engaged: he is concerned for the second meaning of his poem, and he is obviously relishing the fun of playing with its purported meaning. More than one thing is happening at once, and the good reader must be prepared to respond at all levels simultaneously.

The essential doubleness of what is happening in this poem involves the nature of *the metaphoric contract.*

All metaphor is basically a way of speaking of the unknown in terms of the known. The metaphoric formula may thus be stated:

$$X \text{ (unknown)} = Y \text{ (known)}$$

"My luve is like a red rose," says Burns. The reader knows what a red red rose is, but he does not know what "my luve" is in Burns's way of thinking. By applying his known feelings for "red red rose" to his unformed sense of "my luve," however, the reader finds a sense of how Burns feels about his love.

Rarely, however, is X truly equal to Y in any literal sense. If one says, "Richard's eyes are like Peter's," then the unknown (Richard's eyes) may reasonably be taken as exactly equal to the known (Peter's eyes), but such a pure case rarely occurs in poetry. Even in responding richly to Burns' line, one knows very well that "my luve" is substantially unlike a "red red rose." One hopes, for example, that her complexion is not entirely that vivid, that her body is not green and thorny, and that she is not wholly vegetable. The point of similarity, that is to say, is nowhere in the denotation, and in fact must work *in spite of* the denotation. A semantically accurate statement of the case might be: "The connotations released by the concept 'red red rose' may be taken as equivalent to those released by the concept 'my luve.'" The metaphoric formula may better be stated, therefore, as "X does and does not equal Y." The poet, nevertheless, brushes aside such clinical considerations and goes joyously about making metaphors *as if* X did in fact equal Y. His contract is simple: if the reader will bring a fluent and a supple mind to play upon the Y of the metaphor, the poet will engage to give him an experience of the X.

But he will also undertake to give him an experience of the pleasurable interplay of X upon Y. So for Rupert Brooke. He is concerned for both X and Y, and he is further concerned for the happy duplicity of playing one against the other.

In "A Refusal to Mourn the Death, by Fire, of a Child in London" (p. 230), Dylan Thomas says, speaking of his eventual death:

> And I must enter again the round
> Zion of the water bead
> And the synagogue of the ear of corn

This is an especially rich pair of metaphors, but it is only slightly more complex (for being more interesting) than the simple X=Y equation, and the reader still makes use of the given to solve for the unknown, the thing suggested. What Thomas has given us in each metaphor is a ratio with three known parts:

man, water bead [raindrop], round Zion

and

man, ear of corn, synagogue

or

$$\frac{\text{raindrop}}{\text{X}} :: \frac{\text{the man}}{\text{Zion}}$$

and

$$\frac{\text{ear of corn}}{\text{X}} :: \frac{\text{the man}}{\text{synagogue}}$$

X in each case, of course, is the earth, which is equated with Zion (the place of origin and return) for the drop of rain, and the synagogue (source of sustenance and roots) for the corn plant, as the earth is the source of roots and sustenance, and place of return also for the poet.

By not just "coming out and saying" that he would one day die and be buried, Thomas has made it necessary (and possible) for the reader to take part in the realization of the metaphoric statement and thereby to become an actual participant in the poem. The imagination of the reader is engaged, and he is taken out of the role of the passively entertained.

Even beyond this, Thomas tells the reader, by means of the metaphor, that there is an essential kinship between man and raindrop and between man and corn plant, and suggests that the life of man might also come again out of the earth. No part of this experience is possible for the reader who insists that a writer come out and say what he means in the most direct terms possible.

The poet must engage himself in both sides of the metaphor at once. Having undertaken to speak of religion in terms of fish (as Brooke decided to do with his poem "Heaven"), everything he then says must be as true of his X as it is of his Y. If one begins to speak, for example, of "the ship of state," everything he says must be *equally applicable* to both a ship and the state. He may speak of the captain, of the voyage, of the wheelhouse, and depending upon his manipulation, the reader will understand these images as metaphorically apt to a discussion of the state (though they are, of course, clichés by now). But let one begin by speaking of "the ship of state" and of "the captain" and then refer to "the House of Representatives," and all is lost. There has occurred a breach of metaphoric contract. It is as if an actor had undertaken to play the role of, let us say, Hamlet, had found himself incapable of projecting the role, and had stepped out of character to *tell* the audience what his acting was intended to be about. In any theater seriously taken, such an action can call for nothing but tomatoes.

A related violation is the *mixed metaphor*, the situation in which the writer does not abandon metaphor but slides unwittingly from one metaphor to another. "We must put our noses to the grindstone and lift our eyes to the great vision of tomorrow if we truly mean to escape from the quicksands of confusion." There is always likely to be an element of the grotesque in such a mixture. And as in all matters of poetry, mixed metaphor can be used for special effects. Any such instance of a special effect does not, however, cancel the force of the metaphoric contract. Rather, the special effect is possible only because it is a violation of a contract that is in force.

Such mixed metaphors as the following are seen more often than they should be by the editor of any magazine publishing poetry. It should be easy for you to tell specifically what is wrong with each of them without suffering through the entire poems.

> The night comes in like the tide
> and whispers in my ear
> and I rest in its dark and leafy arms
> where there is no fear.

> Our passion is a flame
> in the lap of Venus
> where never land nor ocean
> come between us.

> Your eyes are limpid pools
> and when they wink
> I want to dive into them both
> and happily sink.

Grammatically, "metaphor" signifies an indirect comparison, and "simile" a direct comparison. Thus to say "Richard has a heart like a lion's" is a simile, and to say "Richard the lion-hearted" is a metaphor. The distinction between such direct and indirect comparisons has little meaningful application to poetic practice, and since "metaphor" can readily be made into an adjective, whereas "simile" would require the awkward adjectival form "similitudinous," the terms "metaphor" and "metaphoric" serve for all figurative comparisons in poetry.

"Imagery," however, is a wider term than "metaphor." *Imagery* is best defined as "the total sensory suggestion of poetry." Most of that sensory suggestion is, of course, visual, but metaphoric language can as readily suggest sound, as in Keats' "The silver snarling trumpets 'gan to chide"; or tactile sensation, as in MacLeish's "Dumb/As old medallions to the thumb"; or taste, as in Coleridge's "For she on honey dew has fed/And drunk the milk of Paradise"; or even interior bodily sensation as in Emily Dickinson's "Without a tighter breathing/And Zero at the Bone."

Clearly, however, some of the sensory suggestion of poetry is involved in metaphoric comparisons, and some is not. Simple statements of fact, and even the simple names of things, convery sensory suggestion. One very definite sort of effect can be achieved in poetry by the device called the catalogue, which consists simply of a list of names of things, or of sensory impressions, though in practice the catalogue tends to become a mixture of both names and metaphors. Walt Whitman has used the catalogue more extensively than any poet writing in English. The following passage from "Song of Myself" will illustrate both the basic quality of the catalogue as a simple listing of things, and the tendency for some metaphoric comparison to become involved in the list. As a first exercise, one might do well to underline every element in the catalogue that is simply the name of a thing, and to circle every element that involves some sort of metaphoric comparison.

Song of Myself (26)

Walt Whitman

Now I will do nothing but listen,
To accrue what I hear into this song, to let sounds contribute toward it.

I hear the bravuras of birds, bustle of growing wheat, gossip of flames,
    clack of sticks cooking my meals.
I hear the sound I love, the sound of the human voice,
I hear all sounds running together, combined, fused or following,
Sounds of the city and sounds out of the city, sounds of the day and
    night,
Talkative young ones to those that like them, the loud laugh of work-
    people at their meals,
The angry bass of disjointed friendship, the faint tones of the sick,
The judge with hands tight to the desk, his pallid lips pronouncing a
    death-sentence,
The heave'e'yo of stevedores unlading ships by the wharves, the
    refrain of the anchor-lifters,
The ring of alarm-bells, the cry of fire, the whirr of swift-streaking
    engines and hose-carts with premonitory tinkles and color'd lights,
The steam-whistle, the solid roll of the train of approaching cars,
The slow march play'd at the head of the association marching two and
    two,
(They go to guard some corpse, the flag-tops are draped with black
    muslin.)

I hear the violincello, ('tis the young man's heart's complaint,)
I hear the key'd cornet, it slides quickly through my ears,
It shakes mad-sweet pangs through my belly and breast.

I hear the chorus, it is a grand opera,
Ah this indeed is music—this suits me.

A tenor large and fresh as the creation fills me,
The orbic flex of his mouth is pouring and filling me full.

I hear the train'd soprano (what work with hers is this?)
The orchestra whirls me wider than Uranus flies,
It wrenches such ardors from me I did not know I possessed them,
It sails me, I dab with bare fee, they are licked by the indolent waves,
I am cut by bitter and angry hail, I lose my breath,
Steep'd amid honey'd morphine, my windpipe throttled in fakes of
    death,
At length let up again to feel the puzzle of puzzles,
And that we call Being.

For purposes of more convenient discussion, therefore, one may distinguish between *metaphors* and *properties* as the two sorts of imagery. The term *property* is used in the same sense one has in mind when speaking of a theatrical prop room.

Whitman fathered a large pretense that his catalogues were all inclusive, that every sort of detail was equally welcome to his mind. Obviously, however, certain kinds of images were more welcome to his sensibilities than were others. Whitman tended to welcome without reserve, all images of industrial expansion, of fruitful nature, of the brotherhood of man, of astronomy, of the bustle of urban life, and of physical strength, for example, but one will not find anywhere in his catalogues such satanic images as one may find in Poe or in Baudelaire. One has only to turn to "Prufrock" (p. 78) or to "Dirge" (p. 289) to see two catalogues of properties that would never occur in Whitman, despite his pretense to all-inclusiveness.

There is, that is to say, some *principle of selection* at work. One can see certain kinds of images that occurred readily to Whitman's mind and were welcomed into his poems. And one can locate other sorts of images that not only were pushed away from the poems, but that probably never occurred to the poet's mind.

It follows that a simple tabulation of the kind of image that appears in a man's poetry is one index to his mind. The contents of a prop room can suggest, to some extent at least, what sort of play is being produced. The contents of the poetic catalogue can tell one much more accurately the nature of the poet's mind.

In a sense, moreover, the collected works of any poet are always a catalogue of a sort. There is a kind of image that is natural to one poet and not another. The frequency with which certain kinds of images occur will say a great deal about the poet. Were one to compile a list of the most common images of such a poet as John Donne, for example, he would end with a listing that would certainly include the following:

> knots
> anchors
> royal crowns
> the king's face
> coins
> the king's image on a coin
> candles in darkness

There is no present need to make such a list complete. It is enough to note that this sort of image seems to occur frequently in Donne's poetry. Its very frequency would suggest that it answers the need of something the poet feels and is attempting to express. All these images, moreover, have a common quality: all of them are images that concentrate power in a small space. The knot is the point that concentrates the whole power of the rope. The anchor is the point that concentrates all those forces that keep a ship fast. The royal crown is the symbol of the total power of the sovereign, as is his face, and his image on a coin. The coin is a concentrated image of all wealth. The candle in darkness is the focus of all vision.

One might go through John Donne's poetry and find many more examples of this sort of imagery. Scattered as it is denotatively, all of it has a connotative area in common. And the consistency of that connotation will serve immediately to identify one of the psychic forces of John Donne's vision. He was a man who strained all of his life to concentrate emotional forces, to reach one intense experience that would summarize all of his life's meaning.

Imagery can, therefore, be taken as a language of its own, and one way to establish a first communication with a poet can be reduced to the mechanical exercise of tabulating the images a poet uses in a representative number of poems, noting the frequency with which each image occurs, the area of experience from which the image is drawn (as, for example, war, sports, nature, law), the denotation, the connotation, and whether the image is used metaphorically or as a property.

Some critics have made very elaborate tabulations of this sort, with even more elaborate cross-references. Needless to say the overelaboration of any mechanical method of analysis, when applied to poetry, can very soon run into the law of diminishing returns. Any careful reader, on the other hand, will come to recognize at least those images a given poet tends to use most frequently.

The fact seems to be that in locating the image-making quality of a given poet, one comes close to identifying the center of his character as a poet. Even a relatively simple tabulation may provide clues to a true insight. If, for example, one does no more than to note that in a thousand lines of Poet A, flower images occur twenty-two times but that the flowers are seldom (except for, say, roses and daisies) given their particular names, whereas in a thousand lines of Poet B, flower images occur one hundred thirty-two times and almost invariably with such specific names as orchis, hyacinth, anemone, sweet william, arrowroot, and so on—if one notes no more than that, he will already have a reasonable measure of the importance of actual contact with nature in Poet A and Poet B. Clearly, whatever these two poets may profess of interest in nature, B is the one who has gone more observantly and more often into the fields and woods.

A simple way of making such tabulations is to comb through a representative number of lines by a given poet and to jot each image on a filing card, adding notes at one's own pleasure on the denotation, connotation, area of experience, and whether the image is used metaphorically or as a property. Such cards may then be sorted into many different categories. If, for example, "flowers" seems a natural category for the given poet, then the image "daisy" would be so classified. It may be, however, that as one sorts the filing cards, a more basic category for this poet seems to be "whiteness." In that case, daisy might be classified with snow, swans, albino rabbits, and cumulus clouds. Or it may well be that both "flowers" and "whiteness" are basic to that poet's mind and that "daisy" must be entered in both categories.

The point is that such categories cannot be set in advance. Each poet must suggest his own natural groupings to each reader. It is most precisely in finding those categories that seem most native to the imagery of a given poet that one comes closest to locating the emotional center of his poetic character. The mechanical business of jotting images on filing cards is simply a way of directing one's attention to the possible categories suggested by a given poet. The business must not become an end in itself, for poetry will not yield to such bookkeeper analysis. Undertaken simply as an exercise in increasing one's perception of a single (and very central) quality of the poetry, however, such detailed image analysis can prepare one to encounter the poet's work more meaningfully.

A more direct, and perhaps more rewarding, way of analyzing imagery is to take careful note of the overtone themes of the images within a single poem, in exactly the same way one may note the overtone themes of the diction of the poem.

When the images of a given poem, or of a given passage, are related by their denotations, that poem or that passage is said to be constructed on a *dominant image*. When the images are related by their connotations but range widely in their denotations, that poem or passage is said to make use of *scattered imagery*. John Donne's "A Valediction Forbidding Mourning" may be taken as one of the great masterpieces of imagery in English poetry. Its first six stanzas are constructed on scattered images, its last three stanzas develop one of the most memorable dominant metaphors to be found in English literature.

A word on the situation of the poem will make it more meaningful to the reader not well acquainted with Donne's other poems. John Donne wrote "A Valediction Forbidding Mourning" as a farewell to his wife on the occasion of embarking for a diplomatic mission to France. He tells her not to mourn because mourning would belittle their love. Donne believed fervently in the union of souls in true love. Thus, since their souls remain united no matter what distance separates their bodies, true lovers suffer no real absence.

A Valediction Forbidding Mourning

John Donne

As virtuous men pass mildly away
  And whisper to their souls to go,
Whilst some of their sad friends do say,
  "The breath goes now," and some say, "No";

So let us melt, and make no noise,
  No tear-floods, nor sigh-tempests move;
'Twere profanation of our joys
  To tell the laity our love.

Moving of th'earth brings harms and fears;
  Men reckon what it did, and meant.
But trepidation of the spheres,
  Though greater far, is innocent.

Dull sublunary lovers' love—
  Whose soul is sense—cannot admit
Absence, because it doth remove
  Those things which elemented it.

But we by a love so much refined
  That ourselves know not what it is,
Inter-assured of the mind,
  Care less eyes, lips, and hands to miss.

Our two souls, therefore, which are one,
  Though I must go, endure not yet
A breach, but an expansion,
  Like gold to airy thinness beat.

If they be two, they are two so
  As stiff twin compasses are two;
Thy soul, the fixed foot, makes no show
To move, but doth, if th'other do.

And though it in the center sit,
  Yet, when the other far doth roam,
It leans and harkens after it,
  And grows erect, as that comes home.

Such wilt thou be to me, who must,
  Like th'other foot, obliquely run;
Thy firmness makes my circle just,
  And makes me end where I begun.

The denotations of the images in the first six stanzas scatter over many areas. The poet summons to his image structure (1) the deathbed of a virtuous man, (2) the physical phenomena of melting, making

---

moving of the earth: earthquake. **trepidation of the spheres:** the vibration of the spheres as conceived in the Ptolemaic system. It is the vibration of the spheres that produces heavenly harmony. Thus, though the motion of the heavenly spheres (here equated to the love of true lovers) is vastly greater than that of an earthquake (here equated to the sensuality of merely physical lovers), the higher motion produces no bad consequences. **sublunary:** below the circle of the moon; on earth; earthbound. **elemented it:** made up its elements, those simply physical elements of which such love consists.

noise, floods, and tempests, (3) church hierarchy, (4) earthquake and the vibration of the Ptolemaic spheres, (5) the process of refining what one suspects to be gold, and (6) the process of beating gold into gold leaf. The poet's mind seems to have reached in all directions and to have ranged widely in the search for images that will give force to the experience of the poem.

One is well justified, therefore, in waiving denotation as the unifying principle of selection here, and in concluding that Donne was willing to accept any illustration that carried the emotional connotation he sought. The kind of human behavior that produces a poem, however, is seldom quite that simple. A closer student of Donne could argue with true point and insight, that all these images are from areas of learning that would naturally attract a speculative intellect of Donne's time. The deathbed of a virtuous man is an image suggesting many speculations on the meaning of life and of its relation to the idea of a hereafter. Physical phenomena of every sort suggest speculations into the nature of the world. The comparison between earthquake and the vibration of the Ptolemaic spheres suggests speculations into the nature of the universe. The processes of gold refining and gold beating suggest speculations into the nature of man's technological grip upon the planet. These are all in some sense *metaphysical* concerns, and it is for this quality of his work that Donne is referred to as a "metaphysical poet."

But though one may be tempted to argue that the images of the first six stanzas are united by their metaphysical denotation, one has only to compare them to the single sustained comparison of the last three stanzas to see that they are indeed organized on a different principle. However widely their denotations range, all of these scattered images are connotatively associated in two overtone themes that might, for convenience, be labeled the *true love* and the *merely physical love* themes. Throughout, the poet is clearly in favor of one set of his images, and clearly opposed to another. Those themes may be tabulated thus:

Images of true love (approved)	*Images of merely physical love* (disapproved)
virtuous men pass mildly away (having no fear) the undemonstrative nature of the passing from one state to the other	
melt (imperceptible change)	noise (violent change)
	tear-floods (violence) sigh-tempests (violence)
our joys (high) our love (high)	profanation (low) laity (low)
trepidation of the spheres (high and serene)	earthquake (low and violent)
refined love (high, serene)	dull sublunary lovers (low, coarse)

expansion (imperceptible
   change; high, as gold is a
   symbol of merit; serene)

airy thinness (high, serene)

breach (violent change, low,
   coarse as opposed to "airy
   thinness")

One may see at once, even from so crude a list of jottings, that a development like that of theme and countertheme in music is taking place. The images are entering the poem not only for their own sakes but in response to the images that have preceded them, both those images whose overtones they reinforce, and those whose overtones they oppose. Such imagery, as noted, is "scattered" only in the sense that its denotations range widely. Its connotations are intricately and meaningfully related.

In the last three stanzas, on the other hand, the single image of a compass is sustained and developed in great detail, and every detail is directly related to the way in which a compass draws a circle. The pleasure of such imagery arises not from the way the connotations are musically united into themes, but in the inventiveness and the aptness with which the poet works his image structure for more and more points of fitting comparison. One ends by feeling that the possibilities of the image have been wholly evoked. Certainly, too, one must note that the circle has long been a metaphysical symbol of unity and perfection. That perfect rounding serves to close the metaphysical implications of the whole poem in exactly the way a tonic chord rounds out and resolves a piece of music.

Poems for Study: Metaphor and Statement

Departmental

Robert Frost

An ant on the tablecloth
Ran into a dormant moth
Of many times his size.
He showed not the least surprise.
His business wasn't with such.
He gave it scarcely a touch,
And was off on his duty run.
Yet if he encountered one
Of the hive's enquiry squad
Whose work is to find out God
And the nature of time and space,
He would put him onto the case.
Ants are a curious race;

One crossing with hurried tread
The body of one of their dead
Isn't given a moment's arrest—
Seems not even impressed.
But he no doubt reports to any
With whom he crosses antennae,
And they no doubt report
To the higher-up at court.
Then word goes forth in Formic:
"Death's come to Jerry McCormic,
Our selfless forager Jerry.
Will the special Janizary
Whose office it is to bury
The dead of the commissary
Go bring him home to his people.
Lay him in state on a sepal.
Wrap him for shroud in a petal.
Embalm him with ichor of nettle.
This is the word of your Queen."
And presently on the scene
Appears a solemn mortician;
And taking formal position,
With feelers calmly atwiddle,
Seizes the dead by the middle,
And heaving him high in air,
Carries him out of there.
No one stands round to stare.
It is nobody else's affair.

It couldn't be called ungentle.
But how thoroughly departmental.

QUESTIONS

Check the exact meaning of "Formic," "Janizary," "ichor," "nettle," and "sepal."

Frost has written what purports to be a ritual of the society of ants. That ritual seems clearly enough aimed at dramatizing the ant conception of the relation of the individual to society. How does Frost feel about the ants for being so "thoroughly departmental"? By human standards what is lacking from a "thoroughly departmental" society?

If ant society is a metaphoric X, what is the metaphoric Y? (Do not be in a hurry to make Y equal one thing only.)

At what points does Frost seem to be having most fun in playing X against Y?

As a matter of the metaphoric contract, is the *"hive's"* enquiry squad (line 9) defensible? Do ants live in hives? Or should the phrase have been "the *hill's* enquiry squad"?

Heaven

Rupert Brooke

Fish (fly-replete, in depth of June
Dawdling away their wat'ry noon)
Ponder deep wisdom, dark or clear,
Each secret fishy hope or fear.
Fish say, they have their Stream and Pond;
But is there anything Beyond?
This life cannot be All, they swear,
For how unpleasant, if it were!
One may not doubt that, somehow, good
Shall come of Water and of Mud;
And, sure, the reverent eye must see
A Purpose in Liquidity.
We darkly know, by Faith we cry,
The future is not Wholly Dry.
Mud unto Mud!—Death eddies near—
Not here the appointed End, not here!
But somewhere, beyond Space and Time,
Is wetter water, slimier slime!
And there (they thrust) there swimmeth One
Who swam ere rivers were begun,
Immense, of fishy form and mind,
Squamous, omnipotent and kind;
And under that Almighty Fin
The littlest fish may enter in.
Oh! never fly conceals a hook,
Fish say, in the Eternal Brook,
But more than mundane weeds are there,
And mud, celestially fair;
Fat caterpillars drift around,
And Paradisal grubs are found;
Unfading moths, immortal flies,
And the worm that never dies.
And in that Heaven of all their wish,
There shall be no more land, say fish.

QUESTIONS

Check the exact meaning of "squamous."

As already noted, this poem purports to be about fish but is obviously enough about certain religious attitudes. In conceiving God and heaven in their own image, the fish are illustrating the concept of religious anthropomorphism. Anthropomorphism is that concept which attributes human forms and desires to God. One critic has gone as far as to attack this poem as sacrilegious. What in the poem might have moved him to that opinion?

The X and the Y of Brooke's metaphor are clear enough but one should not fail to note that Brooke is obviously enjoying the process of working out his idea in "fishy" terms. Does Brooke persuade the reader that these are indeed the terms in which a reflective fish might conceive heaven? Does he violate his metaphor at any point by introducing "thoughts" that are inappropriate to a fish?

What is the effect of describing the rewards of faith in terms of "slimier slime," "Paradisal grubs," and "fat caterpillars"?

Arriving

Daniel Halpern

On a day long and wet we fall upon
The city like tramps belched from all-night bus
Depots. Time is porcelain on the wall
As we step into the light. I will call
To the taxi stalling for his crude pay
Outside a bar, and if he comes for us
We will doze through falling streets, moving on
Until the heights break down before the bay.

At Steele's Motel a man behind a sign
Yawns his questions at us in hot clouds
And hands us a key, pointing where the night
Spills a crowd of different throats near a pine.
The cabin is a bed and desk—a shroud
Of moth wings on the screen, starving for light.

We are told in this poem that the speaker and his traveling companion are like tramps, that time is porcelain, and that the wings of moths on the screen are a shroud. What are we meant to understand by these comparisons? That is, what is Halpern telling us that we might not otherwise have known about the two people, about time (as it appears to the speaker), and about the motel room (as it is represented by the screen with its moths)?

Ode on the Death of a Favorite Cat, Drowned in a Tub of Gold Fishes

Thomas Gray

'Twas on a lofty vase's side,
Where China's gayest art had dy'd
  The azure flowers, that blow;
Demurest of the tabby kind,
The pensive Selima reclin'd,
  Gazed on the lake below.

Her conscious tail her joy declar'd;
The fair round face, the snowy beard,
   The velvet of her paws,
Her coat, that with the tortoise vies,
Her ears of jet, and emerald eyes,
   She saw; and purr'd applause.

Still had she gaz'd; but 'midst the tide
Two angel forms were seen to glide,
   The Genii of the stream:
Their scaly armour's Tyrian hue
Thro' richest purple to the view
   Betray'd a golden gleam.

The hapless Nymph with wonder saw:
A whisker first and then a claw,
   With many an ardent wish,
She stretch'd in vain to reach the prize,
What female heart can gold despise?
   What Cat's averse to fish?

Presumptuous Maid! with looks intent
Again she stretch'd, again she bent,
   Nor knew the gulf between.
(Malignant Fate sat by, and smil'd)
The slipp'ry verge her feet beguil'd.
   She tumbled headlong in.

Eight times emerging from the flood
She mew'd to ev'ry watry God,
   Some speedy aid to send.
No Dolphin came, no Nereid stirr'd:
Nor cruel *Tom,* nor *Susan* heard.
   A Fav'rite has no friend!

From hence, ye Beauties, undeceiv'd,
Know, one false step is ne'er retriev'd,
   And be with caution bold.
Not all that tempts your wand'ring eyes
And heedless hearts, is lawful prize;
   Nor all, that glistens, gold.

QUESTIONS

Check the exact meaning of "Genii," "Tyrian," "Nymph," and "Nereid."
What tone do such words set for the poem?

Identify the metaphoric X and Y.

Selima, the cat, reclined and looked into the "lake" below. Why does
Gray call the goldfish bowl a "lake"?

What is the force (in stanza four) of placing as equal statements: "What female heart can gold despise?" and "What Cat's averse to fish?"

How many of the metaphoric implications of the poem flow from the "goldness" of the goldfish? What metaphoric points, that is, would have been lost, or would at least have been much harder to make, had the bowl contained black tropical fish? What was the cat's folly? If that folly is the metaphoric X, what is the metaphoric Y?

Note that Gray abandons his metaphoric pretense from time to time to interject a nonmetaphoric statement, and that he adds a final injunction that might be thought of as altogether (though actually not quite) abandoning the metaphor. Frost and Brooke were much more insistent on keeping their poems entirely within the metaphoric pretense. What is the difference in effect of these two methods?

To a Fair Lady Playing with a Snake

Edmund Waller

Strange that such Horror and such Grace
Should dwell together in one place,
A Fury's Arm, an Angel's Face.

'Tis innocence and youth which makes
In *Chloris's* fancy such mistakes,
To start at Love, and play with Snakes.

By this and by her coldness barr'd,
Her servants have a task too hard,
The Tyrant has a double guard.

Thrice happy Snake, that in her sleeve
May boldly creep, we dare not give
Our thoughts so unconfin'd a leave:

Contented in that nest of Snow
He lies, as he his bliss did know,
And to the wood no more would go.

Take heed, (fair *Eve*) you do not make
Another Tempter of this Snake,
A marble one so warm'd would speak.

QUESTIONS

Waller purports to describe a strange incident he has observed. Does he in all ways intend the incident to be taken as a strange one, or might he intend that, in one sense at least, all "fair ladies" play with some sort of metaphoric snake?

What differences of interpretation might have been stressed had the poem been titled "The Fall of Man"? Or "Beauty and the Beast"? Or "'Twas Ever Thus"?

Note the proportion of metaphors to statements.

It is relatively rare for poems to sustain their metaphoric pretense as faithfully as do "Departmental" and "Heaven." Poems of the order of these two may be thought of as *parables* and in them the author's intent is clearly to state his poem *entirely within the metaphor.* The more usual tendency, as demonstrated by Waller's poem, is to allow a certain amount of plain (single) statement into the metaphoric (double) statement.

At the other extreme there are some poems and even some poets who make practically no use of metaphor. In the course of reading the following poems, mark the lines that contain metaphors.

A Satirical Elegy on the Death of a Late Famous General

Jonathan Swift

His Grace! impossible! what dead!
Of old age too, and in his bed!
And could that Mighty Warrior fall?
And so inglorious, after all!
Well, since he's gone, no matter how,
The last loud trump must wake him now:
And, trust me, as the noise grows stronger,
He'd wish to sleep a little longer.
And could he be indeed so old
As by the news-papers we're told?
Threescore, I think, is pretty high;
'Twas time in conscience he should die.
This world he cumber'd long enough;
He burnt his candle to the snuff;
And that's the reason some folks think,
He left behind *so great a s . . .k.*
Behold his funeral appears,
Nor widow's sighs, nor orphan's tears,
Wont at such times each heart to pierce,
Attend the progress of his herse.
But what of that, his friends may say,
He had those honours in his day.
True to his profit and his pride,
He made them weep before he dy'd.

Come hither, all ye empty things,
Ye bubbles rais'd by breath of Kings;
Who float upon the tide of state,

Come hither, and behold your fate.
Let pride be taught by this rebuke,
How very mean a thing's a Duke;
From all his ill-got honours flung,
Turn'd to that dirt from whence he sprung.

QUESTIONS

What differences of effect may be located in Swift's "Satirical Elegy"
and Frost's "Departmental"? Both poems are clearly enough satirical.
Frost keeps his satire interesting by a careful elaboration of metaphor.
How does Swift keep his satire interesting? What does he use in place
of metaphor? At what points in the poem does he seem to be having the
most fun?

The Latest Decalogue

Arthur Hugh Clough

Thou shalt have one God only; who
Would be at the expense of two?
No graven images may be
Worshipped, except the currency.
Swear not at all; for thy curse
Thine enemy is none the worse.
At church on Sunday to attend
Will serve to keep the world thy friend.
Honor thy parents; that is, all
From whom advancement may befall.
Thou shalt not kill; but need'st not strive
Officiously to keep alive.
Do not adultery commit;
Advantage rarely comes of it.
Thou shalt not steal; an empty feat,
When it's so lucrative to cheat.
Bear not false witness; let the lie
Have time on its own wings to fly.
Thou shalt not covet, but tradition
Approves all forms of competition.

QUESTIONS

Clough has written a clear enough poem but there are, unfortunately,
American readers who will miss some of the turns of his language.
"who/Would be at the expense of two?": who would put himself to the
expense of supporting two Gods? "but need'st not strive/Officiously to
keep alive": Though we are forbidden to kill a man we certainly are not
required to take on the burden of helping him to stay alive.

There is only one metaphor in this poem. Locate it.

What is the structure of each of the ten couplets? One must note at once that each statement is divided into two parts. What is there in the working out of that pattern of statement that can serve to take the place of metaphor?

Three Poems from the Japanese

Yamabe No Akahito

Translated by Kenneth Rexroth

I

I passed by the beach
At Tago and saw
The snow falling, pure white,
High on the peak of Fuji.

II

The mists rise over
The still pools at Asuka.
Memory does not
Pass away so easily.

III

I wish I were close
To you as the wet skirt of
A salt girl to her body.
I think of you always.

Compare the method and the effect of these poems to the following translations from the Chinese.

Written on the Wall at Chang's Hermitage

Tu Fu

Translated by Kenneth Rexroth

It is Spring in the mountains.
I come alone seeking you.
The sound of chopping wood echoes
Between the silent peaks.
The streams are still icy.
There is snow on the trail.
At sunset I reach your grove

In the stony mountain pass.
You want nothing, although at night
You can see the aura of gold
And silver ore all around you.
You have learned to be gentle
As the mountain deer you have tamed.
The way back forgotten, hidden
Away, I become like you,
An empty boat, floating, adrift.

QUESTIONS

The last two lines of this poem obviously contain a metaphor. Is there a metaphor contained in the statement:

> although at night
> You can see the aura of gold
> And silver ore all around you.

Does the poet seem to intend the reader to take "the aura of gold and silver ore" literally? As perhaps a quality of the moonlight? As perhaps a spiritual quality?

A Friend Advises Me to Stop Drinking

Mei Yao Ch'en

Translated by Kenneth Rexroth

In my young days I drank a
Lot of wine. There is nothing
Wrong with the love of drink. Now
I am old and my teeth and
Hairs are few and far between.
I still love to drink, but I
Can't do it as I used to.
Now when I drink it upsets
My stomach. There is not much
Pleasure in it. Today I
Got drunk and could not hold up
My head. The room turned round and round.
Seeking pleasure, I find only
Sickness. This is certainly
Not the way to care for my health.
Maybe I should give it up
Altogether. I am afraid
People will laugh at me. Still,

You say it would be a good
Idea. There is not much pleasure
In a sour stomach and
Bad breath. I really know that I
Ought to stop it. If I don't do it,
I don't know what will happen to me.

QUESTION

The tone and attitude of this poem seem well suited to the sparse and
entirely unmetaphoric quality of the language. In one sense, that is to
say, metaphor is decorative. Why is the sort of statement that this poem
makes best served by removing all decoration?

To a Traveler

Su Tung P'o

Translated by Kenneth Rexroth

Last year when I accompanied you
As far as the Yang Chou Gate,
The snow was flying, like white willow cotton.
This year, Spring has come again,
And the willow cotton is like snow.
But you have not come back.
Alone before the open window,
I raise my wine cup to the shining moon.
The wind, moist with evening dew,
Blows the gauze curtains.
Maybe Chang-O the moon goddess,
Will pity this single swallow
And join us together with the chord of light
That reaches beneath the painted eaves of your home.

QUESTION

"Will pity this single swallow": In Chinese convention, joined swallows,
flying with one wing in common, are a symbol of steadfast love.

What is the significance of the fact that the language becomes
metaphoric when the poet is most thinking of the past, and that
metaphor disappears when he is most thinking of the present?

from **A Bestiary**

Kenneth Rexroth

DEER

Deer are gentle and graceful
And they have beautiful eyes.
They hurt no one but themselves,
The males, and only for love.
Men have invented several
Thousand ways of killing them.

HERRING

The herring is prolific.
There are plenty of herrings.
Some herrings are eaten raw.
Many are dried and pickled.
But most are used for manure.
See if you can apply this
To your history lessons.

LION

The lion is called the king
Of beasts. Nowadays there are
Almost as many lions
In cages as out of them.
If offered a crown, refuse.

YOU

Let Y stand for you who says,
"Very clever, but surely
These were not written for you
Children?" Let Y stand for yes.

QUESTIONS

Rexroth's method in his "Bestiary" is obviously influenced by his interest in Japanese and Chinese poetry. Does it seem apt to say that Rexroth makes the dramatic (and often ironic) juxtaposition of statements serve as a substitute for metaphor?

The Lion stanza contains no phrase that may be identified as a metaphor (with the possible exception of "king of beasts," which as a long-dead metaphor no longer has a metaphor's function), yet it is clearly possible to argue that the whole poem is a single metaphor. Discuss. (What, for example, would the effect have been if the last line had read: "If offered a crown, do not be like the lion, but refuse it or you, too, may end up in a cage"?)

Rexroth is not by any means the only English poet to have been powerfully influenced by Chinese and Japanese poetry. The poetic movement that began just before World War One and that was labeled imagism was deeply indebted to the Japanese and Chinese poets. The work of Amy Lowell, of H.D., and of John Gould Fletcher is characteristic of this movement, as is some of the work of Ezra Pound and of William Carlos Williams. The two following poems by Williams will illustrate.

The Red Wheelbarrow

William Carlos Williams

so much depends
upon

a red wheel
barrow

glazed with rain
water

beside the white
chickens

QUESTION

Is "glazed" a metaphor?

This Is Just to Say

William Carlos Williams

I have eaten
the plums
that were in
the icebox

and which
you were probably
saving
for breakfast

Forgive me
they were delicious
so sweet
and so cold.

The Chinese and Japanese are not the only sources for this sort of poetry. Stephen Crane, an American poet who died in 1900, had developed a similar sort of poem on his own impulse, and certainly was a native influence upon the imagists and on the kind of sparse unmetaphoric poem that developed in part from imagism.

I Saw a Man

Stephen Crane

I saw a man pursuing the horizon;
Round and round they sped.
I was disturbed at this;
I accosted the man.
"It is futile," I said,
"You can never—"
"You lie," he cried.
And ran on.

The Book of Wisdom

Stephen Crane

I met a seer.
He held a book in his hands,
The book of wisdom.
"Sir," I addressed him,
"Let me read."
"Child—" he began.
"Sir," I said,
"Think not that I am a child,
For already I know much
Of that which you hold;
Aye, much."

He smiled.
Then he opened the book
And held it before me.
Strange that I should have grown
    so suddenly blind.

The Heart

Stephen Crane

In the desert
I saw a creature, naked, bestial,
Who, squatting upon the ground,
Held his heart in his hands,

And ate of it.
I said, "Is it good, friend?"
"It is bitter—bitter," he answered;
"But I like it
Because it is bitter,
And because it is my heart."

QUESTIONS

Has Crane allowed any metaphors into these poems?

Is it possible to think of each poem as itself constituting a dramatic metaphor? For example, is the man pursuing the horizon to be taken literally or does the whole incident "stand for" something else? If each of these meetings is taken as a metaphoric X, what might be the metaphoric Y? Is the metaphoric Y specific, or is it better taken as standing for a whole area of experience? May one, that is to say, take each of these meetings—metaphorically sparse as they are in the way they are stated—as symbols?

See p. 240. There an effort was made to distinguish between metaphor and symbol. Both involve a metaphoric X that stands for a metaphoric Y. If each of these poems by Crane is taken to be a symbol, what qualities of the symbolic X and symbolic Y do they suggest as distinct from the metaphoric X and metaphoric Y?

Apply the same criteria to the Japanese and Chinese poems.

Compare the qualities of Crane's poems as symbols with the qualities of the two metaphors that occur in Swift's "Satirical Elegy."

Which of the following two poems profits more from a metaphoric reading?

The Death of the Ball Turret Gunner

Randall Jarrell

From my mother's sleep I fell into the State,
And I hunched in its belly till my wet fur froze.
Six miles from earth, loosed from its dream of life,
I woke to black flak and the nightmare fighters.
When I died they washed me out of the turret with a hose.

"I love you and the rosebush"

Armando Uribe

Translated by Miller Williams

I love you and the rosebush
gives roses. I give feet,
I give hands and eyes.

And the rosebush gives roses.

All the following poems are mixtures of metaphor and *statement*. Metaphor is of course the language of double meaning, it speaks of X in terms of Y. Statement, on the other hand, is single; it speaks of X as X. In each of the poems below underline every statement and bracket every metaphor. The following questions may then be asked of each poem.

QUESTIONS

How much statement does each poet employ as compared to how much metaphor?

A good paragraph tends to have a topic assertion followed by evidence or analysis in support of that assertion, or it tends to present a chain of evidence or analysis which is then summarized in a generalizing state-ment. In certain kinds of more sophisticated writing those opening assertions or closing summaries are omitted, or not so much omitted as left implicit. In all good writing there still tends to be present a relation of assertion (or summary) to evidence.

In each of these poems, does the poet tend to make his assertions or summaries as statements which are supported by metaphors, or does he make his assertions or summaries as metaphors which are sup-ported by statements?

Does the change from statement to metaphor or from metaphor to statement bear any relation to changes in the poet's tone or attitude?

Distinguish, wherever possible, between symbols and metaphors.

The World Is Too Much with Us; Late and Soon

William Wordsworth

The world is too much with us; late and soon
Getting and spending, we lay waste our powers:
Little we see in Nature that is ours;
We have given our hearts away, a sordid boon!
The Sea that bares her bosom to the moon;
The winds that will be howling at all hours,
And are up-gathered now like sleeping flowers;
For this, for everything, we are out of tune;
It moves us not.—Great God! I'd rather be
A Pagan suckled in a creed outworn;
So might I, standing on this pleasant lea,
Have glimpses that would make me less forlorn;
Have sight of Proteus rising from the sea;
Or hear old Triton blow his wreathèd horn.

QUESTIONS

"The Sea that bares her bosom to the moon" may, on one level, be taken simply as a visual image of the sea as a great breast. The metaphor, however, imputes certain qualities to the sea, suggesting that it is a great mother from which the moon sucks its life force. How does that suggestion relate to Wordsworth's assertion that we are losing our life force? And how does it relate to the pagan who sees Proteus and Triton (other life-force symbols) rising from the sea? Note that Wordsworth would not only prefer an outworn creed to ignorance of the life force, but that he would rather be "suckled" in it. Thus the whole poem is animated by the suggestion of the infant (the individual) drawing the life substance from the great mother (nature).

Sonnet LXXIII

William Shakespeare

That time of year thou mayst in me behold
When yellow leaves, or none, or few, do hang
Upon those boughs which shake against the cold,
Bare ruined choirs, where late the sweet birds sang;
In me thou see'st the twilight of such day
As after sunset fadeth in the west,
Which by and by black night doth take away,
Death's second self, that seals up all in rest.
In me thou see'st the glowing of such fire
That on the ashes of its youth doth lie,
As the death-bed whereon it must expire,
Consumed with that which it was nourished by.
This thou perceiv'st, which makes thy love more strong,
To love that well which thou must leave ere long.

QUESTIONS

Sonnet LXXIII consists of three metaphoric comparisons, each of which is stated in four lines, and all of which are summarized in two lines of statement. What is the progression of the metaphors from winter of the year through twilight of the day to last glow of the fire? How does that progression relate to the summarizing statement?

On First Looking into Chapman's Homer

John Keats

Much have I travelled in the realms of gold,
  And many goodly states and kingdoms seen;
  Round many western islands have I been
Which bards in fealty to Apollo hold.
Oft of one wide expanse had I been told
  That deep-browed Homer ruled as his demesne:

Yet never did I breathe its pure serene
Till I heard Chapman speak out loud and bold.
Then felt I like some watcher of the skies
    When a new planet swims into his ken;
Or like stout Cortez when with eagle eyes
    He stared at the Pacific—and all his men
Looked at each other with a wild surmise—
    Silent, upon a peak in Darien.

QUESTION

"Till I heard Chapman speak out loud and bold" is the only statement
in this poem, and even that may be argued to contain metaphoric
elements. The rest of the poem consists of three metaphors: of traveling
in "realms of gold," of an astronomer discovering a new planet, and of
Cortez (Balboa, of course) discovering the Pacific. What do these scat-
tered images have in common and how do they relate to the statement?

Sonnet

Samuel Daniel

Fair is my Love, and cruel as she is fair;
    Her brow shades frowns, although her eyes are sunny,
    Her smiles are lightning, though her pride despair;
    And her disdains are Gall, her favors Honey.
A modest maid, deckt with a blush of honor,
    Whose feet do tread green paths of youth and love,
    The wonder of all eyes that look upon her:
    Sacred on earth, design'd a Saint above.
Chastity and Beauty, which were deadly foes,
    Live reconcilèd friends within her brow:
    And had she pity to conjoin with those,
Then who had heard the plaint I utter now?
    For had she not been fair, and thus unkind,
    My Muse had slept, and none had known my mind.

QUESTION

How does the quality of Daniel's metaphors compare with those of
Keats?

---

design'd a Saint above: designed (so made as) to be a saint in heaven after she departs from
this world. **Sense of the final couplet:** Had she not been beautiful and at the same time as
unkind as I have shown her to be, nothing would have compelled me to write this lament,
and thus no one would have known about her.

Young Reynard

George Meredith

Gracefullest leaper, the dappled fox-cub
Curves over brambles with berries and buds,
Light as a bubble that flies from the tub,
Whisked by the laundry-wife out of her suds.
Wavy he comes, wooly, all at his ease,
Elegant, fashioned to foot with the deuce;
Nature's own prince of the dance: then he sees
Me, and retires as if making excuse.

Never closed minuet courtlier! Soon
Cub-hunting troops were abroad, and a yelp
Told of sure scent: ere the stroke upon noon
Reynard the younger lay far beyond help.
Wild, my poor friend, has the fate to be chased;
Civil will conquer: were 't other 'twere worse;
Fair, by the flushed early morning embraced,
Haply you live a day longer in verse.

QUESTION

Note that Meredith's metaphors are almost exclusively descriptive and
that all his larger implications are made as statements. How does this
order of metaphor contrast with that of Keats in "On First Looking into
Chapman's Homer?"

To a Waterfowl

William Cullen Bryant

Whither, midst falling dew,
While glow the heavens with the last steps of day,
Far, through their rosy depths, does thou pursue
Thy solitary way?

Vainly the fowler's eye
Might mark thy distant flight to do thee wrong,
As, darkly seen against the crimson sky,
Thy figure floats along.

Seek'st thou the plashy brink
Of weedy lake, or marge of river wide,
Or where the rocking billows rise and sink
On the chafed ocean-side?

Sense of lines 5 and 6 of stanza 2: What is wild (the fox) is fated to be chased by what is
man-controlled (the dogs) and what is man-controlled (civil) will conquer. Were it the other
way around, that would be worse.

There is a Power whose care
Teaches thy way along that pathless coast—
The desert and illimitable air—
  Lone wandering but not lost.

All day thy wings have fanned,
At that far height, the cold, thin atmosphere,
Yet stoop not, weary, to the welcome land,
  Though the dark night is near.

And soon that toil shall end;
Soon shalt thou find a summer home, and rest,
And scream among thy fellows; reeds shall bend,
  Soon, o'er thy sheltered nest.

Thou'rt gone, the abyss of heaven
Hath swallowed up thy form; yet, on my heart
Deeply has sunk the lesson thou has given,
  And shall not soon depart.

He who, from zone to zone,
Guides through the boundless sky thy certain flight,
In the long way that I must tread alone,
  Will lead my steps aright.

QUESTION

How does the metaphoric method of "To a Waterfowl" compare with
that of the following poem by Peter Viereck?

Poet

Peter Viereck

> Toute forme créée, même par l'homme, est immortelle.
> Car la forme est indépendente de la matière, et ce ne sont pas les
> molécules qui constituent la forme.
>
> Baudelaire, *"Mon Coeur Mis a Nu"*

I

The night he died, earth's images all came
To gloat in liberation round his tomb.
Now vengeful colors, stones, and faces dare
  To argue with his metaphor;
And stars his fancy painted on the skies
Drop down like swords
                to pierce his too wide eyes.

II

Words that begged favor at his court in vain—
Lush adverbs, senile rhymes in tattered gowns—
  Send notes to certain exiled nouns
And mutter openly against his reign.
While rouged clichés hang out red lights again,
Hoarse refugees report from far-flung towns
That exclamation-marks are running wild
And prowling half-truths carried off a child.

III

But he lives on in Form, and Form shall shatter
  This tuneless mutiny of Matter.
His bones are dead; his voice is horribly strong.
Those famed vibrations of life's dancing dust,
Whose thrice-named pangs are "birth" and "death" and "lust,"
Are but the split iambics of his song.
Scansion of flesh in endless ebb and flow,
The drums of duty and renown's great gong—
Mere grace-notes of that living thousand-year
Tyrannic metronome whose every gear
Is some shy craftsman buried long ago.
What terror crowns the sweetness of all songs?

IV

What hardness leaps at us from each soft tune,
And hammers us to shapes we never planned?
This was a different dying from our own.
  Call every wizard in the land—
Bell, book, and test tube; let the dark be rife
With every exorcism we command.
In vain. This death is stronger than our life.

V

In vain we drive our stakes through such a haunter
Or woo with spiced applaudings such a heart.
His news of April do but mock our Winter
Like maps of heaven breathed on window-frost
By cruel clowns in codes whose key is lost.
Yet some sereneness in our rage has guessed
That we are being blessed and blessed and blessed
When least we know it and when coldest art
  Seems hostile,
              useless,
          or apart.

VI

Not worms, not worms in such a skull
But rhythms, rhythms writhe and sting and crawl.
He sings the seasons round, from bud to snow.
And all things are because he willed them so.

In "Exchange" a wish and a fear are each compared to a constant
drone over the telephone, and the reader is told various ways in which
the comparisons "work," ways in which they really are *like* that. On the
other hand, "Meditation for a Pickle Suite" asks us to see as "pick-
lelike" a number of things we may have trouble associating with pick-
les, and the poet chooses not to help us.

QUESTIONS

How would you defend, one by one, Dillard's pickle comparisons?

Is Stuart successful in defending his telephone similes? That is, were
you convinced that the two sides of the simile in each case are like each
other in some important way, or ways?

It might be useful to consider how alike two things have to be to
serve effectively as sides of a comparison in a poem, and what the
relation is between the thing itself and the characteristic of that thing
pointed to in the comparison. To put it in the form of a question, when
we hear someone described as "a bull," what characteristic of a bull
comes to our minds? as "a bulldog"? as "a mouse"?

Pick several metaphors and similes at random from the poems in this
section and list for each one the characteristics which the two sides
have in common. How many characteristics do you generally find, and
how central are they to the nature of the thing on the right-hand side of
the comparison—the thing brought in to illuminate our understanding
of the left-hand side of the comparison, the thing being talked about?

Exchange

Dabney Stuart

It's always there, like the drone
I hear when I pick up the telephone,
Steady, uninsistent, satisfied
With never having made a vow or lied
Or done anything, in fact, but been
Around, ubiquitous, yet mine.
The wish to die, I mean.

It's always there, like the drone
I hear when the voice at the other end
Hangs up, having said it all
For once. As long as I hang on no other call
Can break through to me, standing alone.
I have to dial to hide that constant tone.
The fear of death, I mean.

Meditation for a Pickle Suite

R. H. W. Dillard

Morning: the soft release
As you open a jar of pickles.
The sun through the window warm
And moving like light through brine,
The shadows of pickles swim the floor.
And in the tree, flowing down the chimney,
The songs of fresh birds clean as pickles.
Memories float through the day
Like pickles, perhaps sweet gherkins.
The past rises and falls
Like curious pickles in dark jars,
Your hands sure as pickles,
Opening dreams like albums,
Pale Polish pickles.
Your eyes grow sharp as pickles,
Thoughts as green, as shining ,
As rows of pickles, damp and fresh,
Placed out in the afternoon sun.

Both the following poems deal metaphorically with a person in bed, being attended by others, waiting for something to happen. In each case the poet has used comparison—spelled out in "Gamecock," barely suggested in "A Timepiece"—to deepen our understanding of the person talked about.

QUESTIONS

Do you feel that one of the metaphors does this more effectively than the other?

Seeing a poem as a performance, which of these do you enjoy more?

Seeing it as an experience you share with the poet, which do you find most exciting to the imagination?

Can you give reasons for your responses?

Gamecock

James Dickey

Fear, jealousy and murder are the same
When they put on their long reddish feathers,
Their shawl neck and moccasin head
In a tree bearing levels of women.
There is yet no thread

Of light, and his scabbed feet tighten,
Holding sleep as though it were lockjaw,
His feathers damp, his eyes crazed
And cracked like the eyes
Of a chicken head cut off or wrung-necked

While he waits for the sun's only cry
All night building up in his throat
To leap out and turn the day red,
To tumble his hens from the pine tree,
And then will go down, his hackles

Up, looking everywhere for the other
Cock who could not be there,
Head ruffed and sullenly stepping
As upon his best human-curved steel:
He is like any fierce

Old man in a terminal ward:
There is the same look of waiting
That the sun prepares itself for;
The enraged, surviving-
another-day blood,

And from him at dawn comes the same
Cry that the world cannot stop.
In all the great building's blue windows
The sun gains strength; on all floors, women
Awaken—wives, nurses, sisters and daughters—

And he lies back, his eyes filmed, unappeased,
As all of them, clucking, pillow-patting,
Come to help his best savagery blaze, doomed, dead-
game, demanding, unreasonably
Battling to the death for what is his.

A Timepiece

James Merrill

Of a pendulum's mildness, with her feet up
My sister lay expecting her third child.
Over the hammock's crescent spilled
Her flushed face, grazing clover and buttercup.

Her legs were troubling her, a vein had burst.
Even so, among partial fullnesses she lay
Of pecked damson, of daughters at play
Who in the shadow of the house rehearsed

Her gait, her gesture, unnatural to them,
But they would master it soon enough, grown tall
Trusting that out of themselves came all
That full grace, while she out of whom these came

Shall have thrust fullness from her, like a death.
Already, seeing the little girls listless
She righted herself in a new awkwardness.
It was not *her* life she was heavy with.

Let us each have some milk, my sister smiled
Meaning to muffle with the taste
Of unbuilt bone a striking in her breast,
For soon by what it tells the clock is stilled.

Poems for Study: Single and Multiple Imagery

The Single Image. The poems that immediately follow all develop a
central theme in terms of a single sustained comparison. They are con-
structed, that is to say, on a dominant metaphor.

As in the case of John Donne's great compass image in the last three
stanzas of "A Valediction Forbidding Mourning," the pleasure of such
sustained comparisons must lie in (a) their aptness to the subject and to
the poet's tone and attitude, (b) the inventiveness with which the poet
draws more and more points of meaningful comparison from his basic
metaphor, and (c) the management of the poet in making his inventions
seem natural, unstrained, and inevitable. If at any point in a poem
constructed on a single dominant metaphor, the poet must violate his
metaphoric structure in order to make his point, that is bound to seem a
breach of metaphoric contract.

Compare the following sonnet by Shakespeare with the rewritten
version that follows it. The rewritten version contains many points at
which the basic comparison of love to a fever is either violated or
loosened. Discuss the effect of those changes.

Sonnet CXLVII

William Shakespeare

My love is as a fever, longing still
For that which longer nurseth the disease,
Feeding on that which doth preserve the ill,
The uncertain sickly appetite to please.
My reason, the physician to my love,
Angry that his prescriptions are not kept,
Hath left me, and I desperate now approve
Desire is death, which physic did except.
Past cure I am, now reason is past care,
And frantic-mad, with evermore unrest;
My thoughts and my discourse as madmen's are,
At random from the truth vainly expressed:
For I have sworn thee fair, and thought thee bright,
Who art as black as hell, as dark as night.

Sonnet CXLVII

(rewritten in order to weaken the dominant metaphor)

My love is as a fever, longing still
For that which longer strengthens the disease,
Lusting for that which doth confirm the ill,
The uncertain fickle passion to appease.
My reason, the inspirer of my love,
Angry that his sage counsels are not kept,
Berates me, and I desperate now approve
Desire is mad, which wisdom did except.
Past hope I am, now all is in despair,
And robbed and stripped of every rag of rest.
My thoughts and my discourse as gossips' are,
At random from the truth vainly expressed:
For I have sworn thee fair, and thought thee bright,
Who are as black as hell, as dark as night.

Note that Shakespeare's sonnet develops the basic metaphor of love as a delirious fever without interruption. The single comparison flows on for twelve lines. It is then abandoned and a final couplet states Shakespeare's reasons for thinking of love in such terms.

Eliot's "The Hippopotamus" also develops a single comparison, but in a different way. The poet constantly interrupts his metaphor in order to apply it. Thus the first two lines of each stanza make a statement

Lines 1–4: Shakespeare compares his love to a fever that seeks to continue itself, thus to preserve the disease rather than to take the prescription of reason. **approve:** prove. Sense: thus in my desperation I prove (demonstrate) that that desire which refuses medicine ("physic did except"; "take exception to") is death.

about the hippopotamus, and the last two lines comment on that statement, usually by making that statement into a direct comparison with the Church. Stanzas seven and eight vary that pattern. What is the effect of changing the pattern at that point in the poem?

The Hippopotamus

T. S. Eliot

Similiter et omnes revereantur Diaconos, ut mandatum Jesu Christi; et Episcopum, ut Jesum Christum, existentem filium Patris; Presbyteros autem, ut concilium Dei et conjunctionem Apostolorum. Sine his Ecclesia non vocatur; de quibis suadeo vos sic habeo.*

S. Ignatii ad Trallianos

And when this epistle is read among you, cause that it be read also in the church of the Laodiceans.

The broad-backed hippopotamus
Rests on his belly in the mud;
Although he seems so firm to us
He is merely flesh and blood.

Flesh and blood is weak and frail,
Susceptible to nervous shock;
While the True Church can never fail
For it is based upon a rock.

The hippo's feeble steps may err,
In compassing material ends,
While the True Church need never stir
To gather in its dividends.

The 'potamus can never reach
The mango on the mango-tree;
But fruits of pomegranate and peach
Refresh the Church from over sea.

At mating time the hippo's voice
Betrays inflexions hoarse and odd,
But every week we hear rejoice
The Church, at being one with God.

* "And likewise let all the deacons be reverenced, as commanded by Jesus Christ; and let the bishop be reverenced, as Jesus Christ, the living son of the Father; also let the presbyters be reverenced, as the council of God and the assembly of the apostles. Without these there can be no church; of these things I persuade you as I can."

Saint Ignatius' third epistle to the Traillians

The hippopotamus's day
Is passed in sleep; at night he hunts;
God works in a mysterious way—
The Church can sleep and feed at once.

I saw the 'potamus take wing
Ascending from the damp savannas,
And quiring angels round him sing
The praise of God, in loud hosannas.

Blood of the Lamb shall wash him clean
And him shall heavenly arms enfold,
Among the saints he shall be seen
Performing on a harp of gold.

He shall be washed as white as snow,
By all the martyr'd virgins kist,
While the True Church remains below
Wrapt in the old miasmal mist.

QUESTIONS

"The Hippopotamus" is obviously written as a satire of what Eliot labels "the True Church." What in the quality of the comparison makes for satire? (Compare Goldsmith's remarks on Homer, p. 119, as one clue.)

Savannas are the tropical grasslands where the hippo roams, the miasmal mist is the mist from the rivers and marshes the hippo inhabits. Why does Eliot say that the hippo will ascend to heaven while the Church takes his place in the miasmal mist?

What is there in the tone of Saint Ignatius' epistle to the Traillians that connects with Eliot's tone in satirizing the True Church as a great ungainly beast?

The poems that follow are all in one way or another built on a single basic image. They are presented without comment as an opportunity for the reader to apply in his own way the criteria that have been developed.

The Flea

John Donne

Marke but this flea, and marke in this,
How little that which thou deny'st me is;
It suck'd me first, and now sucks thee,
And in this flea, our two bloods mingled bee;

Thou know'st that this cannot be said
A sinne, nor shame, nor losse of maidenhead,
   Yet this enjoyes before it wooe,
   And pamper'd swells with one blood made of two,
   And this, alas, is more than we would doe.

Oh stay, three lives in one flea spare,
Where wee almost, yea more than married are.
This flea is you and I, and this
Our marriage bed, and marriage temple is;
Though parents grudge, and you, w'are met,
And cloysterd in these living walls of Jet.
   Though use make you apt to kill mee,
   Let not to that, selfe murder added bee,
   And sacrilege, three sinnes in killing three.

Cruell and sodaine, has thou since
Purpled thy naile, in blood of innocence?
Wherein could this flea guilty bee,
Except in that drop which it suckt from thee?
Yet thou triumph'st and saist that thou
Find'st not thy selfe, nor mee the weaker now;
   'Tis true, then learne how false, feares bee;
   Just so much honor, when thou yeeld's to mee,
   Will wast, as this flea's death took life from thee.

A Simile for Her Smile

Richard Wilbur

Your smiling, or the hope, the thought of it,
Makes in my mind such pause and abrupt ease
As when the highway bridgegates fall,
Balking the hasty traffic, which must sit
On each side massed and staring, while
Deliberately the drawbridge starts to rise:

Then horns are hushed, the oilsmoke rarefies,
Above the idling motors one can tell
The packet's smooth approach, the slip,
Slip of the silken river past the sides,
The ringing of clear bells, the dip
And slow cascading of the paddle wheel.

A Poison Tree

William Blake

I was angry with my friend:
I told my wrath, my wrath did end.
I was angry with my foe:
I told it not, my wrath did grow.

And I water'd it in fears,
Night and morning with my tears:
And I sunnèd it with smiles,
And with soft deceitful wiles.

And it grew both day and night,
Till it bore an apple bright;
And my foe beheld it shine,
And he knew that it was mine,

And into my garden stole
When the night had veil'd the pole:
In the morning glad I see
My foe outstretch'd beneath the tree.

Mind

Richard Wilbur

Mind in its purest play is like some bat
That beats about in caverns all alone,
Contriving by a kind of senseless wit
Not to conclude against a wall of stone.

It has no need to falter or explore;
Darkly it knows what obstacles are there,
And so may weave and flitter, dip and soar
In perfect courses through the blackest air.

And has this simile a like perfection?
The mind is like a bat. Precisely. Save
That in the very happiest intellection
A graceful error may correct the cave.

Multiple Images.   All the poems that immediately follow are built on
many images rather than on a single basic comparison. All of them are

in some sense catalogues, though in some cases the catalogue is more formal than in others.

Since poems constructed of multiple images lack the denotative unity of poems built on a single image, the unity of their images must be found—if at all—in the connotations (overtones) exactly as in the analysis of overtone themes in the diction of the poem. *Any reasonable analysis of poetic overtones, in fact, must combine the overtone themes of the words and the images into a single unity.* In fact, nothing but confusion could follow were one to think in terms of one set of overtones for the diction and of another for the images. Word and image are forever closely related, and they are usually inseparable. These overtones may gather into a single *overtone theme,* or into combinations of theme and countertheme, as in the first six stanzas of Donne's "Valediction."

A *catalogue,* a more or less deliberate listing of metaphors and properties, was dealt with briefly in Chapter Three. Theoretically, a catalogue might be based on a single metaphor, as would be the case were one to write a poem called "The House of Love" in which he compiled a list of all the furnishings of the house as metaphoric equivalents of love. Yet within that single image the catalogue would have to reach in many directions to bring together such disparate elements as roof, fireplace, storehouse, and foundation. Even more importantly, the basic impulse of the catalogue is akin to name magic: the poet writing a catalogue tends simply to *list* his properties without any such metaphoric development and connection of image to image, unlike what one finds in Donne's "Valediction."

A catalogue, then, may be taken to be a *list* of properties under a single topic. The impulse of the poet in making such a list is primarily to *name things.* The topic, moreover, is almost always a *statement* rather than a metaphor. "I hear America singing," states Whitman; he then proceeds to name the many ways in which he hears that singing. So Mrs. Browning asks "How do I love thee?" and then lists the ways. So Rupert Brooke states "These I have loved," and compiles, without much metaphoric development of any one item, the list of his most enduring pleasures.

When, on the other hand, there is no deliberate assertion of a topic, but rather a development from image to image, each succeeding image called into being not by a single original assertion, but by the suggestion of what has gone before it (once again, as in the first six stanzas of Donne's "Valediction")—that method is better taken to be the development of an overtone theme.

The following questions may be asked of all these poems.

QUESTIONS

How many overtone themes are identifiable? What is the connotative quality of each overtone theme? (What is the principle of selection of each overtone theme?)

What progression is observable in the development of each overtone theme? (Do the images go from large to small? From less intense to more intense? Do they develop by some sort of parallelism? By a series of balanced antitheses? From near to far? From relatively concrete to relatively abstract?

If there is more than one overtone theme, are there any image elements common to both themes and, if so, how do they serve to bring the two themes together?

Within each theme what relative proportion of the images are metaphors? Properties? How many of the metaphors are basically sensory and how many tend to be symbols?

What is the proportion of statement to metaphor, and how are the two related?

If the poem is a catalogue, what is its topic assertion? What is the proportion of properties to metaphors? Are any of the metaphors elaborated or is the poet satisfied simply to name his elements? Is there any order of development in the listing or are the details listed at random?

In "Ars Poetica," MacLeish makes a statement that has become famous in literary discussion:

> A poem should not mean
> But be.

That statement concludes three catalogues of images detailing what a poem is. How are the images of each of these following poems related to the "being" (which is to say, the performance) of the poem?

These poems are built at least in part of catalogues. In which of the poems do the lists move through a natural order, such as days of the week or the probable steps in a process? Compare these to the poems in which the list seems most random. Which catalogues do you enjoy more? Look again at the "random" lists and see if you can discover a *rightness* in the grouping of the items and perhaps even in their sequence that you had not seen before.

Ars Poetica

Archibald MacLeish

A poem should be palpable and mute
As a globed fruit,

Dumb
As old medallions to the thumb,

Silent as the sleeve-worn stone
Of casement ledges where the moss has grown—

A poem should be wordless
As the flight of birds.

A poem should be motionless in time
As the moon climbs,

Leaving, as the moon releases
Twig by twig the night-entangled trees,

Leaving, as the moon behind the winter leaves,
Memory by memory the mind—

A poem should be motionless in time
As the moon climbs.

A poem should be equal to:
Not true.

For all the history of grief
An empty doorway and a maple leaf.

For love
The leaning grasses and two lights above the sea—

A poem should not mean
But be.

QUESTION

Assume that "Ars Poetica" had been written without images and that
the following is what is left:

A poem should be palpable, mute,
Dumb,
Silent,
And wordless.

It should be motionless
In a single illuminated
Moment of time.

It should be equal to:
Not true,
Expressing each concept
In a single telling symbol.
Thus
A poem should not mean
But be.

Ignoring the debauchery of the rhythm incident to such manhandling,
what part of the poem's "being" has been removed from it?

How Do I Love Thee?

Elizabeth Barrett Browning

How do I love thee? Let me count the ways.
I love thee to the depth and breadth and height
My soul can reach, when feeling out of sight
For the ends of Being and ideal Grace.
I love thee to the level of everyday's
Most quiet need, by sun and candle-light.
I love thee freely, as men strive for Right;
I love thee purely, as they turn from Praise.
I love thee with the passion put to use
In my old griefs, and with my childhood's faith.
I love thee with a love I seemed to lose
With my lost saints—I love three with the breath,
Smiles, tears, of all my life!—and, if God choose,
I shall but love thee better after death.

QUESTION

Lines 12–13 seem to be offered as a summary of the ways in which the poet loves. Do all the elements in the preceding catalogue fit that summary (that is, does the summary state the unifying principle of the catalogue)?

What the Sonnet Is

Eugene Lee Hamilton

Fourteen small broidered berries on the hem
Of Circe's mantle, each of magic gold;
Fourteen of lone Calypso's tears that rolled
Into the sea, for pearls to come of them;
Fourteen clear signs of omen in the gem
With which Medea human fate foretold;
Fourteen small drops, which Faustus, growing old,
Craved of the Fiend, to water Life's dry stem.
It is the pure white diamond Dante brought
To Beatrice, the sapphire Laura wore
When Petrarch cut it sparkling out of thought;
The ruby Shakespeare hewed from his heart's core;
The dark deep emerald that Rossetti wrought
For his own soul, to wear for ever more.

Circe: the enchantress of the Odyssey who changed men into beasts. **Calypso:** the nymph who detained Odysseus for seven years on her island. **Medea:** the enchantress who helped Jason win the Golden Fleece of Colchis. **drops . . . to water Life's dry stem:** the blood of Christ. One drop would serve to win Faustus' redemption but the Devil (in Marlowe's *Faustus*) would not allow Faustus that drop. **Beatrice:** Dante's symbol of Divine Love. **Laura:** the Lady of Petrarch's sonnets.

QUESTION

Hamilton's sonnet is a catalogue of eight things to which the sonnet is
equated. What have the elements of this catalogue in common in their
denotations? In their connotations?

The Great Lover

Rupert Brooke

I have been so great a lover: filled my days
So proudly with the splendor of Love's praise,
The pain, the calm, and the astonishment,
Desire illimitable, and still content,
And all dear names men use, to cheat despair,
For the perplexed and viewless streams that bear
Our hearts at random down the dark of life.
Now, ere the unthinking silence on that strife
Steals down, I would cheat drowsy Death so far,
My night shall be remembered for a star
That outshone all the suns of all men's days.
Shall I not crown them with immortal praise
Whom I have loved, who have given, dared with me
High secrets, and in darkness knelt to see
The inenarrable godhead of delight?
Love is a flame:—we have beaconed the world's night.
A city:—we have built it, these and I.
An emperor:—we have taught the world to die.
So, for their sakes I loved, ere I go hence,
And the high cause of Love's magnificence,
And to keep loyalties young, I'll write those names
Golden for ever, eagles, crying flames,
And set them as a banner, that men may know,
To dare the generations, burn, and blow
Out on the wind of Time, shining and streaming . . .
These I have loved:
    White plates and cups, clean-gleaming,
Ringed with blue lines; and feathery, faery dust;
Wet roofs, beneath the lamp-light; the strong crust
Of friendly bread; and many-tasting food;
Rainbows; and the blue bitter smoke of wood;
And radiant raindrops couching in cool flowers;
And flowers themselves, that sway through sunny hours,
Dreaming of moths that drink them under the moon;
Then, the cool kindliness of sheets, that soon
Smooth away trouble; and the rough male kiss
Of blankets; grainy wood; live hair that is
Shining and free; blue-massing clouds; the keen
Unpassioned beauty of a great machine;

The benison of hot water; furs to touch;
The good smell of old clothes; and other such—
The comfortable smell of friendly fingers,
Hair's fragrance, and the musty reek that lingers
About dead leaves and last year's ferns. . . .
                      Dear names,
And thousand others throng me! Royal flames;
Sweet water's dimpling laugh from tap or spring;
Holes in the ground; and voices that do sing:
Voices in laughter, too; and body's pain,
Soon turned to peace; and the deep-panting train;
Firm sands; the little dulling edge of foam
That browns and dwindles as the wave goes home;
And washen stones, gay for an hour; the cold
Graveness of iron; moist black earthen mold;
Sleep; and high places; footprints in the dew;
And oaks; and brown horse-chestnuts, glossy-new;
And new-peeled sticks and shining pools on grass;—
All these have been my loves. And these shall pass,
Whatever passes not, in the great hour,
Nor all my passion, all my prayers, have power
To hold me with them through the gate of Death.
They'll play deserter, turn with traitor breath,
Break the high bond we made, and sell Love's trust
And sacramental covenant to the dust.
—Oh, never a doubt but, somewhere, I shall wake,
And give what's left of love again, and make
New friends now strangers. . . .
                    But the best I've known
Stays here, and changes, breaks, grows old, is blown
About the winds of the world, and fades from brains
Of living men, and dies.
              Nothing remains.
O dear my loves, O faithless, once again
This one last gift I give: that after men
Shall know, and later lovers, far-removed
Praise you, "All these were lovely"; say, "He loved."

QUESTIONS

"The Great Lover" centers on the catalogue beginning "These I have loved." Before and after the catalogue the poet explains its importance to him. At the end he points out that all the things he has loved are temporary. There are, for example, no angels, eternal verities, cosmic laws, geometric theorems, or unfading essences among the items of his catalogue. Have those items anything else in common? That is, what principle of selection chooses the items from Brooke's catalogue?

Some of those items are metaphoric and some are properties. What is the connotative force of the metaphoric items? Do the connotations of the properties harmonize with the connotations of the metaphors?

Is the catalogue more interesting in itself than in Brooke's comment on it, before and after?

Compare Brooke's catalogue with that of the following poem by Karl Shapiro. Scyros, it is interesting to note, is the island on which Brooke met his death, and the motto "snuffle and sniff and handkerchief" is from one of Brooke's letters.

Scyros

Karl Shapiro

snuffle and sniff and handkerchief

  The doctor punched my vein
  The Captain called me Cain
Upon my belly sat the sow of fear
    With coins on either eye
    The President came by
And whispered to the braids what none could hear

  High over where the storm
  Stood steadfast cruciform
The golden eagle sank in wounded wheels
    White negroes laughing still
    Crept fiercely on Brazil
Turning the navies upward on their keels

  Now one by one the trees
  Stripped to their naked knees
To dance upon the heaps of shrunken dead
    The roof of England fell
    Great Paris tolled her bell
And China staunched her milk and wept for bread

  No island singly lay
  But lost its name that day
The Ainu dived across the plunging sands
    From dawn to dawn to dawn
    King George's birds came on
Strafing the tulips from his children's hands

  Thus in the classic sea
  Southeast from Thessaly
The dynamited mermen washed ashore
    And tritons dressed in steel
    Trolled heads with rod and reel
And dredged potatoes from the Aegean floor

Hot is the sky and green
Where Germans have been seen
The moon leaks metal on the Atlantic fields
Pink boys in birthday shrouds
Look lightly through the clouds
Or coast the peaks of Finland on their shields

That prophet year by year
Lay still but could not hear
Where scholars tapped to find his new remains
Gog and Magog ate pork
In vertical New York
And war began next Monday on the Danes.

It is clear enough that Shapiro's images were chosen by a principle of selection and for a purpose markedly different from those that chose the images of "The Great Lover." Note that Shapiro gives no explanation for his catalogue but leaves it to stand as itself.

The careful reader will have no difficulty in seeing that Shapiro has reached in many directions for images whose force will express his sense of modern war. Certainly the opening three lines can describe nothing but the scene of a man's induction into the army; and the following three, nothing but a glimpse of the President discussing matters of war policy with the ranking brass. Thereafter all seems to be made of scattered glimpses of destruction flung meaninglessly all over the globe. To emphasize that sense of meaninglessness, Shapiro has built many of his images upon paradoxes and has left out all interrelating statements, even omitting all punctuation except for the final period.

QUESTION

Can Shapiro's images be taken as a simple catalogue illustrating the inhumanity of mechanical war, or should one identify two themes in this poem, one working against the other?

Gee I Like to Think of Dead

E. E. Cummings

gee i like to think of dead it means nearer because deeper
firmer since darker than little round water at one end of
the well   it's too cool to be crooked and it's too firm
to be hard but it's sharp and thick and it loves,   every
old thing falls in rosebugs and jacknives and kittens and
pennies they all sit there looking at each other having the
fastest time because they've never met before

dead's more even than how many ways of sitting on
your head your unnatural hair has in the morning

dead's clever too like POF goes the alarm off and the
little striker having the best time tickling away every-
body's brain so everybody just puts out their finger
and they stuff the poor thing all full of fingers

dead has a smile like the nicest man you've never met
who maybe winks at you in a streetcar and you pretend
you don't but really you do see and you are My how
glad he winked and hope he'll do it again

or if it talks about you somewhere behind your back it
makes your neck feel pleasant and stoopid   and if
dead says may i have this one and was never intro-
duced you say Yes because you know you want it to
dance with you and it wants to and it can dance and
Whocares

dead's fine like hands do you see that water flowerpots
in windows but they live higher in their house than
you so that's all you see but you don't want to

dead's happy like the way underclothes All so differ-
ently solemn and inti and sitting on one string

dead never says my dear,Time for your musiclesson
and you like music and to have somebody play who
can but you know you never can and why have to?

dead's nice like a dance where you danced simple hours
and you take all your prickly-clothes off and squeeze-
into-largeness without one word   and you lie still as
anything   in largeness and this largeness begins to
give you,the dance all over again and you,feel all again
all over the way men you liked made you feel when they
touched you(but that's not all)because largeness tells
you so you can feel what you made,men feel when,you
touched,them

dead's sorry like a thistlefluff-thing which goes land-
ing away all by himself on somebody's roof or some-
thing where who-ever-heard-of-growing and nobody
expects you to anyway

dead says come with me he says(and whyevernot)into
the round well and see the kitten and the penny and
the jacknife and the rosebug

and you say Sure you
say (like that) sure i'll come with you you say for i
like kittens i do and jacknives i do and pennies i do
and rosebugs i do

QUESTIONS

"The poem is a catalogue of the fantasies that go through a young girl's head when she thinks of death, an idea strongly connected in her mind with the idea of sex. The girl, by the very terms in which she thinks, can be identified as living in some large city—almost certainly New York—but it is clear that she has come there from a rural childhood." Discuss this comment.

Is this catalogue connotatively united?

What is the tone of the girl's thinking? Is the tone constant or does it change at any point?

Dirge

Kenneth Fearing

1-2-3 was the number he played but today the number came
   3-2-1;
   bought his Carbide at 30 but it went to 29; had the
   favorite at Bowie but the track was slow—

O, executive type, would you like to drive a floating power,
   knee action, silk-upholstered six? Wed a Hollywood star?
   Shoot the course in 58? Draw to the ace, king, jack?
O, fellow with a will who won't take no, watch out for three
   cigarettes on the same, single match; O democratic voter
   born in August under Mars, beware of liquidated rails—

Dénouement to dénouement, he took a personal pride in the
   certain, certain way he lived his own, private life,
   but nevertheless, they shut off his gas; nevertheless,
   the bank foreclosed; nevertheless, the landlord called;
   nevertheless, the radio broke,

And twelve o'clock arrived just once too often,
   just the same he wore one gray tweed suit, bought one
      straw hat, drank one straight Scotch, walked one short
      step, took one long look, drew one deep breath,
   just one too many,

And wow he died as wow he lived,
   going whop to the office and blooie home to sleep and
      biff got married and bam had children and oof got fired,
   zowie did he live and zowie did he die,

With who the hell are you at the corner of his casket,
and where the hell we going on the right hand silver
knob, and who the hell cares walking second from the
end with an American Beauty wreath from why the hell
not.

Very much missed by the circulation staff of the New York
Evening Post; deeply, deeply mourned by the B.M.T.,

Wham, Mr. Roosevelt; pow, Sears Roebuck; awk, big dipper;
bop, summer rain;
bong, Mr., bong, Mr., bong, Mr., bong.

QUESTIONS

Compare the images in "Dirge," both properties and metaphors, with
those of Whitman's catalogue in "Song of Myself (26)." Both catalogues
are drawn largely from city life, but quite obviously the similarity ends
there. Fearing's images are obviously not of things that Whitman
would welcome into his poem. What is the difference in the two princi-
ples of selection? (If in doubt, make parallel listings of the items in
Whitman's and Fearing's catalogues.) What would two such lists tell
one of the way each poet conceived city life?

On careful reading one cannot fail to note that there are at least two
overtone themes in "Dirge." "Bought his Carbide at 30 but it went to
29," for example, is vastly different in connotation from "O democratic
voter born in August under Mars." Make a list of everything in the
poem that immediately relates to the order of life suggested by
"bought his Carbide at 30 but it went to 29" and another list of every-
thing that immediately relates to "born in August under Mars." Are
there any images that seem to fall into an in-between theme? If "buying
Carbide" is thought of as "mundane" and "born in August under
Mars" as "human aspiration," is there a third theme that might be
labeled "aspirations of the mundane"? Note that all the mundane im-
ages are images of loss. Are all the aspiration images also of loss?

from Hero and Leander

Christopher Marlowe

Her veil was artificial flowers and leaves,
Whose workmanship both man and beast deceives.
Many would praise the sweet smell as she passed,
When 'twas the odor which her breath forth cast;
And therefor honey bees have sought in vain,
And, beat from thence, have lighted there again.
About her neck hung chains of pebble-stone,
Which, lightened by her neck, like diamonds shone. . . .

. . . Buskins of shell all silvered, used she,
And branched with blushing coral to the knee,
Where sparrows perched, of hollow pearl and gold,
Such as the world would wonder to behold;
Those with sweet water oft her handmaid fills,
Which, as she went, would chirrup through the bills.
Some say, for her the fairest cupid pined,
And, looking in her face, was strooken blind.

QUESTIONS

Marlowe piles up a great deal of very peculiar ornamentation in his
description of Hero's dress. Shell boots ornamented with branches of
coral on which are perched jeweled metal birds hardly make for com-
fort, but Marlowe goes further: a serving maid keeps filling the metal
birds with water that makes a sound of chirruping as its passes through
their bills. Strange regalia; do the details of that regalia have anything
in common? Denotatively? Connotatively? Has the catalogue of Hero's
dress anything in common with the description of her physical pres-
ence?

The following poems are presented without additional comment to
allow for further reading and discussion of multiple images, the
catalogue, and overtone themes.

Walter Jenks' Bath
For Rollin Williams

William Meredith

These are my legs. I don't have to tell them, legs,
Move up and down or which leg. They are black.
They are made of atoms like everything else,
Miss Berman says. That's the green ceiling
Which on top is the Robinsons' brown floor.
This is Beloit, this is my family's bathroom on the world.
The ceiling is atoms, too, little parts running
Too fast to see. But through them running fast,
Through Audrey Robinson's floor and tub
And the roof and air, if I lived on an atom
Instead of on the world, I would see space.
Through all the little parts, I would see into space.

Outside the air it is all black.
The far apart stars run and shine, no one has to tell them,

buskins: boots. **strooken:** stricken.

Stars, run and shine, or the same who tells my atoms
Run and knock so Walter Jenks, me, will stay hard and real.
And when I stop the atoms go on knocking,
Even if I died the parts would go on spinning,
Alone, like the far stars, not knowing it,
Not knowing they are far apart, or running,
Or minding the black distances between.
This is me knowing, this is what I know.

A Grasshopper

Richard Wilbur

But for a brief
Moment, a poised minute,
He paused on the chicory-leaf;
Yet within it

The sprung perch
Had time to absorb the shock,
Narrow its pitch and lurch,
Cease to rock.

A quiet spread
Over the neighbor ground;
No flower swayed its head
For yards around;

The wind shrank
Away with a swallowed hiss;
Caught in a widening, blank
Parenthesis,

Cry upon cry
Faltered and faded out;
Everything seemed to die.
Oh, without doubt

Peace like a plague
Had gone to the world's verge,
But that an aimless, vague
Grasshopper-urge

Leapt him aloft,
Giving the leaf a kick,
Starting the grasses' soft
Chafe and tick,

So that the sleeping
Crickets resumed their chimes,
And all things wakened, keeping
Their several times.

In gay release
The whole field did what it did,
Peaceful now that its peace
Lay busily hid.

Ponce de León: A Morning Walk

Al Young

You too if you work hard enough
can end up being the name of a street
in a drowsy little Indian town
a day's drive from Mexico City
where orphans like bold Joselito
hustle in the taxi burro streets,
where cosmetic fragrances mingle
with scents of ripe & overripe fruits
& vegetables, where the smell of breakfast
& dinner are almost the same.

The natural odor of dung & bodysweat
rises from the zócalo into a sky, semi-
industrialized, housing the spirits of
blue señoritas with sun soaking into
their rain-washed skirts dried dustier
& wrinklier than red or green pepper.

While a crazy rooster's crowing late
a brown baby delights in orange & yellow
balloons floating up like laughter
to tenement windows where a whole family
of older kids wave happy soap wands
that yield fat bubbles part air part
water part light that pop in the faces
of prickly straw behatted gents
rambling by below, ragged & alive—

One morning's moment in this ageless
stone thoroughfare named after just one
dead Spaniard who wanted to live forever

Dolor

Theodore Roethke

I have known the inexorable sadness of pencils,
Neat in their boxes, dolor of pad and paper-weight,
All the misery of manilla folders and mucilage,
Desolation in immaculate public places,
Lonely reception room, lavatory, switchboard,
The unalterable pathos of basin and pitcher,
Ritual of multigraph, paper-clip, comma,
Endless duplication of lives and objects.
And I have seen dust from the walls of institutions,
Finer than flour, alive, more dangerous than silica,
Sift, almost invisible, through long afternoons of tedium,
Dropping a fine film on nails and delicate eyebrows,
Glazing the pale hair, the duplicate gray standard faces.

Some Good Things to Be Said for the Iron Age

Gary Snyder

A ringing tire iron
        dropped on the pavement

Whang of a saw
brusht on limbs

        the taste
        of rust.

Between Walls

William Carlos Williams

the back wings
of the

hospital where
nothing

will grow lie
cinders

in which shine
the broken

pieces of a green
bottle

from **The Great Bear Lake Meditations**

J. Michael Yates

NUMBER 13

Legend: The god in the sun made two men. In the hands of one he placed a book. An axe he handed the other.

Decree: In search of one another they shall circle the earth forever.

Curse: May you walk upwind all of your days.

Act: The left hand loses memory of the right. Neither blade nor word gives the feel of gods at this long high noon of the night. The wind, like consciousness, appears only in other things.

NUMBER 22

The wolves say to the dogs what the madman of me says to the citizen.

I need to go fishing until I need to return.

NUMBER 51

Again and again I go away from you and send back only words.

Where I am is very cold and the ice figures I collect for you never somehow survive the transport.

And so these small black tracks upon the page.

Where you are is too warm for me.

This message is a map which shows my exact coordinates at this moment. Follow it. Try to find me. I should like to be here when you arrive, but in this weather it is necessary to keep moving.

The Lost Pictures

Hollis Summers

I am blessed with my location,
Living near the central factory
Of Best Pictures, Inc., Coolville, Ohio.

I recommend the place at Coolville,
But I am a purist; surely other centers exist,
With other names, for studying photography.

Tell the pleasant girl at the desk,
"You have lost my film."
She will ask you when and the name of your camera.

Make up a month, like May or June,
Say, "Instamatic."
Say, "Color."

She will take you to a pleasant morgue,
Air conditioned, full of other pleasant girls
Concerned with found and lost.

Everybody takes the same pictures: the deck of a ship,
A wedding, a beach, fat people at a picnic,
A three-month-old child held in various arms.

In Coolville you are allowed to study all the pictures,
Slowly. "Here we are," you can say,
Knowing you aren't.

Dog

Lawrence Ferlinghetti

The dog trots freely in the street
and sees reality
and the things he sees
are bigger than himself
and the things he sees
are his reality
Drunks in doorways
Moons on trees
The dog trots freely thru the street
and the things he sees
are smaller than himself
Fish on newsprint
Ants in holes
Chickens in Chinatown windows
their heads a block away
The dog trots freely in the street
and the things he smells
smell something like himself
The dog trots freely in the street
past puddles and babies
cats and cigars
poolrooms and policemen
He doesn't hate cops
He merely has no use for them

and he goes past them
and past the dead cows hung up whole
in front of the San Francisco Meat Market
He would rather eat a tender cow
than a tough policeman
though either might do
And he goes past the Romeo Ravioli Factory
and past Coit's Tower
and past Congressman Doyle
He's afraid of Coit's Tower
but he's not afraid of Congressman Doyle
although what he hears is very discouraging
very depressing
very absurd
to a sad young dog like himself
to a serious dog like himself
But he has his own free world to live in
His own fleas to eat
He will not be muzzled
Congressman Doyle is just another
fire hydrant
to him
The dog trots freely in the street
and has his own dog's life to live
and to think about
and to reflect upon
touching and tasting and testing everything
investigating everything
without benefit of perjury
a real realist
with a real tale to tell
and a real tail to tell it with
a real live
      barking
          democratic dog
engaged in real
          free enterprise
with something to say
          about ontology
something to say
         about reality
           and how to see it
              and how to hear it
with his head cocked sideways
          at streetcorners
as if he is just about to have
         his picture taken
           for Victor Records
     listening for

His Master's Voice
and looking
like a living questionmark
into the
great gramaphone
of puzzling existence
with its wondrous hollow horn
which always seems
just about to spout forth
some Victorious answer
to everything

Time Out

Donald Finkel

My mind shrugs off his threadbare winter poems
stone broke   hands in his pockets
he stalks the freeway   not a thought to his name
whistling
April slides her long cool fingers
under his shirt.

An Elegy Is Preparing Itself

Donald Justice

There are pines that are tall enough
Already. In the distance,
The whining of saws; and needles,
Silently slipping through the chosen cloth.
The stone, then as now, unfelt,
Perfectly weightless. And certain words,
That will come together to mourn,
Waiting, in their dark clothes, apart.

CHAPTER SEVEN

THE POEM
IN MOTION

Buick

Karl Shapiro

As a sloop with a sweep of immaculate wings on her delicate spine
And a keel as steel as a root that holds in the sea as she leans,
Leaning and laughing, my warm hearted beauty, you ride, you ride,
You tack on the curves with parabola speed and a kiss of goodbye,
Like a thoroughbred sloop, my new high-spirited spirit, my kiss.

As my foot suggests that you leap in the air with your hips of a girl,
My finger that praises your wheel and announces your voices of song,
Flouncing your skirts, you blueness of joy, you flirt of politeness,
You leap, you intelligence, essence of wheelness with silvery nose,
And your platinum clocks of excitement stir like the hairs of a fern.

But now with your eyes that enter the future of roads you forget;
Where you turned on the stinging lathes of Detroit and Lansing at night
And shrieked at the torch in your secret parts and the amorous tests,
But now with your eyes that enter the future of roads you forget;
You are all instinct with your phosphorous glow and your streaking
  hair.

And now when we stop it is not as the bird from the shell that I leave
Or the leathery pilot who steps from his bird with a sneer of delight,
And not as the ignorant beast do you squat and watch me depart,
But with exquisite breathing you smile, with satisfaction of love,
And I touch you again as you tick in the silence and settle in sleep.

No one who reads this poem can miss the fact that the poet is lovingly concerned with the motion of his saying. A poem exists in time. The first line comes first, the others follow in their order to the last line, and there is no other order in which the lines can be read.

And since a poem has duration, it also has pace. One poem may obviously urge the voice at a faster pace than does another. Within the same poem, moreover, one part may urge itself much more rapidly than another. Even within an individual line, one phrase may clearly be indicated as moving more rapidly or more slowly than another. For just as music carries with it a notation that tells the musician at what rate and with what feeling to play a given passage, so every good piece of writing, and poetry in particular, carries within it a series of unmistakable notations that tell the good reader how any given passage should be read. One of the poet's chief delights is in the manipulation of his pace and its changes. He is deeply involved in the *feeling of his motion.* Since a poem is always about something felt, its motion is certainly part of what it is about, part of what it feels, and, therefore, part of what it "means." Even more importantly, the motion is fundamental to *how* the poem means.

All writing has pace. Poetry has all the notation for pace that one may find in other writing, and it has the additional notation of metrics. "Pace" must be understood to be the more inclusive term, but since metric is the peculiar characteristic of poetry, an understanding of the poem's pace must begin with some understanding of metrics. What follows is in no sense a complete survey of English metrics, but simply a first look at some basic metrical phenomena.

As a working simplification, the basic line of English poetry may be taken to be *iambic pentameter.* "Iambic" indicates the "beat" of the rhythm, "pentameter" indicates the length of the line in terms of feet. A foot is a unit of stressed and unstressed syllables. English line lengths in progression from one-foot to eight-foot are labeled: *monometer, dimeter, trimeter, tetrameter, pentameter, hexameter, septameter,* and *octameter.* The basic English metric feet are *iambic, trochaic, anapestic, dactylic, amphibrachic, pyrrhic, spondaic,* and *monosyllabic.*

The *iamb* (iambic) is a two-syllable foot consisting of an unaccented syllable followed by an accented syllable: ta-*tum.* It is the basic English foot for the idiomatic reason that most English words of two syllables (many exceptions are, of course, to be noted) are accented on the second syllable

$$\overset{-}{re}\text{-}\overset{\prime}{fer},\ \overset{-}{a}\text{-}\overset{\prime}{bout},\ \overset{-}{des}\text{-}\overset{\prime}{troy}.$$

English, moreover, contains many monosyllabic words which when preceded by a monosyllabic article or preposition fall into a natural iambic rhythm. Metric principle does not exist in a vacuum. Iambic has become the basic beat of English poetry and pentameter the basic line length because these measures are most responsive to the qualities of English speech. A great deal of the poetic energy of the sixteenth century in England went into testing the iambic pentameter line (among others) as a vehicle for poetry in English. Some poets, for example, tried to tune English speech to the measures of Latin hexameters, basing their metric on *quantitative* measure (the succession of long and short syllables) rather than on *qualitative* (the succession of accented and unaccented) syllables. Quantitative measure failed in English poetry because it is not adapted to the nature of English speech. By the last quarter of the sixteenth century iambic pentameter was firmly established. One important reason for the great flowering of poetry in Shakespeare's time lay in the fact that such a basic line had been established and that it proved itself capable of such great range and flexibility.

The *trochee* (trochaic) is a two-syllable foot consisting of an accented syllable followed by an unaccented syllable: *tum*-ta, a reversed iambic. The trochee is inevitable in English because so many two-syllable words, despite the general iambic nature of the language, are stressed on the first syllable

        /   – / – / –
       wait-ing, ap-ple, sin-gle.

Note that when such words are preceded by an article or by a monosyllabic preposition, a light-heavy or iambic sequence happens. There is a general tendency in southern mid-western American speech to move the accent forward in the word, that is, toward a trochaic accentuation. If such speech habits continue to spread as they (unfortunately) seem to be doing, the basic meter of American poetry will undergo considerable change.

         /   /
      In Mon-roe, Loo z'ana, which is locally known as part of the
      /   /   /
      U-nited States, the po-lice station is near the the-ay-ta. Get the
      /
      i-dee?

The *anapest* (anapestic) is a three-syllable foot consisting of two unaccented syllables followed by an accented syllable: ta-ta-*tum*. If the iamb is conceived, by a musical analogy, to be in three-eighths time, then the unstressed syllable is an eighth note and the stressed is a quarter note. If the eighth comes before the quarter and is changed to two sixteenths, the result can be taken as analagous to anapestic meter

     – – /   – – /   – – /
     of the day, in a while, lem-on-ade.

There are very few naturally anapestic words in English but many combinations of preposition-article-noun that demand the anapestic beat.

The *dactyl* (dactylic) is, simply enough, a reversed anapest: *tum*-ta-ta. Obviously it bears the same relation to the trochee that the anapest bears to the iamb.

The *amphibrach* is a three-syllable foot consisting of unstressed-stressed-unstressed syllables: ta-*tum*-ta, as in the word

$$\overset{-}{\text{re}}\text{-}\overset{/}{\text{but}}\text{-}\overset{-}{\text{tal}}.$$

The amphibrach may be thought of as a feminine iamb. (See below for the terms *feminine* and *masculine*.)

The *pyrrhic* is a foot consisting of two unstressed syllables. It is possible to construct a theory of metrics in which the pyrrhic does not exist. In conventional metrics, however, it is impossible to scan certain lines without resort to the pyrrhic. A famous example occurs in Shakespeare's much quoted line:

$$\overset{-}{\text{To}}\ \overset{/}{\text{mo}}/\overset{-}{\text{rrow}}\ \overset{-}{\text{and}}\ /\ \overset{-}{\text{to}}\ \overset{/}{\text{mo}}/\overset{-}{\text{rrow}}\ \overset{-}{\text{and}}\ /\ \overset{-}{\text{to}}\ \overset{/}{\text{mo}}\ \overset{-}{\text{rrow}}$$

So scanned, the line is seen to consist of iamb-pyrrhic-iamb-pyrrhic-amphibrach (or feminine iamb).

The *spondee* (spondaic) is a two-syllable foot consisting of two stressed syllables: *tum-tum*. In such a line as "Blow, Blow, ye wintry winds!" it should be obvious that the first two syllables cannot meaningfully be read either as blow-*blow* or as *blow*-blow: they must be given equal and heavy stress.

The *monosyllabic* foot consists of a single stressed syllable. The uncorrupted version of Lady Macbeth's famous lines display richly the dramatic effect that may be achieved by the use of the monosyllabic foot:

$$\overset{/}{\text{Out}},//\ \overset{/}{\text{damn}}\ \overset{-}{\text{ed}}/\ \overset{/}{\text{spot}}!//\ \overset{/}{\text{out}}//\ \overset{/}{\text{I}}\ \overset{/}{\text{say}}!$$
$$\overset{/}{\text{What}},//\ \overset{/}{\text{will}}\ \overset{-}{\text{these}}/\ \overset{/}{\text{hands}}/\ \overset{/}{\text{ne}}\ \overset{-}{\text{ver}}/\ \overset{/}{\text{be clean}}?$$

It is possible to interpret these lines with a somewhat different emphasis and hence with some variation in the scansion. But it should be clear that Shakespeare deliberately used the monosyllabic foot in combination with a basically trochaic meter to indicate more than usual passion (hence a speech rhythm far from normal). Note, too, that the monosyllabic foot falls, in each case, before a double line, the notation for the caesura.

Caesura is an essential term in metrics and labels the internal pauses in a passage. It corresponds to a rest in music. A pause, one must remember, also consumes time, and as one may imagine by analogy to music, can also compensate for missing measures either accented or unaccented.

When a caesura occurs at the end of the line, the line is said to be *end-stopped*. When the voice must continue to the next line without pause, the line is said to be *run on*, or *enjambed*.

Feminine and *masculine* are terms that may be used to describe poetic lines, feet, or rhymes. These elements are feminine if they end on an unaccented syllable; masculine if they end on an accented syllable.

$$\overset{-}{\text{He}}\ \overset{/}{\text{came}}/\ \overset{-}{\text{to}}\ \overset{/}{\text{me}}/\ \overset{-}{\text{and}}\ \overset{/}{\text{told}}/\ \overset{-}{\text{me}}\ \overset{/}{\text{he}}/\ \overset{-}{\text{must}}\ \overset{/}{\text{leave}}\ \overset{-}{\text{me}}$$

is a feminine line (ending in the unaccented "me"). With a slight change it can become the masculine line:

$$\text{Hĕ cáme/ tŏ mé/ ănd tóld/ mĕ hé/ mŭst léave.}$$

English not only tolerates but welcomes such extra light beats, especially before an end stop or a caesura.

These are the most common elements of English metrics, but the practice of individual poets varies widely. It seems best, however, to establish these basic measures and to note variations as they occur.

A mechanically flawless iambic pentameter would read: ta-*tum,* ta-*tum,* ta-*tum,* ta-*tum,* ta-*tum.* English poetry, however, is capable of far more interesting effects than such mechanical regularity. It is useful to think of the pattern of mechanical iambic pentameter as roughly corresponding to the squares on graph paper: the variations of the drawn graph are meaningful only as they work against the fixed norm of the squares. In poetry the mechanical pattern may be thought of as an *expectation.* The metric performance of any line happens in the way it works its variations against the established expectation.

Good poets, moreover, do not work by rule but by ear (their own strictest rule), by feel rather than by meticulous observance of generalizations about metrics. As a starting generalization, however, one may safely say that all poets work against a pattern of expectation (a norm) and vary its dead regularity (1) by slipping in extra, unaccented syllables, (2) by displacing an expected accent, as in the reversed foot, (3) by increasing the number of stresses, primarily by the use of spondees and monosyllabic feet, (4) by grouping stressed or unstressed syllables, and (5) by the manipulation of internal pauses (caesuras), end stops, and run-ons. These are the basic metric devices that speed up or slow down the line and change its voice emphases. A number of nonmetrical devices that serve the same function of speeding up or slowing down the line will be considered as they occur. But for poets, the rule of thumb is still the law of practice.

Alexander Pope's *Essay on Criticism* (an extended poem in rhymed iambic pentameter couplets) offers, among other things, a number of such useful rules of thumb. In one famous passage Pope discusses a number of poetic faults and graces, illustrating each by the line in which he mentions it. He points out, for example, that if all the vowels in a given passage are open, the effect is laborious (hence a nonmetric device for slowing down the line); and in saying so he piles up a succession of open vowels all of equal duration. "These" refers to a class of critics Pope is satirizing:

> These equal syllables alone require,
> Though oft the ear the open vowel tire.

Pope goes on to condemn the pointless expletive *do,* run into a line without grammatical integrity but simply to pad out the syllabic count. Thus instead of writing the normal English "while expletives join (then pronounced "jine") their feeble aid," Pope illustrates:

> While expletives their feeble aid *do* join.

And he concludes the couplet with an example of the general lifelessness of a line that consists of ten equal monosyllables:

> And ten low words oft creep in one dull line.

Later in the same passage he discusses and illustrates the necessity for meaningful change of pace:

> When Ajax strives some rock's vast weight to throw,
> The line, too, labors, and the words move slow:
> Not so when swift Camilla scours the plain,
> Flies o'er th'unbending corn, and skims along the main.

Clearly the first line of this passage is *impeded* ("slowed down") by the effort required to wrestle through the consonantal cluster of "When Ajax strives some rock's." And clearly the fourth line is *accelerated* ("speeded up") by the meter. But slowed down and speeded up from what? Pope's own "dull line" will serve to establish a norm:

> And ten low words oft creep in one dull line.

Nothing could be more regular, and hence more dull.

Pope must certainly have believed that the dullness of this line resulted from the combination of its two chief metrical characteristics: first, that all of the line moves at exactly the same pace, and second, that all of its stressed syllables are equal, as are all of its unstressed syllables. Such lack of variation, however, is not final evidence that any given line is a bad one. Pope, for example, uses its monotony brilliantly to illustrate monotony. The last line of the following poem makes use of ten monosyllables for a tremendous special emphasis. The poet, moved by the mystical quality of El Greco's painting in which the human body is elongated and distorted into flamelike shapes suggesting the enormous upward tug of the spirit, is driven to ask a question of those other-worldly men. If they so yearn to enter the houses of eternity (whose doorway is the tomb) and if that eternity is full of such radiance as they envision, then—and each syllable of the line pounds the question—"Why, does, no, light, come, through, as, those, doors, close"?

El Greco

E. L. Mayo

See how the sun has somewhat not of light
Falling upon those men who stand so tall;
See how their eyes observe some inward sight

And how their living takes no room at all,—
Their passing stirs no air, so thin they are;
Behind them see small houses with small doors;
The light comes from an unfamiliar star
That lights their walls and falls across their floors.

What shall we say when one of those men goes
Into his house and we no longer see
His eyes observing something that he knows.
And if those houses brim with radiancy
Why does no light come through as those doors close?

Any poetic device can be used triumphantly for special effects, and one should be cautious of making categoric assertions about poetry. With that much understood, it is still possible to say that any passage of poetry in which line after line is made up of equally measured monosyllables, or nearly, will tend to monotony. A pianist playing to strict metronomic beat is painful to listen to. One needs the felt variations and compensation of a more human response. So in poetry.

I put my hat upon my head
And strolled into the Strand,
And there I met another man
Whose hat was in his hand.

The lines are metrically perfect, but as lifeless as the metronome. One need hardly be told that the passage is deliberate parody.

Yet part of the insipidity of those lines is certainly due to the insipidity of what they are saying. The following poem is nearly as monosyllabic as the parody above, but it may well be cited as a masterpiece of one sort of pure English lyricism:

With Rue My Heart Is Laden

A. E. Housman

With rue my heart is laden
For golden friends I had,
For many a rose-lipt maiden
And many a light-foot lad.

By brooks too broad for leaping
The light-foot lads are laid.
And rose-lipt girls are sleeping
In fields where roses fade.

The very monosyllabic understatement of the poem is important to its lyrical restraint and success. Yet certainly the gracious variety provided by the adjectives (most of them compounded monosyllables) and by the delicate interplay of feminine and masculine rhymes is inseparable from the poem's success. It is not necessary to have great variation, but some variation there must certainly be. One need only convert Housman's feminine rhymes into masculine counterparts to see how much the little upward flip of the extra feminine syllable at the ends of alternate lines enriches the total effect, and how leaden the effect becomes without such enrichment:

> With rue my heart is laid
> For golden friends I had,
> For many a rose-lipt maid
> And many a light-foot lad.
>
> By brooks too broad to leap
> The light-foot lads are laid.
> And rose-lipt girls now sleep
> In fields where roses fade.

Pope's Ajax, as noted, moves more slowly than does his Camilla. The slowness of the Ajax line is due to nonmetrical impedance caused by the clustering of consonants. Metrically, two causes combine to give the little tripping speed-up to the last line of that passage. The line, it must be noted, is an *alexandrine:* a hexameter used as a final variation in a passage of pentameter lines. Normally the alexandrine, by drawing the line out an extra foot, tends to slow it down. Pope himself has satirized the overreliance of some poets on alexandrines:

> A needless Alexandrine ends the song,
> That, like a wounded snake, drags its slow length along.

Despite the alexandrine's tendency to slow down the line,, however (especially when impeded by caesuras), Pope accelerates the last line of his Ajax-Camilla passage:

> Flíes o'er / th' un bend/ ing córn// and skíms/ a long/
> the main

The first foot of this line has sometimes been scanned as an iamb rather than as a trochee. The present scansion takes the grammatical force of the parallelism in this passage to play *flies* against *skims*: Camilla *flies* over the corn and *skims* across the sea. If the first foot is taken as an iamb, then one must argue that she "flies *o'er*" and "skims *along*"—a reading one may not be able to defend. The first cause of the acceleration is obviously in the anapest of the second foot. Just as sixteenth notes must be played more rapidly than eighths, so the two unaccented syllables of the anapest must be read more rapidly than would be a single unaccented syllable. This first cause is assisted, moreover, by the reversal of the first foot, since that reversal puts three rather than two unstressed syllables in a row. The fundamental basis of all metrical acceleration should be apparent: *the more unstressed syllables are brought together between accents, the faster the line will tend to move.*

The two basic metric devices for impeding the line are the caesura and the grouping of heavily accented syllables. *The more caesuras and the more stressed syllables that occur in a given passage, the slower its pace will tend to be.*

Caesura, by definition, could hardly serve any other purpose than to slow down a passage. One need only observe how it functions in such a passage as the speech in which Macbeth pours out his grief and his death wish:

> I have lived long enough// my way of life
> Is fallen into the sere,// the yellow leaf,//
> And that which should accompany old age//
> As honor,//love,// obedience,//troops of friends,//
> I must not look to have// but, // in their stead//
> Curses,// not loud but deep,// mouth honour,// breath,//
> Which the poor heart would fain deny// and dare not.

One may interpret this passage also in slightly different ways, and argue for the removal of the caesuras after "old age" in line 3, after "but" in line 5, and after "stead" at the end of line 5; but even so interpreted, the passage clearly derives its pace primarily from the heavy incidence of caesuras.

One should note also that as caesuras grow closer and closer together, there must inevitably be less language between them. Since it is the unstressed syllables that tend to be squeezed out (partly compensated for by the pauses), such passages tend to cluster accents, with a consequent greater likelihood of more monosyllabic feet. Since stressed syllables are obviously more emphatic than unstressed, caesural pause is closely linked with especially powerful voice emphasis.

John Donne, one of the most metrically skilled of English poets, was also one of the most passionately religious. Many of his later poems burn with desire for a direct physical experience of God. In the urgency of that desire, Donne pounds and beats his language. In one of his *Holy Numbers* he calls upon God to ravish him. The metrics of that passage, in seeking to find a motion equal to the emotion, makes extraordinary use of the caesura combined with many monosyllabic feet.

> Batt er/ my heart/ three per/ soned God,// for you
> As yet/ but knock// breathe// shine// and seek/ to mend.//
> That I/ may rise,/ and stand// o'er throw me// and bend
> Your powers/ to break// blow// burn// and make/ me new.

The passage is exquisitely controlled and emphasized from the first reversed (trochaic) foot that plunges the voice in with a sharp thrust on the hard *bat* sound, to the final clustering of accents in the iamb-and-spondee combination at the end of line 4.

But if this introduction is not to become a treatise, it will be necessary to pass over many fine points. Metrics, as noted, tends to go by practice rather than by rule. No one has ever compiled a wholly satisfactory set of metric rules. There seem in fact to be many systems of metrics at work in various periods of English poetry. The best way to familiarize oneself with the resources of English metrics is by specific example. Let the poem illustrate the poem.

A Metrical Exercise

To Lucasta, on Going to the Wars

Richard Lovelace

Tell me not, Sweet, I am unkind
    That from the nunnery
Of thy chaste breast and quiet mind
    To war and arms I fly.

True, a new mistress now I chase,
    The first foe in the field;
And with a stronger faith embrace
    A sword, a horse, a shield.

Yet this inconstancy is such
    As you, too, shall adore;
I could not love you, dear, so much,
    Loved I not honour more.

A glance at Lovelace's poem should be enough to make it clear that the poem is built metrically on an iambic norm and consists of alternate tetrameters and trimeters. The complications that Lovelace has worked into his metric pattern may tend momentarily to obscure the essentially iambic base, but one has only to read the last line of the first two stanzas to be reassured that the meter is in fact iambic. Nothing could be more mechanically correct than the iambic trimeter of those lines, and one will do well to note that almost all good poets who use complicated metrics provide such "rest" lines at intervals. Whether or not they do so consciously is more or less irrelevant. The fact seems to be that few good poets actually scan their lines. And why should they?—their ears have been attuned by years of reading and writing, and it is the ear that decides.

The trouble is that the ear decides in ways too subtle for simple rules. The beginner, therefore, must approach metrics by means a bit simpler than the whole truth. If he is a good reader, he will assume the responsibility for carrying these simplifications further, toward a more valid metrical sense. But one must begin somewhere.

Were one to read the first stanza of the Lovelace poem mechanically, ignoring everything but the alternation of stressed and unstressed syllables, the stanza might be scanned so:

Tell me / not, Sweet, / I am / un kind

That from / the nunn / er y

Of thy / chaste breast / and qui / et mind

To war / and arms / I fly.

Such scansion may be called *mechanical*.

Now let the lines be read in a more meaningful and more felt way. Let them be read as nearly as possible without attention to metrical principles, simply as an exercise in locating the voice emphasis of English speech, and let those syllables that must be stressed in such a meaningful rendering be indicated by a caret below the line. One will sense at once that certain syllables, though they are clearly stressed, are stressed more or less heavily than others. A large caret for more emphatically stressed syllables and a smaller one for those less heavily stressed will serve our present purposes. The same lines might then be *meaningfully* scanned as follows:

Tell me not, Sweet, I am unkind
     ^   ^   ^   ^

That from the nunnery
  ^   ^

Of thy chaste breast and quiet mind
 ^   ^   ^   ^   ^

To war and arms I fly.
  ^   ^   ^

Now if the same passage be marked for both the mechanical and the meaningful scansion, it will appear as follows:

Tell me / not, Sweet, / I am / un kind
     ^   ^   ^   ^

That from / the nunn / er y
 ^   ^

Of thy / chaste breast / and qui / et mind
 ^   ^   ^   ^   ^

To war / and arms / I fly.
 ^   ^   ^

With these two scansions thus indicated, one may sense at once that all metric effect must result from the interplay of the mechanical and the meaningful beat. The mechanical beat corresponds roughly to those squares on the graph paper, and the meaningful beat to the variations of the drawn graph against the mechanical pattern.

Comparison of the two patterns shows that *a line may have more or fewer meaningful than mechanical stresses.* The second line, for example, has three mechanical stresses and two meaningful; the third has four mechanical and five meaningful. Such variation is more common than not in English metrics.

Moreover, *the stresses of the mechanical and of the meaningful scansions do not always coincide.* In the first line of the Lovelace passage, for example, three syllables unstressed in mechanical scansion receive meaningful stresses, and three syllables stressed in mechanical scansion receive no meaningful stresses. Such displacement will at once serve to indicate the presence of reversed feet—in this case, the presence of trochaic feet in an iambic line.

Further, *the mechanical and the meaningful stresses may coincide,* as in the fourth line. Such coincidence will serve to indicate a smooth or "rest" line. When a poem is metrically smooth for too long the effect will tend to monotony (an effect that can, of course, be sought deliberately as in part three of Auden's "In Memory of W. B. Yeats," p. 187). Accomplished poets always tend to bring a metrically complicated poem "to rest" from time to time, but inept poets, by keeping the metrics too smooth for too long, tend to produce only a graceless and soporific tick-tock:

> O do not say that dreams are vain
> And love is not the goal of time.
> The soul of man was made to climb
> By love and dreams above the plain
> Where beasts do roam and must remain
> While man aspires to win that clime
> Where soul and soul are made to rhyme
> At home in bliss with Him again.

Once aware of these two patterns, one will be able to understand that conventional metric notation (itself not by any means an infallible measure) is an effort to indicate the interplay of meaningful and mechanical scansion in a single system of notation. He will see, further, that no one system of metrics is likely to serve all cases unless the notation becomes extremely complicated.

The metric interpretation of the first word of Lovelace's poem is a case in point. Is there any sort of stress on "Tell"? One might reasonably argue that some slight stress should be indicated, though not as much as falls on "not"; but to indicate the degree of that stress would require a third size of caret, one smaller than the caret reserved for "not." The next step, obviously, is to evolve a system of caret sizes so complicated as to become more confusing than helpful.

In the case of unstressed syllables, on the other hand, conventional metrics has a useful measure in the very number of unstressed syllables per foot. If, as previously noted, iambic may be taken as corresponding to three-eighths time, then the unaccented syllable of the iambic foot corresponds to an eighth, and the unaccented syllables of an anapestic foot correspond to sixteenths. To keep the discussion within reasonable

limits, nothing has been said of cases in which more than two un-
stressed syllables occur within a foot, though Richard Eberhart's "The
Fury of Aerial Bombardment" (p. 359) will demonstrate such a case.
The poet Gerard Manley Hopkins evolved a metric of his own, largely
on the premise that *there is no certain limit to the number of light syllables
that may be swallowed into a given foot.* Thus the presence of three un-
stressed syllables within a foot would indicate thirty-seconds; of four,
sixty-fourths, and so on.

Conventional metrics, however, does not generally admit a notation
that distinguishes the relative emphases of stressed syllables, but relies
on a single vertical mark ("ictus") to indicate stress. It will be well,
however, by analogy to the carets of meaningful stress to use a double
ictus to indicate exceptionally heavy stress. So indicated, Lovelace's
poem may be scanned as follows:

> Tell me not,/ Sweet,// I am/ un kind
>
> That from/ the nunn/ er y
>
> Of thy / chaste breast / and qui / et mind
>
> To war / and arms / I fly.
>
> True,// a new mis / tress now / I chase,
>
> The first / foe in / the field;
>
> And with / a stron / ger faith / em brace
>
> A sword,/ a horse, / a shield.
>
> Yet this / in con / stan cy / is such
>
> As you/ too/ shall a dore;
>
> I could not / love you,/ dear,/ so much
>
> Loved I not/ hon our / more.

A study of this scansion should make clear that English metrics
consists of a series of variations and compensations that are usually
open to various interpretation. The first line of the second stanza, for
example, might have been scanned in a less controversial way as fol-
lows:

> True, a / new mis / tress now / I chase

If, however, the obvious prose rhythm of the phrasing (as further indi-
cated by the comma) is to be honored, "True" must be a monosyllabic
foot unless one wishes to admit the possibility of a caesura within the
metric foot. That possibility can indeed be considered but will not serve
the present purpose. It is more apt to introduce the arrow, as in the first
scansion, to indicate a special compensation whereby the unstressed

syllable that would normally accompany the stressed "True" is shifted into the next measure.

One may reasonably argue, to take another example, that normal voice stress might put an accent on "And" at the beginning of the third line of the second stanza and that the first foot is, accordingly, a trochee rather than a pyrrhic.

It is the second line of this stanza, however, that deserves most particular attention. Shall it be indicated:

$$\text{The } \overline{\text{first}} \, / \, \acute{\text{foe}} \, \overline{\text{in}} \, / \, \overline{\text{the}} \, \acute{\text{field}}$$

or should it be:

$$\text{The } \overline{\text{first}} / \, \acute{\text{foe}} / \, \overline{\text{in}} \, \overline{\text{the}} \, \acute{\text{field}}?$$

Certainly the prose-rhythm force of the phrasing is such that "in the field" is clearly anapestic. Here is one more case in which an arrow would be useful to indicate a displacement, thus:

$$\text{The } \overline{\text{first}} \, / \, \acute{\text{foe}} / \, \overline{\text{in}} \, \overline{\text{the}} \, \acute{\text{field}}.$$

Such displacement may be taken as a principle of English metrics: *whenever a monosyllabic foot occurs, an unaccented syllable that would accompany the accent in a mechanical scansion may be displaced to the preceding or the following foot.* When the displaced unaccented syllable occurs in the preceding foot, that foot becomes feminine and no further notation is absolutely demanded, though the arrow may still be used as an indication. When the displaced unaccented syllable occurs in the following foot, it is well to indicate that displacement by an arrow.

The first line of Lovelace's poem will illustrate the further metric complication that *the same syllables cannot always be scanned in the same way.* "Tell me not, Sweet, I am unkind" has here been scanned with the first three syllables, "Tell me not," rendered as an anapestic foot. The same phrase in another context, however, might be emphatically trochaic:

$$\acute{\text{Tell}} \, \overline{\text{me}} \, / \, \acute{\text{not}} \, \overline{\text{in}} \, / \, \acute{\text{mourn}} \, \overline{\text{ful}} \, / \, \acute{\text{num}} \, \overline{\text{bers}}.$$

Or it might be iambic:

$$\overline{\text{Tell}} \, \acute{\acute{\text{me}}} \, / \, \overline{\text{not}} \, \acute{\acute{\text{him}}}. \, // \, \overline{\text{Is}} \, \acute{\acute{\text{he}}} / \, \overline{\text{the}} \, \acute{\text{judge}} \, / \, \overline{\text{of}} \, \acute{\text{love}}?$$

The grammatical context, determining as it does the voice emphases of the spoken language (meaningful stress), is never entirely separable from metrics.

One further notation in the scansion of the Lovelace poem needs discussion. The first foot of the first line of the last stanza was marked:

Yet this.

Such notation indicates a *distributed stress*. The foot is not clearly spondaic in the sense that each syllable requires a distinct accent, yet the two syllables are clearly equal and not entirely unaccented. Whatever stress is to be allotted to that foot seems evenly divided between the two syllables.

Many other notations could be introduced into the discussion, but these will suffice for present purposes. One would do well to attempt detailed scansions of some of the following poems, or at least of some of their more interesting passages. Whether or not one undertakes such detailed scansions, he should at least apply the following measures to all of the poems:

QUESTIONS

If the poem is metrical—such a poem as H. D.'s "Socratic" (p. 348), for example, is not—identify the basic meter (iambic pentameter, trochaic trimeter, and so forth).

Place the notation for the mechanical scansion above the line and the carets for the meaningful stresses below the line.

To what extent do the mechanical and meaningful stresses coincide? (Is the metrics smooth or rough?) Note that no matter how rough the metrics of some lines may be, the poet will introduce smooth or "rest" lines from time to time.

Mark the pattern of caesuras and end stops.

Note any tendency for unstressed syllables to fall together.

Note any tendency for stressed syllables to fall together.

Note marginally any nonmetrical devices that tend to accelerate or impede any part of the poem. A number of such nonmetrical devices that contribute to acceleration or impedance will be discussed in connection with some of the poems that follow.

Poems for Guided Study: Acceleration and Impedance

Shapiro's "Buick" (p. 299) is written as a tour de force in anapestic hexameter, a rare meter in English. Sustained anapestic meter is much rarer in English poetry than sustained iambic, and good poets who use such a meter invariably introduce many little variations to keep the voice from being swept entirely away by the flow of tripping unstressed syllables.

No poet in English has relied more heavily upon the anapest than has Swinburne. Long chains of anapests combined with the nonmetrical acceleration produced by heavy alliteration became so characteristic of Swinburne's style that he was moved to write a nonsense poem in self-parody. "Nephelidia" ("Little Clouds") carries both these devices to the point of absurdity for the fun of it and as a pleasant gesture of recognizing one's own weaknesses. The meter is basically anapestic octameter, the eight-foot line serving to exaggerate further the anapestic abuse of the rhythm. The alliteration is beyond description. Meaning is nowhere to be found except in the fun of the trick itself.

In assessing what produces the extraordinary acceleration of this poem, the reader will do well to consider carefully before assigning the effect to any one cause. Metrically, the speed of the poem is certainly due to the anapestic structure and to the fact that Swinburne drags it out through an extraordinary eight-foot line. Nonmetrically, the acceleration is certainly assisted by the heavy alliteration. It is important to bear in mind, however, that all these devices work together in producing the total effect.

Nephelidia

(An excerpt)

Algernon Charles Swinburne

From the depth of the dreamy decline of the dawn through a notable
    nimbus of nebulous noonshine,
  Palid and pink as the palm of the flag-flower that flickers with fear of
    the flies as they float—
Are the looks of our lovers that lustrously lean from a marvel of mystic
    miraculous moonshine,
    These that we feel in the blood of our blushes that thicken and
    threaten with throbs through the throat?
Thicken and thrill as a theatre thronged at appeal of an actor's appalled
    agitation,
    Fainter with fear of the fires of the future than pale with the promise
    of pride in the past;
Flushed with the famishing fullness of fever that reddens with radiance
    of rathe recreation,
    Gaunt as the ghastliest of glimpses that gleam through the gloom of
    the gloaming when ghosts go aghast?
Nay, for the nick of the tick of the time is a tremulous touch on the
    temples of terror,
    Strained as the sinews yet strenuous with strife of the dead who is
    dumb as the dust-heaps of death:
Surely no soul is it, sweet as the spasm of erotic emotional exquisite
    error,
    Bathed in the balms of beatified bliss, beatific itself by beatitude's
    breath.
Surely no spirit or sense of a soul that was soft to the spirit and soul of
    our senses
    Sweetens the stress of suspiring suspicion that sobs in the semblance
    and sound of a sigh;

Only this oracle opens Olympian, in mystical moods and triangular
    tenses—
"Life is the lust of a lamp for the light that is dark till the dawn of the
    day that we die."

The last line of this excerpt is a triumph of fun. Note that it begins
and ends with stressed syllables. Since "Life" must obviously be
stressed, one may be tempted to read the line as that rare thing, a
dactyllic octameter. A second look, however, will make it clear that like
others in the extract, the line is anapestic with a monosyllabic first foot:

$$\overset{//}{\text{Life}}/ \quad \bar{\text{is}}\ \bar{\text{the}}\ \acute{\text{lust}}/ \quad \bar{\text{of}}\ \bar{\text{a}}\ \acute{\text{lamp}}/ \quad \bar{\text{for}}\ \bar{\text{the}}\ \acute{\text{light}}/ \ \text{etc.}$$

The first foot in such lines is *truncated*. In any art form *pattern* exerts a
powerful force. With a strong anapestic pattern established in the first
line, it becomes possible to omit some part of the pattern and still to feel
its force. Suppose, for example, that Swinburne had written the first
foot of every line in full conformity with the pattern: for example, "As
our life." And suppose then that he struck out the first two syllables in
the course of revising the poem. In order to feel free to do so he must
certainly have relied on the fact that his pattern was so strongly estab-
lished that he could easily afford to swallow two syllables without
disrupting the reading. The truncation of those two syllables (whether
or not they ever existed on paper) may be indicated by commas if one
wishes, and the first foot may then be scanned:

$$, , \overset{//}{\text{Life}}/$$

Swinburne's self-parody will do as well as any passage in English to
demonstrate the dangers inherent in the sustained anapest. The meter
trips so fast that it tends to take over from the poet the management of
the poem. The poet is left nothing to do but to turn the crank for more
and more anapests, the meter becoming more and more mechanical.

Alliteration is, of course, inseparable from the total effect of
"Nephelidia." The three poems that follow will demonstrate a number
of nonmetrical devices that affect the motion of the poem.

Sir Beelzebub

Edith Sitwell

WHEN
Sir
Beelzebub called for his syllabub in the hotel in Hell
    Where Proserpine first fell,
Blue as the gendarmerie were the waves of the sea,

    (Rocking and shocking the bar-maid.)

    Nobody comes to give him his rum but the
    Rim of the sky hippopotamus-glum
    Enhances the chances to bless with a benison
    Alfred Lord Tennyson crossing the bar laid
    With cold vegetation from pale deputations
    Of temperance workers (all signed In Memoriam)
    Hoping with glory to trip up the Laureate's feet,

    (Moving in classical meters). . . .

    Like Balaclava, the lava came down from the
    Roof, and the sea's blue wooden gendarmerie
    Took them in charge while Beelzebub roared for his rum.

    . . . None of them come!

   The principal nonmetrical devices for acceleration and impedance are:

1. sound patterns:	alliteration, vowel and consonant sequences, consonantal clusters, rhyme, internal rhyme, repetition of the same word or phrase
2. visual patterns:	the isolation of words as single lines, the separation of words from one another by unusual spacings in the line, the breaking off of lines for special effect
3. punctuation:	in one sense punctuation is a special case of visual pattern. Punctuation must be taken to include the capitalization of whole words or of their first letters, and the use of italics.
4. grammatical structure:	particularly parallel constructions and balanced antitheses as devices for controlling the voice emphases of the speech rhythms

Of these devices, only the first will require special discussion here. The remaining three are obvious and can be cited as they occur in specific poems.

"Sir Beelzebub" makes notable use of sound patterns, but it depends on all the other elements as well for its effect. The isolation of single words in the first two lines and the capitalization of "WHEN" in the first cannot fail to instruct the voice to apply special emphases to these words: they lead into the poem like two slow drumbeats. They are then immediately followed by an enormously accelerated passage. One should note also the special effect of the punctuation in varying the pace of the poem from passage to passage, the function of the two parentheses in varying the pace, and the unusual way in which some of the lines break off on "the."

Unlike the sound patterns of "Nephelidia," however, those of "Sir Beelzebub" run much more to internal rhyme than to alliteration, though some alliteration assists the total effect. The internal rhymes, moreover, tend to involve more than one syllable: "Beelzebub/syllabub," "enhances/chances," "benison/Tennyson." What would have been the difference of effect had those rhymes involved a single syllable only?

> WHEN
> Sir
> Glub called for his tub in the hotel in Hell . . .

Which of the nonmetrical devices listed above work for acceleration in "Sir Beelzebub," and which work for impedance? How concerned is the poet for ringing the changes from impedance to acceleration?

Apply the same measures to the two poems that follow.

Lenox Avenue Mural

Langston Hughes

HARLEM

What happens to a dream deferred?

Does it dry up
like a raisin in the sun?
Or fester like a sore—
And then run?
Does it stink like rotten meat?
Or crust and sugar over—
like a syrupy sweet?

Maybe it just sags
like a heavy load.

Or does it explode?

GOOD MORNING

Good morning, daddy!
I was born here, he said,
watched Harlem grow
until colored folks spread
from river to river
across the middle of Manhattan
out of Penn Station

dark tenth of a nation,
planes from Puerto Rico,
and holds of boats, chico,
up from Cuba Haiti Jamaica,
in buses marked New York
from Georgia Florida Louisiana
to Harlem Brooklyn the Bronx
but most of all to Harlem
dusky sash across Manhattan
I've seen them come dark
   wondering
   wide-eyed
   dreaming
out of Penn Station—
but the trains are late.
The gates open—
but there're bars
at each gate.

What happens
to a dream deferred?

Daddy, ain't you heard?

SAME IN BLUES

I said to my baby,
Baby, take it slow.
I can't, she said, I can't!
I got to go!

There's a certain
amount of traveling
in a dream deferred.

Lulu said to Leonard,
I want a diamond ring.
Leonard said to Lulu,
You won't get a goddamn thing!

A certain
amount of nothing
in a dream deferred.

Daddy, daddy, daddy,
All I want is you.
You can have me, baby—
but my lovin' days is through.

A certain
amount of impotence
in a dream deferred.

Three parties
On my party line—
But that third party,
Lord, ain't mine!

There's liable
to be confusion
in a dream deferred.

From river to river
Uptown and down,
There's liable to be confusion
When a dream gets kicked around.

COMMENT ON CURB
You talk like
they don't kick
dreams around
downtown.

I expect they do–
But I'm talking about
Harlem to you!

LETTER

Dear Mama,
*   Time I pay rent and get my food*
and laundry I don't have much left
but here is five dollars for you
to show you I still appreciates you.
My girl-friend send her love and say
she hopes to lay eyes on you sometime
*   in life.*
Mama, it has been raining cats and
*   dogs up*
here. Well, that is all so I will close.
*   Your son baby*
*   Respectably as ever,*
*   Joe*

ISLAND

Between two rivers,
North of the park,
Like darker rivers
The streets are dark.

Black and white,
Gold and brown—
Chocolate-custard
Pie of a town.

Dream within a dream,
Our dream deferred.

Good morning, daddy!

Ain't you heard?

How Jack Found that Beans
May Go Back on a Chap

Guy Wetmore Carryl

Without the slightest basis
For hypochondriasis
    A widow had forebodings which a cloud around her flung,
And with expression cynical
For half the day a clinical
    Thermometer she held beneath her tongue.

Whene'er she read the papers
She suffered from the vapors,
    At every tale of malady or accident she'd groan;
In every new and smart disease,
From housemaid's knee to heart disease,
    She recognized the symptoms as her own!

She had a yearning chronic
To try each novel tonic,
    Elixir, panacea, lotion, opiate, and balm;
And from a homeopathist
Would change to an hydropathist,
    And back again, with stupefying calm!

She was nervous, cataleptic,
And anemic, and dyspeptic:
    Though not convinced of apoplexy, yet she had her fears.
She dwelt with force fanatical
Upon a twinge rheumatical,
    And said she had a buzzing in her ears!

Now all of this bemoaning
And this grumbling and this groaning
    The mind of Jack, her son and heir, unconscionably bored.
His heart completely hardening,

He gave his time to gardening,
  For raising beans was something he adored.

Each hour in accents morbid
This limp maternal bore bid
  Her callous son affectionate and lachrymose good-bys.
She never granted Jack a day
Without some long "Alackaday!"
  Accompanied by rolling of the eyes.

But Jack, no panic showing,
Just watched his beanstalk growing,
  And twined with tender fingers the tendrils up the pole.
At all her words funereal
He smiled a smile ethereal,
  Or sighed an absent-minded "Bless my soul!"

That hollow-hearted creature
Would never change a feature:
  No tear bedimmed his eye, however touching was her talk.
She never fussed or flurried him,
The only thing that worried him
  Was when no bean-pods grew upon the stalk!

But then he wabbled loosely
His head, and wept profusely,
  And, taking out his handkerchief to mop away his tears,
Exclaimed: "It hasn't got any!"
He found this blow to botany
  Was sadder than were all his mother's fears.

The Moral is that gardeners pine
Whene'er no pods adorn the vine.
Of all sad words experience gleans
The saddest are: "It *might* have beans."
  (I did not make this up myself:
  'Twas in a book upon my shelf.
  It's witty, but I don't deny
  It's rather Whittier than I!)

To observe the effect of rhymes running to more than one syllable, compare the following lines with the first two stanzas of Carryl's poem:

Without the slightest need
For feeling off her feed
  A widow had forebodings which a cloud aroung her flung,
And with a look like brass
For half a day a glass
  Thermometer she held beneath the tongue.
Whene'er she read the news

> She suffered from the blues,
>   At every tale of malady or accident she'd groan;
> In every new and smart ill
> From housemaid's knees to flu-chill,
>   She recognized the symptoms as her own.

Rhyme can function very importantly in affecting the motion of the poem. In general the heavier and more complicated the rhymes (whether internal or at the end of the line) the more they will tend to accelerate the pace. Poets, in fact, shun especially complicated rhymes in serious poems. They do so because the cleverness and the acceleration of such rhymes seems incompatible with *seriousness.* Such tricky rhyme sequences, therefore, remain the almost exclusive device of light-verse writers.

While the discussion is on rhyme it seems pertinent to mention some of the devices introduced into English rhymes by more recent poets, even though those devices are not intimately connected with the pace of the poem. Traditional English rhyme is *syllabic.* That is, it rhymes the final syllable of each rhyme word. Examples of syllabic rhyme are: "dove/love"; "and/hand"; "clever/never"; "intellectual/hen-pecked-you-all." Within English convention, and for reasons that need not be discussed here, a number of common rhymes are merely *visual.* Examples of such visual rhymes are: "love/move"; "wind/mind"; "has/was." Obviously, such rhymes are intended to function as syllabic.

English convention also has a certain tolerance, though bad poets are forever abusing that tolerance, for *false rhyme.* True rhyme pairs stressed syllable with stressed syllable. False rhyme offers an unstressed syllable as a rhyme for a stressed syllable. Examples of false rhymes are: "apple/full"; "sea/eternity"; "widow/snow." Few poetic abuses can be drearier than the rhyming of a poet who keeps pairing such monosyllabic and simple rhymes as "sea" with such easy, large poeticisms as

"ecstacy," "infinity," "inconstancy,"

and with such adverbs as

"exultantly," "mystically," "imponderably."

But, as was observed in the discussion of Frost's "Stopping by Woods on a Snowy Evening," English is a rhyme-poor language. Inevitably certain rhymes tend to pair up, with a consequent sense of dull predictability. And inevitably the poets will cast about for ways of refreshing their rhymes.

One resort of the past and one still importantly current is to abandon rhyme altogether. When the poetry is metrically regular but unrhymed, it is referred to as *blank verse.* Almost all blank verse of the past was written in iambic pentameter, but many twentieth-century poets and some of their forerunners have dropped not only rhyme but metrical regularity to write what has become known as *free verse*.

Rhyme, however, is too valuable a device to be abandoned permanently, and many more recent poets have worked to vary their rhyme methods rather than to eliminate rhyme altogether. The principal variations from syllabic rhyme are consonantal, assonantal, and approximate rhyme.

Of these variations, *consonantal rhyme* is perhaps the most immediately apt to the quality of English speech. It has the further advantage of being every bit as strict as syllabic rhyme. Consonantal rhyme, however, does not rhyme the syllable (which consists generally of a vowel-and-consonant sound group, though it may consist of a single vowel) but rhymes instead the consonants that enclose the last syllable while varying the vowel. Examples of consonantal rhyme are: "run/ran"; "maid/mud"; "hill/hall." Note especially, however, that consonantal rhymes tend to run in readily available chords: "run/ wren/ran/Rhine/rune/ruin," or "maid/mid/Maud/mud/mad," or "hill/hale/heil/hall/hole/who'll," and so forth. No poet as yet has systematically worked out the possibilities of such chords as the rhymes for whole stanzas (Wilfred Owen, killed at twenty-five in World War One, comes closest to having done so), but certainly the chords make possible special stanzaic effects. Combined with syllabic rhymes, consonantal rhymes make possible extended progressions of rhyme, as for example, "rain/wren/when/wan/dawn/dine/mine/main/ rain." Consonantal rhyme is often used in combination with syllabic, assonantal, or approximate rhyme.

Assonantal rhyme reverses the procedure of consonantal rhyme and pairs simply the vowel sound without regard to the consonants. Examples of such rhyme are: "hat/mad; shine/smile; gruff/dud," but more characteristically: "shine/eye; heel/sea; grave/day;" the second rhyme of an assonantal pairing, that is to say, seems to work best when the vowel is not closed in by a final consonant. Assonance is native to French poetry because of the number of words in French that lend themselves to such treatment. It seems doubtful that assonance will ever become a major device of English poetry though it can contribute certain grace notes to the poetic structure.

Approximate rhyme is a more indeterminate name for all rhymes that are not quite syllabic, not quite consonantal, and not quite assonantal, but that obviously pair words of somewhat related sound. Approximate rhymes tend to occur most naturally around such strong sounds as "x" as in: "depicts/fix; lacks/fox; tax/tanks." They may, however, occur in combinations of all other English sounds. Wilfred Owen made extensive use of approximate rhymes in combination with others. Here, for example, are the rhyme sequences of the first twenty-one lines of Owen's "Strange Meeting" (p. 141): "escaped/scooped/groined/ groaned / bestirred / stared / eyes / bless / hall / Hell / grained / ground / moan / mourn / years / yours / wild / world / hair / hour / here."

To return to the discussion of rhyme as it affects the pace of the poem, it seems to be a general rule that heavy rhyme (a sequence of more than two rhymes), especially when it occurs in poems with short lines, tends to produce acceleration and emphasis together, as in a rapid and staccato liturgy. In such a poet as John Skelton, for example, the short, rough line that might have resulted in a heavily emphasized slowing of the pace because of the natural tendency of the voice to pause at the end of the line, is hurtled along by the heavy pounding of the rhyme. Skelton, it must be borne in mind, died in 1529, and English pronunciation has changed markedly since his time. Skelton's movement will be better approximated if one reads

/   /   /   /

joyously, maidenly, womanly, demeaning.

Thus part of the effect may be seen to reside in the fact that one must swallow many light syllables en route to a heavy final accent.

To Mistress Margaret Hussey

John Skelton

Merry Margaret
As midsummer flower,
Gentle as falcon
Or hawk of the tower;
With solace and gladness,
Much mirth and no madness,
All good and no badness;
So joyously,
So maidenly,
So womanly,
Her demeaning,
In every thing
Far far passing
That I can indite
Or suffice to write
Of merry Margaret,
As midsummer flower,
Gentle as falcon
Or hawk of the tower.

As patient and as still,
And as full of good will,
As the fair Isyphill,
Coriander,
Sweet pomander,
Good Cassander,
Steadfast of thought,

That I can indite: that which I can write. **Isyphill:** Hypsipyle, a beautiful woman of Greek legend. **Coriander:** an aromatic herb. **pomander:** a sachet. **Cassander:** Cassandra, daughter of King Priam of Troy.

Well made, well wrought.
Far may be sought
Ere that ye can find
So courteous, so kind,
As merry Margaret,
This midsummer flower,
Gentle as falcon
Or hawk of the tower.

But rhyme may also function for emphasis or to slow down a passage. Yeats uses internal rhyme for stunning emphasis in the sixth line of the following poem. "Supreme theme" is clearly a climactic assertion. Yeats emphasizes it not only metrically but by the heavy rhyme sounds that occur with nothing between them.

After Long Silence

William Butler Yeats

Speech after long silence; it is right
All other lovers being estranged or dead,
Unfriendly lamplight hid under its shade,
The curtains drawn upon unfriendly night,
That we descant and yet again descant
Upon the supreme theme of Art and Song:
Bodily decrepitude is wisdom; young
We loved each other and were ignorant.

The impedance of forward movement here is due in part to the repetition of "descant." Repetition will generally tend to slow a line down, but such repetition is not essentially different from the way rhyme works on the lines, since it still amounts to an increase in a poem's internal echoes.

Compare the effects of rhyme on motion in the two previous poems with the effect Hopkins achieves in this heavily rhymed poem.

Spring and Fall
(To a Young Child)

Gerard Manley Hopkins

Márgarét, are you gríeving
Over Goldengrove unleaving?
Leáves, líke the things of man, you
With your fresh thoughts care for, can you?
Áh! ás the heart grows older
It will come to such sights colder
By and by, nor spare a sigh

Though worlds of wanwood leafmeal lie;
And yet you wíll weep and know why.
Now no matter, child, the name:
Sórrow's spríngs áre the same.
Nor mouth had, no nor mind, expressed
What heart heard of, ghost guessed:
It ís the blight man was born for,
It is Margaret you mourn for.

In "The Grindstone," Robert Frost uses an unusual final rhyme for emphasis. The poem concludes:

What if it wasn't all it should be? I'd
Be satisfied, if he'd be satisfied.

The reader is forced to punch down hard on the "I'd" rhyme, in part because it is an unusual rhyme, and in part because of the unusual placement of the word (visual pattern). Then, having been forced to emphasize "I'd," the reader must emphasize "he'd" in the next line, as demanded by the force of the parallel grammatical construction.

To these nonmetrical devices for emphasis, one must add the metrical force of "I'd" as a monosyllabic foot. The metric situation of the monosyllabic foot is well worth a particular look. Note the following examples:

'Tis with/ our judg/ ments as/ our wa tches, // none
Go just / a like,// yet each/ be lieves/ his own.

(Alexander Pope)

Bod' ly/ de crep/ i tude/ is wis dom;// young
We loved/ each o ther// and were ig/ nor ant.

(W. B. Yeats)

What if/ it was/ n't all / it should be?// I'd
Be sat/ is fied/ if he'd/ be sat/ is fied.

(Robert Frost)

The second line of the Yeats excerpt is metrically very complicated. One may also scan the line as follows:

We loved/ each o/ ther// and / were ig/ nor ant

with the third foot rendered as a pyrrhic containing a caesura within it. If the line must be brought to five feet at all costs it seems far more reasonable to take the caesura as a foot all by itself (a full-measure rest) than to render a "split pyrrhic," whatever that might be. The fact is that Yeats' line (it is the last line of the poem) is constructed for a deliberately falling rhythm. And might almost be rendered:

$$\bar{}\ /\quad\bar{}\ /\quad\bar{}\quad\bar{}\quad\bar{}\ /\quad\bar{}\quad\bar{}$$
We loved/ each o ther//and were ig nor ant.

Certainly the stress on the last syllable of "ignorant" is hardly more than formal as compared to the stress on the first syllable. Note, however, that despite all variation, the syllable count is full and the mechanical scansion presents no difficulties:

$$\bar{}\ /\quad\bar{}\ /\quad\bar{}\ /\quad\bar{}\ /\quad\bar{}\ /$$
We loved/ each o/ ther and/ were ig/ nor ant.

In each of these passages the final monosyllabic foot at the end of the first line is used in exactly the same way. That metric pattern may be represented thus:

$$\bar{}\ /\ \bar{}\ //\ /\ /$$

Note that in each case there is an extra unstressed (feminine) syllable immediately before the caesura. Obviously, a light syllable has been displaced from the last foot to the preceding foot, and one might use the arrow as the notation for such displacement, thus:

$$\bar{}\ /\ \overset{\frown}{\bar{}\ //}\ /\ /$$

The need for such a light syllable preceding the caesura will be evident at once if one substitutes, in the three examples, "clocks" for "watches," "wise" for "wisdom," and "I'd hoped" for "it should be." The result would not be increased emphasis but awkwardness. *The normal pattern for a final monosyllabic foot requires an unstressed syllable before the caesura that divides the foot from the line.*

The next to last line of the following passage will illustrate that there will be an exception to this rule *when the last two feet are both monosyllabic:*

Voice of the Studio Announcer
from The Fall of the City

Archibald MacLeish

Ladies and gentlemen:
This broadcast comes to you from the city.
Listeners over the curving air have heard
From furthest off frontiers of foreign hours

> Mountain Time: Ocean Time: of the islands:
> Of waters after the islands   some of them waking
> Where noon here is night there: some
> Where noon is the first few stars they see or the last one.

The next to last line may be scanned:

$$\overset{-}{\text{Where}}\overset{\prime}{\text{ noon}}/\overset{\prime\prime}{\text{ here}}/\overset{-}{\text{ is}}\overset{\prime}{\text{ night}}/\overset{\prime\prime}{\text{ there:}}//\overset{\prime\prime}{\text{ some}}$$

The extraordinary metrics of this line obviously reflects MacLeish's special concern for the staccato quality of the radio announcer's way of speaking. Note how important caesura is to the special effect of the entire passage.

Pause, whether achieved by metrical or nonmetrical devices, is fundamental to the quality of any poetic line. The nature of the poetic line itself, however, must be considered. A poetic line is not simply a quantity of language. One might, for example, write in flawless syllabic count without remotely approaching poetry:

> I bought some shoes and then I put them on
> My feet and took a walk and they felt good.

The deadness of such lines results not only from the fact that they are metronomic, but that *they are not true units of phrase.* Compare the following individual lines from many sources:

> When in disgrace with fortune and men's eyes

> Yet once more, O ye laurels, and once more

> Since there's no help, come, let us kiss and part

> It is morning, Senlin says, and in the morning

> Full fathom five thy father lies

> Bid me to live and I will live

> Bob Southey! You're a poet—Poet Laureate

> Whenas in silks my Julia goes

> The mellow ousel fluted in the elm

Such lines are not only metrical units but natural units of language. They are metrical units for reasons that should now be clear. They are units of language because they seem to fit naturally onto the tongue and the breath groupings of English-speaking people, and to fit as rounded phrases rather than as fragments of phrases. To resort once more to a musical analogy, the lines seem to be not simply quantities of notes, but discrete and sufficient musical phrases: stop them anywhere short of their own end and one has not a phrase but a fragment of a phrase. One may note also that the lines powerfully suggest how they should read, even as isolated lines.

One part of the suggestion of a true poetic line is its general tendency to bring the voice to rest at the line ending. Such lines are referred to as end-stopped. Inevitably, however, there will be situations in which the poet finds it necessary to urge the voice on to the next line without an end stop. A poet's way of handling end stops and run-ons can have a great deal to do with the pace of his poem.

In the two following poems mark every end stop and every run-on. (A down-curving arrow is a useful notation for a run-on line.)

Then, preferably with ink or pencil of a different color, mark all internal pauses. Which poem has more internal pauses? Is there any observable relation between internal pauses and end stops, or between internal pauses and run-ons? Which poem seems more colloquial in its speech rhythms and which more formal? Have the pauses (both internal and end stop) and the run-ons any discernible relation to the differences of the speech rhythms?

My Last Duchess

Robert Browning

That's my last Duchess painted on the wall,
Looking as if she were alive. I call
That piece a wonder, now: Frà Pandolf's hands
Worked busily a day, and there she stands.
Will't please you sit and look at her? I said
"Frà Pandolf" by design, for never read
Strangers like you that pictured countenance,
The depth and passion of its earnest glance,
But to myself they turned (since none puts by
The curtain I have drawn for you, but I)
And seemed as they would ask me, if they durst,
How such a glance came there; so, not the first
Are you to turn and ask thus. Sir, 'twas not
Her husband's presence only, called that spot
Of joy into the Duchess' cheek: perhaps
Frà Pandolf chanced to say, "Her mantle laps
Over my Lady's wrist too much," or "Paint
Must never hope to reproduce the faint
Half-flush that dies along her throat"; such stuff
Was courtesy, she thought, and cause enough
For calling up that spot of joy. She had
A heart—how shall I say?—too soon made glad,
Too easily impressed; she liked whate'er

She looked on, and her looks went everywhere.
Sir, 'twas all one! My favor at her breast,
The dropping of the daylight in the West,
The bough of cherries some officious fool
Broke in the orchard for her, the white mule
She rode with round the terrace—all and each
Would draw from her alike the approving speech,
Or blush, at least. She thanked men,—good; but thanked
Somehow—I know not how—as if she ranked
My gift of a nine-hundred-years-old name
With anybody's gift. Who'd stoop to blame
This sort of trifling? Even had you skill
In speech—(which I have not)—to make your will
Quite clear to such an one, and say, "Just this
Or that in you disgusts me; here you miss,
Or there exceed the mark"—and if she let
Herself be lessoned so, nor plainly set
Her wits to yours, forsooth, and made excuse,
—E'en then would be some stooping, and I choose
Never to stoop. Oh, sir, she smiled, no doubt,
Whene'er I passed her; but who passed without
Much the same smile? This grew; I gave commands;
Then all smiles stopped together. There she stands
As if alive. Will't please you rise? We'll meet
The company below, then. I repeat,
The Count your master's known munificence
Is ample warrant that no just pretence
Of mine for dowry will be disallowed;
Though his fair daughter's self, as I avowed
At starting, is my object. Nay, we'll go
Together down, sir! Notice Neptune, though,
Taming a sea-horse, thought a rarity,
Which Claus of Innsbruck cast in bronze for me!

from Crass Times Redeemed by Dignity of Souls

Peter Viereck

II

The tenderness of dignity of souls
Sweetens our cheated gusto and consoles.
It shades love's lidless eyes like parasols
And tames the earthquake licking at our soles.
Retunes the tensions of the flesh we wear.
Forgives the dissonance our triumphs blare.
And maps the burrows of heart's buried lair

Where furtive furry Wishes hide like moles.
O hear the kind voice, hear it everywhere
(It sings, it sings, it conjures and cajoles,
Prompting us shyly in our half-learnt rôles.
It sprouts the great chromatic vine that lolls
In small black petals on our music scrolls
(It flares, it flowers—it quickens yet controls).
It teaches dance-steps to this uncouth bear
Who hops and stumbles in our skin and howls.

The weight that tortures diamonds out of coals
Is lighter than the skimming hooves of foals
Compared to one old heaviness our souls
Hoist daily, each alone, and cannot share:
To-be-awake, to sense, to be aware.
That even the dusty dreams that clog our skulls,
The rant and thunder of the storm we are,
The sunny silences our prophets hear,
The rainbow of the oil upon the shoals,
The crimes and Christmases of creature lives,
And all pride's barefoot tarantelle on knives
Are but the search for dignity of souls.

As always, one device tends to work with another. "Crass Times Redeemed by Dignity of Souls" is not so much a colloquially spoken as an incantatory poem. The poet wants the poem intoned in a mechanical, litanized way. Such a reading requires a full stop at the end of each line (and with that pause as the dominant voice punctuation, such a reading requires little internal pause, since internal pause would make the end pauses less emphatic). Especially in the second verse-paragraph of the excerpt, however, the meaning does not come to a rest at the end of each line and normally the voice would run on to the next. Here the poet makes the rhyme function as additional emphasis. Repetition, as already noted, is a natural means of emphasis.

Viereck, by picking up in his second paragraph the heavy sequence of strong "oles" rhymes which he established in the first, instructs the voice to pause at the end of the first three lines where it would normally run on. He also eliminates all internal pause in these lines. In the fourth, both the sense of the line and the final colon are pause enough, and he can accordingly change rhyme scheme and allow caesuras in the line without losing his incantatory effect. The rhyme assistance is not needed in lines 4 to 10 since the meaning comes to its own pause at the end of each, but note that after a variation into internal pause in lines 4 and 5, the lines once more march straight to their end stop, reemphasizing the incantatory effect. Finally, there would be a normal tendency to run on in the next to the last line were one to depend upon the meaning alone, and here Viereck once more returns to much heavier and closer rhyme than he has been using in the immediately preceding lines. "Knives/lives" are strong sounds and close together. As further instruction to the reader Viereck isolates the last line into a special sense by italicizing it. It is impossible to miss his voice instruction (which is, of course, his control of pace) if one takes these clear indications into account. It is pertinent, however, to ask again how the poem could mean what it means without that incantatory insistence of the rhythm. A related question may be useful in locating this idea: would a prayer mean what it means if, without changing any of its words, its normal intonations were syncopated into a jazz beat?

Poems for Individual Analysis: Acceleration and Impedance

The End of the World

Archibald MacLeish

Quite unexpectedly as Vasserot
The armless ambidextrian was lighting
A match between his great and second toe
And Ralph the lion was engaged in biting
The neck of Madame Sossman while the drum
Pointed, and Teeny was about to cough
In waltz-time swinging Jocko by the thumb—
Quite unexpectedly the top blew off.
And there, there overhead, there, there, hung over
Those thousands of white faces, those dazed eyes,
There in the starless dark, the poise, the hover,
There with vast wings across the canceled skies,
There in the sudden blackness, the black pall
Of nothing, nothing, nothing—nothing at all.

The Traveler's Curse after Misdirection

(from the Welsh)

Robert Graves

May they wander stage by stage
Of the same vain pilgrimage,
Stumbling on, age after age,
Night and day, mile after mile,
At each and every step, a stile;
At each and every stile, withal,
May they catch their feet and fall;
At each and every fall they take,
May a bone within them break;
And may the bones that break within
Not be, for variation's sake,
Now rib, now thigh, now arm, now shin,
But always, without fail, THE NECK.

from The Rubáiyát of Omar Khayyám

Translated by Edward FitzGerald

I

A Book of Verses underneath the Bough,
A Jug of Wine, A Loaf of Bread—and Thou
    Beside me singing in the Wilderness—
Ah, Wilderness were Paradise enow!

II

I sometimes think that never blows so red
The Rose at where some buried Caesar bled;
    That every Hyacinth the Garden wears
Dropt in her Lap from some once lovely Head.

III

Think in this battered Caravanserai
Whose Portals are alternate Night and Day,
    How Sultan after Sultan with his Pomp
Abode his destined Hour and went his way.

IV

Ah, my Beloved, fill the Cup that clears
Today of past Regret and future Fears:
    Tomorrow!—Why, Tomorrow I may be
Myself with Yesterday's Sev'n Thousand Years.

V

For some we loved, the loveliest and the best
That from his Vintage rolling Time hath prest,
    Have drunk their Cup a Round or two before,
And one by one crept solemnly to rest.

VI

Myself when young did eagerly frequent
Doctor and Saint, and heard great argument
    About it and about: but evermore
Came out by the same Door where in I went.

VII

With them the seed of Wisdom did I sow,
And with mine own hand wrought to make it grow;
    And this was all the Harvest that I reaped—
"I came like Water, and like Wind I go."

VIII

The Moving Finger writes; and, having writ,
Moves on: nor all your Piety nor Wit
    Shall lure it back to cancel half a Line,
Nor all your Tears wash out a Word of it.

IX

Ah Love! could you and I with Him conspire
To grasp this sorry Scheme of Things entire,
    Would we not shatter it to bits—and then
Remould it nearer to the Heart's Desire.

X

Come, fill the Cup, and in the fire of Spring
Your Winter-garment of Repentance fling:
    The Bird of Time has but a little way
To flutter—and the Bird is on the Wing.

XI

Some for the Glories of This World; and some
Sigh for the Prophet's Paradise to come;
    Ah, take the Cash and let the Credit go,
Nor heed the rumble of a distant Drum!

XII

The Worldly Hope men set their Hearts upon
Turns Ashes—or it prospers; and anon,
    Like Snow upon the Desert's dusty Face,
Lighting a little hour or two—is gone.

XIII

Why, all the Saints and Sages who discussed
Of the Two Worlds so wisely—they are thrust
   Like foolish Prophets forth; their Words to Scorn
Are scattered, and their Mouths are stopt with Dust.

XIV

A Moment's Halt—a momentary taste
Of Being from the Well amid the Waste—
   And Lo!—the phantom Caravan has reached
The Nothing it set out from—Oh, make haste!

XV

There was the Door to which I found no Key;
There was the Veil through which I might not see:
   Some little talk awhile of Me and Thee
There was—and then no more of Thee and Me.

L'Allegro

John Milton

Hence, loathed Melancholy
   Of Cerberus and blackest Midnight born,
In Stygian cave forlorn
   'Mongst horrid shapes, and shrieks, and sights unholy!
Find out some uncouth cell
   Where brooding Darkness spreads his jealous wings
And the night-raven sings;
   There under ebon shades, and low-browed rocks
As ragged as thy locks,
   In dark Cimmerian desert ever dwell.
But come, thou goddess fair and free,
In heaven yclept Euphrosyne,
And by men, heart-easing Mirth,
Whom lovely Venus at a birth
With two sister Graces more
To ivy-crownéd Bacchus bore;
Or whether (as some sager sing)
The frolic wind that breathes the spring,
Zephyr, with Aurora playing,
As he met her once a-Maying—
There on beds of violets blue
And fresh-blown roses washed in dew
Filled her with thee, a daughter fair,
So buxom, blithe, and debonair.

Haste thee, Nymph, and bring with thee
Jest and youthful Jollity,
Quips and Cranks and wanton Wiles,
Nods and Becks and wreathèd Smiles,
Such as hang on Hebe's cheek
And love to live in dimple sleek;
Sport that wrinkled Care derides,
And Laughter holding both his sides.
Come, and trip it as you go
On the light fantastic toe;
And in thy right hand lead with thee
The mountain-nymph, sweet Liberty;
And if I give thee honor due
Mirth, admit me of thy crew,
To live with her, and live with thee
In unreprovèd pleasures free;
To hear the lark begin his flight
And singing startle the dull night
From his watch-tower in the skies,
Till the dappled dawn doth rise;
Then to come, in spite of sorrow,
And at my window bid good-morrow
Through the sweetbriar, or the vine,
Or the twisted eglantine:
While the cock with lively din
Scatters the rear of darkness thin,
And to the stack, or the barn-door,
Stoutly struts his dames before:
Oft listening how the hounds and horn
Cheerly rouse the slumbering morn,
From the side of some hoar hill,
Through the high wood echoing shrill;
Sometime walking, not unseen,
By hedge-row elms, on hillocks green,
Right against the eastern gate
Where the great Sun begins his state,
Robed in flames and amber light,
The clouds in thousand liveries dight;
While the ploughman, near at hand,
Whistles o'er the furrowed land,
And the milkmaid singeth blithe,
And the mower whets his scythe,
And every shepherd tells his tale
Under the hawthorn in the dale.
Straight mine eye hath caught new pleasures
Whilst the landscape round it measures:
Russet lawns, and fallows gray,
Where the nibbling flocks do stray;
Mountain, on whose barren breast

The laboring clouds do often rest;
Meadows trim with daisies pied,
Shallow brooks, and rivers wide.
Towers and battlements it sees
Bosomed high in tufted trees,
Where perhaps some beauty lies,
The cynosure of neighboring eyes.
Hard by, by a cottage chimney smokes
From betwixt two aged oaks,
Where Corydon and Thyrsis met
Are at their savory dinner set
Of herbs, and other country messes
Which the neat-handed Phillis dresses;
And then in haste her bower she leaves,
With Thestylis to bind the sheaves;
Or, if the earlier season lead,
To the tanned haycock in the mead.
   Sometimes with secure delight
The upland hamlets will invite,
When the merry bells ring round,
And the jocund rebecks sound
To many a youth and many a maid,
Dancing in the chequered shade;
And young and old come forth to play
On a sunshine holy-day,
Till the livelong daylight fail:
Then to the spicy nut-brown ale,
With stories told of many a feat,
How faery Mab the junkets eat:—
She was pinched, and pulled, she said;
And he, by friar's lantern led,
Tells how the drudging Goblin sweat
To earn his cream-bowl duly set,
When in one night, ere glimpse of morn,
His shadowy flail hath threshed the corn
That ten day-laborers could not end;
Then lies him down the lubber fiend,
And, stretched out all the chimney's length,
Basks at the fire his hairy strength;
And crop-full out of doors he flings,
Ere the first cock his matin rings.
Thus done the tales, to bed they creep,
By whispering winds soon lulled asleep.
Towered cities please us then
And the busy hum of men,
Where throngs of knights and barons bold,
In weeds of peace, high triumphs hold,

friar's lantern: will-o'-the-wisp. **lubber:** oafish.

With store of ladies, whose bright eyes
Rain influence, and judge the prize
Of wit or arms, while both contend
To win her grace, whom all commend.
There let Hymen oft appear
In saffron robe, with taper clear,
And pomp, and feast, and revelry,
With mask, and antique pageantry;
Such sights as youthful poets dream
On summer eves by haunted stream.
Then to the well-trod stage anon,
If Jonson's learnéd sock be on,
Or sweetest Shakespeare, Fancy's child,
Warble his native wood-notes wild.
  And ever against eating cares
Lap me in soft Lydian airs,
Married to immortal verse,
Such as the meeting soul may pierce,
In notes with many a winding bout
Of linkéd sweetness long drawn out,
With wanton heed and giddy cunning,
The melting voice through mazes running,
Untwisting all the chains that tie
The hidden soul of harmony;
That Orpheus' self may heave his head
From golden slumber, on a bed
Of heaped Elysian flowers, and hear
Such strains as would have won the ear
Of Pluto, to have quite set free
His half-regained Eurydice.
  These delights if thou canst give,
Mirth, with thee I mean to live.

Il Penseroso

John Milton

Hence, vain deluding Joys,
  The brood of Folly without father bred!
How little you bested
  Or fill the fixéd mind with all your toys!
Dwell in some idle brain,
  And fancies fond with gaudy shapes possess
As thick and numberless
  As the gay motes that people the sunbeams,
Or likest hovering dreams,
  The fickle pensioners of Morpheus' train.

---

sock: the slipper worn by comic actors.

But hail, thou goddess sage and holy,
Hail, divinest Melancholy!
Whose saintly visage is too bright
To hit the sense of human sight,
And therefore to our weaker view
O'erlaid with black, staid Wisdom's hue;
Black, but such as in esteem
Prince Memnon's sister might beseem,
Or that starred Ethiop queen that strove
To set her beauty's praise above
The sea-nymphs, and their powers offended.
Yet thou are higher far descended:
Thee bright-haired Vesta long of yore
To solitary Saturn bore;
His daughter she; in Saturn's reign
Such mixture was not held a stain:
Oft in glimmering bowers and glades
He met her, and in secret shades
Of woody Ida's inmost grove,
While yet there was no fear of Jove.
  Come, pensive Nun, devout and pure,
Sober, steadfast, and demure,
All in a robe of darkest grain
Flowing with majestic train,
And sable stole of cypress lawn
Over thy decent shoulders drawn.
Come, but keep thy wonted state,
With even step, and musing gait,
And looks commercing with the skies,
Thy rapt soul sitting in thine eyes:
There, held in holy passion still,
Forget thyself to marble, till
With a sad leaden downward cast
Thou fix them on the earth as fast.
And join with thee calm Peace, and Quiet,
Spare Fast, that oft with gods doth diet,
And hears the Muses in a ring
Aye round about Jove's altar sing:
And add to these retired Leisure
That in trim gardens takes his pleasure:—
But first and chiefest, with thee bring
Him that yon soars on golden wing
Guiding the fiery-wheeléd throne,
The cherub Contemplatión;
And the mute Silence hist along,
'Less Philomel will deign a song
In her sweetest saddest plight,
Smoothing the rugged brow of Night,

While Cynthia checks her dragon yoke
Gently o'er the accustomed oak.
Sweet bird, that shunn'st the noise of folly,
Most musical, most melancholy!
Thee, chauntress, oft the woods among
I woo, to hear thy even-song;
And missing thee, I walk unseen
On the dry smooth-shaven green,
To behold the wandering Moon
Riding near her highest noon,
Like one that had been led astray
Through the heaven's wide pathless way,
And oft, as if her head she bowed,
Stooping through a fleecy cloud.
   Oft, on a plat of rising ground
I hear the far-off curfew sound
Over some wide-water'd shore,
Swinging slow with sullen roar;
Or, if the air will not permit,
Some still removed place will fit,
Where glowing embers through the room
Teach light to counterfeit a gloom;
Far from all resort of mirth,
Save the cricket on the hearth,
Or the bellman's drowsy charm
To bless the doors from nightly harm.
   Or let my lamp at midnight hour
Be seen in some high lonely tower,
Where I may oft out-watch the Bear
With thrice-great Hermes, or unsphere
The spirit of Plato, to unfold
What worlds or what vast regions hold
The immortal mind that hath forsook
Her mansion in this fleshly nook;
And of those Daemons that are found
In fire, air, flood, or underground,
Whose power hath a true consent
With planet, or with element.
Sometime let gorgeous Tragedy
In sceptered pall come sweeping by,
Presenting Thebes, or Pelops' line,
Or the tale of Troy divine;
Or what (though rare) of later age
Ennobled hath the buskined stage.
   But, O sad Virgin, that thy power
Might raise Musaeus from his bower,

Cynthia: the moon. **unsphere:** call down from the spheres of Heaven. **buskined:** wearing the heavy shoe of tragic actors.

Or bid the soul of Orpheus sing
Such notes as, warbled to the string,
Drew iron tears down Pluto's cheek
And made Hell grant what Love did seek!
Or call up him that left half-told
The story of Cambuscan bold,
Of Camball, and of Algarsife,
And who had Canace to wife,
That owned the virtuous ring and glass,
And of the wondrous horse of brass,
On which the Tartar king did ride;
And if aught else great bards beside
In sage and solemn tunes have sung,
Of tourneys, and of trophies hung,
Of forests, and enchantments drear,
Where more is meant than meets the ear.
  Thus, Night, oft see me in thy pale career,
Till civil-suited Morn appear,
Not tricked and frounced as she was wont
With the Attic boy to hunt,
But kerchiefed in a comely cloud
While rocking winds are piping loud,
Or ushered with a shower still,
When the gust hath blown his fill,
Ending on the rustling leaves
With minute-drops from off the eaves.
And when the sun begins to fling
His flaring beams, me, goddess, bring
To arched walks of twilight groves,
And shadows brown, that Sylvan loves,
Of pine, or monumental oak,
Where the rude axe, with heavéd stroke,
Was never heard the nymphs to daunt
Or fright them from their hallowed haunt.
There in close covert by some brook
Where no profaner eye may look,
Hide me from day's garish eye,
While the bee with honeyed thigh,
That at her flowery work doth sing,
And the waters murmuring,
With such consort as they keep,
Entice the dewy-feathered Sleep;
And let some strange mysterious dream
Wave at his wings in airy stream
Of lively portraiture displayed,
Softly on my eyelids laid:

him that left half-told: Chaucer.

And, as I wake, sweet music breathe
Above, about, or underneath,
Sent by some spirit to mortals good,
Or the unseen Genius of the wood.
   But let my due feet never fail
To walk the studious cloister's pale
And love the high-embowéd roof,
With antique pillars massy proof
And storied windows richly dight,
Casting a dim religious light:
There let the pealing organ blow
To the full-voiced quire below
In service high and anthems clear,
As may with sweetness, through mine ear,
Dissolve me into ecstasies,
And bring all Heaven before mine eyes.
   And may at last my weary age
Find out the peaceful hermitage,
The hairy gown and mossy cell
Where I may sit and rightly spell
Of every star that heaven doth shew,
And every herb that sips the dew;
Till old experience do attain
To something like prophetic strain.
   These pleasures, Melancholy, give,
And I with thee will choose to live.

How They Brought the Good News from Ghent to Aix

Robert Browning

I sprang to the stirrup, and Joris, and he;
I galloped, Dirck galloped, we galloped all three;
"Good speed!" cried the watch, as the gatebolts undrew;
"Speed!" echoed the wall to us galloping through;
Behind shut the postern, the lights sank to rest,
And into the midnight we galloped abreast.

Not a word to each other; we kept the great pace
Neck by neck, stride by stride, never changing our place;
I turned in my saddle and made its girths tight,
Then shortened each stirrup, and set the pique right,
Rebuckled the cheek-strap, chained slacker the bit,
Nor galloped less steadily Roland a whit.

'Twas moonset at starting; but while we drew near
Lokeren, the cocks crew and twilight dawned clear;

At Boom, a great yellow star came out to see;
At Duffeld, 'twas morning as plain as could be;
And from Mecheln church-steeple we heard the half-chime,
So Joris broke silence with, "Yet there is time!"

At Aershot, up leaped of a sudden the sun,
And against him the cattle stood black every one,
To stare through the mist at us galloping past,
And I saw my stout galloper Roland at last,
With resolute shoulders, each butting away
The haze, as some bluff river headland its spray;

And his low head and crest, just one sharp ear bent back
For my voice, and the other pricked out on his track;
And one eye's black intelligence—ever that glance
O'er its white edge at me, his own master, askance!
And the thick heavy spume-flakes which aye and anon
His fierce lips shook upwards in galloping on.

By Hasselt, Dirck groaned; and cried Joris, "Stay spur!
Your Roos galloped bravely, the fault's not in her,
We'll remember at Aix"—for one heard the quick wheeze
Of her chest, saw the stretched neck and staggering knees,
And sunk tail, and horrible heave of the flank,
As down on her haunches she shuddered and sank.

So we were left galloping, Joris and I,
Past Looz and past Tongres, no cloud in the sky;
The broad sun above laughed a pitiless laugh,
'Neath our feet broke the brittle bright stubble like chaff;
Till over by Dalhem a dome-spire sprang white,
And "Gallop," gasped Joris, "for Aix is in sight!"

"How they'll greet us!"—and all in a moment his roan
Rolled neck and croup over, lay dead as a stone;
And there was my Roland to bear the whole weight
Of the news which alone could save Aix from her fate,
With his nostrils like pits full of blood to the brim,
And with circles of red for his eye-sockets' rim.

Then I cast loose my buffcoat, each holster let fall,
Shook off both my jack-boots, let go belt and all,
Stood up in the stirrup, leaned, patted his ear,
Called my Roland his pet-name, my horse without peer;
Clapped my hands, laughed and sang, any noise, bad or good,
Till at length into Aix Roland galloped and stood.

And all I remember is—friends flocking round
As I sat with his head 'twixt my knees on the ground;

And no voice but was praising this Roland of mine,
As I poured down his throat our last measure of wine,
Which (the burgesses voted by common consent)
Was no more than his due who brought good news from Ghent.

The Charge of the Light Brigade

Alfred, Lord Tennyson

Half a league, half a league,
Half a league onward,
All in the valley of Death
   Rode the six hundred.
"Forward the Light Brigade!
Charge for the gun!" he said.
Into the valley of Death
   Rode the six hundred.

"Forward, the Light Brigade!"
Was there a man dismayed?
Not though the soldier knew
   Someone had blundered.
Theirs not to make reply,
Theirs not to reason why,
Theirs but to do and die.
Into the valley of Death
   Rode the six hundred.

Flashed all their sabers bare,
Flashed as they turned in air
Sabring the gunners there,
Charging an army, while
   All the world wondered.
Plunged in the battery-smoke
Right through the line they broke;
Cossack and Russian
Reeled from the saber-stroke
   Shattered and sundered.
Then they rode back, but not,
   Not the six hundred.

Cannon to right of them,
Cannon to left of them,
Cannon behind them
   Volleyed and thundered;
Stormed at with shot and shell,
While horse and hero fell,

They that had fought so well
Came through the jaws of Death,
Back from the mouth of hell,
All that was left of them,
   Left of six hundred.

When can their glory fade?
O the wild charge they made!
   All the world wondered.
Honor the charge they made!
Honor the Light Brigade,
   Noble six hundred.

"To be, or not to be"
from Hamlet

William Shakespeare

To be, or not to be: that is the question:
Whether 'tis nobler in the mind to suffer
The slings and arrows of outrageous fortune,
Or to take arms against a sea of troubles,
And by opposing end them. To die: to sleep;
No more; and by a sleep to say we end
The heart-ache, and the thousand natural shocks
That flesh is heir to. 'Tis a consummation
Devoutly to be wish'd. To die, to sleep;
To sleep? Perchance to dream! aye, there's the rub;
For in that sleep of death what dreams may come,
When we have shuffled off this mortal coil,
Must give us pause: there's the respect
That makes calamity of so long life;
For who would bear the whips and scorns of time,
The oppressor's wrong, the proud man's contumely,
The pangs of despised love, the law's delay,
The insolence of office, and the spurns
That patient merit of the unworthy takes,
When he himself might his quietus make
With a bare bodkin? who would fardels bear,
To grunt and sweat under a weary life,
But that the dread of something after death,
The undiscovered country from whose bourn
No traveler returns, puzzles the will,
And makes us rather bear those ills we have
Than fly to others that we know not of?
Thus conscience does make cowards of us all,
And thus the native hue of resolution

Is sicklied o'er with the pale cast of thought,
And enterprises of great pith and moment
With this regard their currents turn awry
And lose the name of action.

"For God's sake, let us sit upon the ground"
from King Richard the Second

William Shakespeare

For God's sake, let us sit upon the ground,
And tell sad stories of the death of kings:
How some have been deposed; some slain in war;
Some haunted by the ghosts they have deposed;
Some poisoned by their wives; some sleeping killed;
All murdered:—for within the hollow crown
That rounds the mortal temples of a king
Keeps Death his court; and there the antick sits,
Scoffing his state, and grinning at his pomp;
Allowing him a breath, a little scene,
To monarchize, be feared, and kill with looks;
Infusing him with self and vain conceit—
As if this flesh, which walls about our life,
Were brass impregnable; and humored thus,
Comes at the last, and with a little pin
Bores through his castle-wall, and—farewell king!

"Under the greenwood tree"
from As You Like It

William Shakespeare

Under the greenwood tree
Who loves to lie with me,
And turn his merry note
Unto the sweet bird's throat—
Come hither, come hither, come hither!
    Here shall he see
    No enemy
But winter and rough weather.

Who doth ambition shun
And loves to live i' the sun,
Seeking the food he eats
And pleased with what he gets—
Come hither, come hither, come hither!
    Here shall he see
    No enemy
But winter and rough weather.

"Full fathom five"

from The Tempest

William Shakespeare

Full fathom five thy father lies:
  Of his bones are coral made;
Those are pearls that were his eyes:
  Nothing of him that doth fade,
But doth suffer a sea-change
Into something rich and strange.
Sea-nymphs hourly ring his knell:
  Hark! now I hear them,—
    Ding, dong, Bell.

In a Time of Pestilence

Thomas Nashe

Adieu, farewell earth's bliss.
This world uncertain is;
Fond are life's lustful joys,
Death proves them all but toys.
None from his darts can fly;
I am sick, I must die.
    Lord, have mercy on us!

Rich men, trust not in wealth,
Gold cannot buy your health;
Physic himself must fade;
All things to end are made;
The plague full swift goes by.
I am sick, I must die.
    Lord, have mercy on us!

Beauty is but a flower
Which wrinkles will devour;
Brightness falls from the air;
Queens have died young and fair;
Dust hath closed Helen's eye.
I am sick, I must die.
    Lord, have mercy on us!

Strength stoops unto the grave,
Worms feed on Hector brave;
Swords may not fight with fate;
Earth still holds ope her gate;

Come, come! the bells do cry.
I am sick, I must die.
> *Lord, have mercy on us!*

Wit with his wantonness
Tasteth death's bitterness;
Hell's executioner
Hath no ears for to hear
What vain art can reply.
I am sick, I must die.
> *Lord, have mercy on us!*

Haste therefore each degree
To welcome destiny;
Heaven is our heritage,
Each but a player's stage.
Mount we unto the sky.
I am sick, I must die.
> *Lord, have mercy on us!*

Socratic

H. D.

"They cut it in squares,
sometimes it comes
in little jars—"

"O—?"

"Under the trees—"

"Where?"

"By his *sheep*-pen."

"Whose?"

"The man
who brings eggs:
he put it
in a basket with moss."

"What?"

"Why,
the little jar."

"What for?"

"Why,
to carry it over—"

"Over where?"

"The fields to Io's house."

"Then?"

"*Her* mother took it out
of the moss,
opened it—"

"What?"

"The little jar."

"And then?"

"We each *had* some."

"What?"

"Why the thing
in the little jar
they got
from the straw huts."

"What huts?"

"Why,
the little huts under the apple-trees,
where they live—"

"Who live?"

"Why,
the *bees*."

The Negro

James Emanuel

Never saw him.
Never can.
Hypothetical,
Haunting man:

Eyes a-saucer,
Yessir bossir,
Dice a-clicking,
Razor flicking.

The-ness froze him
In a dance.
A-ness never
Had a chance.

Kubla Khan

Samuel Taylor Coleridge

In Xanadu did Kubla Khan
   A stately pleasure-dome decree:
Where Alph, the sacred river, ran
Through caverns measureless to man
   Down to a sunless sea.
So twice five miles of fertile ground
With walls and towers were girdled round:
And here were gardens bright with sinuous rills,
Where blossomed many an incense-bearing tree,
And here were forests ancient as the hills,
Enfolding sunny spots of greenery.

But oh! that deep romantic chasm which slanted
Down the green hill athwart a cedarn cover!
A savage place; as holy and enchanted
As e'er beneath a waning moon was haunted
By woman wailing for her demon-lover!
And from this chasm, with ceaseless turmoil seething,
As if this earth in fast thick pants were breathing,
A mighty fountain momently was forced,
Amid whose swift half-intermitted burst
Huge fragments vaulted like rebounding hail,

Or chaffy grain beneath the thresher's flail:
And 'mid these dancing rocks at once and ever
If flung up momently the sacred river.
Five miles meandering with a mazy motion
Through wood and dale the sacred river ran,
Then reached the caverns measureless to man,
And sank in tumult to a lifeless ocean:
And 'mid this tumult Kubla heard from far
Ancestral voices prophesying war!

    The shadow of the dome of pleasure
    Floated midway on the waves;
    Where was heard the mingled measure
    From the fountain and the caves.
It was a miracle of rare device,
A sunny pleasure-dome with caves of ice!

    A damsel with a dulcimer
    In a vision once I saw:
    It was an Abyssinian maid,
    And on her dulcimer she played,
    Singing of Mount Abora.
    Could I revive within me
    Her symphony and song,
    To such a deep delight 'twould win me,
That with music loud and long,
I would build that dome in air,
That sunny dome! those caves of ice!
And all who heard should see them there,
And all should cry, Beware! Beware!
His flashing eyes, his floating hair!
Weave a circle round him thrice,
And close your eyes with holy dread,
For he on honey-dew hath fed,
And drunk the milk of Paradise.

Song

Thomas Carew

Ask me no more where Jove bestows,
When June is past, the fading rose;
For in your beauty's orient deep
These flowers, as in their causes, sleep.

Ask me no more whither do stray
The golden atoms of the day;
For in pure love heaven did prepare
Those powders to enrich your hair.

Ask me no more whither doth haste
The nightingale when May is past;
For in your sweet dividing throat
She winters and keeps warm her note.

Ask me no more where those stars 'light
That downwards fall in dead of night;
For in your eyes they sit, and there
Fixèd become as in their sphere.

Ask me no more if east or west
The Phœnix builds her spicy nest;
For unto you at last she flies,
And in your fragrant bosom dies.

Why So Pale and Wan?

Sir John Suckling

Why so pale and wan, fond lover?
    Prithee, why so pale?
Will, when looking well can't move her,
    Looking ill prevail?
    Prithee, why so pale?

Why so dull and mute, young sinner?
    Prithee, why so mute?
Will, when speaking well can't win her,
    Saying nothing do't?
    Prithee, why so mute?

Quit, quit for shame! This will not move;
    This cannot take her.
If of herself she will not love,
    Nothing can make her:
    The devil take her!

Early Evening Quarrel

Langston Hughes

Where is that sugar, Hammond?
I sent you this morning to buy?
I say, where is that sugar
I sent you this morning to buy?
Coffee without sugar
Makes a good woman cry.

> *I ain't got no sugar, Hattie,*
> *I gambled your dime away.*
> *Ain't got no sugar, I*
> *Done gambled that dime away.*
> *But if you's a wise woman, Hattie,*
> *You ain't gonna have nothin to say.*

I ain't no wise woman, Hammond.
I am evil and mad.
Ain't no sense in a good woman
Bein' treated so bad.

> *I don't treat you bad, Hattie,*
> *Neither does I treat you good.*
> *But I reckon I could treat you*
> *Worser if I would.*

Lawd, these things we women
Have to stand!
I wonder is there anywhere a
Do-right man?

from Essay on Criticism

Alexander Pope

A little learning is a dang'rous thing;
Drink deep, or taste not the Pierian spring:
There shallow draughts intoxicate the brain,
And drinking largely sobers us again.
Fir'd at first sight with what the Muse imparts,
In fearless youth we tempt the heights of arts,
While from the bounded level of our mind,
Short views we take, nor see the lengths behind;
But more advanc'd, behold with strange surprise
New distant scenes of endless science rise!
So pleas'd at first the tow'ring Alps we try,

Mount o'er the vales, and seem to tread the sky;
Th' eternal snows appear already past,
And the first clouds and mountains seem the last;
But, those attain'd, we tremble to survey
The growing labours of the lengthen'd way,
Th' increasing prospect tires our wand'ring eyes,
Hills peep o'er hills, and Alps on Alps arise!

from Epistle to Dr. Arbuthnot

Alexander Pope

Shut, shut the door, good John! fatigu'd, I said.
Tie up the knocker! say I'm sick, I'm dead.
The dog-star rages! nay, 'tis past a doubt,
All Bedlam, or Parnassus, is let out:
Fire in each eye, and papers in each hand,
They rave, recite, and madden round the land.
What walls can guard me, or what shades can hide?
They pierce my thickets, through my grot they glide.
By land, by water, they renew the charge,
They stop the chariot, and they board the barge.
No place is sacred, not the church is free,
Ev'n Sunday shines no Sabbath-day to me:
Then from the Mint walks forth the man of rhyme
Happy! to catch me just at dinner-time.

Is there a parson much be-mus'd in beer,
A maudlin poetess, a rhyming peer,
A clerk, foredoom'd his father's soul to cross,
Who pens a stanza when he should engross?
Is there, who, lock'd from ink and paper, scrawls
With desp'rate charcoal round his darken'd walls?
All fly to Twit'nam, and in humble strain
Apply to me, to keep them mad or vain.

What Riddle Asked the Sphinx

Archibald MacLeish

In my stone eyes I see
The saint upon his knee
Delve in the desert for eternity.

In my stone ears I hear
The night-lost traveller
Cry *When?* to the earth's shadow: *When?*   *Oh Where?*

Stone deaf and blind
I ponder in my mind
The bone that seeks, the flesh that cannot find.

Stone blind I see
The saint's eternity
Deep in the earth he digs in.   Cannot he?

Stone deaf I hear
The night say *Then!* say *There!*
Why cries the traveller still to the night air?

The one is not content
With silence, the day spent;
With earth the other. More, they think was meant.

Stone that I am, can stone
Perceive what flesh and bone
Are blind and deaf to?
                          Or has hermit known,
Has traveller divined,
Some questions there behind
I cannot come to, being stone and blind?

To all who ken or can
I ask, since time began,
What riddle is it has for answer, Man?

The Anniversarie

John Donne

All Kings, and all their favorites,
  All glory of honors, beauties, wits,
The Sun itselfe, which makes time, as they passe,
Is elder by a yeare, now, than it was
When thou and I first one another saw:
All other things, to their destruction draw,
  Only our love hath no decay;
This, no to morrow hath, nor yesterday,
Running it never runs from us away,
But truly keepes his first, last, everlasting day.

Two graves must hide thine and my coarse,
    If one might, death were no divorce.
Alas, as well as other Princes, wee,
(Who Prince enough to one another bee,)
Must leave at last in death, these eyes, and eares,
Oft fed with true oathes, and with sweet salt teares;
    But soules where nothing dwells but love
(All other thoughts being inmates) then shall prove
This, or a love increased there above,
When bodies to their graves, soules from their graves remove.

And then wee shall be thoroughly blest,
    But we no more, than all the rest;
Here upon earth, we'are Kings, and none but wee
Can be such Kings, nor of such subjects bee.
Who is so safe as wee? where none can doe
Treason to us, except one of us two.
    True and false feares let us refraine
Let us love nobly, and live, and adde againe
Yeares and yeares unto yeares, till we attaine
To write threescore: this is the second of our raigne.

South End

Conrad Aiken

The benches are broken, the grassplots brown and bare,
the laurels dejected, in this neglected square.
Dogs couple undisturbed. The roots of trees
heave up the bricks in the sidewalk as they please.

Nobody collects the papers from the grass,
nor the dead matches, nor the broken glass.
The elms are old and shabby; the houses, around,
stare lazily through paintless shutters at forgotten ground.

Out of the dusty fountain, with the dust,
the leaves fly up like birds on a sudden gust.
The leaves fly up like birds, and the papers flap,
or round the legs of benches wrap and unwrap.

Here, for the benefit of some secret sense,
warm-autumn-afternoon finds permanence.
No one will hurry, or wait too long, or die:
All is serenity, under a serene sky.

Dignity shines in old brick and old dirt,
in elms and houses now hurt beyond all hurt.
A broken square where little lives or moves;
these are the city's earliest and tenderest loves.

Nude Descending a Staircase

X. J. Kennedy

Toe upon toe, a snowing flesh,
A gold of lemon, root and rind,
She sifts in sunlight down the stairs
With nothing on. Nor on her mind.

We spy beneath the banister
A constant thresh of thigh on thigh—
Her lips imprint the swinging air
That parts to let her parts go by.

One-woman waterfalls, she wears
Her slow descent like a long cape
And pausing, on the final stair
Collects her motions into shape.

The Altar

George Herbert

A broken ALTAR, Lord thy servant rears,
Made of a heart, and cèmented with teares:
   Whose parts are thy hand did frame;
   No workman's tool hath touch'd the same.
        A HEART alone
        Is such a stone,
        As nothing but
        Thy pow'r doth cut.
        Wherefore each part
        Of my hard heart
        Meets in this frame,
        To praise thy Name:
  That, if I chance to hold my peace,
  These stones to praise thee may not cease.
O let thy blessed SACRIFICE be mine,
And sanctify this ALTAR to be thine.

Do the Dead Know What Time It Is?

Kenneth Patchen

The old guy put down his beer.
Son, he said,
   (and a girl came over to the table where we were:
   asked us by Jack Christ to buy her a drink.)
Son, I am going to tell you something

The like of which nobody was ever told.
    (and the girl said, I've got nothing on tonight;
    how about you and me going to your place?)
I am going to tell you the story of my mother's
Meeting with God.
    (and I whispered to the girl: I don't have a room,
    but maybe . . .)
She walked up to where the top of the world is
And He came right up to her and said
So at last you've come home.
    (but maybe what?
    I thought I'd like to stay here and talk to you.)
My mother started to cry and God
Put His arms around her.
    (about what?
    Oh, just talk . . . we'll find something.)
She said it was like a fog coming over her face
And light was everywhere and a soft voice saying
You can stop crying now.
    (what can we talk about that will take all night?
    and I said that I didn't know.)
You can stop crying now.

CHAPTER EIGHT
THE POEM IN COUNTERMOTION

A poem, by the very fact of its existence in time rather than in space, has *duration* and *pace*. Since a good poem does not move throughout at exactly the same pace (unless the poet is trying for a special effect, and doubtfully then), the poem must also have *change of pace;* one part moves more rapidly or more slowly than another. All such changes of pace, it must be noted, are relative to one another: an anapest introduced into an iambic line accelerates that part of the line; an anapest in an anapestic line sustains the already accelerated pace, but does not accelerate it further. All the rhythms of poetry achieve their effect by the way they play against one another. They exist in countermotion.

Similarly, *all* the elements of a poem are engaged in a series of countermotions. Meter and rhythm are only two of the elements that may be involved. Diction, imagery, rhyme, line length, vowel quantities, consonant sequences, and grammatical structure are some of the other principal elements. From these elements the poem builds complexes of poetic structures, each related to all the others. The motion of these poetic structures, each against the others, is what ultimately determines the poem's performance. One simple rule seems to apply to the play of all such countermotions: *whenever in the course of a poem the poet changes either his tone or his attitude, some change will occur in the handling of the technical elements.* That change in the technical handling of the poem may be slight or it may be marked, but some change must occur. Conversely, any change in the handling of the technical elements in the course of the poem will indicate that a change has taken place in the poet's tone or attitude. Attitude, one will recall, is taken to signify "the way the poet takes his subject"; tone, "the way he takes himself."

The following little poem will serve as a convenient first illustration:

The Span of Life

Robert Frost

The old dog barks backward without getting up.
I can remember when he was a pup.

Note that neither line is a poem by itself. It is not a poem to say "The old dog barks backward without getting up." That much is only a statement. Nor is it a poem to say "I can remember when he was a pup." That much is only a comment. But a poem does happen when the two lines are said one after the other. It must follow that the poem exists in the countermotion of the two lines, in the way the second line (in this case the comment) makes something of what has been established in the first line (in this case the statement). Nor do the two lines simply run together: there is some point of balance between the end of the first and the beginning of the second, a pause, a meditative silence like a rest in music. The poem enters that pause with one attitude (in this case a relatively detached specific observation of the old dog) and after a moment of meditation it comes out of the pause with a different attitude (in this case a double change involving, first, a fonder, a sadder, and a more general recollection of the dog, and, second, a metaphoric implication, as reinforced by the title, that the comment is not only about the old dog but about all of life).

For convenience such a point of balance (and silence) may be called a *fulcrum* and may be indicated by the symbol <. Thus:

The old dog barks backward without getting up.

                                        <

I can remember when he was a pup.

Such countermotion is inseparable from what the poem is and what the poem means; it is in fact *how* the poem means. In briefest form, *a poem is one part against another across a silence.* To understand this characteristic of the poem is to understand the theory of poetic form. To be able to respond to it in a poem is to understand the practice of poetry.*

---

*It was pointed out earlier that every shift in tone or attitude is accompanied by some shift in the handling of the technical elements. That shift is relatively difficult to establish in so brief a poem since it involves the metrical differences between two lines each of which is unusual. The norm is, of course, anapestic, and one will do well to note at least some of the ways in which these lines vary in their play against that norm. The first line may be scanned:

$$\_ \ \_ \ / \ \ / \ \ / \ \ \_ \ \_ \ / \ \ \_ \ \_ \ /$$
The old dog   barks back   ward wi thout   ge tting up.

Yet certainly there is good reason for wishing to distribute the stress of the first foot over both "old" and "dog," thus:

$$\_ \ \overgroup{\text{old dog}} \ / \ \ / \ \ \_ \ \_ \ / \ \ \_ \ \_ \ /$$
The old dog   barks back   ward wi thout   ge tting up.

The Frost poem is as simple an example of poetic countermotion as one may well find. The following poem will illustrate the same sort of countermotion with rather more marked changes occurring across the fulcrum. The poem is one of the most memorable of the anonymous ballad snatches surviving from the early sixteenth century or perhaps earlier. Like most folk balladry, it survives in variant forms. The following is a modernized version.

O Western Wind

Anonymous

O Western wind, when wilt thou blow
That the small rain down may rain?
                                        <
Christ, that my love were in my arms,
And I in my bed again.

As indicated by the fulcrum, the poem, like "The Span of Life," consists of two parts. The first two lines are a cry of anguish to the western wind (in England, the wind of spring). The lament issues without any statement of cause for the speaker's anguish. The second two lines snap off that generalized lament and utter an angry and specific protest. The poet's tone has undergone an emphatic change.

As in "The Span of Life," one may note at once that neither of the halves is a poem. Whatever is being experienced is not complete in either the first two or the last two lines, but achieves its completion only in their countermotion across the silence of the fulcrum. Now if one will study the differences in technical handling on either side of the fulcrum, and if he will then relate them to the emotional force of the poem, he will be approaching the poem as its own performance, as its own act of itself, without resort to confusion by paraphrase.

For though paraphrase may be useful in helping to explain a specific difficulty in the phrasing of a poem, it is unfailingly a destructive method of discussion if one permits the illusion that the paraphrase is more than a momentary crutch, or that it is in any sense the poem itself. No poem means anything that any paraphrase is capable of saying. For,

---

The fact that one must pause after saying "old" in order to form the "d" sound of dog, tends to force a heavy stress on both words. The similarity of the vowels tends to make the words equal. And the repetition of "b" and "k" sounds around a similar (not identical) vowel sound in "barks back" once more heightens the pattern. Thus one is tempted to cluster four heavy accents on "old dog barks back."

The second line, on the other hand, has only one complication and that in the first (monosyllabic) foot. After the first foot the line progresses to the close in flawless anapests (the norm).

$$// \quad - \quad - \quad / \quad - \quad - \quad / \quad - - \quad /$$
I   can re mem   ber when he   was a pup.

Note the unusually heavy accent at the beginning of the second line (in this case a monosyllabic foot). Though it is not an invariable rule, there is a strong tendency in English and American poetry for the line after a fulcrum to begin with an unusually heavy stress, a monosyllabic foot, a spondee, a reversed foot, or some combination of these accents that produces a cluster of heavy stresses.

as noted, the poem exists in time and it exists in balance and counter-motion across a silence. That timing and that counterthrust are insepar-able from the emotional force of the poem, and it is exactly that timing and counterthrust that paraphrase cannot reproduce. The question to put to the poem is not "What does it mean?" but "How does it mean?" "What does it mean?" inevitably invites paraphrase and inevitably leads away from the poem. "How does it mean?" is best asked by absorbing the poetic structure as a poetic structure, as a countermotion across a silence, and thus leads the analysis to the poem itself.

In "O Western Wind" the two most notable differences between the lines before and after the fulcrum are (1) the pace, as determined by the metrics, by the consonant-vowel sequences, and by the rhetorical struc-ture; and (2) the diction, which changes from formal hortatory in the first two lines, to colloquial in the second two.

The shift in the quality of the diction is clear enough. The first two lines are a generalized hortatory question phrased in terms that might do for an invocation to some minor deity of the wind; the second two lines are specific and bitter exclamation phrased in the simplest lan-guage of common speech.

It is the metric pattern accompanying that shift of diction that is worth special attention:

O Wes / tern wind, / / when wilt / thou blow
That the small / rain down / may rain?
Christ, / / that my love / were in / my arms,
And I / in my bed / again.

The first two lines make use of two spondees in seven feet, and of two series of three heavy stresses in a row. The second two lines make use of no spondees, there is no point in them where even two heavy stresses fall together, there are two anapests in them as opposed to one in the first line, and there is a pyrrhic to add two more unstressed sylla-bles between accents. The only unusual emphasis in the second two lines occur in the monosyllabic foot at the beginning of line 3.* After that initial emphasis the meter becomes not only smooth but acceler-ated. It is as if that initial stress had consumed all the force of despair and passion, after which the voice can only slide forward into its grief.

Thus, one has located a first difference in the technical handling: the first two lines are metrically impeded and the second two lines are not only smooth but slightly accelerated. Having located that difference, one who wishes to experience poetry rather than simply to talk around it, will do well to consider that a fast passage in music is not the equivalent of a slow one, nor of the same passage repeated slowly. In the same way, a good poem does not change its pace without meaning

* See Frost's use of the same device after the fulcrum in "The Span of Life," and see the footnote on pp. 355-356.

something by that change. The rhythm is one part of the performance of the poem's meaning.

The first two lines of the present poem, moreover, are impeded not only by the meter but by the six lingering "w" sounds followed by the open vowels of "thou blow" (which pick up the open vowel of the vocative at the beginning of the line), thus:

O WEHstern WInd HWEn WIlt thOU blOW.

With this much observed, one may identify the essence of the poem's performance of itself. It begins with a heavily impeded generalized invocation to the western wind of spring. The poet draws out his cry as if tortured by the thought, carrying it on a rising inflection throughout the first two lines and leaving it suspended. The cry ends and the poet pauses, silent. Suddenly, within that silence, the terms of his grief change inside him. A second voice of his despair surges in him and lashes forth with a cry to heaven. The voice resumes with a hammer beat of anguish on the first syllable. Then, as if that first hammered syllable had drained the last strength of the speaker's anger, the voice slides off into a numb personal statement of the poet's exact grief, that grief now simply stated, no longer volatile and angry but defeated, and the metric line accordingly runs smooth and even accelerates in response to the fact that the poet no longer struggles against the truth, but closes on a dying fall.

The foregoing paragraph is not a paraphrase of the poem, but rather a simplified description of the details of the poetic performance. The function of such description is not to replace the poem but to direct the attention to it by pointing out the emotional sequences of the poem in time and the accompanying shifts in technical management. The question to be addressed is always *How* — not *What* — does a poem mean?

In both "The Span of Life" and "O Western Wind" the poetic structure is built across a single fulcrum and the units on either side of the fulcrum are equal in length. The following poem will illustrate a different case. Before one reads it, he needs to know that the poet served as an instructor in aerial gunnery during World War Two and that an essential part of such gunnery training consisted of memorizing the nomenclature of the many parts of a Browning .50-caliber machine gun. Obviously a gunner must be able to order repair parts from rear area depots, and if he is to receive the right part he must be able to give its exact technical name, no matter how complicated. The "belt-feed-lever" and the "belt-holding-pawl" of the last line are two of the many items of nomenclature that student gunners were required to learn. The poet is bemused by the resemblance of such vocabulary exercises from the school for death to the exercises all children are assigned in the school of innocence.

The Fury of Aerial Bombardment

Richard Eberhart

You would think the fury of aerial bombardment
Would rouse God to relent; the infinite spaces
Are still silent. He looks on shock-pried faces.
History, even, does not know what is meant.

<3

You would feel that after so many centuries
God would give man to repent; yet he can kill
As Cain could, but with multitudinous will,
No farther advanced than in his ancient furies.

<2

Was man made stupid to see his own stupidity?
Is God by definition indifferent, beyond us all?
Is the eternal truth man's fighting soul
Wherein the beast ravens in his own avidity?

<1

Of Van Wettering I speak, and Averill,
Names on a list whose faces I do not recall.
But they are gone to early death, who late in school
Distinguished the belt-feed-lever from the belt-holding-pawl.

The principal fulcrum of this poem quite clearly occurs, as marked, between the third and the fourth stanzas. There are lesser fulcrums within the first three stanzas, but they are better left for later discussion. The point to note is that there is no reason for two statements to be of the same length in order to have the same emotional weight. It is a working convention of the English sonnet, for example, to balance the final couplet against the twelve preceding lines, the couplet usually reversing the tone and attitude. Thus the main fulcrum would occur, in such sonnets, between the first twelve lines and the last two.

The first three stanzas of "The Fury of Aerial Bombardment" are made up of enormous rhetorical statements and questions addressed to no less a subject than man's fate upon the planet. In stanza four the address suddenly changes from a rhetoric for abstract man to an understated elegy for two boys named Van Wettering and Averill, boys who sought no universal meaning but simply distinguished the belt-feed-lever from the belt-holding-pawl, and died of their schooling, into the anonymities of fate. They are not even faces: they are names on a list. The only point at which they touch larger significance is that they are gone to early death. Thus, they are unknowing heirs to all human waste: their death is their one real illustration of the universal questions the poem begins with. Yet the implication is clear that their death is both man's tragedy and failure. The boys are the least of men in one sense, faceless and forgotten; yet their deaths accuse all of mankind, the more so in that these who die are so insignificant.

There can be no mistaking that the author has changed both his attitude toward the subject and his personal tone in going from one side of the fulcrum to the other. The opening attitude is one of the most intense moral indignation; the opening tone is rhetorical and resonant enough for the loftiest pulpit. The closing attitude drops the high moral indignation in favor of the simplest sort of sorrow, and the tone changes from high rhetoric to a conversational understatement. Inevitably the whole quality of the language changes from the Latinate diction of moral abstraction to the colloquial and less Latinate diction of simple statement.

The change in the pace and the rhythm is as marked as the change in diction. Each of the first three stanzas divides between masculine and feminine rhymes, the effect of the feminine rhymes being to leave the voice suspended on a rising inflection. The fourth stanza uses no feminine rhymes, each line closing on a masculine word. The voice is brought down firm to the falling inflection.

The change in the quality of the metrics from one side of the fulcrum to the other is even more emphatically marked. Eberhart's meter is unusual for the number of light syllables allowed into a single foot. One should sense at once that the poem is written in pentameters, and despite great variation, that the norm is iambic. (The next to last line, though lengthened to a hexameter, is made up entirely of iambics, and may be taken as the rest line of the poem, the line in which the norm is most clearly asserted. When in doubt it is wise to look for such rest lines.) Against that norm, however, the voice must swallow many accelerated syllables. So in the opening line:

$$\_\ \_\ \acute{}\ /\ \_\ \_\ \acute{}\ /\ \_\ \acute{}\ /\ \_\ \_\ \acute{}\ /\ \_\ \_\ \acute{}\ \_$$
You would think / the fu ry / of ae / ri al / bom bard ment

Line 9 can be scanned only by allowing a double feminine foot at the end:

$$\_\ \acute{}\ /\ \acute{}\ \acute{}\ /\ \_\ \_\ \acute{}\ /\ \_\ \acute{}\ /\ \_\ \acute{}\ \_\ \_$$
Was man / made stu / pid to see / his own / stu pid it y.

And line 10 runs to seven light accents in the second and third feet:

$$\_\ \acute{}\ /\ \_\ \_\ \_\ \acute{}\ /\ \_\ \_\ \acute{}\ /\ \_\ \_\ \_\ \acute{}\ /\ \_\ \acute{}$$
Is God / by de fin i tion / in di ffe rent, / / beyond / us all?

The characteristic of Eberhart's metric in the first three stanzas is extraordinary acceleration checked by relatively heavy caesura. The voice is thus required to lash out and stop, lash out and stop. The metric effect, when combined with the voice thrust suggested by the vastness of the concepts being declared, is clearly oratorical. The rhythm thrusts like the voice of a man delivering a powerful, outraged sermon, and being carried away by it. Note also that the sermon concludes with the voice rising on a double feminine, appropriately in a question:

$$\overset{\frown}{}\ \_\ \acute{}\ /\ \acute{}\ \_\ \_\ \_\ \acute{}\ /\ \_\ \acute{}\ \_\ \_$$
Where in / the beast / ra vens / in his own / a vi di ty?*

---

* The first foot may with equal reason be taken as a pyrrhic. The syllables are equal whether taken as stressed or unstressed.

Across the fulcrum, on the other hand, there is only one case in which three light syllables fall together. The extraordinary accelerations have disappeared, the metric is much smoother, and the pace is further slowed by the fact that the last two lines have become hexameters. The extra foot of the hexameter in English seems almost invariably to slow the pace by drawing out the line.

Of Van / We tter ing / I speak, / and A / ver ill,

Names/on a list, / / whose fa ces / I do not / re call.*

But they are gone / to ear / ly death, / / who late / in school
Dis tin / guished the belt / feed le ver / / from the / belt hold / ing
pawl.

Were the discussion of the poem to stop here, it would still be apparent that such changes in pace are not only relevant to the meaning of the poem, but so inseparably involved in the meaning that there can be no communication of the poem's essential experience until the voice has responded to the changes. Many sensitive readers are able to make such a response without being able to analyze why they have so responded; such attunement is the happy result of extensive and sensitive reading. It is possible, that is to say, to receive a poem without this sort of analysis. It is not possible, however, to *discuss* the poetic structure meaningfully without recognizing the countermoving balance of that structure across the fulcrum and the attendant change in the handling of the poetic elements. It is precisely because paraphrase is incapable of taking these elements and their counterweights into account that one must go the long way round to the discussion if he truly wishes to know what the poem is doing with itself.

There still remains to be considered the matter of the lesser fulcrums in the structure of Eberhart's poem, the fulcrums numbered 2 and 3 as distinct from the major fulcrum numbered 1. Thus far the discussion has all been of central fulcrum points, of the poem divided in two. The suggested image of the poetic structure has been that of a scale arm balanced across a single fulcrum. That image needs now to be expanded into something more like a piece of mobile sculpture, a structure possessing, to be sure, a single main point of balance, but containing further lesser balances within the parts.

Those lesser balances can become so intricate that to pursue all of them would lead to more confusion than clarity. Certainly, however, one may readily note that the first three stanzas of the Eberhart poem, though they constitute a single side of the central balance, are themselves divided into two units, one of which is divided once again.

---

* The beginning of line 2 may be scanned more regularly as a trochee followed by an iamb. There can be no doubt, however, that the normal speech rhythm of English makes "on a list" an anapest.

Represented as a diagrammatic mobile sculpture, with the numbers on the weights corresponding to the stanza numbers and F labeling the main fulcrum, the poem might be imagined thus:

One has only to observe the carefully repeated pattern of stanzas one and two to recognize their close relationship. The first line of each stanza is a run-on, and the voice continues without pause to a caesura after the third foot of the second line. After that caesura, the second line of each stanza again runs on, the voice in both cases coming to rest after the second foot of the third line. Then once more the voice moves forward for three feet and comes to rest again. And though the fourth line of the first stanza differs from the fourth line of the second by a small caesural effect around "even," the two lines are still more than sufficiently close to keep the pattern firm. Leaving that small caesural ripple around "even" out of consideration, one may diagram the pattern thus:

```
-----------------------------          m    f
-----------------//--------            f    m
--------//------------------//         f    m
-------------------------//            m    f
```

The rhyme ("m" for masculine and "f" for feminine) changes position from the first stanza (first column) to the second stanza in a perfect reversed pattern. As if to leave no possible doubt that the stanzas are exactly related, the poet has added an unmissable and unusual internal rhyme, "relent/repent," just before the first caesura in each stanza.

Such patterning of pauses and effects may again be recognized as characteristic of the rhetorician. The very parallel construction of the sentences—"You would think" in the first stanza, "You would feel" in the second, and again "Would rouse God" in the first, and "God would give" in the second—is a device of the same rhetorical impulse.

Then, having established his pattern with such care, the poet breaks from it. The third stanza has a much more definite tendency to run the line straight to a full end stop without internal pause, and thus the whole pattern of the pauses changes. A principal point of the present discussion, to repeat once again, is that such changes can only happen in response to a change in the poet's tone or attitude or both. He may realize exactly what change he is making, or he may simply follow the dictates of his feelings without analysis or need for analysis, but the changes themselves do not occur without cause. One can, of course, see at a glance that the voice has changed from making statements to asking questions. But given no more than the scansion of the poem and its pattern of pauses, without a word of the text, one would still be able to tell that the voice had undergone some change in response to a change in the poet's tone and attitude.

If every poem is constructed on such countermotions across a fulcrum, and if the handling of the technical elements always changes from one unit of the poetic structure to another, the method of analysis here suggested must inevitably lead to a fuller understanding of that poetic structure. One need only locate the principal fulcrum, the lesser fulcrums within the main units of the structure, and then analyze the differences in the handling of the poetic elements within each unit and subunit. To do that much, however, is not to have achieved the poem, but rather to have prepared oneself to achieve it. Any method of analysis is designed only to assure one that he is giving his human attention to the poem itself rather than to some nonpoetic paraphrase of its unenacted meaning. In every good poem there is some final echo of nuance and feeling that lies beyond explanation and analysis.

Not all poems, however, make their countermotions immediately apparent. So it is necessary to distinguish between what may be called *balanced* and *truncated* poems. Balanced poems are of the order already discussed: they exist in countermotion across inner fulcrum points. Truncated poems, on the other hand, travel in a straight line outward from the opening statement and seem to lack the counterthrust of an opposing passage. The following is an example.

My Papa's Waltz

Theodore Roethke

The whiskey on your breath
Could make a small boy dizzy;
But I held on like death:
Such waltzing was not easy.

We romped until the pans
Slid from the kitchen shelf;
My mother's countenance
Could not unfrown itself.

The hand that held my wrist
Was battered on one knuckle;
At every step you missed
My right ear scraped a buckle.

You beat time on my head
With a palm caked hard by dirt,
Then waltzed me off to bed
Still clinging to your shirt.

Despite its seeming lightness, "My Papa's Waltz" is a poem of terror, all the more terrible because the boy is frightened and hurt by the father even in play. "We romped," the poet says, but the romp is a dizzying succession of painful glimpses: the house is shaking, the mother is frowning, the father's hand is scarred by violence, every misstep in the dance scrapes the father's belt buckle painfully across the boy's ear, and the boy's head is being pounded by that huge, hard palm. It is a romp, but the boy must cling like death until he is finally dumped into bed.

The terror, however, mounts in a straight line, detail upon detail, with no countermotion across a fulcrum *because there is no change either in tone or in attitude*. The poem clearly breaks into four parts, as indicated by the stanza breaks, but the parts follow one another with no sense that one stanza break is more important than another. And as one might suspect in such a case, there is no marked difference in the handling of the poetic elements from stanza to stanza. Metrics, pace, diction, imagery, grammatical structure—all are very nearly constant throughout. Even the pattern of pauses is the same from stanza to stanza with only one variation in the extra pause at the end of the third line of stanza one: with that exception all the stanzas move without pause to the end of the second line, and then move forward again without pause to the end of the fourth line. And though there are two feminine rhymes in the first and third stanzas, even they fall into a neatly repeated pattern. The whole, disregarding the extra pause in stanza one, may be diagrammed thus:

```
-------------------------------   m   m   m   m
------------------------------//  f   m   f   m
------------------------------    m   m   m   m
----------------------------//    f   m   f   m
```

The poem seems to lack a fulcrum. The fact is that the poem does indeed work against a fulcrum, but that *the fulcrum occurs after the last line*. Imagine, as a horrible example, that the poet had written an additional summarizing stanza in his first draft, and imagine that it had run to some such sad stuff as the following:

> Ah, that was long ago.
> Now, his first terrors shed,
> This dancer turns to go
> Calm, to the fearless dead.

Miserable and cliché-ridden poeticizing to be sure, but had such a stanza existed, one would have had no hesitation in placing the fulcrum between it and the preceding poem, or in identifying the metric shift wherein three of the last four lines begin with monosyllabic feet.

The poet may very well have been tempted at first writing to add some such summarizing stanza. If so, he wisely put by the temptation in the secure sense that nothing could be said in such an addition that was not already better said by silence worked upon by the implications of the preceding lines. For silence, too, is communication when placed in context. Thus *the fulcrum exists outside the poem, between the enacted experience and the silence that follows it.*

The following poem, on the other hand, is a fair example of a poem that overran its silence into six lines of "tacked-on moral," all the more painful in view of the extraordinary sharpness and economy of most of the poem up to those last six lines:

Before Disaster

Yvor Winters

Evening traffic homeward burns,
Swift and even on the turns,
Drifting weight in triple rows,
Fixed relation and repose.
This one edges out and by,
Inch by inch with steady eye.
But should error be increased,
Mass and moment are released;
Matter loosens, flooding blind,
Levels driver to its kind.

Ranks of nations thus descend,
Watchful to a stormy end.
By a moment's calm beguiled,
I have got a wife and child.
Fool and scoundrel guide the State.
Peace is whore to Greed and Hate.
Nowhere may I turn to flee:
Action is security.
Treading change with savage heel,
We must live or die by steel.

A metric note is necessary before the discussion of the countermotions of this poem. The pattern of scansion for all lines is the same and may be represented thus:

$$/ - / - / - /$$

Each line, that is, begins and ends with a heavy stress and each consists of four such heavy stresses enclosing three unstressed syllables. In such a case one may be uncertain whether to take the line as iambic or trochaic. The fact is that many English poets who have written in tetrameters have welcomed this effect as pleasing. The voice begins and ends each line on a stressed syllable and proceeds through each line without internal pause, the metronomic quality of such metrics producing an especially incantatory effect. It is relevant that this stress-to-stress pattern of the tetrameter line rarely, if ever, occurs when caesuras are used.

Traditionally such lines are referred to as *catalectic* (noun form: *"catalexis"*) from Greek roots signifying "to stop short." Since what is stopped short of must come at the end, catalexis implies a trochaic base with something missing from the last foot:

$$\text{É}\text{ve ning/ tra ffic/ home ward/ burns,}$$
$$\text{Swift and/ e ven/ on the/ turns.}$$

The large fulcrum after the last couplet is labeled 1 to indicate that it is the major point of balance. The lesser fulcrums are both labeled 2 to indicate that they are of equal value. One may, if he wishes, argue for a lesser fulcrum after the sixth line, but it seems more important to stress that the first ten lines are a single unit.

That first unit of the poem is a dispassionate description of evening traffic seen primarily as a problem in physics: the tone of the passage is set by the implicit image of physical particles (detached from all human feeling) in motion. Rank on rank the particles move forward in their dangerous precision.

Across the first of the lesser fulcrums, the poet suddenly strikes a balance against his first image, amplifying the idea from literal description of traffic to an image-related idea of the condition of nations. "Nations" must certainly receive an unusually heavy stress by the logic of the implicit parallel construction. Ranks of particles move toward collision and ranks of *nations* to do exactly the same thing. The first shift then is from description to comment.

Having made a first comment on the largest scale, the poet pauses, and suddenly strikes a further balance with his material by applying it wryly to himself in the most personal terms. "By a moment's calm" (fixed relation and repose) and like nations, the poet says, *I* have also been beguiled. The three operative emphases are physical particles, nations, and I.

A triumphant poem thus far, a poetic structure lodging itself in a powerfully suggestive way against its following silence.

But at the end the moralist triumphs over the poet and the poem is blurred by six empty lines of abstract moralizing. "Fool," "scoundrel," "State," "Peace," "Greed," "Hate" (and capitalized for emphasis) are terms that might have tempted such a pompous moralizer as Henley. There can certainly be no doubt that they constitute a change in the quality of the diction, but they are unfortunately a change for the worse.

For a poem must finally be seen as a formal structure in which the countermotions of the units release into the silences they create a force of contained emotional perception beyond the power of statement. The key terms are: *release into silence, contained emotional perception,* and *statement.* The poetic structure *releases* its meaning; it does not *say* it.

Hawk's Way

Ted Olson

This was the hawk's way. This way the hawk
Nested a moment on the incredible
Crag of the wind, sitting the wind like rock.
This was the perilous, lovely way the hawk fell

Down the long hill of the wind, the anarch air
Shaped by his going: air became visible, bent
To a blade of beauty, cruel and taut and bare,
A bow of ecstasy, singing and insolent.

And the heart, too, bent to breaking; the heart was rent
Like a cloth, and did not care.

Then air deployed again, and was only air
On the empty way the hawk in his beauty went.

Compare this poem with Yvor Winters' "Before Disaster." The
editors believe that this poem, like Winters' could be much more
effective without the added comment. The first two stanzas capture the
hawk's way of going in a magnificent rhythm that closes upward on
the rising inflection of "singing and insolent." Had the poem been
brought firmly to rest against its own charged, following silence, could
the reader fail to sense that the author was indeed moved and that the
air seemed empty once the hawk was gone from it? Could a poet
capture the dive of a hawk into so moving a rhythm unless his "heart"
was involved?

Poems for Study: Countermotion

A number of the following poems have specific suggestions for study
attached. In all of them, whether or not accompanied by specific
notation:

1. Mark the fulcrums, identify their relative importance, and
   identify the poem as balanced or truncated.
2. In your own words and as economically as possible, identify
   the tone and attitude of each division of the poem.
3. Identify every technical device you can locate in each division.
4. Identify and specify every change in the handling of given
   technical devices across the fulcrum.
5. Reread the poem with these analyses accomplished.

Those who desire further exercises in analyzing the countermotions of poetry may apply these measures to any poem in the present volume, though it may be found that the length of the narrative poems in Chapter Three makes such analysis of them cumbersome.

On the Vanity of Earthly Greatness

Arthur Guiterman

The tusks that clashed in mighty brawls
Of mastodons, are billiard balls.

The sword of Charlemagne the Just
Is ferric oxide, known as rust.

The grizzly bear whose potent hug
Was feared by all, is now a rug.

Great Caesar's bust is on the shelf,
And I don't feel so well myself.

QUESTIONS

The humor of this poem is obviously a result of its countermotions. Each couplet builds up to its dividing comma in the largest possible diction, and then counterthrusts with an idea that seems incongruously small by comparison.

Is there any progression in this series of thrusts and counterthrusts?

See the somewhat similar series of thrusts and counterthrusts in Reed's "Naming of Parts," p. 192.

War Poet

Roy Fuller

Swift had pains in his head.
Johnson dying in bed
Tapped the dropsy himself.
Blake saw a flea and an elf.
Tennyson could hear the shriek
Of a bat. Pope was a freak.
Emily Dickinson stayed
Indoors for a decade.
Water inflated the belly
Of Hart Crane, and of Shelley.
Coleridge was a dope.
Southwell died on a rope.

Byron had a round white foot.
Smart and Cowper were put
Away. Lawrence was a fidget.
Keats was almost a midget.
Donne, alive in his shroud,
Shakespeare, in the coil of a cloud,
Saw death very well as he
Came crab-wise, dark and massy.
I envy not only their talents
And fertile lack of balance
But the appearance of choice
In their sad and fatal voice.

QUESTIONS

Everything in Fuller's catalogue of the oddness of the English and American poets is true, at least in some sense, but it is stated in the most irreverent terms. How does the poem develop from its irreverence to its final tone?

Why the irreverence?

Herself

John Holmes

Herself listening to herself, having no name,
She walked in an airy April sun, clothes close on her
And thin and of some printed green;
A girl came nearer and nearer, came
Carrying white and yellow flowers.

Girls are smooth with sleep in the morning
And before they dress up out of naked bed,
Stand open to all airs,
Next to the world's body as the world's to theirs.
In the evening and at midnight, light
Curves round a girl, reaches to brush her cheek,
Her lips, loose hair, or breast or knee.
Outlining her with shining that cannot speak.

Ann at midnight and three midnights heard a voice
Saying, When you come back you will not find me here.
Or Hulda. Not Ruth. Perhaps Elizabeth
Who read next year's news in a letter, all the accidents

Donne, alive in his shroud: the Sunday before his death, John Donne, then Dean of St. Paul's, arose from his death bed and, dressed in his shroud, preached what amounted to his own death sermon.

Postmarked, and lost it. No one believed her.
It was a dead man if you know what it is to be dead.
Eleanor, he said, or Janet Janet Janet do you dream me?

QUESTIONS

What is the force of "printed green" on line 3? "Printed" green as distinct from what other kind of green?

The third stanza may reasonably be taken as a reconstruction of the dream life of "Herself" ("At midnight and three midnights heard a voice"). What is the effect of running so many girls' names in, as if at random?

Unemployment

William Mills

A young hound howls.

I am almost slumbering
In a rocking chair.
The soft rain pats
A Mississippi road.

I feel like the road.

My Luve

Robert Burns

O my luve is like a red, red rose,
    That's newly sprung in June:
O my luve is like a melodie,
    That's sweetly played in tune.

As fair art thou, my bonie lass,
    So deep in luve am I;
And I will luve thee still, my dear,
    Till a' the seas gang dry.

Till a' the seas gang dry, my dear,
    And the rocks melt wi' the sun:
And I will luve thee still, my dear,
    While the sands o' life shall run.

And fare thee weel, my only luve!
    And fare thee weel a while!
And I will come again, my luve,
    Tho' it were ten thousand mile.

Ozymandias

Percy Bysshe Shelley

I met a traveler from an antique land,
Who said: Two vast and trunkless legs of stone
Stand in the desert. Near them, on the sand,
Half sunk, a shattered visage lies, whose frown,
And wrinkled lip, and sneer of cold command,
Tell that its sculptor well those passions read,
Which yet survive, stamped on these lifeless things,
The hand that mocked them, and the heart that fed:
And on the pedestal these words appear:
"My name is Ozymandias, King of Kings:
Look on my works, ye Mighty, and despair!"
Nothing beside remains. Round the decay
Of that colossal wreck, boundless and bare
The lone and level sands stretch far away.

The Passionate Shepherd to His Love

Christopher Marlowe

Come live with me and be my love,
And we will all the pleasures prove,
That valleys, groves, hills and fields,
Woods or steepy mountain yields.

And we will sit upon the rocks,
Seeing the shepherds feed their flocks
By shallow rivers, to whose falls
Melodious birds sing madrigals.

And I will make thee beds of roses,
And a thousand fragrant posies,
A cap of flowers and a kirtle
Embroidered all with leaves of myrtle;

A gown made of the finest wool,
Which from our pretty lambs we pull;
Fair-linèd slippers for the cold,
With buckles of the purest gold;

A belt of straw and ivy buds,
With coral clasps and amber studs;
And if these pleasures may thee move,
Come live with me and be my love.

The shepherd swains shall dance and sing
For thy delight each May morning;
If these delights thy mind may move,
Then live with me and be my love.

The Nymph's Reply to the Shepherd

Sir Walter Raleigh

If all the world and love were young
And truth in every shepherd's tongue,
These pretty pleasures might me move
To live with thee and be thy love.

Time drives the flocks from field to fold
When rivers rage and rocks grow cold,
And Philomel becometh dumb;
The rest complain of cares to come.

The flowers do fade and wanton fields
The wayward winter reckoning yields;
A honey tongue, a heart of gall,
Is fancy's Spring, but sorrow's Fall.

Thy gowns, thy shoes, thy beds of roses,
Thy cap, thy kirtle, and thy posies
Soon break, soon wither, soon forgotten,
In folly ripe, in reason rotten.

Thy belt of straw and ivy buds,
Thy coral clasps and amber studs,
All these in me no means can move
To come to thee and be thy love.

But could youth last and love still breed,
Had joys no date nor age no need,
Then these delights my mind might move
To live with thee and be thy love.

The Baite

John Donne

Come live with mee, and bee my love,
And wee will some new pleasures prove
Of golden sands, and christall brookes,
With silken lines, and silver hookes.

There will the river whispering runne
Warm'd by thy eyes, more than the Sunne.
And there the'inamored fish will stay,
Begging themselves they may betray.

When thou wilt swimme in that live bath,
Each fish, which every channell hath,
Will amorously to thee swimme,
Gladder to catch thee, than thou him.

If thou, to be so seene, beest loath,
By Sunne or Moone, thou darknest both,
And if myself have leave to see,
I need not their light, having thee.

Let others freeze with angling reeds,
And cut their legges, with shells and weeds,
Or treacherously poor fish beset,
With strangling snare, or windowie net:

Let coarse bold hands, from slimy nest
The bedded fish in banks out-wrest,
Or curious traitors, sleavesilk flies
Bewitch poore fishes wandering eyes.

For thee, thou needst no such deceit,
For thou thyself are thine owne bait;
That fish that is not catch'd thereby,
Alas, is wiser farre than I.

Many readers have trouble reading John Donne because they fail to solve his grammatical sense (which is not a random eccentricity but a device for forcing voice emphasis primarily through the weight of parallel constructions and balanced antitheses). The last line of the third stanza, for example, is a parallel construction. Rendered with all its implications stated it would read: "[Each fish will be] gladder to catch thee, than thou [wilt be to catch] him." With that understood, the voice must punch the parallel elements with unusual emphasis, thus: "Gladder to catch *thee,* than *thou* him." No poet in English has used grammatical structure so extensively for metric effect.

That grammatical control of voice stresses can be confusing, the first two lines of the fourth stanza attest. Certainly the grammar instructs the voice to read with the stress as follows:

If THOU, to be so SEENE, beest *loath,*
By *Sunne* or *Moone,* thou *dark*nest BOTH.

The italicized syllables receive normal stress, those printed in capitals acquire especially heavy stresses because of the grammatical force.

Unfortunately some grammatical difficulty is likely to follow, but a willing reader should not find Donne's grammar a stumbling block for long. As an illustration of this sort of difficulty, these two lines may be taken to mean, in more usual grammar: If thou beest loath to be so seene by either the Sunne or the Moone (a double meaning here equivalent in the second sense to "by day or night") then thou darknest both (and in both senses).

To His Coy Mistress

Andrew Marvell

Had we but world enough, and time,
This coyness, lady, were no crime.
We would sit down, and think which way
To walk, and pass our long love's day.
Thou by the Indian Ganges' side
Should'st rubies find: I by the tide
Of Humber would complain. I would
Love you ten years before the Flood,
And you should, if you please, refuse
Till the conversion of the Jews.
My vegetable love should grow
Vaster than empires, and more slow.
An hundred years should go to praise
Thine eyes, and on thy forehead gaze:
Two hundred to adore each breast:
But thirty thousand to the rest;
An age at least to every part,
And the last age should show your heart.
For, lady, you deserve this state,
Nor would I love at lower rate.
   But at my back I always hear
Time's wingéd chariot hurrying near:
And yonder all before us lie
Deserts of vast eternity.
Thy beauty shall no more be found;
Nor, in thy marble vault, shall sound
My echoing song: then worms shall try
That long-preserved virginity,
And your quaint honor turn to dust,
And into ashes all my lust.
The grave's a fine and private place,
But none, I think, do there embrace.
   Now, therefore, while the youthful hue
Sits on thy skin like morning dew,
And while thy willing soul transpires
At every pore with instant fires,

Now let us sport us while we may;
And now, like amorous birds of prey,
Rather at once our Time devour,
Than languish in his slow-chapt power.
Let us roll all our strength and all
Our sweetness up into one ball,
And tear our pleasures with rough strife
Through the iron gates of life.
Thus, though we cannot make our Sun
Stand still, yet we will make him run.

You, Andrew Marvell

Archibald MacLeish

And here face down beneath the sun
And here upon earth's noonward height
To feel the always coming on
The always rising of the night

To feel creep up the curving east
The earthly chill of dusk and slow
Upon those under lands the vast
And ever-climbing shadow grow

And strange at Ecbatan the trees
Take leaf by leaf the evening strange
The flooding dark about their knees
The mountains over Persia change

And now at Kermanshah the gate
Dark empty and the withered grass
And through the twilight now the late
Few travelers in the westward pass

And Baghdad darken and the bridge
Across the silent river gone
And through Arabia the edge
Of evening widen and steal on

And deepen on Palmyra's street
The wheel rut in the ruined stone
And Lebanon fade out and Crete
High through the clouds and overblown

And over Sicily the air
Still flashing with the landward gulls

And loom and slowly disappear
The sails above the shadowy hulls

And Spain go under and the shore
Of Africa the gilded sand
And evening vanish and no more
The low pale light across that land

Nor now the long light on the sea—

And here face downward in the sun
To feel how swift how secretly
The shadow of the night comes on. . . .

The Tyger

William Blake

Tyger! Tyger! burning bright
In the forests of the night,
What immortal hand or eye
Could frame thy fearful symmetry?

In what distant deeps or skies
Burnt the fire of thine eyes?
On what wings dare he aspire?
What the hand dare seize the fire?

And what shoulder, and what art,
Could twist the sinews of thy heart?
And when thy heart began to beat,
What dread hand? and what dread feet?

What the hammer? what the chain?
In what furnace was thy brain?
What the anvil? what dread grasp
Dare its deadly terrors clasp?

When the stars threw down their spears
And watered heaven with their tears,
Did he smile his work to see?
Did he who made the Lamb make thee?

Tyger! Tyger! burning bright
In the forests of the night,
What immortal hand or eye
Dare frame thy fearful symmetry?

"And what is love? Misunderstanding, pain"

J. V. Cunningham

And what is love? Misunderstanding, pain,
Delusion, or retreat? It is in truth
Like an old brandy after a long rain,
Distinguished, and familiar, and aloof.

"Lady, of anonymous flesh and face"

J. V. Cunningham

Lady, of anonymous flesh and face
In the half-light, in the rising embrace
Of my losses, in the dark dress and booth,
The stripper of the gawking of my youth,
Lady, I see not, care not, what you are.
I sit with beer and bourbon at this bar.

The Second Coming

William Butler Yeats

Turning and turning in the widening gyre
The falcon cannot hear the falconer;
Things fall apart; the centre cannot hold;
Mere anarchy is loosed upon the world.
The blood-dimmed tide is loosed, and everywhere
The ceremony of innocence is drowned;
The best lack all conviction, while the worst
Are full of passionate intensity.

Surely some revelation is at hand;
Surely the Second Coming is at hand.
The Second Coming! Hardly are those words out
When a vast image out of *Spiritus Mundi*
Troubles my sight: somewhere in sands of the desert
A shape with lion body and the head of a man,
A gaze blank and pitiless as the sun,
Is moving its slow thighs, while all about it
Reel shadows of the indignant desert birds.

Spiritus Mundi: The Spirit of the World. Yeats was a believer in a mystical system largely of
his own invention. In that system *Spiritus Mundi* is the name of a place somewhere between
the Earth and Sun. It is there the souls of the dead go.

The darkness drops again; but now I know
That twenty centuries of stony sleep
Were vexed to nightmare by a rocking cradle,
And what rough beast, its hour come round at last,
Slouches toward Bethlehem to be born?

Sailing to Byzantium

William Butler Yeats

I

That is no country for old men. The young
In one another's arms, birds in the trees,
—Those dying generations—at their song,
The salmon-falls, the mackerel-crowded seas,
Fish, flesh, or fowl, commend all summer long
Whatever is begotten, born, and dies.
Caught in that sensual music all neglect
Monuments of unaging intellect.

II

An aged man is but a paltry thing,
A tattered coat upon a stick, unless
Soul clap its hands and sing, and louder sing
For every tatter in its mortal dress,
Nor is there singing school but studying
Monuments of its own magnificence;
And therefore I have sailed the seas and come
To the holy city of Byzantium.

III

O sages standing in God's holy fire
As in the gold mosaic of a wall,
Come from the holy fire, perne in a gyre,
And be the singing-masters of my soul.
Consume my heart away; sick with desire
And fastened to a dying animal
It knows not what it is; and gather me
Into the artifice of eternity.

IV

Once out of nature I shall never take
My bodily form from any natural thing,
But such a form as Grecian goldsmiths make

Of hammered gold and gold enameling
To keep a drowsy Emperor awake;
Or set upon a golden bough to sing
To lords and ladies of Byzantium
Of what is past, or passing, or to come.

Byzantium (what is now Istanbul) became for Yeats the symbol of all that was desirable in this world. He had a mystic nostalgia for what he considered Byzantium's golden age, when possibly, as he put it, "never before or since in recorded history, religious, aesthetic, and practical life were one." "Perne in a gyre" is Yeats' term for "spinning in a spiral motion." Perne will be found in the dictionary as a noun, "pirn." Yeats likes the word and reshaped it into the verb he needed.

MATERIALS FOR FURTHER STUDY

A Poem in Progress

Following is the history of the creation of a poem by Wilfred Owen: a record of the poem's coming to be. Owen was a British soldier killed in action in World War One. As a lieutenant of infantry, he saw men die in the fields and the trenches, far from England and the rituals they had known and would have expected for their own funerals had they died at home and in peace. The poem takes form as Owen looks about the battleground for the elements of war that might be made to substitute for the elements of a funeral mass in the Church of England. As he takes wailing shells for the choir and the sound of the rifle for the chant of the priest, he begins to build a metaphoric service.

The force of the poem lies to a large degree in the ironic similarities between the worlds of peace and war as they come together in death, but to point out the irony would not be enough. Nothing in a poem can be effective if the language is not, and Owen worked and reworked his lines with great care through what amounts to nine known drafts of the poem.

These were not neatly written versions on nine separate sheets of paper, but have been reconstructed from marked-out and overwritten lines on four worksheets. After Owen had made some initial changes in the first version of the poem, he asked his friend and fellow poet Siegfried Sassoon for suggestions—as poets are likely to do—and since it ought to be of some interest to see which of these suggestions the author took and which ones he rejected, Sassoon's suggestions are presented as the changes in the third draft of the poem.

The changes in the poem are shown line by line, so that the development of each line can be more easily observed. There should not be any difficulty in the reading of an entire draft, however; to follow the fourth version, for example, simply read each line d as it comes in

sequence. Line i read through in sequence adds up to the finished
poem, which is given intact on the page following the drafts.

The following is the first draft:

first draft of **Anthem for Doomed Youth**

Wilfred Owen

What mind's bells for these who die so fast?
—Only the monstrous anger of our guns.
Let the majestic insults of their iron mouths
Be as the priests' words at their burials.
Of choristers and holy music, none,
Nor any voice of mourning, save the wail,
The long-drawn wail of high, far-sailing shells.
What candles may we hold for these lost souls?
Not in the hands of boys, but in their eyes
Shall many candles shine, and He will light them:
Women's wide-spreaded arms shall be their wreaths,
And pallor of girls' cheeks shall be their palls.
The flowers, the tenderness of old men's minds,
And every dusk, a drawing down of blinds.

The following diagram gives, line by line, the nine different drafts of
the poem—from first through final versions. As will be seen, not all
lines were revised nine times. Siegfried Sassoon's suggested changes
are given in line c.

LINE 1

a) What mind's bells for these who die so fast?
b) "   passing- "   "   "   "   "   "   "
c) "   "   "   "   "   "   "   "   "
d) "   "   "   " you   "   " in herds?
e) "   "   "   "   "   "   "   "   "
f) "   "   "   " these dumb-dying cattle?
g) "   "   "   "   " who die as   "
h) "   "   "   "   "   "   "   "   "
i) "   "   "   " these   "   "   "   "

LINE 2

a) — Only the monstrous anger of our guns.
b) — "   "   "   "   "   "   "
c) — "   "   "   "   " the   "
d) — "   "   "   "   " more   "
e) — "   "   "   "   " the   "
f) — "   "   "   "   " more   "

g) — "   "   "   "   "   the   "
h) — "   "   "   "   "   "   "
i) — "   "   "   "   "   "   "

LINE 3

a) Let the majestic   insults of their iron mouths
b) "   "   "   "   "   "   "   "
c) "   "   blind   insolence "   "   "   "
d) Only " stuttering rifles'   rattled   words
e) "   "   "   "   "   "
f) "   "   "   "   rapid   rattle
g) "   "   "   "   "   "
h) "   "   "   "   "   "
i) "   "   "   "   "   "

LINE 4

a) Be as the priests' words at their burials.
b) "   "   " requiem   of   "   "
c) "   "   " organs   "   the old requiem
d) Can patter out your hasty orisons.
e) "   "   "   "   "   "
f) "   "   "   their "   "
g) "   "   "   "   "   "
h) "   "   "   "   "   "
i) "   "   "   "   "   "

LINE 5

a) Of choristers and holy music, none,
b)   "   "   "   "   "
c) "   "   "   "   "   "
d) No chants   for   you,   nor balms, nor wreaths, nor   bells
e) "   "   "   "   "   "   "   "   "   choirs
f) "   "   "   them; "   "   " asphodels
g) " mockeries   "   "   from prayers or   bells,
h) "   music   "   "   "   "   "   "
i) " mockeries now   "   "   no   "   nor   "

LINE 6

a) Nor any voice of mourning, save the   wail
b) "   "   "   "   "   "   "   "
c) "   "   "   "   "   "   "   "
d) "   "   "   "   "   "   " choirs
e) "   "   "   "   "   "   " shells
f) "   "   "   "   "   "   " choirs,—
g) "   "   "   "   "   "   "   "
h) "   "   "   "   "   "   "   "
i) "   "   "   "   "   "   "   "

LINE 7

a)   The long-drawn wail of high, far-sailing shells
b)   "   "   "   "   "   "   "   "   ·"
c) & "   "   kiss   " lonely   "
d)   " shrill   demented choirs of wailing   "
e) "   long-drawn   sighs   "   "   "
f)   " shrill   demented   "   "   "   "
g)   "   "   demonic   "   "   "   "
h)   "   "   demented   "   "   "   "
i)   "   "   "   "   "   "   "

LINE 8

a)   (no line here in first three drafts)
b)
c)
d) And bugles calling for   you   from sad shires.
e)   "   "   "   "   "   "   "   "
f)   "   "   "   "   them   "   "   "
g)   "   "   "   sad across the   "
h)   "   "   "   for them from sad   "
i)   "   "   "   "   "   "   "   "

LINE 9

a) What candles may we hold for these lost souls?
b)   "   "   "   "   " to light "   " ?
c)   "   "   "   " " "   "   "   " ?
d)   "   "   "   " " " " speed you all ?
e)   "   "   "   " " " "   "   " ?
f)   "   "   "   " " " "   " them" ?
g)   "   "   "   " " " "   "   " ?
h)   "   "   "   " " " "   "   . "   " ?
i)   "   "   " be held "   "   "   " ?

LINE 10

a) Not in the hands of boys, but in their eyes
b) " " "   "   "   "   " "   "   "
c) " " "   "   "   "   " "   "   "
d) " " "   "   "   "   " "   "   "
e) " " "   "   "   "   " "   "   "
f) " " "   "   "   "   " "   "   "
g) " " "   "   "   "   " "   "   "
h) " " "   "   "   "   " "   "   "
i) " " "   "   "   "   " "   "   "

LINE 11

a) Shall many candles shine, and he will light them:
b)   "   shine the many flames, no holy   tapers
c)   "   "   "   "   "   "   "   "
d)   "   "   "   holy   lights of long good-byes.
e)   "   "   "   "   "   " our   "
f)   "   "   "   "   gleams " their   "
g)   "   "   "   "   glimmers "   "
h)   "   "   "   "   "   "   "
i)   "   "   "   "   "   "   "

LINE 12

a) Women'swide-spreaded arms shall be their wreaths
b)   "   "   spread   "   "   "   "   "
c)   "   "   "   "   "   "   "   "
d) (This line is dropped with the third draft)

LINE 13

a)   And pallor of girls' cheeks shall be their palls.
b)   "   "   "   "   "   "   "   "   "
c)   "   "   "   "   "   "   "   "   "
d) The   "   "   "   brows   "   " your pall
e)   "   "   "   "   "   must "   "   "   comrade!
f)   "   "   "   "   cheeks shall " their   "
g) &   "   "   "   "   brows   "   "   "   "
h)   "   "   "   "   "   "   "   "   "
i)   "   "   "   "   "   "   "   "

LINE 14

a) The flowers, the tenderness of old   men's minds,
b) "   "   "   "   " rough   "   "
c) "   "   "   "   " rough   "   "
d) Your   "   "   "   "   mortal   "
e)   "   "   "   "   "   broken   "
f) Their   "   "   "   "   silent   "
g)   "   "   "   "   " sweet white   "
h)   "   "   "   "   "   silent   "
i)   "   "   "   "   "   patient*   "

---

* "comrade's" was also interlineated early as a possible word to describe the quality of the mind of those left to live on. Owen had apparently settled on "silent" (his temporary substitution of "sweet white" suggests that he wanted both the sibilant and the long "i" as echoes in the line), but he decided finally on "patient," very likely as a further suggestion from Siegfried Sassoon, to whom Owen showed the poem again after it was finished—except, possibly, for that change.

LINE 15

a) And every dusk, a drawing down of blinds.*
b)   " each slow " "   "   "   "   "
c)   "   "   "   "   "   "   "   "   "
d)   "   "   "   "   "   "   "   "   "
e)   "   "   "   "   "   "   "   "   "
f)   "   "   "   "   "   "   "   "   "
g)   "   "   "   "   "   "   "   "   "
h)   "   "   "   "   "   "   "   "   "
i)   "   "   "   "   "   "   "   "   "

Here is the poem after final revision:

Anthem for Doomed Youth

Wilfred Owen

What passing-bells for these who die as cattle?
    Only the monstrous anger of the guns.
    Only the stuttering rifles' rapid rattle
Can patter out their hasty orisons.
No mockeries now for them; no prayers nor bells,
    Nor any voice of mourning save the choirs,—
The shrill, demented choirs of wailing shells;
    And bugles calling for them from sad shires.

What candles may be held to speed them all?
    Not in the hands of boys, but in their eyes
Shall shine the holy glimmers of good-byes.
    The pallor of girls' brows shall be their pall;
Their flowers the tenderness of patient minds,
And each slow dusk a drawing-down of blinds.

In choosing "patient" over "silent" or "sweet white" in the next-to-last line of the poem, Owen sacrificed sound for sense. Often it is impossible to find the word that serves sound and sense equally well, and many word choices involve a sacrifice of one to the other. If sense is always sacrificed to sound, the result is a nonsense jingle; if sound is always sacrificed to sense, the result is a probably dull piece of reporting. The poet has to decide in each instance whether sound play or exact meaning seems more vital at the particular place in a poem's development. What other moments in this poem can you find when Owen seems to have been making such a decision?

---

* There is an old custom, once generally practiced—and still observed in some small towns in the United States as well as England—of lowering the blinds in a home visited by death as a way of putting the whole house and all within it into mourning.

Note that as the poem develops, there is a general movement toward:

distance between the poet and his subject;
understatement, ordinary language, and a quiet voice;
consistency of tone;
a clear pattern of rhyme;
a controlled series of stresses giving the poem a compelling sense of forward motion (rhythm);
a clear development of the idea of the poem, true to the poem's own internal logic.

An example of the development of the idea of the poem through the poem's internal logic is the use in the first part of words suggesting speed, with a shift in the last few lines to words suggesting slowness, as the movement of the lines slows down at the same time. What instances can you find exemplifying the other five major directions in which the poem moves?

Translation as Laboratory

When a translator sets out to carry a poem from one language to another, he finds himself serving two masters who quite often disagree about what he should do. A poet writing his own work must be true to his own language and what he wants to say, but what he wants to say may change any number of times during the writing of a poem. Frequently the exigencies of the language itself will turn the direction of his statement, and the poet will follow along to see where the new direction takes him. In translating, on the other hand, the poet has to be true to the deeper syntax of his own language and to what the first poet finally said, and there's no altering that. The first poem is already written.

The compromises made word by word in translation are even more excruciating than those made by the writer of his own work, but one standard of judgment hangs as a backdrop behind all a translator's compromises: the poem must first of all be a good poem in his own tongue, as if it were originally his poem. A poem carried from Spanish into English is worth nothing to the English reader if it is not a good English poem by the time he reads it. Probably no test shows a writer's skill in his language so clearly as his ability to build a worthy poem under these circumstances, and few circumstances present the student with so excellent an opportunity to observe the effects of word choice and the meaning of sacrifice.

The following poem is by Goethe, a German poet who lived from 1749 until 1832. If you know someone who reads German, even if you don't understand it yourself, it would be a good idea to listen to the poem read aloud, to see how much of its effect is in the way it sounds.

Dauer im Wechsel

Johann Wolfgang von Goethe

Hielte diesen frühen Segen
Ach, nur Eine Stunde fest!
Aber vollen Blütenregen
Schüttelt schon der laue West.
Soll ich mich des Grünen freuen,
Dem ich Schatten erst verdankt?
Bald wird Sturm auch das zerstreuen,
Wenn es falb im Herbst geschwankt.

Willst du nach den Früchten greifen,
Eilig nimm dein Teil davon!
Diese fangen an zu reifen,
Und die andern keimen schon;
Gleich mit jedem Regengusse
Ändert sich dein holdes Tal,
Ach, und in demselben Flusse
Schwimmst du nicht zum zweitenmal.

Du nun selbst! Was felsenfeste
Sich vor dir hervorgetan,
Mauern siehst du, siehst Paläste
Stets mit andern Augen an.
Weggeschwunden ist die Lippe,
Die im Kusse sonst genas,
Jener Fuß, der an der Klippe
Sich mit Gemsenfreche maß,

Jene Hand, die gern und milde
Sich bewegte wohlzutun,
Das gegliederte Gebilde,
Alles ist ein andres nun.
Und was sich an jener Stelle
Nun mit deinem Namen nennt,
Kam herbei wie eine Welle,
Und so eilts zum Element.

Laß den Anfang mit dem Ende
Sich in Eins zusammenziehn!
Schneller als die Gegenstände
Selber dich vorüberfliehn.
Danke, daß die Gunst der Musen
Unvergängliches verheißt,
Den Gehalt in deinem Busen
Und die Form in deinem Geist.

The following is a translation of this poem, prepared with great care by a scholar who knows both the German language and the work of Goethe. His purpose in doing the translation—at the request of the editors—was to convey to the English reader as precisely as possible the line-by-line rational content of the poem. When a choice had to be made between sound and sense, the choice was always for sense—the literal sense of Goethe's words. *What* the poem means has been separated—inasmuch as possible—from *how* it means. How much poetry is there in the English?

Permanence in Change

Johann Wolfgang von Goethe

Transliterated by Mark J. Doyle

Oh! if but a single hour
Could hold fast this early blessing!
But already the west wind
Is scattering showers of blossoms.
Will I still find pleasure in the verdure
That I, till now, have been grateful to for shade?
Soon the storm will disperse that, too,
When it trembles, sere, in autumn.

If you would reach out for the fruit,
Then take your share in haste!
For these are beginning to ripen
And the others are going to seed.
With each torrent of rain
Your lovely valley changes
And, alas, you do not swim
A second time in the same stream.

Now you yourself! What once was
Manifest to you, as firm as rock—
Palisades you see, see palaces,
Always with a different eye.
Gone from sight forever is the lip
Which once found joy in kissing,
The foot that on the precipice
Rivaled the mountain goat's in boldness.

Gone too the hand that willingly and bounteously
Stretched forth for kindness' sake.
The structured order of the parts—
The whole is now a different thing.

What is that fixed place
Now calls itself by your name,
Came breaking once like a wave
And hastens to the primal element.

Let the beginning and the end
Contract into a single thing!
Faster than the objects of your vision,
Let your self flee past.
Give thanks that the muses' favor
Promises one unchanging thing—
Its substance in your breast
And its form within your spirit.

Now read a translation of the German poem into English poetry. John Nims has set out to make the English-speaking reader feel the response that he believes the German-speaking reader felt. Much of what the reader of German responded to was rhythm and sound play, image and suggestion, metaphor, and simply good turns of phrase. So, as well as the paraphrasable statement of the poem, Nims has built his translation also on these elements, and sometimes, as you will see if you compare the exact line-by-line "sense" of the following to the preceding, he has sacrificed literal sense to sound. It is a testimony to Nims' ability as a translator that the literal sense is so nearly intact, and the general sense of the poem perfectly so. A large part of what a poem says lies in the experiencing of the poem itself, as a reader moves through turns and patterns of language. This is what Nims has put back in the poem.

Permanence in Change

Johann Wolfgang von Goethe

Translated by John Nims

Early blossoms—could a single
Hour preserve them just as now!
But the warmer west will scatter
Petals showering from the bough.
How enjoy these leaves, that lately
I was grateful to for shade?
Soon the wind and snow are rolling
What the late Novembers fade.

Fruit—you'd reach a hand and have it?
Better have it then with speed.
These you see about to ripen,
Those already gone to seed.

Half a rainy day, and there's your
Pleasant valley not the same.
None could swim that very river
Twice, so quick the changes came.

You yourself! What all around you
Strong as stonework used to lie
—Castles, battlements—you see them
With an ever-changing eye.
Now the lips are dim and withered
Once the kisses set aglow;
Lame the leg, that on the mountain
Left the mountain goat below.

Or that hand, that knew such loving
Ways, outstretching in caress,
—Cunningly adjusted structure—
Now can function less and less.
All are gone; this substitution
Has your name and nothing more.
Like a wave it lifts and passes,
Back to atoms on the shore.

See in each beginning, ending,
Double aspects of the One;
Here, amid stampeding objects,
Be among the first to run,
Thankful to a muse whose favor
Grants you one unchanging thing:
What the heart can hold to ponder;
What the spirit shape to sing.

Study and compare the five following renderings into English of the first twenty-one lines of Dante's *Inferno*. The Allan Gilbert rendering can be taken to serve as a "transliteration," against which the "literalness" of the "translations" can be measured. Which translation do you imagine must convey to the English reader most of what an Italian reader of the late middle ages must have felt when he read the lines?

Notice that Dante wrote in three-line groups (you can see this from the original without knowing any Italian), which rhyme in an interlocking fashion so that rhymes are in threes—a very difficult thing to achieve in English, as English doesn't have nearly so many rhyme sounds as Italian does. Some translators have ignored the form altogether, but the numbers on which Dante builds his epic poem (all threes and multiples of three) have such symbolic significance and are so much a part of the way in which the poem means that most translators have not been willing to give up the "three-ness" of the poem without a struggle. Read all of the renderings to see what word choices have been made, and simply how good a piece of writing the poem as rendered seems to be in English. Imagine that what you are reading was written in English as an original poem, and see how it fares. Then look to the handling of the three-ness of the form, and see what you think about the ways in which the various translators have dealt with that problem. If you will do this carefully, you should come out of it with a clearer sense not only of the problems of language and diction and the sometimes inimical demands of form, but of the nature of language as a tool of communication and even of the nature of poetry as an art form.

Canto I
from The Inferno (lines 1-21)
Dante Alighieri

Nel mezzo del cammin di nostra vita
  mi ritrovai per una selva oscura,
  chè la diritta via era smarrita.
Ahi quanto a dir qual era è cosa dura
  esta selva selvaggia e aspra e forte
  che nel pensier rinnova la paura!
Tant' è amara che poco è più morte;
  ma per trattar del ben ch' io vi trovai,
  dirò de l' altre cose ch' io v' ho scorte.
Io non so ben ridir com' io v' entrai,
  tant' era pieno di sonno a quel punto
  che la verace via abbandonai.
Ma poi ch' i' fui al piè d' un colle giunto,
  là dove terminava quella valle
  che m' avea di paura il cor compunto,
guardai in alto, e vidi le sue spalle
  vestite già de' raggi del pianeta
  che mena dritto altrui per ogni calle.
Allor fu la paura un poco queta
  che nel lago del cor m' era durata
  la notte ch' io passai con tanta pieta.

Canto I
from The Inferno (lines 1-21)
Dante Alighieri
Translated by Allan Gilbert

[NARRATOR] In the midst of my journey through this life of ours, I was in a dark forest, because I had lost the right road. Oh, how hard it is to tell of what sort this forest was—so wild, rugged, and difficult that as I remember it my fear returns! It so afflicts me that death is little less bitter. But that I may deal with the good which there I found, I shall write of all the things I saw. I cannot in any way report how I got into it—so overcome with sleep I was at the moment when I left the true road. But on reaching the foot of a hill at the edge of that lowland which had pierced my heart with fear, I looked up and saw its ridges already lighted by the rays of the planet which leads us straight on every path. Then the fear in the bottom of my heart, which had lasted through the night I passed so wretchedly, was a little subdued.

Canto I
from The Inferno (lines 1–21)

Dante Alighieri

Translated by Charles S. Singleton

Midway in the journey of our life I found myself in a dark wood, for the straight way was lost. Ah, how hard it is to tell what that wood was, wild, rugged, harsh; the very thought of it renews the fear! It is so bitter that death is hardly more so. But, to treat of the good that I found in it, I will tell of the other things I saw there.

I cannot rightly say how I entered it, I was so full of sleep at the moment I left the true way; but when I had reached the foot of a hill, there at the end of the valley that had pierced my heart with fear, I looked up and saw its shoulders already clad in the rays of the planet that leads men aright by every path. Then the fear was somewhat quieted that had continued in the lake of my heart through the night I had passed so piteously.

Canto I
from The Inferno (lines 1–21)

Dante Alighieri

Translated by Dorothy L. Sayers

Midway this way of life we're bound upon,
　　I woke to find myself in a dark wood,
　　Where the right road was wholly lost and gone.

Ay me! how hard to speak of it—that rude
　　And rough and stubborn forest! the mere breath
　　Of memory stirs the old fear in the blood;

It is so bitter, it goes nigh to death;
      Yet there I gained such good, that, to convey
      The tale, I'll write what else I found therewith.

How I got into it I cannot say,
      Because I was so heavy and full of sleep
      When first I stumbled from the narrow way;

But when at last I stood beneath a steep
      Hill's side, which closed that valley's wandering maze
      Whose dread had pierced me to the heart-root deep,

Then I looked up, and saw the morning rays
      Mantle its shoulder from that planet bright
      Which guides men's feet aright on all their ways;

And this a little quieted the affright
      That lurking in my bosom's lake had lain
      Through the long horror of that piteous night.

Canto I
from The Inferno (lines 1–21)

Dante Alighieri

Translated by John Ciardi

Midway in our life's journey, I went astray
      from the straight road and woke to find myself
      alone in a dark wood. How shall I say

what wood that was! I never saw so drear,
      so rank, so arduous a wilderness!
      Its very memory gives a shape to fear.

Death could scarce be more bitter than that place!
      But since it came to good, I will recount
      all that I found revealed there by God's grace.

How I came to it I cannot rightly say,
      so drugged and loose with sleep had I become
      when I first wandered there from the True Way.

But at the far end of that valley of evil
      whose maze had sapped my very heart with fear!
      I found myself before a little hill

and lifted up my eyes. Its shoulders glowed
  already with the sweet rays of that planet
  whose virtue leads men straight on every road,

and the shining strengthened me against the fright
  whose agony had wracked the lake of my heart
  through all the terrors of that piteous night.

Canto I
from The Inferno (lines 1–21)

Dante Alighieri

Translated by Jefferson Butler Fletcher

Upon the journey of our life midway
  I came unto myself in a dark wood,
  For from the straight path I had gone astray.
Ah, how is hard the telling what a drear
  And savage and entangled wood it was,
  That in the very thought renews the fear!
So bitter is it death is little more;
  But to show forth what good I gathered there,
  I tell what else for me it held in store.
How I had entered there I scarce can say,
  So full was I of slumber at the point
  At which I first abandoned the true way.
But when I reached the rising of a hill,
  Whereunder came that valley to an end
  Which on my heart had laid its deadly chill,
I looked, and saw the shoulders of the height
  Mantled already with the planet's rays
  That each in every pathway guides aright.
Then was the fear a little quieted
  That in the deep recesses of my heart
  Outlived the night so piteously led.

INDEX OF TOPICS

INDEX OF POETS AND POEMS